Contributio Archaeology

Volume 40

Series editor

Charles E. Orser, Jr., Albany, USA

For further volumes:
http://www.springer.com/series/5734

Gilly Carr

Legacies of Occupation

Heritage, Memory and Archaeology in the Channel Islands

Springer

Gilly Carr
St. Catharine's College
Cambridge
UK

ISSN 1574-0439
ISBN 978-3-319-37975-3 ISBN 978-3-319-03407-2 (eBook)
DOI 10.1007/978-3-319-03407-2
Springer Cham Heidelberg New York Dordrecht London

Springer is part of Springer Science+Business Media (www.springer.com)

To my grandparents, Mark and Margaret Plummer, who were evacuated; my great-grandparents, Inez and Herbert Plummer, who were occupied; and to Bertram, Lily, Robin, Harold, Edith and Eva Bartlett, and Gus Bradshaw, who were deported to Biberach civilian internment camp

Acknowledgments

During the six years of fieldwork I was helped by numerous people in each of the Channel Islands who gave up their time to talk to me and to visit Occupation sites of all description with me in all kinds of weather. Together we have gone 'bunkering' on hot sunny days and in the biting cold of winter; we've toured memorials in the pouring rain; museum cabinets have been opened up for me in the last light of day after the tourists have left; and the celebrations of Liberation Day has been shared with me. Islanders have even waded through the undergrowth of former labour camps with me and shown me the traces. They have fed me and made me endless cups of tea; they've put me up and put up with me, and answered my numerous letters and emails between visits over the entire period of my fieldwork. A large number of them have become my friends, and for that I am deeply grateful and honoured. To all of these people, I owe a debt of gratitude. By sharing their knowledge about the Occupation with me, they have enabled me to understand local attitudes towards its legacies, and how these have changed over the last 70 years. They have also helped me to form new interpretations, gathered by in-depth research, which have countered the more superficial and sometimes damaging earlier misconceptions about Channel Islanders and the way they treasure and guard their past.

In particular I would like to thank Michael and Josephine Ginns in Jersey for their friendship and hospitality, for letting me stay with them on numerous occasions, and for their constant willingness to answer my letters (Michael) and for the legendary gâche melée and slices of cakes (Josephine). I would also like to thank warmly Mark 'Liberation' Lamerton for diligently sending me newspaper cuttings for the last few years (I owe you a small fortune in postage), for your emails, for sharing your archive with me, and for checking the facts in my chapter on Liberation Day in this volume. Mark: thank you so much. You've been fantastic and I am deeply grateful.

In Guernsey I would like to give a special mention to Richard Heaume, who has always been willing to welcome me into his museum, to let me photograph his Occupation artefacts, to give me a cup of tea and a slice of gâche, and to bring me up to date with the latest Occupation-related news. I also want to thank Jonathan Bartlett, who let me stay with him for most of my Guernsey-based fieldwork, and who has become my husband and 'anthropological informant'. Jon, you are an 'unexpected outcome of research' of the very best kind!

I would also like to thank warmly the following people, about whom I wish I had the space to say more: Chris Addy (formerly Jersey War Tunnels and now National Trust for Jersey); Val Nelson, Doug Ford, Neil Mahrer, Olga Finch, Jon Carter (Jersey Heritage) and Linda Romeril and Stuart Nicolle and other members of staff (Jersey Archives); Damien Horn (Channel Islands Military Museum); Paul Simmonds (formerly of Jersey War Tunnels); Eric Blakeley (Channel TV); John Mesch (Council for the Protection of Jersey's Heritage) and Tom Bunting. Also, members of the Channel Islands Occupation Society (Jersey branch), including: Bob Le Sueur, Paul Burnal, Matthew Costard, Jeremy Hamon, Tony Chalker, Tony Pike, David Maindonald and Colin Isherwood. I would also like to thank the following Jerseymen for letting me interview them: Graeme Delanoe, Alan Allix, Martin Walton, Tony Titterington, Peter Le Vesconte, Ian Channing and Kevin Mayne, Gary Font, Freddie Cohen, Rod McLoughlin and Bruce Willing.

In Guernsey, I would like to extend my heartfelt thanks to Jason Monaghan, Matt Harvey, Josephine Dowding, Lisa Burton, Helen Glencross and Helen Conlon (Guernsey Museum and Art Gallery); Darryl Ogier and Nathan Coyde (Guersey Archives); Amanda Bennett, Sue Laker, Jean Vidamour, and other staff members of the Priaulx Library; Mike O'Hara (Department of Culture and Leisure); Peter Sirett; and Peter and Paul Balshaw (La Valette Military Museum). I would also like to thank the following members of the Channel Islands Occupation Society (Guernsey branch): Ian Brehaut, Paul Le Pelley, Ken Tough, Phil Martin, Paul Bourgaize, Michael Lanyon and Molly Bihet.

My thanks also to Michael Beaumont (Seigneur of Sark); Richard Axton (Société Serquiaise); and Danny Wakley, Richard Dew, and Paul Armorgie in Sark; and to Frances Jeens (Alderney Museum); and Colin Partridge and Trevor Davenport in Alderney.

I would also like to thank the following former Bailiffs of Guernsey and Jersey for granting me interviews: Sir De Vic Carey (Guernsey), Sir Geoffrey Rowland (Guernsey) and Sir Philip Bailhache (Jersey).

My fieldwork in the Channel Islands has been made possible by funding from the British Academy, the McDonald Institute for Archaeological Research (University of Cambridge) and the Société Jersiaise Millennium History Grant.

The following people very kindly read and commented on different chapters of the book and I thank them warmly: Britt Baillie, Philip Stone, Sharon McDonald, Susan Pearce, Chris Addy and Mark Lamerton, although I take full responsibility for any mistakes. Rebecca Montague greatly eased my task by transcribing many interviews with great promptness. Thank you.

Finally, I would like to take this opportunity to thank Nick Saunders, the man who first introduced me to the concept of conflict archaeology and trench art, who converted me away from a life in prehistoric archaeology, and who has been a great mentor and supporter of my work over the last few years. The experience of writing this book has been emotionally and intellectually rewarding and literally life changing in so many ways. Nick, if I hadn't met you, then this book would never have been written—a cliché, but entirely true. Thank you.

Some of the ideas in Chap. 3 have been reproduced from my paper 'Shining a light on dark tourism: German bunkers in the British Channel Islands', which appeared in 2010 in *Public Archaeology* 9(2): 65–86, published by Maney Publishing (www.maneypublishing.com/journals/pua and www.ingentaconnect.com/content/maney/pua). Similarly, parts of Chap. 4 have been used in 'The hidden heritage of forced and slave labour: examining the commitment to remembering in the Channel Islands', edited by Marek Jasinski (forthcoming), *Painful Heritage: The Falstad Symposia*. Trondheim: The Royal Norwegian Society of Sciences and Letters. The first part of Chap. 6 was first published by Taylor & Francis in 2012, in 'Examining the memorialscape of occupation and liberation: a case study from the Channel Islands', *International Journal of Heritage Studies* 18(2): 174–193 (http://www.tandfonline.com/doi/abs/10.1080/13527258.2011.606330). I would also like to thank the Jersey Evening Post, the Guernsey Museum and Art Gallery, Jonathan Bartlett, Brian Green, Richard Heaume, Tony Titterington, the family of Richard Mayne, Peter Sirett and Gary Font for granting permission for me to reproduce a number of photos in this book, and Ian Taylor for drawing the maps so expertly.

Contents

Author Biography

Dr. Gilly Carr is a Senior Lecturer and Academic Director in Archaeology at the University of Cambridge's Institute of Continuing Education. She is also a Fellow and Director of Studies in Archaeology and Anthropology at St Catharine's College, Cambridge. She has published widely on the subject of the heritage of the German Occupation of the Channel Islands and her subsequent volume, Protest, Defiance and Resistance in the Channel Islands, 1940–1945, co-written with Paul Sanders and Louise Willmot, will be published in 2014. She recently curated Occupied Behind Barbed Wire, an exhibition on the arts and crafts made by the 2,200 Channel Islanders interned in Germany during the war, for Guernsey Museum (2010) and Jersey Museum (2012). She co-edited with Harold Mytum, The Cultural Heritage of POWs: Creativity Behind Barbed Wire (2012) and Prisoners of War: Archaeology, Memory and Heritage of 19th- and 20th-Century Mass Internment (2013). She is currently working on a coedited volume with Keir Reeves entitled 'Islands of War, Islands of Memory'.

Abbreviations

CIOS	Channel Islands Occupation Society
GEP	Guernsey Evening Press
GP	Guernsey Press and Star
JEP	Jersey Evening Post
JH	Jersey Heritage
JWT	Jersey War Tunnels
OT	Organisation Todt

Lager Wick, Jersey

Chapter 1
Legacies of Occupation

Introduction

The Channel Island of Guernsey has always been, for me, a second home—the land of my ancestors, my mother's family and my childhood. I used to spend school holidays in Guernsey, staying with my grandparents and playing on the beaches with my cousins. Although the remnants of the Occupation in the form of concrete bunkers were seemingly everywhere—we children used them as impromptu toilets or changing rooms at the beach—I just accepted their presence. I knew from childhood that the Channel Islands were the only part of the British Isles to be occupied during the Second World War. I knew that certain places in Guernsey were still haunted by ghosts of German soldiers, because I had heard the stories. I knew, too, that my grandfather had joined the army and left the island just before the Germans came and that my pregnant grandmother had evacuated a few days afterwards, unwilling to be separated from him. I knew that my grandfather's parents had stayed during the Occupation, continuing to run their bakery in St Peter Port, and looking after my grandparents' house when, in their absence, it was requisitioned by German soldiers. My strict great-grandmother, so the family story went, made sure the soldiers wiped their feet before entering the house.

I was also dimly aware that several members of my father's family, who had moved to Guernsey before the First World War, were deported to a German civilian internment camp, but this was never spoken about. Only a torn and bent photograph in my father's old RAF trunk gave testimony to this fact. Written on its reverse, in pencil, was a list of those in the photo and the note that it was taken in '1945 on release of Guernsey prisoners from Biberach'. Even though everyone in the photo was smiling, my father's cousin, Robin, who caught tuberculosis in the camp, looked dreadfully thin.

This was more or less my sum childhood knowledge about the Occupation years as it affected my family. What I did not know until long after I really should have done was that the Channel Islands were not the only places in Europe to be occupied. I remember feeling utterly astounded when I discovered this fact in late childhood. The way that the Occupation was presented in local museums and

G. Carr, *Legacies of Occupation*, Contributions To Global Historical Archaeology 40,
DOI: 10.1007/978-3-319-03407-2_1, © Springer International Publishing Switzerland 2014

talked about generally gave the impression—to a child at least—that they were the only place in Europe to have experienced such a fate. Such was the focus of heritage then (and still now to a lesser extent) upon the island experience, coupled with their inward-looking nature and almost complete disregard for the European context, that my ignorance was, perhaps, understandable.

The Channel Islands' experience of Occupation was my baseline against which all other Occupations were later measured. Or rather, I assumed that the way in which their ongoing relationship (not to say, obsession) with the Occupation manifested itself was normal and natural. When I began my research in this area in 2006, moving away from my study of the Roman Occupation of Britain, I began to discuss my work with my academic colleagues. It was then that I realised quite how unusual and sometimes a little odd (to outsiders) the Channel Islands' relationship was. I had grown up seeing mannequins of German soldiers and swastika flags in bunkers; I had seen how newspaper cartoons (posted to me by my grandmother) and daily life were still infused with references to the Occupation. I had also observed the continuing local cultural currency and potency of the iconic symbols of Occupation: the German helmet and V-for-victory symbol.

To me, the overwhelming predominance of both the German soldier and nostalgic references to the Occupation (always spelled locally with a capital O) in local heritage discourse (both professional and amateur) was normal and to be expected. It is sometimes hard to question—or see anything questionable—about what one grows up with. Not until I began my research and visited war museums and sites throughout Europe did I fully appreciate the narratives that were not explored in the Occupation heritage of the Channel Islands. Only then, after witnessing the surprised reaction of not just my academic colleagues but also my students, some of whom came from other formerly occupied countries, did I begin to query their reaction—and my own. Why does the obsession with the Occupation manifest itself the way that it does? How has it evolved since the islands were liberated? And how and why has the Occupation become an important part of local identity? What has been the role of memory and the heritage of Occupation within this construction of identity? This book attempts to answer these questions.

At one level, my central aim is to chart and understand the legacies of Occupation in the Channel Islands to help place them within a European context. At another, it is my intention to contribute more generally to wider debates surrounding the response of cultural heritage to military Occupation and conflict, especially to that of the Second World War. While this volume considers *how* heritage responds to conflict, we might also ask precisely *how long* heritage continues to respond to war or Occupation after the conflict ends. How long—and why—does it continue to be a living force, provoking addition, restoration, destruction or reinterpretation? When does it become fossilised, ignored or is no longer valued by a society? For Maria Tumarkin, who has studied what she terms 'traumascapes'—places across the world marked by traumatic legacies of violence, suffering and loss—'the past is never quite over. Years, decades after the event, the past is still unfinished business'. Traumascapes are spaces where 'events are experienced and re-experienced across time'; they are places where the past 'continues to inhabit and refashion the present' (2005: 12). If this is so, and if the Channel Islands can be seen as traumascapes—and I believe that they can—then this particular past will never quite be over.

It is, however, still too early to know, nearly 70 years after the Second World War, how cultural heritage responses will continue to evolve after the death of those who experienced it first-hand. Certain phases in the evolution of the politics of war memory in many countries have been explored and analysed (e.g. Evans and Lunn 1997; Ashplant et al. 2000; Müller 2002; Bell 2006; Lebow et al. 2006; Jarausch and Lindenberger 2007; Pakier and Stråth 2010). Research has shown how cultural heritage can support, reflect or respond to these phases, emphasising different narratives at different times. Sometimes heritage even constructs war narratives in the first place, even if there is a tension between state-supported and private heritage enterprises.

While short- and even medium-term predictions can be made about the likely future direction of war memory and heritage, this cannot be done with any accuracy for the long term. I have been surprised many times at the strength of feeling of the post-war generation, and their desire to keep alive and honour the memory of their parents. While it is possible that this desire may wane with each subsequent generation, the degree to which the Occupation has become part of local identity in the Channel Islands means that this heritage response may continue to evolve beyond the edge of living memory. As I write, plans for the commemoration of the centenary of the start of the First World War are well underway at museums across Europe, and it will be interesting to observe whether and how heritage and memory will continue to evolve after 2018. The growth in popularity of Conflict Archaeology over the last decade, which takes the study of the First World War as a original theme (e.g. Saunders 2003, 2004, 2007; Saunders and Cornish 2009), is one indication of how and why memory and subsequent heritage will continue to develop and flourish beyond the centenary.

I believe that the memory of Occupation will not immediately lose its potency when the last of the Occupation generation has gone. The war years are still so present and valued in the islands that it is likely that this will continue for a period; perhaps for as long as first-hand memory of this generation exists, extending potency for another generation or two. Already, control of Occupation heritage is slowly moving from the hands of indigenous enthusiasts and volunteers into those of professionals who are often incomers to the islands. Although currently, in the early twenty-first century, the two are working together, we may be living through the period of handover. The baton is moving from personal or family memory to that which is gleaned from written accounts. It is also in a period of transition from what might be perceived by enthusiasts as 'authentic' memory to one which must be interpreted and re-interpreted through artistic installations. The heritage of the Occupation is going through a process of change and evolution.

The research presented in this volume has changed focus and direction throughout the years of fieldwork. At the outset, my intention was to study only the handmade material culture of the Occupation years. Through studying the objects made by islanders, soldiers, foreign workers, prisoners and deportees, I hoped to be able to understand and analyse the multiple experiences of Occupation. As I built up a large database of information about objects, I began to form friendships with the collectors of Occupation militaria and paraphernalia who owned them. I soon realised that the collectors themselves and their experiences of collecting since childhood in the fifties, sixties and seventies were an important story to tell. I heard accounts of swapping hand grenades and bayonets in the school playground and of breaking into sealed fortifications in search of German helmets. I also learned of the trade in souvenirs with friends in other islands, and of the never-ending search for authentic items with a cast-iron local provenance. I realised that here, among these men (I never found any female collectors), was a fascinating, unwritten social history of the fate of German militaria since 1945. This gave me an insight into how and why people can spend a lifetime by collecting such material without having neo-Nazi sympathies (as is so often presumed by those who do not collect). I wondered to what extent this lifetime devotion or obsession for collecting was shared among formerly occupied people all over Europe as a desire to recreate or re-experience an exciting (albeit dreadful) period in their history that they had missed through being born after the war. Perhaps the stimulus to the vast worldwide trade in Nazi memorabilia was actually triggered by such people and their collections.

At an early stage in my research, I saw that many collectors owned their own private museums. Whether these were in their houses and for their own personal enjoyment, or whether they were open to the public, these spaces spoke to me of how the Occupation is locally perceived and mediated through objects. The objects chosen for display made it clear whose stories were told and whose were not deemed interesting or worthy enough to tell; whose objects were worth collecting and whose were not. But why were German swastikas favoured over clogs belonging to slave workers? Why did German militaria and the German experience of Occupation predominate over even the local experience? Who was the intended audience? I wanted to know whether this had any bearing on why it was always referred to as the *German* and not the *Nazi* Occupation, as elsewhere in Europe. I also wondered why victims of Nazism (especially foreign ones) were almost entirely ignored and how and to what extent this was replicated in other forms of Occupation heritage.

Of the Occupation museums which are open to the public, a fair number are housed in German bunkers, the concrete fortifications which make up the Atlantic Wall in the Channel Islands. In fact, museums are just one example of the reuse of the bunkers which line the coasts of Guernsey and Jersey, as I discovered as I followed the trail of artefacts on display inside many of them. While the majority of bunkers in Alderney are neglected, vandalised, overgrown and empty, I wanted to understand why so many in Guernsey and Jersey had been converted or restored. There was clearly a difference of perception both between islands and over time. What was once a blot on the landscape was now an important historic monument. The tension between destruction and preservation had passed, but there are still some who argue strongly that bunkers are an ethically non-neutral arena for reuse. While some find it acceptable to restore a bunker, complete with swastikas and pictures of Hitler, others argue that their only legitimate use today should be as a space for condemning the Nazi regime. Should they be reused for cafes, general storage and public toilets, or is it more appropriate to use them only for heritage? In comparison with bunkers elsewhere in Europe, I wanted to know how unusual the Channel Islands are in their restoration of these structures. Such issues are most controversial in Jersey, where opinion is very sharply divided between the local bunkers enthusiasts and the heritage professionals. In Guernsey, the two groups work together and these issues are not (yet) of concern.

As I observed the interconnectedness of objects, collectors, museums and bunkers, I began to think about the aspects of the Atlantic Wall that are rarely mentioned in Occupation museums. What of the slave, forced and 'volunteer' labourers who built the bunkers—how were they treated and where did they live? How were they perceived by local people and were locals forced to build bunkers too? While such questions were often ignored, marginalised or only briefly alluded to in private museums, I was relatively advanced in my fieldwork before I appreciated that the third largest island of Alderney was not the only Channel Island upon which labour camps were built to house workers. Yet no camps are visible in the other islands and none of them is a heritage site. It puzzled me why many bunkers, which foreign labourers helped to build, were now restored and promoted to tourists, and yet the labour camps where many lived had long since been removed from the landscape. I wanted to know why the remains of not a single one had become a memorial or heritage site and why their original locations were so difficult to find and known by so few. How typical was this invisibility in other formerly occupied countries in Western Europe? I wanted to know why the preservation and promotion of camps as heritage, memorial and educational places occurred only in some countries and not in others. How and why did the nationality of the workers involved influence the narratives told about the camps and the way in which they were memorialised? These are still ongoing questions for my own research, yet are not seemingly of much concern in the Channel Islands.

Over six years, I spent many fieldwork trips visiting, photographing, cataloguing and researching memorials and monuments to the different groups of the Occupation years. I observed similarities among how different categories of victims of Nazism (such as foreign workers, deportees and Jews) had been memorialised. On the whole, they tended to have the smallest, most recent and most marginal memorials. The major anniversaries of Liberation Day, on the other hand, seemed to be marked by large monuments in the middle of St Peter Port and St Helier, the capital towns of Guernsey and Jersey. I wanted to discover what lay behind the patterning, and how it shaped or was shaped by the islands' war narrative. Was there a link between the marginalisation of the memory of foreign labourers in both Occupation museums and memorialisation? Did this pattern spill over into other aspects of Occupation heritage?

Several times I attended Holocaust Memorial Day in Guernsey and Jersey and saw the startling difference in both the size of the crowd and the memorials at the focus of the two ceremonies. While Guernsey's honoured the Jews who were deported from the island in 1942, Jersey's ceremony focused on the island's deported political prisoners who did not return from penal prisons and concentration camps after the war. Perhaps the traditional rivalry between these two largest islands was enough to explain the lack of similarity between the ceremonies; or perhaps Occupation histories differed between the two islands sufficiently for Occupation memory and heritage to also differ. On the other hand, dissimilarities could have been due to the memorial instigators or organisers involved. Maybe there was insight to be gained from comparing the way that Liberation Day is celebrated on the two islands and observing the place of victims of Nazism at this time. I wanted to see what grand narratives were passed down to the next generation on such days.

Memorialisation, commemorations and celebrations, too, are intertwined aspects of Occupation heritage, and those who organise them, propose them and attend them are often the same guardians of memory, interest groups and stakeholders, linked to each other by ties of family and friendship, as those who collect memorabilia, restore bunkers and own museums. How and why has this wider group become involved in their heritage and how have they decided which legacies of Occupation to turn into heritage?

Different legacies of Occupation within this volume speak both to distinct and overlapping issues within cultural heritage studies and Conflict Archaeology. The analysis of memorials and the celebrations of Liberation Day illustrate how these forms of heritage can reinforce both historical narratives and political legitimacy. In the Channel Islands, these narratives focus on military victory and liberation but not victimhood. The neglect of sites of labour camps shows the success of these narratives. The Channel Islands Occupation Society (CIOS), the official Occupation specialists in the islands, states that it's aims are to 'study and investigate' and 'preserve and record all aspects' of the Occupation by 'recording, safeguarding and preserving relics of the period'.[1] This is clearly not entirely accurate, given that they have shown little interest in preserving certain aspects of the Occupation, but I wanted to dig deeper and understand what governed their choices.

But how have both grass-root narratives and those supported by local government elites come to converge? Were they imposed from above as some sort of quasi-Churchillian diktat which demanded that narratives of military heroism, endurance and victory be remembered above all others? Or did the ordinary islanders themselves independently choose to preserve and present traumatic memory in a certain way? Was Occupation memory constructed from below and fostered by local government? Or has there been tension in the way in which ordinary enthusiasts and professionals in local government wish to present their history and heritage? I wanted to discover how this has manifested itself in heritage presentation, and, precisely, how such narratives are chosen, constructed and supported by heritage. By focusing on a range of forms of cultural heritage,

---

[1] http://www.ciosjersey.org.uk/ciosrules.htm, accessed 13 August 2012, http://www.occupied.guernsey.net/index.html, accessed 13 August 2012.

I show how the combination, when taken together, can reveal a more nuanced picture than the study of one form alone.

Any war or military Occupation leaves behind it a varied legacy. For the Channel Islands, the German Occupation left behind a particular post-Occupation landscape of barbed wire, mined beaches, toppled monuments, vandalised properties, labour camps, concrete fortifications, ruined coastlines and traumatised populations. The local occupied populations had witnessed or suffered widespread panic followed by the rapid evacuation of tens of thousands of residents and the later forced deportation to Germany of over two thousand civilians. They had also observed or suffered anti-Jewish legislation and the imprisonment of those who committed acts of resistance. Everyone had faced the confiscation of wireless sets that had provided the only serious contact with the outside world. They knew of and often saw the ill-treatment of slave and forced workers. Many experienced the mass requisitioning of property, and there was no escaping the increased hunger and starvation for all. It was no wonder that for the first few decades after the war, people did not want to look back or talk about the Occupation, except to tell humorous anecdotes about outwitting the occupiers. This generation was notoriously silent about the grim reality of the years of Occupation and wanted to face the future with a determination to restore the islands to their former state as far and fast as possible. But as the years passed and the post-war generation grew up, the anecdotes, snatches of stories, and German helmets used as a flower pots in the back garden only fuelled their desire to discover the real details of the Occupation years. It was this that stimulated the desire for the collection of militaria, many examples of which were found in abandoned bunkers and other fortifications. There appears to have been a domino effect in terms of where the interest in exploring the past began (i.e. with militaria) and where it led (to bunkers, then to museums, commemorations and memorials), and I have at times felt as if I were retreading that same path myself. I have come to understand why some legacies have been turned into heritage and why some have not and were instead neglected. One day another generation may pull back the metaphorical and literal undergrowth to open up the pathways which lead to other legacies too dark to face at the moment.

Sites of Memory, Sites of Occupation

It is apparent that a self-selecting group among the post-war generation—which I will broadly define for convenience as those born between the mid-1940s and mid-1960s—has been largely (with notable exceptions) responsible for the choice and the creation of sites of memory in the Channel Islands. A *lieux de mémoire* or 'site of memory' is a concept coined by Pierre Nora to mean 'any significant entity, whether material or non-material in nature, which by dint of human will or the work of time has become a symbolic element of the memorial heritage of any community' (Nora 1996a: xvii). The sites of memory within the French nation included *lieux* as diverse as places, songs, dates, books and ceremonies (see Nora 1996b, 1997). While for Nora the subject of his study was France and the search for a certain 'ineffable quality called 'Frenchness'' (Winter 1995: 10), it is those who live in the Channel Islands who are the subject of this book. Their memorial heritage and landscape of the German Occupation makes up the public 'occupationscape' of the islands today.

The occupationscape, like Nora's *lieux de mémoire*, also concerns itself with symbolic elements of memorial heritage. Nora was concerned with important French historical *lieux*, ranging from the *Marseillaise*, the French flag and the Pantheon, to the pilgrimage of Lourdes and de Gaulle's funeral at Notre Dame, and to Bastille Day, and the Liberation parade down the Champs-Elysées. For Nora, the national history of France 'traversed the network' of *lieux de mémoire* (1989: 23). I have coined a new term to understand the landscapes of Occupation still surviving in Europe. The occupationscape is more than just a random or holistic collection of heritage sites or types. Rather, it includes only certain elements or legacies; a cultural landscape selected for survival and heritage incorporation by members of the local population to speak for them, their identity and their memory of Occupation.

The sites of memory of the occupationscape discussed in this volume depart from Nora's cultural heritage of France in three key ways. First, while they are unique to the Channel Islands in their precise manifestations, they can be compared and contrasted with each other and with other occupationscapes throughout Europe. Second, my aim is to avoid presenting an uncritical, reverential, nostalgic or rose-tinted view of the Occupation and its sites of memory, even though some of the people whom I study may perceive the past and its legacies in this way. Rather, I include these sites because of their value in helping us to understand why particular legacies of Occupation have been perceived as important cultural and memorial heritage and how they both shape and have been shaped by the Channel Islands' Occupation narratives. My aim is deconstruction, rather than construction or reification of those narratives. Third, while Nora has been criticised for his lack of sites of counter-memory (Tai 2001; Legg 2005b), these are included here because of the important insight they provide into power relations between elites and non-elites, between official and popular memory, and because they allow us to see who uses which *lieux* to what end. As Legg argues, it is only by combining 'an analysis of national *lieux de memoire* with spaces of memory contestation and survival that complete and inclusive conception of the spaces of the nation can be created' (2005a: 500).

While this book is not exhaustive, it charts the trajectory of the most prominent and publically visible sites of Occupation heritage that have made up the occupationscape from 1945 to the present day. They include anniversaries, commemorations, objects, monuments and museums which have become *lieux* through having been affected by the 'will to remember' and also 'invested with a symbolic aura' by the imagination (Nora 1989: 19). As we shall see, just as with sites of memory in France, the fundamental purpose of *lieux* in the Channel Islands is to 'stop time, to stop the work of forgetting' (ibid). This has been fundamental to collectors of militaria and bunker restorers in particular.

While the Occupation of the Channel Islands was, to a certain extent, similar to that elsewhere in Western Europe, the heritage sites and war narratives have led to different occupationscapes. For example, war museums throughout Europe are called 'resistance museums' (e.g. in Copenhagen, Brussels, Oslo, Esch-sur-Alzette in Luxembourg and Amsterdam), emphasising the importance of such narratives in these countries. Although resistance and deportation were realities in the Channel Islands, museums of this type are usually called 'Occupation' or 'military museums' here, showing the shift of emphasis on to the experience of the occupiers who dominate several aspects of Occupation heritage in the islands.

While there were no Gestapo torture cells in the islands, many islanders in Jersey were beaten up by the *Geheime Feldpolizei* in St Helier to extract confessions at their headquarters, Silvertide (Mière 2004; Sanders 2004). This building survives today, entirely unmarked and unremarkable. The islands' prisons also housed political prisoners who were arrested for acts of resistance; these buildings have since been demolished. A hospital has been built on the site of Jersey jail in St Helier, and the Royal Court and its offices of government now stand upon the site of the prison in St Peter Port in Guernsey. The absence of places such as these in the Channel Islands' sites of memory also tells us much about the way in which the Occupation is remembered here.

There are also important ways in which the specificities of Occupation throughout Western Europe diverged and this, too, has led to different occupationscapes in different countries. There are many historical dissimilarities between wartime events in the Channel Islands and elsewhere in Europe. For example, the Channel Islands avoided resistance reprisals such as were seen at Oradour-sur-Glane in France (Farmer 2000) and at the Fosse Ardeatine in Rome (Portelli 2003). The differences with Eastern Europe are even more marked. For example, no Jewish ghettos such as those in Krakow, Warsaw or Prague were created in the Channel Islands, although legislation was enacted against the islands' Jews (Cohen 2000). No villages were razed or put to the torch, although many islanders' houses were knocked down by the occupiers because they were in the line of sight of the big gun emplacements, as recorded by many diarists. While no massacres took place in the islands and no islanders were executed by firing squad, a small plaque marks the place in St Ouen's manor in Jersey where Frenchman François Scornet was executed after having escaped from France with a group of his compatriots. The islands also lacked partisan groups and forest settlements, such as those which existed in Belorussia (e.g. Tec 2008); but this, perhaps, is mainly because there are no forests in the Channel Islands and many of the young men had gone to England to join the armed forces before the arrival of the Germans. Many of the differences between the islands and the nations of Europe are simply a function of their size. Others are due to the fact that mainland Britain was not occupied and remained a fighting force, with all the associated implications of potential reprisals against severe wrongdoing by the occupiers.

The specific war narratives told by different nations, both those which are state-sponsored and those which are nurtured by self-appointed guardians of memory, have an impact upon which legacies of Occupation are turned into heritage in order to construct and support national and local narratives. For some countries, narratives of victimhood and martyrdom have been stressed (e.g. Lagrou 2000). This has happened through the selection and heritagisation of sites of memory such as concentration camps, the construction of memorials and museums to resistance workers, and a focus on narratives of suffering, resistance and deportation (Berger 2010: 123). For other places, such as the UK, narratives of endurance (e.g. Noakes 1997; Connelly 2004) and victory are reflected in the important sites of memory of those places. As Regula Ludi (2006: 239) has observed, the Nazi era and its legacies has become a 'thorn in the flesh of all European societies, with no closure in sight'. It remains as a defining period in European history that continues to shape memory, narratives of war and cultural heritage into the twenty-first century.

Beyond the core occupationscape discussed here, there is a wider range of legacies and heritage of the Occupation today which are visible or accessible to the public. These *lieux* are restricted to significant and symbolic elements, involving more than just memorials, museums, bunkers, camps and ceremonies. They also comprise dates, places, buildings and memories. We might include important objects such as the iconic German helmet; areas of land on which key events took place; and particular well-known published wartime diaries. There are also living members of the Occupation generation, their specific memories, and their double vision which enables them to see the islands both as they are *now* and as they were *then*. These members of the community, through dint of a combination of their longevity, good memory, knowledge of the Occupation years, and a long period of speaking publically about their experiences, have become living heritage in their own right. Several of these figures have been invaluable to me during my fieldwork.

Added to this list are local archives; the handful of annual commemorations and celebrations that have their roots in the war years; the folk tales of haunted bunkers; and certain liberation-related street names. These are wider aspects of the public occupationscape. One might ask precisely what is excluded from the concept of the occupationscape as every legacy of the Occupation is seemingly meaningful or symbolic for somebody. Here, we can distinguish between public and private (or personal) versions of the concept, as that which is private is individually meaningful, even though it can overlap with that which is public. Private occupationscapes can vary throughout the lifetime of the individual, particularly as they learn more about their own family's Occupation history or as and when they become involved with Occupation heritage. The public occupationscape, too, is in flux as it deals only with what is current common currency; what legacy of Occupation each generation values, selects and deems appropriate to speak for them. There is great potential for certain aspects of cultural heritage to move in and out of focus.

For most people, the Occupation holds meaning today as a receptacle for memories, family stories and artefacts, and these are shared between islanders as a way of expressing their own sense of belonging and right to local identity. However, while these stories and artefacts are often inherited and passed down through the generations, they are also lost, sold, embellished or forgotten as they diminish or increase in value as the distance from the Occupation years increase.

But just as there are sites of memory, there are also sites of forgetting or oblivion, which Nancy Wood has labelled *lieux d'oubli*. Such sites are those that 'public memory has expressly avoided because of the disturbing affect that their invocation is still capable of arousing' (Wood 1999: 10). In emphasising memories that are denied expression or recognition, Wood places particular stress on the intentionality of their avoidance (ibid: 10 and 12, n27). In the consideration of such sites in the Channel Islands, we must explore this, for while there are sites that have indeed been ignored (such as forced and slave labour camps), to be true *lieux d'oubli,* we must demonstrate that they have been deliberately shunned. The dismantling and destruction of many camps after the Occupation and the continuing neglect of their memory is surely an indication of such intentionality. During fieldwork, I have also witnessed conversations among some members of the post-war generation that suggested to me that memorials associated with forced and slave labourers have been deliberately avoided, especially on days such as Liberation Day. But these very memorials are also sites of memory for many, demonstrating that a site can be one of both forgetting and remembering for different people at the same time.

Nora further classifies *lieux* according to how they were created. 'Dominant' sites are often imposing and imposed from above by government or some official organisation from the beginning. One is summoned to them to attend official ceremonies. Those which are 'dominated', on the other hand, tend to become durable sites of memory almost unintentionally. Nora sees them as places of refuge and spontaneous devotion and pilgrimage (1996b: 19; 1989: 23). Here, we can contrast the grand monuments commemorating the act of liberation and imposed by government with those erected to forced and slave labourers. These latter memorials started in Jersey as humble, portable plaques upon which flowers were laid by former labourers who wanted to keep faith with their dead comrades once a year. Stephen Legg would no doubt call these memorials, and the former burial grounds upon which they were placed, 'sites of counter-memory', the 'times and places in which people have refused to forget' which can 'rebut the memory schema of the dominant class, caste, race or nation, providing an alternative form of remembering and identity' (Legg 2005b: 181).

These types of sites of memory are often in flux in their designation, depending on political expediency and events, local campaigners, archaeological fieldwork and sometimes a combination of these working in unison or against each other. I have even, at times, found myself acting as an activist or campaigner in support of the memory of certain victim groups of Nazism, but have been aware that I that I am potentially contaminating the field which I am trying to study. An awareness of my potential impact, however, has been important in testing hypotheses. By putting forward my own views, I have seen how deeply held are the views of those I have interviewed and worked with. Similarly, these people have made an impact on me and I have learned a very great deal from them, not least a deep respect for the work that they have done in salvaging the remnants of the Occupation.

Between them, the three concepts of memory, forgetting and counter-memory have their own overlapping memory communities in the Channel Islands who conspire to promote or forget certain *lieux*, and this book explores these groups as a way of understanding and analysing not just the sites that they curate, but also their intentions, histories and motivations. Modern Channel Islands' identity and a sense of belonging have been created by intervening over the last 70 years in the legacies of Occupation to claim them as heritage. Similarly, more recent immigrants to the Channel Islands who cannot claim any relationship to the Occupation or its memory or heritage often feel excluded by not sharing ownership in these sites and memories. Some (mostly from the UK) have sought inclusion by joining local societies and developing an interest and knowledge in this area. This process of heritage and identity creation is examined in this volume.

The majority of this book focuses upon the two largest islands of Jersey and Guernsey and, to a lesser extent, on the third largest island of Alderney. It will not escape the reader's notice that the spotlight rarely focuses upon Sark or Herm. Both of these islands have very small populations and are mostly lacking in the key aspects of the occupationscape discussed in this volume. Herm, which is half a mile by one and a half miles in size, saw little of the Occupation. It has no bunkers, collectors, museums, labour camps or memorials (Fig. 1.1).

The population of Sark today is around 600 and the island has a small Occupation museum. While a couple of collectors in the island were interviewed for this book, there are no Occupation memorials, sites of labour camps or bunkers. Liberation Day is celebrated on 10 May, but the nature of the small community festivities on this day makes it less amenable for analysis and grand narratives are not as much in evidence. This is not to say that residents of Sark will not have their own personal or island-specific occupationscapes. However, these are likely to comprise *lieux de mémoire* which would be locally relevant but which would not necessarily have their counterparts in, or be applicable to, other islands.

The Transition from Legacy to Heritage

While the bunkers and material culture of Occupation are, without doubt, part of the heritage of the Occupation of the Channel Islands, I argue in chapter four that the term 'heritage' should not be used indiscriminately to describe the leftover general legacy or debris of (in this case) Occupation. To turn something into heritage is an active choice, a decision about what is of value and what a community is happy to embrace as a part of its identity. What remains as a legacy and what is chosen as heritage makes a statement about who you are or want to be and how you are happy to be seen and judged by others. But more than a choice or a decision, for a legacy to become heritage requires *intervention*. A forgotten bunker covered with ivy is a legacy; it requires cleaning up, preserving, restoring or

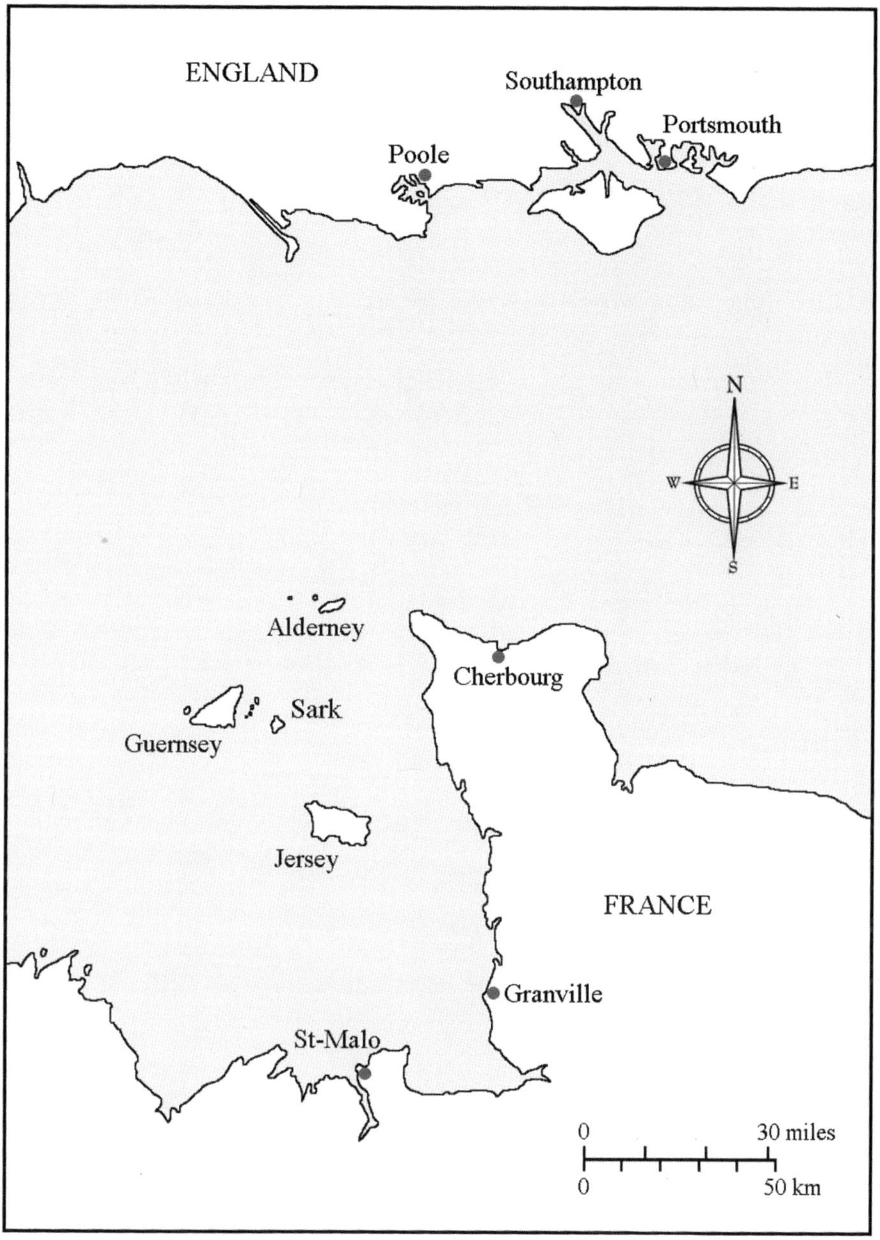

Fig. 1.1 Map of the Channel Islands, courtesy of Ian Taylor

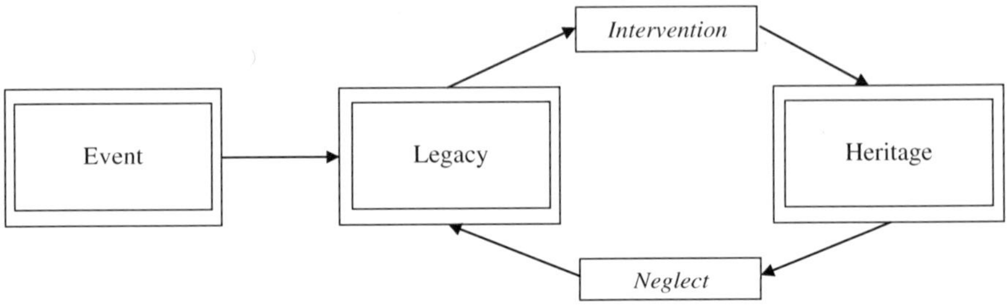

Fig. 1.2 The lifecycle of the event, legacy and heritage

showing off to tourists—in other words, it requires becoming imbued with value—to become part of heritage. Even something less tangible and more ephemeral such as a memory—of deportation, for example—can be turned into heritage by an intervention in that memory as it fades. It can become manifest in stone as a memorial, or perhaps reimagined as a museum exhibition (Fig. 1.2).

If the wooden huts of a forced labour camp are removed and the land turned over to another use, it will be too late for this legacy to become heritage unless an intervention is made, even if it is archaeological. The site of the camp can become marked with a plaque; it can be added to tourist maps. It can become heritage. And yet this transition from a legacy to heritage is not linear. Heritage can fall out of favour. Funding may cease. A memorial can be neglected, moved, removed or destroyed. The brambles can once again grow over a bunker. A museum exhibition can change and its objects sold. A commemorative ceremony can cease or change in structure and meaning as those who support it pass away and another generation with its own agenda takes up the baton. Heritage can turn back into a forgotten legacy. All that is needed for this to happen is a lack of intervention or just neglect—a removal of the direct agency that keeps it a valued part of cultural currency. And yet even this return to legacy status need not be its final destination (should such a state exist). The transition between legacy and heritage can, in theory, move back and forth over time, especially for individual sites of memory. Each site should be considered to be in flux, as is emphasised later in this volume with reference to bunkers. Heritage can be made and unmade. This process should not be confused with a heritage that is vandalised, attacked or destroyed while it is still valued and in vogue even if not everyone values it. Such heritage will be restored if possible at the earliest opportunity, sometimes compromising the authenticity of the site in the process. Restoration usually happens as soon as money becomes available and allocated to the project, or after conflict has ceased, should destruction happen during war. Sometimes repair or restoration can take many generations if the destruction itself becomes a symbol of identity and the ruins display the martyrdom of the people.

Not every designation as 'heritage' is universally appreciated or supported among a community, as the case studies in this book demonstrate. Many sites are controversial, even provocative, and can be the cause of community or intergenerational tension. For some sites, the lifecycle of the transition between legacy and heritage (and back again) may be ongoing over many generations. At 70 years after the Occupation, we may be observing only the early stages of this process.

Transitions between the two states are often not fast. It is usually a gradual affair, especially when the legacy in question relates to conflict. In the Channel Islands, the legacies of the German Occupation were, for a long time, taboo. While children were permitted to collect items of militaria, this was a less accepted pastime for adults, as discussed in chapter two. In general (although with notable exceptions), it was not until the post-war generation of collectors had reached adulthood that it was deemed acceptable for them to put their collections on display in their own private museums. Thus, this particular legacy took a generation to become heritage. This same generation was responsible for restoring bunkers and, as is discussed in chapter three, this work did not begin to be politically acceptable until the late 1970s.

When it comes to the erection of memorials in the Channel Islands, such projects can happen relatively quickly—within a year or two of the idea—or can take a lifetime of campaigning to achieve. Both extremes have occurred in the islands and have been affected by the controversies surrounding both the personality of the campaigner, their role during the Occupation, and the narrative of the group in question to be remembered. Like the examples above, the role of taboo plays a strong part in dictating the period of time that it takes for a legacy to become heritage.

Some legacies of the Occupation, such as the sites of slave and forced labour camps, have still not been turned into heritage. This raises the question of whether every legacy will become heritage in due course; whether the time will ever be right or if the taboo will ever lose its potency. I do not believe that this is by any means a certain outcome. While some legacies will never be seen as important enough to bring to life in public memory, there is a period after which it can be too late. Some legacies depend on the memory which individuals have of the event to keep them alive. What happens when all eyewitnesses are dead? What happens to legacies for which there is no material (or archaeological) trace and no archival record for later generations to resurrect? These are likely to fade entirely, meaning that some legacies have a definite lifespan which can sometimes match that of those involved. For those legacies that last longer due to the length of survival of archaeological traces, even these remains are fragile and dependent on the land remaining undeveloped and the traces remaining intact. The lifecycle of legacies and heritage is largely dependent on the role of people who take it upon themselves to intervene. This is especially apparent in small communities such as the Channel Islands, where individuals are not anonymous, can easily garner media attention and can make an impact. To a certain extent, it also depends on the public support of individual projects to ensure the success of the transition from legacy to heritage.

Structure and Themes

In this book, I consider six key aspects of the occupationscape over five consecutive chapters: militaria, museums, bunkers, labour camps, memorials and Liberation Day commemorations. My aim is to examine what has happened to these legacies of Occupation since 1945, how they have been treated and why: what has been turned into heritage, what has been rejected, and how narratives of Occupation have been constructed through the medium of heritage.

Within these five chapters, I consider first, in chapter two, the Occupation artefacts: those who collect them and the untold history of objects that they represent. The museums in which these objects reside, and the way that they are used to reconstruct the past, are likewise important loci for giving an insight into the way in which these post-war or first-generation guardians of memory remember and value the Occupation and wish to portray it to others.

In the third chapter, I examine how bunkers are perceived and chosen as suitable vehicles for carrying Occupation memory, whether in the form of Occupation museums or as restored and refurbished time capsules. At the same time, I explore why they are places that currently largely exclude those who helped to construct them. This gives an insight into the way that certain victims of Nazism can be marginalised in popular narratives. These same victims are also denied a voice at their other potential place of memory, the labour camps where many of them lived, which I discuss in chapter four. Where victims have been remembered, memorials have been erected, yet the location, date of erection and size of these are telling. These elements are often beyond the control of those who champion them. Where they have been accepted into the memorialscape, official narratives of Occupation memory can be 'read' from these collections of memorials of the capital towns of the three largest Channel Islands. The choice of such placing has often been dictated, guided, created and shaped by the changing commemorations of Liberation Day over the last 70 years, as I discuss in chapter five. As a form of 'memory-acupuncture', these memorials have been placed at certain key nodes of memory as a way of cementing those memories in granite. They act to guide and focus the movement and attention of people at key times of the year, as I explore in chapter six. Their healing role, however, is unclear and uncertain. Like the memorials, celebrations today are re-enacted at their original locations on Liberation Day in an attempt to heal traumatic memories by diverting attention and focusing on the celebration of victory and not the commemoration of victimhood.

Each of these six legacies of Occupation is also an important vector or carrier of Occupation memory in the Channel Islands and can be used to examine the developments in that memory over the last 70 years. Henry Rousso, who charted the memory of the French of their Occupation, argues that carriers of memory can be 'any source that proposes a deliberate reconstruction of an event for a social purpose' (1991: 219)—something that applies to nearly all the elements of the occupationscape that I discuss in this volume. As labour camps are *not* used to reconstruct the Occupation in the Channel Islands but are instead excluded from

Fig. 1.3 The author on fieldwork in Guernsey in front of a German bunker (copyright Jonathan Bartlett)

memory, they cannot be said to be a carrier of Occupation memory according to Rousso's definition. Their very exclusion from collective memory is in itself of value in understanding the construction of that memory.

Rousso used carriers of memory of the French Occupation as a way of gauging the 'temperature' (ranging from 'calm', through 'bouts of fever' to 'acute crises') of the obsessions of the 'Vichy syndrome' as it passed through its various phases since 1944 (1991: 220). While I observe similar moments of fever and crisis in the legacies and heritage of Occupation, most especially with regards to bunkers and memorials, my primary purpose is to record and analyse the nature of that heritage today and to understand how and why it came to take the particular form that it did in the Channel Islands. In other words, I want to chart the phases in the formation of Occupation memory over the last 70 years as expressed through heritage, and I return to this question in the conclusion.

As I noted earlier, my intention is also to understand the source and point of creation of Occupation heritage, the memory it narrated and the cottage industry it spawned. Did it originate with islanders or was it imposed from mainland Britain? Has state-supported narratives and heritage professionals influenced self-appointed guardians of memory and local Occupation enthusiasts or was it the other way around? Have they instead found a middle ground of heritage compromise and co-existence? And what might this tell us about the creation of Occupation heritage elsewhere in Europe and the role that it has played in helping countries come to terms with their traumatic past? By critically exploring this case study within a

European setting, I suggest future avenues for Channel Islands heritage inspired by current and emerging practices elsewhere. I also show how the construction of the occupationscape has at the same time constructed modern Channel Islands identity.

References

Ashplant, T. G., Dawson, G., & Roper, M. (Eds.). (2000). *The politics of war memory and commemoration*. London and New York: Routledge.

Bell, D. (Ed.). (2006). *Memory, trauma and world politics: Reflections on the relationship between past and present*. New York: Palgrave Macmillan.

Berger, S. (2010). Remembering the Second World War in Western Europe, 1945–2005. In M. Pakier & B. Stråth (Eds.), *A European memory? Contested histories and politics of remembrance* (pp. 119–136). New York and Oxford: Berghahn Books.

Cohen, F. (2000). *The Jews is the Channel Islands during the German Occupation, 1940–1945*. Jersey: Jersey Heritage Trust.

Connelly, M. (2004). *We can take it! Britain and the memory of the Second World War*. Harlow: Longman/Pearson.

Evans, M., & Lunn, K. (Eds.). (1997). *War and memory in the Twentieth Century*. Oxford: Berg.

Farmar, S. (2000). *Martyred village: Commemorating the 1944 massacre at Oradour-sur-Glane*. London: University of California Press.

Jarausch, K. H., & Lindenberger, T. (Eds.). (2007). *Conflicted memories: Europeanizing contemporary histories*. New York and Oxford: Berghahn Books.

Lagrou, P. (2000). *The legacy of Nazi Occupation: Patriotic memory and national recovery in Western Europe, 1945–1965*. Cambridge: Cambridge University Press.

Lebow, N., Kansteiner, W., & Fogu, C. (Eds.). (2006). *The politics of memory in postwar Europe*. Durham and London: Duke University Press.

Legg, S. (2005a). Contesting and surviving memory: Space, nation and nostalgia in *Les Lieux de Mémoire. Environment and Planning D: Society and Space, 23*, 481–504.

Legg, S. (2005b). Sites of counter-memory: The refusal to forget and the nationalist struggle in colonial Delhi. *Historical Geography, 33*, 180–201.

Ludi, R. (2006). What's so special about Switzerland? Wartime memory as a national ideology. In N. Lebow, W. Kansteiner, & C. Fogu (Eds.), *The politics of memory in postwar Europe* (pp. 210–248). Durham and London: Duke University Press.

Mière, J. (2004). *Never to be forgotten*. Jersey: Channel Island Publishing.

Müller, J. W. (2002). *Memory and power in post-war Europe: Studies in the presence of the past*. Cambridge: Cambridge University Press.

Noakes, L. (1997). Making histories: Experiencing the blitz in London's museum in the 1990s'. In M. Evans & K. Lunn (Eds.), *War and memory in the Twentieth Century* (pp. 89–104). Oxford: Berg.

Nora, P. (1989). Between memory and history: Les Lieux de Memoire. *Representations, 26*, 7–25.

Nora, P. (1996a) From Lieux de mémoire to realms of memory. In D. Kritzman (Ed.), *Realms of memory: Rethinking the French past. Volume I: Conflicts and divisions* (pp. xiv–xxiv). New York: Columbia University Press (English language edition with a foreword by L. D. Kritzman, trans. Arthur Goldhammer).

Nora, P. (1996b) General introduction: Between memory and history. In D. Kritzman (Ed.), *Realms of memory: Rethinking the French past. volume I: Conflicts and divisions* (pp. 1–20). New York: Columbia University Press (English language edition with a foreword by L. D. Kritzman, trans. Arthur Goldhammer).

Nora, P. (1997) *Realms of memory: Rethinking the French past. Volume 2: Traditions*. New York: Columbia University Press (English language edition with a foreword by L. D. Kritzman, trans. Arthur Goldhammer).

Nora, P. (ed.) (1984–1992). *Les Lieux de Mémoire*. Paris: Gallimard (7 vols.).

Pakier, M., & Stråth, B. (Eds.). (2010). *A European memory? Contested histories and politics of remembrance*. New York and Oxford: Berghahn Books.

Portelli, A. (2003). The massacre at the Fosse Ardeatine: History, myth, ritual and symbol. In K. Hodgkin & S. Radstone (Eds.), *Contested pasts: The politics of memory* (pp. 29–40). London: Routledge.

Rousso, H. (1991). *The Vichy syndrome: History and memory in France since 1944*. Cambridge: Harvard University Press.

Sanders, P. (2004). *The ultimate sacrifice*. Jersey: Jersey Heritage Trust.

Saunders, N. J. (2003). *Trench art: Materialities and memories of war*. Oxford and New York: Berg.

Saunders, N. J. (2004). *Matters of conflict: Material culture, memory and the First World War*. London and New York: Routledge.

Saunders, N. J. (2007). *Killing time: Archaeology and the First World War*. Stroud: Sutton Publishing.

Saunders, N. J., & Cornish, P. (2009). *Contested objects: Material memories of the Great War*. London and New York: Routledge.

Tai, H.-T. H. (2001). Remembered realms: Pierre Nora and French national memory. *The American Historical Review, 106*(3), 906–922.

Tec, N. (2008). *Defiance: The Bielski Partisans*. New York: Oxford University Press.

Tumarkin, M. (2005) *Traumascapes: The power and fate of places transformed by tragedy*. Victoria: Melbourne University Press.

Winter, J. (1995). Sites of memory, sites of mourning: The great war in European cultural history. Cambridge: Cambridge University Press.

Wood, N. (1999). *Vectors of memory: Legacies of trauma in post-war Europe*. Oxford and New York: Berg.

Chapter 2
Militaria: Collecting the Debris of War

1940 to The Present Day

Two German helmets, featuring images painted on the side, entered the collecting market in the Channel Islands in 2009. They had apparently been painted by Bert Hill, a cartoonist who worked for the Guernsey Evening Press during the Occupation. The images were two well-known Bert Hill classics: A V-sign next to a Guernsey donkey, who was kicking a German soldier out of the island (Fig. 2.1). *The words 'Liberation, 8 May 1945' were written underneath. The second helmet featured a lion, dressed as a British Tommy, breaking a chain which shackled a Guernsey donkey to a swastika. The figure of Churchill stood looking on in the background. Above this scene were written the words: 'Freedom! 1 July 1945'.*

These helmets caused instant controversy. Were they genuine? Were they forgeries? Did Bert Hill paint them or were they copies done by someone else more recently? Were they worth what the collector paid for them? For me, an archaeologist with an interest in trench art, it was not important whether the helmets were forgeries or not, nor whether Bert Hill did the cartoons. What was important was that classic and locally significant symbols of victory, freedom and liberation had been painted on top of the ultimate symbol of oppression and occupation. Some collectors in the Channel Islands disagreed: whoever did the cartoons had potentially ruined two good helmets, but perhaps if they were real Bert Hills, then this might be partially excused. In any case, the helmets would now be of more interest to a Guernsey collector than one from Jersey. Besides, they said, the cartoons were not technically very good—not quite as good as Bert Hill's originals, which did not help. And the new owner of the helmets, a Jersey collector with an interest in liberation souvenirs, was thought to have paid over the odds for them. There was also something suspect about the markings on the helmet—were they really from German soldiers who had served in the Channel Islands?

This case study proved instrumental in giving me an insight into local concepts of value and authenticity. A German helmet, that most symbolic of all items of militaria from the Second World War, could clearly be valued in a number of ways. Even between collectors within the islands, different features of the same helmets attracted some and put off others.[1]

[1] The helmets are currently on display in the German Occupation Museum in Guernsey.

G. Carr, *Legacies of Occupation*, Contributions To Global Historical Archaeology 40,
DOI: 10.1007/978-3-319-03407-2_2,

Fig. 2.1 Trench art German helmet (© Gilly Carr)

Introduction

No visit to the Channel Islands today is complete without a trip to an Occupation Museum. Since 1946 and over the decades that have followed, a number of these museums have opened, primarily as venues for the display of collections, but also as tourist facilities. Nearly all of them have followed a formulaic pattern of display since the earliest days, where pride of place is given to uniforms, swastikas, guns and sometimes even pictures of Hitler. For those visitors from outside the islands, and especially from outside Britain, such exhibits can be faintly shocking, especially for the priority and dominance given to the material culture of the occupier (or 'perpetrators of Nazism'), rather than its victims (Vitaliev 1998: 4).

The aim of this chapter is to explore the phenomenon of collecting German militaria in the Channel Islands. Rather than using superficial interpretations of political incorrectness or interpreting militaria as symbols of closet neo-Nazism, I approach this chapter from a contextual and historical vantage point with the intention of understanding the motives behind this long-lived interaction and interception in the biography of objects which date to the Occupation. The vast majority of the kinds of objects or artefacts discussed in this chapter are items of German militaria such as helmets, guns, badges and paperwork (such as photographs, the *Soldbuch* and the *Wehrpass*).

The history of the post-war biography of these objects has not been written down before now; rather, it lies in the past and present actions, collections and memories of collectors in the islands today. They have been the people who, from childhood, have tracked down and 'rescued', 'liberated' or 'souvenired' the objects, swapped them in the school playground, and persuaded friends and relations to part with them or source them and who continue to trade them today. Thus, the prime source of information in this chapter has been gleaned from interviews with the collectors today.

In conducting interviews with collectors, my aim has not been to analyse or interpret individual private collections or museums, interesting though this would have been. Rather, I wanted to discover five key things. First and foremost, what has been this history, the collective 'biography', of items of German militaria between the Occupation and the present day? How have they come to survive in the islands until today? Second, how can we understand and interpret the collection of German militaria over time? Third, how does the trade in militaria 'work' in the Channel Islands, and what does this tell us about the associated concepts of authenticity and value? Fourth, where collections have been placed in private museums, what does their content tell us about visions of the past and how this has been affected by nostalgia? Fifth, finally and in their own words, why have collectors decided to collect such potentially controversial items? Why have they sought to own and trade the very instruments and symbols which once were part of a system of oppression enacted against their own people? Is this how they see them or have these collectors been thoroughly misunderstood by passing journalists (e.g. Vitaliev 1998: 4) who have been critical and uncomprehending of this all-consuming hobby?

In order to find out the answers to these questions, I have taken two lines of enquiry. First, I have carried out interviews with thirteen collectors of varying degrees of prominence in Jersey, Guernsey and Sark and the son of one of the best-known but deceased Jersey collectors. A young but active collector in Guernsey who has played an important role in inter-island trade declined to be interviewed and so his role unfortunately cannot be documented here. No collectors in Alderney were identified as part of this study, although one of the Guernsey collectors was active in his youth in collecting items from this island. Given the limited number of collectors available to interview on these small islands today, the interviews have been analysed for their qualitative and not quantitative content. These people were self-selecting or were recommended to me by others.

Each of the collectors interviewed has very specific interests or sub-fields of speciality within the wider range of militaria or objects dating to the Occupation (e.g. guns, medals, helmets or ammunition boxes, etc.) and has built up specialised knowledge such that many of these collectors also consider themselves to be local historians. When items come into their possession which fall outside their specific interests, those objects will often be sold or traded in order to acquire items which will stay in their collections.

These collectors have all expressed a cultural conservatism when it comes to collections and museums. All remember the days of their youth, before the beginning of modern, professional museums. They express great nostalgia for the small, private Occupation Museum which was packed full of German equipment which could be touched or handled. There was no need for 'interpretation' or information panels in these museums: they presented an image which is perceived today as 'authentic', as if the Germans had just left. They had the all-important 'atmosphere' which they believe cannot be synthetically produced in modern museums through the use of computer screens or artistic/architectural installations.

My second source of information has been the Occupation museums of the Channel Islands. While collectors often refer to earlier collectors who have died, or other museums which have now closed, these have been incorporated into the story of collecting only in so far as they remain present in the memories of current collectors. While some museums which have closed have left behind a photographic record of their collections, or are accessible today through old guidebooks, I focus mostly on those still open. The names of collectors have not been anonymised at their own request: they are proud of their collections and the role they have personally played in the history of their islands in saving these objects for posterity.

It is also important to explore who these collectors are. The average collector of Occupation artefacts or German militaria in the islands today is male. As most of the collections began in childhood, to facilitate playing soldiers, one of the collectors expressed the gender division in simple terms: '*It was a natural thing, I suppose, as boys. Girls weren't interested but of course all the boys got excited*'.[2] Another echoed the gender division in similarly stereotyped terms: '*As you grow up, girls have dolls and boys play British and Germans*'. Some of the German equipments were sealed up in dark tunnels after the war, and while this did not deter schoolboys from breaking into them, one collector commented to me, tongue in cheek, '*of course, you'd never have got a girl doing that, would you?*'. Another remarked that, in the 1950s, '*I didn't find any girls in the tunnels [collecting militaria]. I must admit their interest was not in that particular stuff*'.[3]

The link between gender and collecting has been explored by Belk and Wallendorf (1994: 251), who have found that 'gender is a component of collecting activity' and is 'reflected in ... the objects that are collected'. Pearce, too, has noted that militaria and weapons are very common collecting material for men and that seldom do people collect outside the gender roles on offer to them (1995: 212 and 219). It would be both a generalisation and a stereotype to say that men are more likely than women to collect weapons and instruments of war; however, this observation is true for the Channel Islands, for historically specific reasons that will be explored here. It will also not escape the reader that women are virtually excluded from this chapter, including by the use of gender-exclusive language. This is simply a reflection of the reality of collecting German militaria in the Channel Islands. Those who encouraged, facilitated or helped young collectors were also almost exclusively male, particularly male members of the family. Those who played a cameo role in the history of collecting in the Channel Islands, perhaps by running antiques or collectables shops, or who dealt privately in German equipment, were similarly male.

Only one collector talked about the help they had received from their mother, and I observed that another collector's mother runs his museum for him. It is likely that the exclusion of women from this study is more apparent than real. I did not hear references to any female collectors or dealers in German militaria in the Channel Islands, which is not to say that they may not exist somewhere; they are not, however, discussed by the male collectors who I interviewed.

---

[2] Interview between author and Alan Allix, 21 June 2009.

[3] Interview between author and Richard Heaume, 16 March 2009.

The age of collectors is also significant. None of the collectors interviewed was younger than 45 years old. The oldest were children during the Occupation, making them what Suleiman (2006: 179) refers to as the '1.5' generation, who she defines as being fourteen years old or younger during the war. For Suleiman, this generation was, specifically, the 'child survivors of the Holocaust, too young to have had an adult understanding of what was happening to them, and sometimes too young to have any memory of it at all, but old enough to have *been there* during the Nazi persecution of Jews'. It can be seen that, in a Channel Islands context, it could be used to describe the children who lived through the Occupation and who were old enough to have *been there*, even if they did not understand all that they experienced.

In their study of fifty years of memory politics since the Second World War, Fogu and Kansteiner (2006: 297) observed four overlapping age cohorts, each united by a common experience rather than by age. They list these as 'the war generation proper, that is, men and women who were in their thirties and forties or older during the war and thus politically responsible for it; the war-youth generation, those born before the war but too young to be responsible for the war and Nazism; the first postwar generation, those born during or right after the war and coming of age between the late 1960s and early 1980s; and the second postwar, or boom, generation, those born in the 1960s and currently coming of age'.

It can be seen that Fogu and Kansteiner's war-youth generation and first post-war generation overlaps with Suleiman's '1.5 generation'. This chapter focuses predominantly on the war-youth, first and the second post-war generations. As will be seen, each of these generations had different experiences with and attitudes towards German militaria, but was heavily influenced by those who came before them. My first aim is to chart and analyse this. As these are the three generations of collectors who are still alive in the Channel Islands today to be interviewed, it is likely and, indeed, inevitable that I have placed undue emphasis on their role in collecting, ignoring those who were adults during the Occupation—the 'war generation proper'. However, interviews with collectors today have led me to conclude that this generation was not nearly as active at collecting as those who followed. While they may have kept some items as souvenirs or for personal use, very few—with notable exceptions—actually acquired them for collecting's sake.

When questioned about why younger people in the islands—the third post-war generation—are not interested in collecting today, the answer seems to be fivefold. The first reason was suggested to me by collector Damien Horn. '*It's a disposable world. You don't keep anything now … collecting came about because people had nothing come the end of the war. Things became important … you gathered things up because you never had things. As we've got more money and things have moved on, people don't keep anything now*'.[4] The second reason is that things from the Occupation are no longer circulating among the general population, in the home or in bunkers. The vast majority are now in the hands of increasingly smaller numbers

[4] Interview between author and Damien Horn, 8 April 2010.

of private collectors. Third, they are now too expensive and cannot be paid for with pocket money. Fourth, young people are perceived as being interested only in computer games; they can play out their fantasies on particular war-themed computer games and so do not need to dress up or act out their games with real items; they are all available online. Also, neither their parents nor (increasingly) their grandparents lived through the Occupation; the crucial first-hand link has disappeared, leaving nothing to fire their interest or imagination in the war years.

The role of first-hand stories of the Occupation should not be ignored. For most collectors, they provided the crucial impetus which started their interest in the Occupation; these years held a certain amount of 'glamour' for a generation or more of schoolboys. Many grew up believing that they had missed the most 'exciting' thing ever to happen in the Channel Islands.[5] As we shall see later, their desire to collect was wound up in a similar desire to recreate or relive the event that they had missed.

It is also important to define what I mean by the term 'collector', a term which does not preclude the collector also working as a dealer or trader in militaria in order to finance their collection. One of the collectors in particular was strict in his definition, describing his collecting bug in terms of addictive drug [a common feature among collectors, as noted by Belk (1994: 319)]. '*Twenty-four hours a day, seven days a week. That's me … If it was cocaine or heroin I would be getting all the help in the world and I would be being looked after!*'[6] Another collector also phrased it in similar terms. '*Once you start collecting there is a little bit of the hunter-gatherer which goes on, of course. You do get a bit of a high if you're hunting for something and you suddenly actually come across it. Once you've got it the interest drops quite dramatically*'.[7]

For some collectors, collecting (even if you can no longer afford to do so), and seriously and proactively searching for new items, was part of the definition of what made a serious collector. While not all of the men interviewed could fit such stringent criteria and acknowledged that they had a life outside of collecting, there are several different shades of 'collector' in the Channel Islands, as summarised in Table 2.1. Over six years of fieldwork in the islands, it is clear that while very few people today fit into criteria 1 or 2 (and nearly all of the collectors discussed here do so), it is probably correct to say that most island families (excluding immigrants who have come to the islands since the war—although one of the collectors interviewed fits this criteria) would qualify for criteria 4 or 5, although they would not qualify as 'collectors' strictly defined in the purest sense. While the objects in question in category 4 may be items of militaria (loosely defined), in that they once belonged to German soldiers, items from category 5 tend to belong to the civilian realm. Items in categories 4 and 5 play an important role as memory objects in recounting a family story relating to the Occupation.

---

[5] E.g. Interview between author and Martin Walton, 31 August 2009.

[6] Interview between author and Damien Horn, 8 April 2010.

[7] Interview between author and Martin Walton, 31 August 2009.

Table 2.1 Criteria of collectors, collections and owners of Occupation objects in the Channel Islands

Smallest numbers of islanders	1. People who freely admit to being proactive and obsessed about collecting
	2. People who continue to regularly add to their collection when items 'come their way'
	3. People who have a small collection of items dating from their childhood or later, and who infrequently or rarely add to their collections but still retain a latent interest
	4. People who have a German object from the Occupation that they keep as a souvenir and/or as a working/practical item (e.g. binoculars, spade, helmet)
Largest numbers of islanders	5. People who have a non-German souvenir of some sort from the German Occupation, perhaps kept in the family as an heirloom (e.g. ID card, jam jar of bramble tea, reheeled shoes)

It is useful at the outset to define what I mean by a collection. I favour a common-sense approach which dictates that a collection is only a collection when the owner perceives it to be such. Pearce suggests that, 'at some point in the process the objects have to be deliberately viewed by their owner or potential owner as a collection, and this implies intentional selection, acquisition and disposal. It also means that some kind of specific value is set upon the group by its possessor' (1994a: 159).

Throughout this chapter, I also differentiate between the 'collection' and the 'souvenir'. At its most superficial level, and in the way that I have observed it in the Channel Islands, the primary distinction is in the number of objects owned: it takes many souvenirs to form a collection. However, there is something special about the souvenir. They are 'intrinsic parts of a past experience … they alone have the power to carry the past into the present. Souvenirs are samples of events which can be remembered but not relived' (Pearce 1994b: 195). They are keepsakes, often reminders of childhood, mnemonic objects that trigger memories in the owner of a nostalgic, bitter-sweet past which, in this case, is preferably *directly* related to the Occupation. A souvenir is *personal* and linked to the self and personal history in a different way to other items in the collection. Most of the collectors interviewed here referred to souvenirs as the most precious things in their collection. On the memory of being given such an item, one collector remembered it as '*a rare event in my life and one I am sure will not be repeated*',[8] clearly stating that the souvenir in question would never be for sale.

Lest it be thought that a collection is *only* a larger group of souvenirs, in practice a collector will only own a few such special objects linked to specific personal memories, as will be discussed later. The majority of items in the collection will be anonymous or ideally linked to specific German soldier or Occupation-related story. This is probably why Susan Stewart argues that 'While the point of the souvenir may

[8] Email to author from Damien Horn, 25 July 2011.

be remembering … the point of the collection is forgetting—starting again in such a way that a finite number of elements create, by virtue of their combination, an infinite reverie' (1984: 152). The experience of the collectors I interviewed, however, undermines Stewart's distinction between the souvenir and the collection. While items may be sourced, traded and sold on, potentially mitigating against memory and promoting an 'infinite reverie', the small number of collectors in the Channel Islands and the degree to which they trade among themselves means that a relatively large number were able to identify items that once belonged to them in the collections of others; they also remembered how they acquired them. While these biographies may not be attached to particularly 'special' objects, we may perhaps distinguish between the types of memories associated with souvenirs and those with non-souvenir items in the collection.

Although I discuss this issue later in the chapter, it is important to iterate at the outset that the items of German militaria in a collection, referred to by collectors as 'bits and pieces' of German 'stuff', 'gear', 'kit' or 'relics', are never referred to, by those I interviewed, as 'Nazi' equipment. This would lend it a connotation that it rarely possesses for collectors, despite perceptions to the contrary of some other islanders or visitors. As collector Damien Horn says, '*I always collected German kit, stuff, memorabilia. It's never Nazi. It's never been Nazi. It's just German. It's German military, it's not a political thing, it's just German kit. They were German and they were here and that's what they had*'.[9] Similarly, the German Occupation itself, and all the debris it left behind, is similarly rarely referred to as 'Nazi'. It is probable that this is due to the fact that islanders lived in very close proximity to German soldiers, often in the same house, throughout the Occupation and inevitably got to know many of them. They do, however, make the distinction between the soldiers or officers who expressed Nazi sympathies and the 'ordinary German soldiers' who were seen as '*plain, simple country folk who were just doing what they were told to do. The average man on the street*',[10] who '*didn't want to be in the army*' or who '*would rather have been back on the farm*'.

The Birth of an Obsession: The History of Collecting in the Channel Islands

Phase 1: Militaria as Pilfered Booty

The thirst for collecting militaria began during the Occupation itself and, in its first incarnation, was spawned through the relationships between German soldiers and small boys or teenagers. Where the relationship was a positive one, it was not uncommon for soldiers billeted in islanders' houses to make and give small gifts to

[9] Interview between author and Damien Horn, 8 April 2010.

[10] Interview between author and Damien Horn, 8 April 2010.

island children. These were often toys or items of recycled war matériel, such as trench art [as defined by Saunders (2003: 11)]. Soldiers in the street, too, would sometimes give casual gifts to children, such as the soldier who threw an empty cartridge case to the young Leo Harris, who was watching him carry out a drill (Harris 2000: 36). Children were also responsible for souveniring 'military junk' from air crashes in the islands (e.g. Harris 2000: 117), and shrapnel and leaflets dropped by the RAF (e.g. Winterflood 1980: 12).

King (1991: 28) suggests that schoolchildren were especially vulnerable to the German presence as they were sometimes given gifts of food and sweets and taken for rides in cars and military vehicles. He describes, perhaps with a little artistic licence, how 'boys were soon practising and playing at soldiers, doing the German drills, the goosestep, and marching four abreast, bowing from the waist, heel-clicking and glorying in it!'

There are only a few collectors in the islands today who belonged to this age group. Alan Allix from Jersey is one of them. He explained how the German soldiers would never or rarely give away any of their military equipment. '*If they lost anything, even a button off their jacket, they had to account for it. And woe betide them if they lost any small arms or anything like that … if any of the soldiers fell foul of either the law or regimental orders, their feet didn't touch the ground*'.[11]

Many accounts exist of schoolboys who stole items from Germans, such as caps, helmets or guns (e.g. Harris 2000: 130–131 and 134–135, 2002: 63 and 83; Willmot 2000: 71). While some were taken as souvenirs, others were taken as an adventure or an act of patriotism (Harris personal communication 2010). Sometimes weapons were taken with the intention of keeping them until the Allies arrived, after which time they could fight alongside them. While it never occurred to some of the schoolboys that they could get caught (Harris personal communication 2010), many teenage boys were arrested by the *Geheime Feldpolizei* and imprisoned locally or deported to the continent for such thefts. Not all of these boys survived their imprisonment.

After the Occupation, the appetite for militaria continued. The Germans left behind huge amounts of items of all kinds in their billets, in their fortifications and in *Soldatenheime*. These were salvaged and souvenired by islanders who had been brought to their knees by five long years of occupation. Anything that could be reused in the home, such as furniture, blankets, clothes, tools, binoculars and typewriters, was taken. Guns, shells, German helmets and other militaria were quickly collected, as described in rich detail by Michael Marshall in *The Small Army* (1957), an autobiographical account of his post-war activities in Guernsey with his gang of friends after they returned from evacuation on the mainland. This book is especially valuable as it gives an unparalleled insight into the activities of the 1.5 generation: those who had been affected by war as children.

---

[11] Interview between author and Alan Allix, 21 June 2009.

Marshall described how he and his friends 'set about their pilfering of German equipment with relish. All areas which had been occupied by the German garrison were systematically searched and combed for anything of value. In these operations the boys received some support from the British detachments tackling the huge task of clearing up the mess' (ibid.: 171 and 173). Although the pilfering of stocks of militaria for war trophies continued in the early post-war era, pilfered items were also beginning to be seen as souvenirs.

Phase 2: Militaria as Souvenir

It seems that both departing German prisoners of war and the British liberating soldiers actually stimulated the trade in souveniring. Collector Martin Walton recalls that '*Sometimes they [people] had been given them [souvenirs] by German officers before they left [the island] … I had a Luger which was given to the local garage proprietor in St Martin's by an officer before he went off … they had got to know each other over the years and he just handed it over and said 'I won't be with this very much longer, it's a nice thing''*.[12]
Alan Allix[13] recalls, '*I remember when the Tommies first came here, they were always asking kids, if they saw you … they'd give you a sweet or something and say to you "do you know where there's this?" They were always on the lookout for souvenirs. I clearly remember British troops asking my brother if he could get them whatever it was that they were looking for—usually a Luger or something like that … and they would give him American cigarettes to take to our father … Gee! What a prize!*' Boys would be happy to sacrifice objects from their newly acquired collections for cigarettes because at that time, German equipment was easily replaceable, but cigarettes were hard to come by.

In the immediate post-war period, after years of hardship and shortages, adults took items left behind by the Germans that they could use. Peter Le Vesconte remembered that '*People used to keep all the leather and the boots and shoes for repairs*'.[14] Paul Balshaw was able to vouch for the acquisition of German boots through the story of a friend of theirs. '*When the King and Queen came to visit just after the war, his dad took him. But his father had to stand behind everybody else because he had on a pair of jackboots and he didn't want the King to see them! His father realised he was standing there in a pair of jackboots!*'[15]

A lot of German items were simply left behind in the islands. Richard Heaume suggested that '*people had held on to things because there was so much German material around; Germans billeted on households and on the farms; the things people had collected in the bunkers … the Germans couldn't take anything with*

[12] Interview between author and Martin Walton, 31 August 2009.

[13] Interview between author and Alan Allix, 21 June 2009.

[14] Interview between author and Peter Le Vesconte, 6 April 2010.

[15] Interview between author and Paul Balshaw, 16 March 2009.

Fig. 2.2 British soldier standing in Ho1 alongside anti-aircraft guns, which are about to be sealed inside the tunnel complex, February 1946 (© and courtesy Jersey Evening Post)

them apart from their personal belongings, so all that stuff was still in the island … there was still a sizeable amount of stuff in the island in people's private possessions … and I was able to get a fair chunk of it'.

With all the militaria hanging around in the islands, post-war tourists also played their part in encouraging islanders to trade. Ian Channing remembers a period from his own childhood in the 1950s. '*We used to play cowboys and Indians and everybody had German helmets. And this visitor came up to my mate and he said "Oh, would you sell me that helmet? I'll give you two bob for it". And within ten minutes there were about six kids there giving them another one*'.[16]

As part of the clear-up operations, boat loads of German mines, shells, bombs, mortars, machine guns, ammunition and landmines were dumped at sea, in the Hurd's Deep which lies just off the island of Alderney. At least, this was where they were supposed to have been dumped, but former shipwreck diver, Tony Titterington, saw large numbers of 10-cm gun barrels half a mile out in St Brelade's Bay in Jersey. '*As soon as the Navy cleared the harbour, they waited till they got past Noirmont Point and then started flinging stuff over so they could get back quicker to their beer in the evening! They said, in those days, once it was in the sea in about 60–70 ft of water, nobody wanted to know about it*'.[17]

During the clear-up, the British army presented to the States of Jersey one example of every type of weapon used by the Germans with a view to setting up a war museum. Although the weapons were accepted, they were supposed to be kept in a room at Mont Orgueil Castle, in the east of the island, but were actually placed instead in the German tunnel *Hohlgangsanlagen* 1 (Ho1) for 22 years (Fig. 2.2).[18]

16 Interview between author and Ian Channing, 2 May 2010.

17 Interview between author and Tony Titterington, 10 April 2010.

18 Interview between author and Tony Titterington, 10 April 2010.

Eventually, they were put on display at the Hougue Bie Occupation Museum in 1968 (Ginns 1985: 42).

The guns fixed in bunkers were rendered inoperative and left in position, but many of the light artillery pieces and anti-tank guns were thrown off the cliffs (Ginns 1978: 73). Some of these are still visible today. Such destruction of items that later were to become valuable to collectors can easily be understood: not only were many dangerous but the population could not wait to get rid of the hated machinery of oppression and occupation. As Allix recalled, '*Most adults weren't interested, so kids had a field day … I suppose understandably people were fed up with the sight of the stuff*'.[19]

The son of a collector who lived through the Occupation remembers his father telling him that, for the first few years after the war, on 5 November every year, Guy Fawkes was dressed in a German uniform and perched on top of the bonfire before it was lit.[20] This epitomised the relationship between adults and many items of German militaria in the post-war period.

But not all adults felt this way. While much valuable material was being consigned to the bottom of the sea or burnt, the local population began to complain in the local press about the waste when they, themselves, were still in such need. A halt was called to the destruction, and auction sales were arranged. Those interested were able to purchase not just ordinary items such as knives, bowls, scrubbing brushes, chairs, scissors and lamps,[21] but also 'relics' of the German Occupation to replace items lost or broken during the war years or to build up their collections. As traumatic as the Occupation had been, items of militaria were beginning to be recognised as souvenirs with a value.

Although adults had mixed feelings about these objects, youths had very clear attitudes towards items of militaria, as shown by an event that took place just five months after the end of the Occupation, described by Marshall (1957: 178–179). His aim, and that of his gang of teenage boy soldiers, was to track down and punish 'Guernsey Quislings'. After successful looting, they dressed in a mixture of German and British uniforms and 'now drilled in the public roads, to the amusement of the islanders, the Tommies and the German prisoners of war … On one occasion Marsh marched the whole of his Army, wearing German steel helmets, calf-skin packs and green camouflage smocks, up the Grange, the busiest thoroughfare of St Peter Port'. Such a description sounds shocking to us today, but it seems that such roaming gangs of armed and uniformed teenage boys, probably traumatised by war, were probably not atypical of the post-war era; Marshall alone lists around 60 boys in his wider gang (ibid.: 195).

During this period, as in later years, the urge for youths to acquire military equipment was, in part, a desire to play (at times in a very serious way) at soldiers. While it was relatively easy for the young to acquire actual loaded weapons for

[19] Interview between author and Alan Allix, 21 June 2009.

[20] Interview with author, name withheld, 26 August 2009.

[21] 'Captured German Material Sold', Jersey Evening Post, 15 February 1946.

their war games in the immediate post-war era, with time these became scarcer, and the danger they posed to islanders who had acted as informers or who had made a profit on the black market lessened. As Marshall puts it, 'the boys had grown up. They now had to earn their living. Life was more than just careering about with pistols and knives ... the glamour had disappeared. Like the spirit of the British people after the war, enthusiasm petered out' (1957: 193).

While this may have been the case for older teenagers, who were slowly acquiring the responsibilities of adulthood, younger boys continued to play with German militaria. Local papers published 'dire warnings of the legal consequences' to 'large numbers of island youths in possession of a considerable quantity of German weapons and ammunition' and announced an amnesty if the 'souvenirs' were handed in Marshall (1957: 191). Having sold much of their extensive stores to scrap merchants, Marshall's gang handed over what they had left. Within their combined collections, they has 'high precision optical instruments, pistols, steel helmets, compasses, radio sets with accessories ... a motor-cycle and side-car, complete with a water-cooled machine gun'. One member of the gang even slept with two stick grenades under his pillow (ibid.: 186). Alan Allix also recalls similar advertisements in the Jersey papers, calling in all German military equipment. '*There was a notification in the paper: anyone that had obtained German equipment by whatever means had to hand it all in ... but children of course have their ways of hiding things!*'[22]

The late 1940s and 1950s became an era of salvaging and souveniring, such was the density of artefacts still sitting around. What had once belonged to the enemy was fair game and was not considered stealing; rather, it constituted the spoils of war (Marshall 1957: 178). Islanders still remember this period with fondness. Richard Heaume, owner of the German Occupation Museum in Guernsey, recalled that, in the 1950s, '*most of the bunkers were open and phones and doors were still attached to walls. They and the German tunnels were Aladdin's caves ... These were the exciting places to visit and were where some of the contents of my museum came from. It was the thing to go treasure hunting then*'.[23] Alan Allix remembers swapping '*Anything ... bayonets ... any equipment if you could get hold of it, not necessarily arms ... bullet pouches and belts, caps, things like that. There were always swaps going on in the schools*'.[24] Tom Remfrey, Chair of the Guernsey Deportee Association, had similar memories. He recalled crawling down ventilation shafts of bunkers and retrieving bayonets.[25]

In the 1950s, collecting had not yet become the serious pastime that it is today, and most items of militaria continued to circulate in the domain of children and teenagers rather than adults. For adults, such items were still seen as souvenirs rather than collections. Those few who did collect in this decade were '*considered*

[22] Interview between author and Alan Allix, 21 June 2009.

[23] Informal conversation between author and Richard Heaume, summer 2007.

[24] Interview between author and Alan Allix, 21 June 2009.

[25] Informal conversation between author and Tom Remfrey, summer 2007.

a bit of a crank',[26] although to keep souvenirs or, even better, to give them away to the young was quite acceptable.

Children were able to acquire many souvenirs from the adults who owned them, a practice that went on for decades. Many of the collectors interviewed particularly valued these early gifts from adults. It was indicative that they and their collections were being taken seriously and not just treated as a childish hobby.

It seems clear that children and adults valued them differently in the 1940s and 1950s. For many of the children, their interest in the early days was not '*so much on collecting; it was on finding and exploring*'.[27] And while it was acceptable for children and teenagers to use militaria in war games, this would have been seen in a very different way had adults used them for the same thing. But, with the passing of time, even this has become acceptable—although controversial—today. A number of the collectors I interviewed are members of vintage arms' associations or have been involved in living history or re-enactment which has involved dressing up in German uniform.

Between the 1940s and 1970s, it was perfectly acceptable for adults to give weapons and other equipment to children, something that would be unacceptable today. Richard Heaume recalled that '*my parents were very supportive in the early 1960s to accommodate my hobby. My father used to come out and help me salvage things with the tractors and my mother actively used to go around asking her friends who were here during the Occupation if they had any souvenirs, and she brought back all sorts of interesting items, including guns*'.[28] Mark Lamerton, too, remembers the role of adults in his family in getting him items. '*My grandfather … had these containers full of German motor oil which he still used, and he gave me an empty container once and I was over the moon with this … and I can remember an uncle of mine going into in his workshop and finding a wooden box for a fire extinguisher … and I said, "Can I have it?", and he said "I'll give it to you for your birthday", and on my birthday I got this big thing wrapped up … that was the way I got a number of things, I'd get them for birthdays and Christmas*'.[29]

For Damien Horn, his father would make enquiries on his behalf of friends and customers at his men's clothing shop in St Helier. '*Dad would ask, "Have you got anything?", and people would come into the shop and we'd always get talking to the locals and ask them if they had anything. And we'd pop up on a weekend and see what they'd had on their farm or in their sheds, and inevitably … I was given quite a lot of kit. My dad would take me to see his mates if they had something, and the odd bits he'd always pick up. I remember him coming back from the pub one night and he'd played darts with a guy for a German helmet*'.[30]

[26] Interview between author and Ian Channing, 2 May 2010.

[27] Interview between author and Richard Heaume, 16 March 2009.

[28] Interview between author and Richard Heaume, 16 March 2009.

[29] Interview between author and Mark Lamerton, 8 May 2009.

[30] Interview between author and Damien Horn, 11 May 2010.

Although adults sometimes gave their souvenirs to children as gifts, or parents were able to buy or trade on behalf of their children, the actual *trade* in militaria was kept going by children and teenagers in the 1950s. '*It was quite difficult in those times*', Martin Walton remembers. '*Apart from Dickie Mayne who started it off, there weren't really any collectors as such ... there were one or two antique shops in town who used to have some military things but a lot of it didn't appear on the market until later years. I would buy things from other schoolboys. I do remember that*'.[31]

Swapping objects in the school playground was popular, although teachers tried to ban this practice. Alan Allix remembered that '*you weren't physically searched but they used to look you over when you came into see if you had any stuff on you*'.[32] If they were found with objects, they would be told to take them back home. Tony Titterington, on the other hand, who was a little older, recalls that there were so many children bringing German equipment into school that nobody worried about it. Perhaps the teenagers were given a freer hand than the younger boys to indulge their hobbies.

Smuggling militaria into the school playground is something that continued in Jersey until the 1970s, and almost all of the collectors interviewed remembered doing this. Speaking of the 1950s, Martin Walton recalled that '*They didn't bother to smuggle them, particularly! Obviously they didn't wave them in front of the teacher's face ... you just kept it under covers ... Not that much came through the school to be honest. It was mainly someone said "Oh, I've got this", and then you'd go round to their home*'.[33] Collector Peter Le Vesconte remembers, in the 1960s, '*one kid coming to school with a cross band of live ammunition wrapped around his body, and the police arriving up there and taking it off, and another kid coming to school with a pistol. I do remember that*'.[34] At school in the same decade, Mark Lamerton recalled that '*it seemed at school that everybody had something relating to the Occupation ... I remember having a Walther P38 pistol and having to hide it from my parents ... by the time I was ten my bedroom was covered with it [German equipment]; I had tables with artefacts on them or underneath, or hanging up or whatever*'[35] (Fig. 2.3). By the 1970s, collecting had come full circle; some of those teachers who had been schoolboys during the Occupation were interested to see the German items that their pupils brought in.[36] It was not unknown for teachers to actually donate items to their pupils outside school grounds.[37]

The situation in Guernsey, at least at some schools, was very different; here, teachers were much stricter about what was brought into school. Richard Heaume

---

[31] Interview between author and Martin Walton, 31 August 2009.

[32] Interview between author and Alan Allix, 21 June 2009.

[33] Interview between author and Martin Walton, 31 August 2009.

[34] Interview between author and Peter Le Vesconte, 6 April 2010.

[35] Interview between author and Mark Lamerton, 8 May 2009.

[36] Interview between author and Graeme Delanoe, 25 May 2010.

[37] Interview between author and Paul Balshaw, 16 March 2009.

Fig. 2.3 Collector Mark Lamerton as a schoolboy with his fledgling collection of German militaria, 1969 (© and courtesy Jersey Evening Post)

remembers his school days at Elizabeth College in the 1950s, where the principal declared that '*Any boys collecting German militaria or going in German tunnels and bringing stuff to school would face expulsion*'.[38] This followed the accidental shooting of a policeman by a schoolboy several years earlier, and so collecting had to be done secretly. '*I found other people interested in collecting these things and we used to go round together and explore German bunkers and German tunnels and we collected things. We formed a little society in 1956 … we used to meet in the farmhouse, in the attic, about once a month. We planned activities and outings and it was a very organised group of youngsters, and everything was done with almost military precision … so the society was called the German Occupation Research Department, after the departments we had at the college—we thought we'd add an extra one! A secret one! … and we always met outside school*'.[39]

Guernsey was not the only island where accidents among schoolboys took place. Alan Allix remembers that, in Jersey, '*In about '45 or '46, this boy was playing with bullets. What he'd done, he'd put one in a vice and hit it and taken three fingers off. Well, we were all at it. We thought he was a hero!*'[40] Tony Titterington recalled a similar incident. '*Several of my friends shot themselves with guns … one was sold a Polish cavalry officer's pistol by our school barber … there was probably something wrong with it … it went off and the bullet went into his liver and they couldn't get it out. He very nearly died. There was another one later on, he had a nice little German pistol. A friend came to see him and they were playing with it and his friend shot him. He died*'.[41]

[38] Interview between author and Richard Heaume, 16 March 2009.

[39] Interview between author and Richard Heaume, 16 March 2009.

[40] Interview between author and Alan Allix, 21 June 2009.

[41] Interview between author and Tony Titterington, 10 April 2010.

Any discussion of the era of souveniring, especially by schoolboys, would not be complete without an account of the important role played by the German tunnels. These were one of the key sources of militaria in the Channel Islands, and nearly every collector discussed in this chapter has broken into them at one time or another in search of objects. This is because, during the clean-up of the Channel Islands after the war, the galleries of German tunnels became ideal places to dispose German equipment that the British army did not have time to dump at sea, such as anti-tank guns, anti-aircraft guns, steel helmets, field kitchens, range finders and gas cylinders. The ends of the galleries were then blown up, and the tunnel entrances sealed (Ginns 1993: 16 and 18). Although much of this material was later removed by scrap merchants, the tunnels were destined to become places of pilgrimage to generations of schoolboys intent on hunting for treasure. The key tunnels which all collectors mention are those in St Peter's Valley in Jersey, principally Ho2,[42] and Ho12, the tunnel under St Saviour's Church in Guernsey.

Tony Titterington, who was a young teenager in the late 1940s, recalled how he and his friends used to cycle at weekends to St Peter's Valley to explore the tunnels. '*They'd been sealed up, but very poorly, simply by piling earth at the entrances, so we scrambled over the hump [of earth] and there were all kinds of things in there … they were very good … but we were only interested in guns*'.[43] Martin Walton recalled of the 1950s that '*at that time the tunnels were fairly free and accessible; people used to go up on their bicycles and if you'd gone outside the tunnels you'd see bits of German relics in a trail down the valley road*'.[44]

The trade between schoolboys was so keen in the 1950s that, incredibly, young teenagers could walk around quite openly with weapons and equipment without getting into trouble. Walton remembers trying to acquire a Panzerfaust (a type of rocket launcher) from a friend when he was about 12. '*I was determined to buy this thing from him… I couldn't take it on my bicycle … so I went up there by bus to buy the thing off him … then I got onto the bus with this thing standing up and I wasn't thrown off by the conductor or anything. I took the bus all the way down to St Helier, changed buses, and then came up to St Martin's and then walked down the road from the bus stop at St Martin's Church with this thing above me … it didn't get very much comment at that time*'.[45]

The German tunnels in Jersey became harder to break into in the early 1950s after an incident. After their torch failed, two boys got lost overnight in Ho2[46] (Fig. 2.4). Although the entrance to the tunnel was sealed immediately after they were found, this did not deter those who were searching for equipment, who promptly made a hole in the sealed entrance. Between 1954 and 1962, the Public Works Department in the island spent more than £500 on continual efforts to keep

---

[42] '*Ho*' is an abbreviation of 'Hohlgangsanlagen' or 'cave-passage-installations'.

[43] Interview between author and Tony Titterington, 10 April 2010.

[44] Interview between author and Martin Walton, 31 August 2009.

[45] Interview between author and Martin Walton, 31 August 2009.

[46] *Jersey Evening Post*, 19 March 1952.

Fig. 2.4 Schoolboys peering inside the lower entrance of Ho2, 1962 (© and copyright, Jersey Evening Post)

the tunnel sealed, but each time the concrete was put in place, at night someone would remove it before it had time to dry (Ginns 1993: 21). By 1960, it was not unusual to see anything up to 20 bicycles outside the tunnel entrance as their owners explored the interior (ibid.: 19).

The dangers of these tunnels were no more off-putting to young boys in Guernsey. Richard Heaume remembers one occasion when he was in St Saviour's tunnel in 1958. '*I was there on a wet afternoon when the people were actually sealing the front of the tunnel with concrete, and I'd slid in down an eight-foot shaft and I couldn't see the light to get out … but I knew that if I made a commotion to these workmen then they would not report me because I made them feel irresponsible for not having checked the tunnel … it was a nasty fright!*'

Teenage boys were determined to get into the tunnels, no matter that they were being sealed up as fast as they broke into them again. Peter and Paul Balshaw recalled the methods used. '*They'd seal it up every week but before the next weekend, the boys had unsealed it … [they used] bricks and concrete blocks. And then you'd kick it in again … you'd go at night-time with a hammer and chisel … they'd come back a week later and seal it up again … kids were still going in up till ten years ago. You won't stop them … if you put a notice saying "free entry", they won't go in. If you brick it up, they'll want to go in. "Please keep out" means you want to go in, doesn't it?*'[47] Lest it be thought that the Balshaws were the only collectors to do this, even the most respected of collectors interviewed here

[47] Interview between author and Paul and Peter Balshaw, 16 March 2009.

Fig. 2.5 Richard Heaume removing horse-drawn ammunition trailer from the St Saviour's tunnels in the late 1960s (© and courtesy Brian Green and German Occupation Museum, Guernsey)

admitted to similarly breaking into the tunnels. '*We had to physically dig in all the tunnels*', confirmed Richard Heaume.[48]

The St Saviour's tunnel was still well stocked with equipment in the 1950s. '*Mostly ammunition, boxes, belts, a lot of German helmets. Thousands of German helmets, which was a prize thing … and there was a lot of bigger things: horse-drawn equipment, still on wheels*'.[49] Later on, when Richard Heaume returned to Guernsey from agricultural college at the end of 1963, he began to collect more seriously. He opened his museum in 1966 and, in 1969, gained permission from the church authorities to open up the tunnels under the church and purchase all the equipment there[50] (Fig. 2.5). '*There were all manner of items … it was all things to be scrapped or disposed of, as most of the things of value had actually gone for sale … or people had taken as souvenirs … It was the debris of war; it was the scrap things which had very little interest for most people*'.[51]

---

[48] Interview between author and Richard Heaume, 16 March 2009.

[49] Interview between author and Richard Heaume, 16 March 2009.

[50] The law in the Channel Islands dictates that the contents of underground tunnels or bunkers belong to the person who owns the land above them.

[51] Interview between author and Richard Heaume, 16 March 2009.

The German tunnels did not lose their allure with time, even though their contents were beginning to decay. Ian Channing remembers visiting the tunnel in St Peter's Valley in Jersey around 1960. '*They were full of gear … and there was a white mould over everything so it was like a grotto when you went in there … the stuff was thrown in there and kids searching for stuff were throwing stuff all over the place, and you had drums of oil, big drums with a big eagle and swastika on the top … but when that stuff's all piled up you've got to be careful because it's rotten. You stand on stuff and the next thing you've fallen through it … when you touched stuff it was all crumbling, so you knew it was like walking through a minefield*'.[52] However, not all the items were decaying at an equal rate. 'Some of it was like new', Ian Channing told me. '*It was amazing. You could pick stuff up—there were hundreds and thousands of boxes, ammunition boxes, full of little spares and bit and pieces like that, and everybody was looking for guns. So the kids would go in and pick up the boxes … and there was a wall of helmets, but over the years, all the kids climbing over them and looking in them had pulled them down*'.

On 27 May 1962, two teenage boys died of carbon monoxide poisoning after exploring inside tunnel Ho2 for souvenirs. This time the authorities built a concrete wall over the makeshift upper entrance, but it was soon breached. As it was realised that boys would continue to find their way inside the tunnel as long as German equipment remained, much of the tunnels were emptied and sold off in 1970s and 1980s (Ginns 1993: 21–22).

Tony Titterington took part in the clearance of the tunnel in 1972 (Fig. 2.6). '*We were given a lorry to fill up, to save the stuff like tin hats for example. We found a whole big pile of tin hats that we hadn't known were there … they were covered with petrol tins and junk … and if you could bang them together and no hole came, then we kept them. If a hole appeared, we flung them. About six or seven lorries of tin hats went to St Ouen's to be buried and we kept 2,200. That will show you the scale … I don't know what happened to them in the end*'.[53] Collector Graeme Delanoe was able to tell me about the tin hats taken to be buried in the parish of St Ouen. He was just beginning his collection as an 11 year old at that time. '*A lot of the kids that were in the know went out there and dug the stuff up again and that's how it appeared in circulation*'.[54] In this way, cycles of burial and excavation by adults and children meant that militaria continued to stay in the public domain.

While a lot of the German equipment in good condition that came out of the tunnels at that time was taken to Elisabeth Castle in St Helier, some of it was sold on and other pieces were stored in a large room in the castle. However, after some items were stolen,[55] everything that remained was moved on. The majority was taken to the house of collector Martin Walton after his friend and fellow collector, Paul Clothier, was given permission to take them. From there, after they had been

[52] Interview between author and Ian Channing, 2 May 2010.

[53] Interview between author and Tony Titterington, 10 April 2010.

[54] Interview between author and Graeme Delanoe, 25 May 2010.

[55] Interview between author and Tony Titterington, 10 April 2010

Fig. 2.6 German militaria inside Ho2, 1972 (© and courtesy Tony Titterington)

restored, items were moved into the new island Fortress Museum in St Helier. In the early 1980s, Clothier was also given permission from the landowner of Ho2 to finally clear what remained in the tunnel. Martin Walton was present at the opening. '*It was a big event for me to go into the tunnel at the re-opening. And the only thing that was really there were these field kitchens … they'd left half the field kitchens in*'.[56] The young Graeme Delanoe, also present, was overwhelmed with the anticipation of entering the tunnel after hearing so many stories about them. '*It was like Aladdin going into the cave with all the jewels and things! But unfortunately by the time we were going in there it was just what people had pulled out from corners to try and find the good stuff that people had neglected. There were machine gun belts, gas mask cases, remains of helmets, optical range finders … nothing that you could class as valuable and important*'.[57]

Although the war-youth generation and first post-war generation to enter the tunnels were in search of souvenirs, as these boys grew up, their pile of souvenirs began to become serious collection and they took their hobby more seriously. Thus, it is to the era of militaria as serious collection that we must turn next.

[56] Interview between author and Martin Walton, 31 August 2009.

[57] Interview between author and Graeme Delanoe, 25 may 2010.

Phase 3: Militaria as Serious Collection

By the early 1960s, equipment was circulating in huge numbers around schoolboy collectors (who regularly visited the German tunnels) and, increasingly, adults. Many of the first post-war generation of collectors had reached adulthood and began to be more serious about building up their collections in both quantity and quality. Although today's collectors look back at the 1960s and 1970s as a halcyon age of ubiquity and volume of material, Ian Channing remembers thinking, in 1960, '*It's finished now, it's been too long since the Occupation; I'm only getting 20 or 30 pieces a week*'.[58] Compared to later decades, these numbers were huge.

For those who had established a reputation as collectors, items of German militaria were flooding into the market and directly into their hands. In Guernsey, Richard Heaume recalled that '*a lot of things people were happy to dispose of for a nominal sum. They were not looking at the value of things then; the value was not so great because there was so much of it around, you couldn't put a value on anything*'.[59] A generation after the Occupation, people were getting rid of the souvenirs they had earlier acquired; they were still perceived as neither particularly desirable nor valuable to the wider population.

The late Richard 'Dickie' Mayne was a well-known collector and museum owner who played a large role on the Jersey collecting scene. His son recalls that the Occupation became a predominant obsession for him because it was commercial. '*In the early 1960s, there was only the German Underground Hospital—they had a very extensive collection. There was La Hougue Bie [Occupation Museum] which had some artefacts … tourism was really in its heyday … because he'd lived through the Occupation, he had a foot in it already, had a good network of acquaintances … And I think he saw a niche that he could open up somewhere and collect, which would satisfy his collector's side but was also a way of making money*'.[60]

Richard Mayne is acknowledged by other collectors as having been one of the first serious adult collectors who did not start in childhood. He established the St Peter's Bunker War Museum in 1965 (Fig. 2.7). As with Richard Heaume in Guernsey, once people knew that Mayne was interested, they brought items to him. '*Either they came along with a pair of German leather boots and asked "what are these worth?" or … a number of people who had arms … because their father had got them or their grandfather had got them or whatever, or it was under the bed or it was in a box or in the loft … and what do you do with it? What do you do with a German horse's saddle? Or a German horse's gas mask?… All they do is sit, usually in the garage or in a loft, gathering dust … and I think maybe it was*

[58] Interview between author and Ian Channing, 2 May 2010.

[59] Interview between author and Richard Heaume, 16 March 2009.

[60] Interview with author, name withheld, 26 August 2009.

Fig. 2.7 Interior of St Peter's bunker in its heyday (© and courtesy of the family of Richard Mayne)

families moving or people dying, and their lofts were being cleared out, and they knew someone who was collecting and so might be interested'.[61]

While some islanders had hung onto items of German equipment as souvenirs, others were using them on their farms. Peter Le Vesconte recalled that there was still a lot of German equipment on farms in the 1970s. '*My father said that during the Occupation, a German lorry went past him and they dropped a bundle of spades … so my father had this German spade. He was using it right up until the 70s. He'd never even told me it was German! And in the 70s, he said to me "that's a German spade, that", so I nicked it out of his garage!*'[62] Damien Horn also acquired items from farms and farmers. '*I know a lot of farmers used the stuff … I know farmers used the Germans*' Zeltbahn, *camouflaged ponchos the German soldiers wore. They buttoned them together and they used them for covering the cows in the bad weather as cow covers! They were utilised and that's why they're still in existence, whereas most stuff was burned, buried and dumped … A lot of people kept binoculars because there weren't any around at the end of the Occupation and they were useful … We used to find bayonets on farms because they used to use them for cutting cauliflowers … Anything from the farm that had been used was the secondary part of your collection. It was never the best*'.[63]

The era of the souvenir did not end when the serious collectors began; they continued to stimulate the market for decades. What was once a souvenir was slowly becoming a family heirloom. Damien Horn contrasted the situation between the 1970s and the present day: '*The stuff was still hidden away [in the 1970s]. People had taken it and put it away and weren't ready to let it go. A lot of people took German helmets as souvenirs, and 20–25 years ago they still had them as a souvenir. They weren't at a stage in their life where they're thinking "what do I want this rubbish for?" … People say "I'm keeping it for the grandkids" …*

[61] Interview with author, name withheld, 26 August 2009.

[62] Interview between author and Peter Le Vesconte, 6 April 2010.

[63] Interview between author and Damien Horn, 11 May 2010.

[but] in some cases it comes your way in a few years' time anyway, because the grandkids don't care about it and they do want a few quid … or it goes back to the grandkids and it stays there until they reach a stage in their life where they decide, 20 years down the line, "what do I want it for?" I don't think there are many people hanging on to kit who had it passed down from grandparents … if you say 100 grandparents gave their children something, I think you'd be very lucky to find two or three who actually do hang on to it for a lifetime'.

In the 1970s, the prices were rising and militaria was still circulating in quantity. Peter Le Vesconte, who opened his own collectables shop in the mid-1970s, described collecting during the 1970s as '*easy then, because there was just so much stuff around … You'd pick up a good German helmet for about twenty, twenty-five quid, which at the time for me was two weeks' wages, which was affordable … every single week we were picking up two or three items. I was buying from three different antiques shops at that time*'.[64] Items were still so ubiquitous that even serious collectors did not hang on to items permanently. Tony Titterington explained that '*you collected something and then you swapped it on within a few months when you got tired of it. And there was so much going around, it wasn't hard. I mean, you didn't hold on to a thing as if it was a jewel*'.[65]

The opening of antiques and collectables shops in the 1970s took the trade and collection of militaria to a new level. Martin Walton recalled how Peter Le Vesconte '*had a tremendous contact with people who had German relics, because he was buying all the time. He was the only person dealing in it at the time, he had a tremendous amount of material going through his hands from everyone who knew that he was working*'.[66] Other collectors in the antiques business would also pass items on to him. Once items were for sale at such a venue, many items were sold to visiting tourists, English collectors and collectors from other islands. The previous militaria economy which thrived on gift-giving, barter and exchange between family, friends, neighbours and acquaintances had now expanded to include sale between strangers.

Although by the 1970s many of the first-generation schoolboy collectors were now adults with still-growing collections, museums or shops out of which they conducted a trade in German militaria, the age of the schoolboy collector was still continuing thirty years after the end of the Occupation. The second post-war generation, born in the 1960s, was probably the last to experience this phenomenon. Their experiences still had much in common with the schoolboys of earlier decades, although the items available were less ubiquitous and not in such good condition as the adults passed on to them less valuable pieces.

Graeme Delanoe remembers buying items from the respected Richard Mayne in the late 1970s, when he was still a teenager. '*There was an area [in his attic] where it was tradable pieces and stuff that wasn't so significant … but I had the*

[64] Interview between author and Peter Le Vesconte, 6 April 2010.

[65] Interview between author and Tony Titterington, 10 April 2010.

[66] Interview between author and Martin Walton, 31 August 2009.

pick of these boxes, I was just told to go up there and he would just say "Yep, you can have that, you can have that", and so when I left this house the first time, it was like I'd gone to heaven. It was an amazing experience. And when I look back at it now and see the stuff I was given compared to what I had in the collection in later times, you could see why Richard had passed it on. Because to me it was gold; to him it was silver'.[67]

Damien Horn testified that boys were still bringing militaria into school in the 1970s. '*People were bringing in German helmets and different bits and pieces that their parents and grandparents had given them… A lot of the stuff when I was seven or eight was just rusty stuff, stuff that had come from the German tunnels and, not knowing any different, I thought that all German stuff from the war was in that condition, because that's all I ever saw … different stuff was coming to school all the time and I was trading for it [with] marbles, sweets, money, whatever was wanted … I ended up with a small collection of rusty German equipment*'.[68] Children of the 1970s also had to look harder for their items of militaria. Damien recalled that '*as time went on, I got to know people who had the better stuff … in garages and sheds and tracked it down any way I could … I'd go cycling in the countryside, and as you cycled past you see, in garages and sheds, German helmets hung up or a carbide lamp or a field telephone*'.[69]

Another stimulus to trade and collecting in the 1970s was the market for mass produced Occupation and Liberation souvenir kitsch, some of which was available at a price that children could afford. The kinds of items produced were invariably souvenirs marketed to be released at the time of Liberation Day each year.

An indication of taste among collectors at this time is perhaps best exemplified by an item which came out in 1973. This framed plaque, designed in the same colour scheme as the swastika flag, incorporated historic quotations relating to the Channel Islands made by King George VI, Churchill and Hitler. At the top, flanking a German eagle with a swastika in its talons, were the dates of occupation. The plaque was designed by Michael de Havilland Geraghty, a former public relations consultant, who gave copies to island leaders and to the German Chancellor, Herr Willy Brandt.[70] It is perhaps fortunate that history does not record what they thought of it.

On the twenty-fifth anniversary of liberation, souvenir swords, knives and daggers were produced, but in the years that followed, these were replaced by ash trays, mugs, plates, plaques, thimbles, coins, Zippo lighters, key rings and teddy bears.[71] Such tourist kitsch to commemorate war has parallels with the items produced in America following national disasters such as the Oklahoma bombings and the destruction of the World Trade Centre. These have been documented by

---

[67] Interview between author and Graeme Delanoe, 25 May 2010.

[68] Interview between author and Damien Horn, 11 May 2010.

[69] Interview between author and Damien Horn, 11 May 2010.

[70] *Jersey Evening Post*, 10 May 1973: 11.

[71] My thanks to Mark Lamerton for showing me the liberation souvenir items in his collection.

Marita Sturken, who interpreted them as objects produced for what she calls 'tourists of history', a 'particular mode through which the American public is encouraged to experience itself as the subject of history through consumerism … souvenirs, popular culture … a form of tourism that has as its goal a cathartic "experience" of history'. Sturken is particularly concerned with the subjectivity of the tourist of history, 'for whom history is an experience once or twice removed, a mediated and reenacted experience, yet an experience nevertheless' (2007: 9).

This description is not entirely inappropriate for members of the post-war generation, for whom history (or the Occupation) was experienced second hand or at a distance, mediated through material culture. However, there are differences between the role of souvenir kitsch in America and in the Channel Islands, with the former being used as part of a 'comfort culture', to encourage people to see themselves as innocent victims of unprovoked attacks and the latter playing upon a long tradition of souveniring and collecting war trophies.

Phase 4: Collecting as an Investment/Currency

Although those who still collect have remained every bit as passionate about their collections, many have detected a change in the collecting scene in the Channel Islands from about the mid-1980s onwards. The chief problem is that fewer and fewer items are now circulating. Martin Walton has observed that '*there is a lot less about and some of the people who used [to collect] … the contacts I had … are always saying, "ah, it's finished, it's finished, it's all gone now, it's finished, there's nothing around", but they keep popping up with the odd thing actually, but not to the extent that it used to be—no, you'd have something turning up almost every week about 20 or 30 years ago*'.[72] Damien Horn has also observed this. '*The number of collectors in the last ten years has dropped right off. There was always a sort of group of maybe six or eight people who were collecting … most people have really quietened off in the last ten years. It's died, it's died. There's been a couple of people who've packed up and between us we've kept the ball rolling. There was always something new, always a turnover. There was always something turning up that one or the other wanted, and that meant that something else came out. But now it's gone really quiet*'.[73]

The number of collectors has sharply dwindled, which Peter Le Vesconte puts down to price. '*If you wanted a nice German helmet, you'd be looking at £550, £600 … recently a German paratroop helmet came up for sale, and it fetched £3,600. Those prices, your ordinary person can't afford them*'.[74] As Graeme

---

72 Interview between author and Martin Walton, 31 August 2009.

73 Interview between author and Damien Horn, 11 May 2010.

74 Interview between author and Peter Le Vesconte, 6 April 2010.

Table 2.2 Summary of phases of perception of militaria among those who collect it

Phase 1 (1940s)	Militaria as pilfered booty/war trophy
Phase 2 (1940s to present)	Militaria as souvenir and (later) heirloom
Phase 3 (1950s/1960s to present)	Militaria as serious collection
Phase 4 (1980s/1990s to present)	Militaria as investment/currency

Delanoe commented to me, '*it's got to a stage that you're not going to get new collectors now because it's too expensive*'.[75]

As is clear to all collectors, the cost and value of items of militaria have only increased with time. Those who still collect now view their collections as valuable investments. Some are involved in the trade of German militaria nationally and internationally, and will buy and sell items surplus to their requirements in order to fund the purchase of items that fit their collecting criteria.[76] These collections are highly unlikely to be donated to local island museums or archives in the future, but are instead perceived as pensions[77] or nest eggs for retirement. Those who have sold their entire collections speak of using German helmets (used in this sense as a metaphor for all types of equipment) as a currency for conversion into holidays or time with the family.[78]

When asked about the future of his collection, Damien Horn said that, '*at the end of the day, with no local interest, I may be faced with putting the collection to a major auction to be sold off in Europe where I would be assured that the items would firstly all sell and secondly attain the true worth on the day and set my kids up with a few quid to get them started*'.[79] The perception is that, at some point in the future, the collection can be cashed in.

The time has already arrived when some island collectors are forced to source their items overseas, from Germany, within the families of former soldiers of occupation. They have to look outside the islands in order to 'bring home' or 'rescue' any and all surviving local objects. Although a very small numbers of souvenirs from local families are still entering the market, these are few and far between. Increasingly, collectors are sitting on treasuries of their local heritage and an end to the intra- and inter-island trade in militaria is already in sight.

While the way in which German militaria has been perceived has changed through time in a series of overlapping phases (Table 2.2), this can also been seen as a series of stages which describe the flow of military goods in the islands between tunnels, museums and antiques shops, and between adults and children (Table 2.3). Although the tables are not directly equivalent, chronologically we

[75] Interview between author and Graeme Delanoe, 25 May 2010.

[76] E.g. www.festungjerseymilitaria.com, accessed 24 July 2011.

[77] Telephone interview with Danny Wakley, 26 July 2011.

[78] Interview between author and Graeme Delanoe, 25 May 2010.

[79] Email from Damien Horn to author, 24 July 2010.

Table 2.3 The typical flow of German equipment in the Channel Islands

Stages	Domain of adults	Domain of children/teenagers
1	Militaria in the hands of German soldiers	Militaria pilfered
2	Militaria stockpiled by liberating forces and souvenired by adults	Militaria pilfered
3	Militaria sealed in tunnels/stowed in attics and barns	Militaria stolen from tunnels and circulated among children
4	Tunnels emptied in successive waves and contents buried or removed	Militaria excavated, given or pilfered and circulated among children
5	Militaria taken to museum/shop	Militaria continues to circulate; some acquired from adults
6	Heyday of museum; some items sold to collectors	Militaria continues to circulate; some acquired from adults
7	Museum closes; items sold to collectors or other museums	Militaria continues to circulate; some acquired from adults
8	Number of museums and collectors diminish; increasing amounts of items in hands of the few	Militaria becomes too expensive and scarce to collect

can broadly equate Phase 1 to Stage 1 and 2; Phase 2 to Stage 3 onwards; Phase 3 to Stage 4 onwards; and Phase 4 to Stage 8.

Table 2.3 shows the typical flow of German equipment in Jersey and Guernsey in a series of chronological stages. While some of these stages took place only days apart, others were separated by years. At each stage, the impression gained from talking to collectors is that, unofficially and at all stages, certain items of militaria in the adult domain were being diverted from their supposed path and disappearing into private collections. From there, a few items were given to children, thus fuelling their own collections, or were even sold abroad or to tourists.

There is yet one final stage to the analysis and interpretation of how and why militaria was being collected and understood by different generations. This involves the four-phase model of Table 2.2 being boiled down into two groups: the collecting experiences of those who had some experience of the Occupation (i.e. the war-youth generation) and those who did not (the first and second post-war generation).

The War-Youth Generation: Collecting as a Coping Mechanism

Interviews with those who collected or played with German militaria during or soon after the Occupation clearly show how important this activity was for the young in the Channel Islands. During the Occupation, it was an activity that was driven by children themselves, with no input from adults other than German soldiers. However, after the liberation, adults were much more active in encouraging this activity, although they were perhaps unaware of the full extent of the social worlds young boys were creating with their arsenal of weapons and equipment. Even though adults were often responsible for 'seeding' collections, the degree to which the collections grew out of hand is indicated by the need either to be circumspect about the items brought to school or to keep such activities away from the playground altogether, as collectors Richard Heaume and Martin Walton discovered.

The influence of specific childhood or adolescent experiences on choice and type of collections has been noted by Baekeland (1994: 212–213) and by Belk and Wallendorf (1994) and is something that we must bear in mind as the strongest influence on the collectors discussed in this chapter. Gabriel Moshenska has also explored an example of such collecting in his exploration of the collection of shrapnel among British schoolchildren in the Second World War. He has argued that such collecting was a 'coping mechanism, a means for children to control or domesticate the material culture of violence by integrating it into their social practices and thereby negating its violent and alien qualities'; it was also 'a way for children to feel involved and actively in the world at war on a par with the adults around them' (2008a: 109). The illusion of control of material culture is achieved through ownership and by arranging, classifying and manipulating collections. As Belk and Wallendorf (1994: 248) explain, 'rather than reflecting the real life of the collector in microcosm, collections also offer the collector an opportunity to construct a fully controllable world of objects in which … reality can be manipulated'.

Although many Channel Island children who had been through the Occupation had not experienced the trauma of such regular bombing raids as their English cousins, they had been through a period just as terrifying. A large number of island children had actually spent the war years as evacuees in the United Kingdom, and the relationship of youngsters like Michael Marshall and his friends towards militaria is arguably more shocking than that of their friends who were not evacuated. Children (and, indeed, adults) of the 1940s and 1950s were clearly normalised towards militaria; they had grown up surrounded by real weapons and soldiers in large numbers and felt little fear in handling, firing, dressing up in and collecting the relics of war. Like their counterparts in Britain who collected shrapnel, the obvious danger in collecting such items made it a more thrilling, subversive activity (Moshenska 2008: 116).

The First and Second Post-war Generation: Objects, Stories and Collecting as Nostalgia

By the time the post-war generation had begun collecting, particular differences can be seen in the reasons and meanings of their collection. In order to understand this generation, I explore and extend Marianne Hirsch's concept of 'postmemory' or inherited memory. Hirsch coined the term postmemory to better understand the experience of children of Holocaust survivors who grew up 'dominated by narratives that preceded their birth, whose own belated stories are evacuated by the stories of the previous generation, shaped by traumatic events that can neither be fully understood nor re-created' (1996: 659). These stories are 'so powerful, so monumental, as to constitute memories in their own right' (1999: 8). This description has strong resonances with my perception of the post-Occupation generation born between the mid-1940 and the mid-1960s, who grew up in an era dominated by stories of the Occupation, stories which took the place of their own experiences.

As I see it, where postmemory differs between Hirsch's children of survivors and the post-Occupation generation is in three key areas. First, for the children of survivors, the world of their parents had been violently erased or irreparably changed. For Channel Islanders, the landscape of occupation continued to exist all around them. Much of it is still intact today although affected by the passage of time and prevailing modes of heritage presentation. Second, the traumatic events of Holocaust survivors cannot be recreated by their children; in the Channel Islands, some events of the occupation can be and regularly are recreated and re-enacted. Third, while memories are mediated by family photos for children of the Holocaust survivors, for Channel Islanders it is mediated by objects, principally, souvenirs and items of militaria.

Both Hirsch's children of survivors and the post-Occupation generation share the fact that their connection to the event which affected both their parents and themselves is 'mediated not through recollection but through imaginative investment and creation' (1996: 662). Again, this is especially apparent in the post-war youth who played imaginative games with the souvenirs of war that they had stolen, found or had received from adults. Their collections of militaria were later translated into Occupation museums where their imagination of war was given free rein, as I discuss later.

Objects and Stories

While family photographs are central to Hirsch as the 'building blocks', the 'medium connecting first- and second-generation remembrance, memory and postmemory' (1997: 2–3), in the Channel Islands the key medium of memory is artefactual, as I noted above. Stories are told through the medium of objects, whether they are carefully curated in the home for the regular telling of stories or whether they are abandoned in the garage, field or attic, waiting until the time that the curious child finds it and starts to ask questions. Artefacts and stories (or, where stories were missing, an imaginative mind) have always gone together for children who wished to learn about the Occupation.

Damien Horn recalled that '*everybody [who was] asked if they had something German [to sell] always had a story*'. Graeme Delanoe emphasised the importance of stories from older siblings and friends. '*You'd speak to older brothers and sisters and friends and everything and they would be telling you how they had helmets from their schooldays… I had friends at school who had bits and pieces, legacies from parents and grandparents left lying around, stories from visiting grandparents*'.[80]

As Martin Walton's family evacuated before the Germans arrived, he heard his Occupation tales from local farmers who lived nearby. '*I would approach them and ask them … the Occupation was a medium and this is all to do with part of the collecting—you got hands on… It's much easier to relate to something if there's something you can hold or look at, And then the imagination works on it*'. Ian Channing also emphasised the importance of imagination. In talking about German helmets, he said '*They were everywhere … it was just something that fired the imagination. And everything you got out of there [the tunnels] was free … it was the excitement*'.

Collector Martin Walton remembers a time in the late 1950s, a generation before bunkers began to be excavated and restored. '*The fortification part was not really very readily explained at that time, so there was this mystery about what happened under the German Occupation … but the guns were immediately available at that time … a lot of these kinds of artefacts stirred the imagination quite a bit*'. So even when other aspects of the Occupation were not being talked about, the ubiquity of German equipment was a way in which children could begin to explore the lost world of the Occupation through their imagination. For example, in talking about a gun battery near his house after the war, Martin remembers that '*a lot of the battery was still intact at that time and when you're very small and you're walking along trenches and suchlike, the whole thing takes on an out-of-world experience … it's something very mysterious … and then you have war stories which you get about the Occupation which people were giving you at that time and my interest went in the direction of small arms, guns, firearms, artillery. From quite an early start I was interested in collecting various types of weapons*'.

Ian Channing saw the early post-war years in the same way. He got involved in collecting '*same as other people in the Channel Islands who were brought up hearing stories of … the Occupation and so forth. And if you're interested in that sort of thing you obviously listen and get interested … you were brought up on it all … I was just fascinated and one thing led to another and you … start collecting and swapping … everybody thought that "oh, I wish I was there"*'. '*I'd love to go back*', agreed Mark Lamerton, '*because I've got so many questions*'.[81]

This desire of the first and second post-war generation to have experienced the Occupation or even the liberation can be seen as a nostalgic longing for a time before they were born, a longing for the world that their parents or grandparents inhabited and spoke about afterwards when our collectors were growing up. This was a world that they had created through imaginative play during their childhood, a world that they had touched while venturing inside the German tunnels and bunkers and in collecting militaria. It was also a world that some of them would one day recreate inside their Occupation museums.

---

[80] Interview between author and Graeme Delanoe, 8 April 2010.

[81] Interview between author and Mark Lamerton, 8 May 2009.

Svetlana Boym defines nostalgia as 'the longing for a home that no longer exists or has never existed', a 'sentiment of loss and displacement', a 'romance with one's own fantasy' (2001: xiii), but also a 'yearning for a different time—the time of our childhood' (ibid.: xv). These are precisely the forms of nostalgia experienced by the first and second post-war generation of collectors in the Channel Islands. Like the nostalgic who desires 'to revisit time like space' (ibid.: xv), collectors are able to relate to the items of German equipment in their collections in a way that enables them to encounter the Occupation. However, nostalgia can be dangerous and lead to the confusion of the actual past and an imaginary one.

In her analysis of nostalgic perceptions of the Communist past in Budapest, Nadkarni (2003: 205) defines nostalgia as 'the uncritical attempt to resurrect past presence and imagined origins that forgets everything that was painful and difficult about that era'. This strikes me as a very good description of the nostalgia which surrounds the collection of German militaria. Although collectors present many good reasons to explain why they collect objects which others might perceive as lacking in taste or as politically incorrect (as I discuss later), here I interpret the desire to possess these objects as a nostalgic desire to re-experience an event that they missed: to recapture some of the excitement experienced by teenage boys both during and immediately after the Occupation.

Their nostalgia is for a very specific part of the Occupation. They do not long to recapture the oppression, the food shortages and the hardship, or to witness the ill-treatment of Jews or foreign workers, the deportations or the imprisonment of those who disobeyed the orders of the occupying power. Like the people of Budapest, they tune out all that was 'painful and difficult about that era'. Their nostalgia is for quite specific 'exciting' experiences of boys or young men during the Occupation.

When asked whether they would like to have lived through the Occupation themselves, nearly all responded positively, but drew a selective image of what age they would have liked to be or what they would like to have experienced. Richard Heaume, born towards the end of the Occupation, said, '*I know quite a few boys who were youngsters during the Occupation, and they had an exciting time in a way … the Germans almost were amused with them and quite friendly … for some people it was no joke, because the older people felt the hardship … it was drudgery for some … but for some of the youngsters it was quite exciting … it would have been an experience*'.[82] Damien Horn, born almost 20 years after the end of the Occupation, puts it thus: '*life sounds more exciting [during the Occupation] … you've got that other dimension, as in the unknown … you've got that fear and anxiety of not knowing what's going to happen next … if you were 16, 17, 18, there was excitement to be had*'.[83]

For some collectors, their desire to have experienced the Occupation is, unsurprisingly, object-oriented. Damien Horn imagined himself present on

[82] Interview between author and Richard Heaume, 16 March 2009.

[83] Interview between author and Damien Horn, 11 May 2010.

Liberation Day, '*... in the bunkers carrying out arms full of German rifles and helmets, that sort of thing*'.[84] Mark Lamerton was similarly focused on the objects. '*I'd be saying "you've got to save that, you can't get rid of that, put that aside"*'.[85]

Boym (2001: xviii) distinguishes between two kinds of nostalgia. The first, restorative nostalgia, 'attempts a reconstruction of the lost home'. It does not think of itself as nostalgia, rather 'as truth and tradition'. It manifests itself in total reconstructions of monuments of the past and has 'no use for the signs of historical time—patina, ruins, cracks, imperfections' (ibid.: 45). Reflective nostalgia, on the other hand, 'focuses on the longing itself' and 'lingers on ruins, the patina of time and history, in the dreams of another place and another time' (ibid.: 41).

When observing the interests and priorities of our collectors in childhood and teenage-hood, we can see that their appreciation of objects began with a reflective nostalgia, where rust and the 'signs of historical time' were important. Graeme Delanoe, one of the younger collectors I interviewed, recalled his schooldays in the early 1970s. '*In those days we were collecting anything as long as it was rusty. It had to be rusty! Because we couldn't afford non-rusty equipment ... So my first collection of equipment was empty ammo cans, drum magazines, bullet belts, but [in] the condition that you would throw away today ... you know, if we found an ammo can, in today's standards we'd look at it and throw it away. Well, to us that was the biggest find we could ever imagine*'.[86] Mark Lamerton, born five years before Graeme, explained the importance of the rust: '*If something had a bit of rust on it, you could virtually guarantee that it was the genuine article*'.[87] Rust was thus appreciated and valued by younger collectors. However, as they grew into adulthood and began to have more spending power, they made a transition from reflective to restorative nostalgia in their appreciation and valuation of German equipment.

Many collectors belonged or belong to one of the several vintage military arms or vintage military vehicle associations in the Channel Islands and put much value on restoring or maintaining their collection in full working order. Collector Damien Horn, for example, has a Stoewer, the last Occupation-era German vehicle left in the Channel Islands today (Fig. 2.8). His website boasts that it was a '*rusting wreck*' when he acquired it, but it has now been '*fully restored and put back on the Island's roads. As a member of the Jersey Military Vehicle Club I take the car out on various events throughout the year*'.[88]

Our collectors' collections are not just for display; quite the contrary. For some, they are to be handled, admired and used. Some collectors are also often scathing of modern Occupation museums which have different interests and priorities; some took the opportunity of the interview to express their disapproval of museums where items were going rusty or damp or were not looked after or appreciated.

---

[84] Interview between author and Damien Horn, 11 May 2010.

[85] Interview between author and Mark Lamerton, 8 May 2009.

[86] Interview between author and Graeme Delanoe, 25 May 2010.

[87] Interview between author and Mark Lamerton, 8 May 2009.

[88] www.festungjerseymilitaria.com, accessed 9 July 2011.

Fig. 2.8 Collector Damien Horn driving his Stoewer on Liberation Day 2009 (© Gilly Carr)

Such lack of maintenance can lead to an item losing aesthetic and financial value, even when rust can also be associated with authenticity.

Nostalgia also plays a role in the value of objects in other ways, where those which are somehow closest to the past are more valuable than those deemed to be more recent. This is articulated most clearly by Martin Walton, talking about the items in his collection which he has had since childhood. '*My most treasured provenances are the earliest, partly because of nostalgia for youth and when the "sun always shone", but also because the people involved were closer to the event and seem so much more interesting in character*'.[89] The relationship between 'closeness to the event' and value is clear.

However, unless they are forged or are reproductions, all of the objects with which we are dealing here date to the time of the Occupation, but the ability of collectors to come within touching distance of the Occupation is all important. For this, they must, as far as possible, be the first (rather than, say, the fifth) owner of the object. '*They all want to be the first one*', says Ian Channing. '*There's like an aura … it's like one-upmanship*'.[90] For Graeme Delanoe, like other collectors, the importance of having the item 'first hand' means being the first owner of an object since its original wartime or post-war owner, whether that person acquired it as a souvenir or because it was useful on their farm. '*That's real provenance. And that is sometimes the only thing that I will actually believe in, because I know the source*'.[91] This means that lists or stories of which collectors have previously owned the object in question—whose hands it has passed through—are positively undesirable. There is little prestige to be gained through owning an object that had previously been in another's collection unless there is some guarantee that that

89 Email to author from Martin Walton, 21 April 2010.

90 Interview between author and Ian Channing, 2 May 2010

91 Interview between author and Graeme Delanoe, 25 May 2010.

person obtained it directly or indirectly from a German soldier. Belk (1994: 321) refers to this kind of object as 'sacred' by virtue of having been 'contaminated (in a positive sense) by contact with prominent persons'. Sacred items would rarely leave the collection or at least would greatly boost its value.

In addition to an item becoming sacred or acquiring added value for being closer to the Occupation in this way, it must similarly at least be a local piece, i.e. used by a German soldier in the Channel Islands (as opposed to elsewhere), and preferably from the island where the collector lives, in order to be worth collecting at all. This is of fundamental importance to most of the collectors I interviewed. '*If it's got nothing on it and it doesn't say "Channel Islands", then I can let it go and I can use the money or a direct exchange for something that has a connection*', says Damien Horn.[92] Danny Wakley from Sark remarked to me that '*if it comes from Sark, it makes it more valuable*'.[93] Others are scathing about the importance of such notions of what constitutes 'local'. Ian Channing gives the example of a helmet worn by a German soldier who had served in France, then in Jersey and then on the Eastern Front, in Russia. '*Those helmets were in Jersey. Now they're in Russia. Before that they were in France. How does that make it local?' … They go 'Oh, it's a beautiful local piece, this helmet comes from Jersey'. I say, 'That's funny, I thought it came from Germany'. Where do you start? Is it Jersey only when it comes to Jersey?*'[94]

Some collectors and dealers have brought items into the islands from other formerly occupied European countries, such as France or Norway; after the fall of the Berlin Wall, items from Eastern Europe also entered the market.[95] This can cause problems for the unwary collector, although there are ways of telling the provenance of some items. Every gun that was imported, for example, had to be marked as such.[96] Because of the added value of a secure provenance and the associated importance of 'closeness to the event', many dealers or collectors often do not reveal the list of previous owners of an item in case it puts off a buyer, especially if the list is a long one. Graeme Delanoe elaborates on this. '*The worst thing about collectors is they're very secretive. Collectors will never give any information out [about where they acquired a piece] … people are very guarded about their sources*'.[97]

Thus, the role of nostalgia in collecting can be a powerful influence in determining the value of items of militaria. Just as the brand of nostalgia experienced by collectors is focused on a particular aspect of the past, on the particular memory of youth and the experience of the 'excitement' of the Occupation in the Channel Islands, so collectors value objects which are guaranteed to date from this time and this place or at least which are closer to the Occupation by dint of having been

---

[92] Interview between author and Damien Horn, 11 May 2010.

[93] Telephone interview between author and Danny Wakley, 26 July 2011.

[94] Interview between author and Ian Channing, 2 May 2010.

[95] Interview between author and Mark Lamerton, 8 May 2009.

[96] Interview between author and Peter Le Vesconte, 6 April 2010.

[97] Interview between author and Graeme Delanoe, 8 April 2010.

received first hand from a trusted source or from a German soldier directly—the 'glamour of association' is valued. I now wish to explore the concept of 'closeness to the Occupation' a little more deeply.

The Social Life of German Militaria

Drawing upon her fieldwork among the Kodi people of Sumba in Indonesia, anthropologist Janet Hoskins introduced the concept of the 'biographical object' as an object which is 'endowed with the personal characteristics of their owners'; the 'lines between persons and things can blur and shift' (1998: 7). Such an object can be a 'metaphor for the self' and can 'mediate for the person' (ibid.: 3). I would suggest that the 'aura' that Ian Channing referred to above, associated with items which are in first-hand ownership since the Occupation, i.e. have an unmistakable provenance as they are owned by the person who acquired it from a German soldier in one way or another, is because these particular items of militaria are perceived to be 'endowed with the personal characteristics of their [original] owners'. As Martin Walton explained it to me, *'If it is an item named to an individual, this adds enormously to its interest'*.[98] In other words, if an item can be linked directly to a German soldier, the aura is stronger and the item accrues more value for collectors. Its provenance is strong, and it is 'closer to the Occupation'. However, if the provenance is unclear and an item has passed through the hands of many collectors, an item becomes vaguely contaminated and very quickly loses its value as a biographical object.

Following the work of sociologist Morin (1969: 137–138), Hoskins (1998: 8) contrasts biographical objects with 'public commodities', which are 'not formative of its owner's or user's identity'. 'At the spatial level, the biographical object limits the concrete space of its owner and sinks its roots deeply into the soil. It anchors the owner to a particular time and place. The public commodity, on the other hand, is everywhere and nowhere, marking not a personal experience but a purchasing opportunity'. Thus, for our collectors in the Channel Islands, I would suggest that once items of militaria begin to change hands, they pass rapidly from the status of biographical object to public commodity. For those that stay with the original or first-hand owners, i.e. the people listed in categories 4 and 5 in Table 2.1, they remain as biographical objects as long as they are kept with those owners.

To stay on the subject of the meaning of an object during its life trajectory, anthropologist Arjun Appadurai stated that 'even if our own approach to things is conditioned necessarily by the view that things have no meanings apart from those that human actions, attributions and motivations endow them with, the anthropological problem is that this formal truth does not illuminate the concrete, historical circulation of things. For that we have to follow the things themselves, for

[98] Email to author from Martin Walton, 19 April 2010.

their meanings are inscribed in their forms, their uses, their trajectories. It is only through the analysis of these trajectories that we can interpret the human transactions and calculations that enliven things' (1986: 5). If we follow Appadurai, we must come to the conclusion that for our collectors of militaria, the objects themselves have no meanings apart from those with which they endow them and which can be interpreted by observing their trajectories and their use.

While we might have no problem with this position, Peter Pels, in his study of the fetish, encourages us to look closer. For him, the fetish is an 'object of abnormal traffic', which I take to mean a rare or strange object that, in trade, follows an unusual trajectory or is treated differently, because of its abnormal status. We might assign to items of German militaria this status, as they are 'abnormal' objects which are certainly treated fetishistically by collectors, according to their own rules. Pels suggests that such items possess a 'spirit of matter' and can 'act, emit messages and meanings on their own'; they can 'communicate their own message' (1998: 94). The ability of the 'materiality itself ... to speak and to act' is something that we can connect to the 'aura' referred to by Ian Channing earlier. Collector Martin Walton also suggested to me that many items can '*speak for themselves*'.[99]

Quite how objects are able to speak or act is expressed by Pels; thus, a souvenir can suddenly 'change our everyday rhythm, to connect it with a memory or a history that is commonly absent'. This also happens when we are 'confronted with the difference from everyday life presented by strange museum objects or other curiosities' (1998: 100). Thus, the item of German militaria can act as a trigger for collectors (and others) and connect them with a memory of the Occupation or of their youth, a period when they roamed around their island, searching for items of militaria and having adventures among the debris of war left behind by the occupiers. Even as children, many collectors commented on the ability of these objects to fire their imagination about the war years. Just as people can shape the trade in objects, the trade in objects can also shape people.

I think it important to stress at this point that the perception by collectors of some items of German militaria during their life cycle as 'biographical objects', and the ability of some objects to 'speak' or 'act' or trigger memories, is something that is very Channel Island specific. This is not to say that those who live elsewhere in the world do not see German militaria as biographical objects (indeed, the family of former soldiers of occupation may well see the helmet of their family member in this way); nor is this to argue that people living in the United Kingdom or elsewhere, who buy a military badge or gun in the islands, cannot be sent off into a reverie by handling the object. Rather, my intention is to stress that the memory or sensory perceptions of Channel Islanders in handling these objects will be very specific to their own particular history, and the meanings and values with which they imbue first-hand items of militaria are culturally

[99] Email to author from Martin Walton, 30 April 2010.

specific. Thus, an item traded out of the Channel Islands will lose the meanings that island collectors hold dear.

I now wish to consider the range of biographies of items of German militaria in the Channel Islands. The purpose of a biographical approach (Kopytoff 1986) is that it allows us to understand the changing meaning of the social actions which involved these objects during their existence; they cannot be fully understood at just one point in time during their life history. It also illuminates the links between people and things and the ways 'meaning and values are accumulated and transformed' (Gosden and Marshall 1999: 170 and 172). In short, it clarifies the numerous possible trajectories that militaria can take and the resultant changing meanings and attitudes attached to it by different people. As Kopytoff argues, 'the same thing may be treated as a commodity at one time and not at another … the same thing may, at the same time, be seen as a commodity by one person and as something else as another' (1986: 64).

We have already seen how, by Hoskins' definition, an item may move rapidly from being a biographical object into being perceived as a public commodity. What other transformations are possible and regularly take place among objects of German militaria? Once an item of militaria becomes a candidate for commodity status, is there any turning back? Can it be decommoditised? What, in the perception of our collectors, constitutes an ideal 'career' for militaria and what would be considered an undesirable career?

First of all, how are we to define a commodity? For Kopytoff, it is a 'thing that has a use value and that can be exchanged in a discrete transaction for a counterpart, the very fact of exchange indicating that the counterpart has, in the immediate context, an equivalent value' (1986: 68), i.e. an object intended for exchange. A commodity can be contrasted with a gift, with its associated implications of reciprocity, links and obligations which bind people together.

In small societies such as the Channel Islands, and especially among small groups such as collectors of militaria, the trade and exchange of commodities occurs among people who are already bound together by links of kinship, friendship, membership of the same clubs, proximity and island identity. This muddies the water when contrasting the two types of exchange because, especially when bartering or swapping items as opposed to paying for them with money, collectors will remember who has had the better deal, to whom they owe favours and who behaved appropriately during a transaction.[100]

The links of island identity can be important when considering with whom to trade. Ordinarily, people from one island will preferentially trade with each other rather than with someone from a rival island, although they will prefer to trade with another Channel Islander than with an outsider. To openly trade outside the islands rather than with a friend or neighbouring collector who wishes to acquire the same piece can be a matter of insult or can cause offence. Generally, selling a collection

[100] Some collectors expressed a disapproval of the way that some of their fellow collectors conduct themselves in their search for and negotiation of objects.

outside the Channel Islands has negative connotations. Not only does this constitute a loss of heritage and the sale of items to people for whom it does not have the same meaning or who would not appreciate it, but there is the danger that the collection could be split up, a notoriously difficult concept for a collector to handle.

There are, of course, exceptions to this rule. Sometimes a better price can be gained from an outsider. If the item in question does not have a Channel Island provenance, then it is perfectly acceptable to trade with whomsoever one wishes. Additionally, as time moves on, there are fewer and fewer collectors operating in the Channel Islands. Sometimes collectors are forced to seek new trading partners elsewhere if they are to avoid the endless circulation of the same objects within their social circle. Because of the small circle of collectors, it can even become necessary to sell some items outside the islands. In order to acquire a piece, a collector may have to say that it will go in their personal collection, where it will be kept safe. They would then not be able to sell it locally in case the person who gave it to them saw it.

In this chapter, items of militaria have been considered at different points in their life history, at times during which they were seen as commodities and in periods when they were given as gifts, used as toys and kept as souvenirs or when they left commodity status and entered a museum. Clearly, commoditisation (if that is to be our focus) is best 'looked upon as a process of becoming rather than as an all-or-none state of being', as Kopytoff (1986: 73) puts it.

Appadurai (1986: 13) proposed that 'the commodity situation in the social life of any "thing" be defined as the situation in which its exchangeability (past, present or future) for some other thing is its socially relevant feature'. As one of the key questions in this chapter is to examine, document and understand the trade in militaria in the Channel Islands, we will accept Appadurai's proposal, while not forgetting that commodity trade is just one part of the biography of these items. As Appadurai himself notes, 'things can move in and out of the commodity state, such that movements can be slow or fast, reversible or terminal, normative or deviant' (1986: 13).

As shown in Tables 2.4 and 2.5, in a series of steps, I consider what might be perceived in the Channel Islands as both an ideal and a non-ideal biography of a German helmet, which is most iconic of items of German militaria. The diversion of objects from their 'proper path' was considered by Appadurai (1986: 26) as something which could happen due to crises such as warfare, theft or economic hardship. For our collectors, of course, warfare was the very thing that produced the objects in the first place. Still, there was certainly something to be gained in the post-war period in selling an item, whether to a liberating British soldier or to a tourist, as collector Alan Allix recalled from his youth.

To view militaria in the way I show it in Tables 2.4 and 2.5 highlights not only how it moved in and out of the commodity state through time, but also how it changed in meaning and use, throughout its life history, depending on the owner. The original intention of the first owner may not have been to trade the item in question; the predestined path of the item may have been diverted because of the death of the owner, a desire not to have items on the property which reminded the

Table 2.4 Ideal biography of a German helmet (after Walters 1997: 72)

Begins life as functional head protection issued to soldier
Becomes a souvenir after the war
Becomes a gift for a schoolboy
Becomes a commodity to be traded in the playground
Becomes a toy to be used in playground games
Becomes a collectable item and kept out of marketplace
Re-enters commodity state to be traded in the Channel Islands
Leaves commodity status for non-traded permanent collection
Becomes a museum item
Becomes a symbol of Occupation and oppression for tourists

Table 2.5 Non-ideal biography of a German helmet

Begins life as functional head protection issued to soldier
Becomes souvenir after the war
Becomes a commodity and sold to visitor to islands due to economic hardship
Leaves the Channel Islands
Remains a commodity outside the islands and loses context
Becomes stolen from collector/souvenir hunter owner
Breaks/becomes damaged/becomes junk/loses value
Remains a commodity but leaves collectors' market and sold in junk shop/flea market

owner of a difficult time, or because of economic hardship (Appadurai 1986: 25–26), and this would have resulted in a change in meaning of the item. It may also have lead to the item being eventually put in a museum, where it may have been permanently decommoditised, becoming a kept object and remaining out of circulation (Weiner 1985)—at least for the lifetime of that museum or museum owner.

Tables 2.4 and 2.5 deal only with authentic, original objects. As I have already noted, such items are, not surprisingly, valued more highly than fakes. An increasing problem with German militaria is not just the entry into the market of items from Eastern Europe, but more seriously, the growth in forgeries. It can be notoriously difficult to tell the difference between a 'right' and 'wrong' (to use local parlance) German helmet, for example. Helmets are especially vulnerable to forgery because of the high prices they can command. As collector Martin Walton explained, '*helmets used to be about thirty bob or two pounds in the 1960s … and now a paratrooper helmet is two or three thousand; an ordinary helmet is … six, seven hundred pounds or something like that if someone thinks that it's particularly good*'. It is also almost impossible to tell a reproduction German helmet after it has been weathered.[101]

Collectors consider the ability to discern a real German helmet from a fake as a matter of skill and pride. Peter Le Vesconte told me that '*the most important thing is handling the stuff and having a feel for it. I'm really one of the last few people …*

[101] Interview between author and Martin Walton, 31 August 2009.

bring me a good German helmet and a wrong [i.e. forged] one, I'll tell you straight away. And there's hardly anyone who can do that now. Now you see on Ebay, there's stuff for sale all the time. And they're all fake'.[102] But such skills are not without their problems. As Ian Channing put it, '*you do get a feel for the stuff, but you try convincing somebody else! But you've got the same problem when you've got something genuine … I've got an old saying: "There's none as blind as don't want to see"*'.[103]

Collectors are unwilling to admit to having forgeries in their collection, as it reflects badly on their own ability of discernment. As Martin Walton put it, '*be wary of asking collectors about how you can tell a reproduction, because they are going to immediately say, "well, nothing I've got is reproduction!"*'[104]. As for collectors who also have a reputation for skill in the arts of restoration and reproduction, additional problems exist; other collectors become wary of trading with them. As one such collector-dealer put it to me, '*you could walk up to them with Hitler's pyjamas that you'd got off his mother and they'd go "You made them!" You can't win*'.[105]

Thus, while authenticity is cherished and of considerable importance, it is difficult to distinguish real items from fakes—or even between objects which came from other formerly occupied countries and those which came to the Channel Islands with the German army. The skill of discernment is one that a collector will claim to raise his status and level of respect within the circle of collectors, and there are perceived to be increasingly few collectors who have this skill. Because only the older collectors can claim to have been alive at a time when only genuine items were circulating, they can legitimately be the only ones who can claim to be able to distinguish between real and fake, local (i.e. with a Channel Island provenance) and non-local.

For collectors outside the Channel Islands who buy items online from Channel Island dealers, concepts of local versus non-local are likely to be less important. For these people, what is of value is that the item of militaria dates from the Second World War. For the casual visitor or tourist, however, people without the necessary skills to discern reproduction from real, what matters is that they are buying war memorabilia, perhaps perceived as 'a little piece of the Occupation' because, after all, it was purchased in the Channel Islands. The items that visitors tend to ask about or wish to purchase are the iconic German helmets or iron crosses.[106] Like the trade in Vietnam Zippos explored by Walters (1997: 66), 'the boundary between genuine and fake vanishes entirely in the merchandising'. For veterans or their family members who travel to Vietnam in search of '*that* place, the place of war, the place of their youth, or their dad's youth, or whatever, these

[102] Interview between author and Peter Le Vesconte, 6 April 2010.

[103] Interview between author and Ian Channing, 2 May 2010.

[104] Interview between author and Martin Walton, 31 August 2009.

[105] Name of collector withheld.

[106] Phone call between author and Damien Horn, 23 July 2011.

Table 2.6 Occupation museums in the Channel Islands

Name of museum	Year of opening	Island
German Underground Hospital	1946 (now Jersey War Tunnels)	Jersey
La Hougue Bie	1947 (now a memorial to forced labourers)	Jersey
German Underground Hospital	1954	Guernsey
St Peter's Bunker War Museum	1965-2000 (now closed)	Jersey
German Occupation Museum	1966	Guernsey
Island fortress Occupation Museum	1982-2006 (now closed)	Jersey
La Valette Military Museum	1988	Guernsey
Channel Islands Military Museum	1989	Jersey
Sark Occupation and Heritage Museum	1994	Sark
Jersey War Tunnels	2001	Jersey

things are the mementoes. They are from Vietnam … They must be real. They *are* real. No questions asked. No issue of fake arises'.

It is only among our small group of collectors that locally specific concepts of fakery, authenticity and value prevail. These are firmly wrapped up in historically specific nostalgic memories. And it is all of these concepts and memories which have been put on display in Occupation museums.

Occupation Museums, Nostalgia and Memory

Since the end of the Occupation, there have been at least ten key Occupation museums in the Channel Islands. This list is not exhaustive; there have been other venues which contain items from this era but which also function as a museum for the whole island, such as Alderney Museum. Jersey and Guernsey museums are excluded from this list as they are not Occupation museums even though they own and sometimes display objects in their archives which are similar or identical to those in the collections of the collectors interviewed here. There have, at various times, been objects of German militaria placed on display in places which do not quite conform to museum status (e.g. the St Saviour's tunnels in Guernsey as described in Ginns (1993: 58–59). Additionally, several of the museums discussed here have metamorphosed from museum to memorial; have closed and later opened again under new ownership; or have undergone massive renovation and rebranding, changing from one extreme of Occupation Museum type (as described in Table 2.6) to another. While some of these museums are singled out in this section for further comment, they are mostly described as a single phenomenon.

Display, Design, Poetry and Authenticity

The design of a display in any museum is important; however, among the collectors of militaria, there is a recognised poetry to their own collections and in those of others. This poetry is recognised by collector Martin Walton, who is worth quoting at length. '*The mass of the individual collections are a kind of formulation, almost an artistic display. I mean, when I collected a lot of the items I quite often have in my mind a presentation … I can see the presentation in front of me. The way you put together these things is very much an individual thing … you have enthusiasts here [in Jersey] who have put their life and soul into it and they present it in a way that they have done individually and personally researched … [the bigger museums are] soulless, absolutely soulless. They are done in what is perceived to be the best way to present things as to what the public will relate to most easily. And the little museums have individuality and personality that you are totally losing now. I do think that the small private museums have a very important place because they are being interpreted by people who have invested quite a lot of their life into it. It's not just a job*'.[107]

The different kind of poetry, individuality or personality referred to by Walton reflects the collecting interests of the individual collector who has built up a reputation for a certain style or method of collecting. For Peter Le Vesconte, for example, large numbers of the same kinds of items were important. As he recounted to me, '*by the time I started work, which was about 1970, I had about 60 bayonets, much to my father's disgust because I drilled holes in the walls and put them in rows down the walls*'. Around the same time, he recalled, '*I had the biggest collection of German helmets on the island. I had 116*'.[108] Graeme Delanoe's collecting rationale was different. '*One thing I used to do was, if I found something, I would try to complete it … I would find every accessory to go with it*'.[109] For Damien Horn, on the other hand, the structuring logic of the collection in his museum is less obvious. '*The museum doesn't start … pre-war, it doesn't go to the immediate Occupation and it doesn't end up with the liberation. It's just evolved: what fits into a room, what I can get into that cabinet … what I've got to put on display fits into that space. It would be nice to put everything into chronological order and have the various bits in their own separate cabinets, but the museum doesn't give itself to that; I haven't got the space*'.[110]

In examining collections of militaria in the Channel Islands, preferences for certain kinds of militaria were obvious. While most aimed at artistic display, the constraints of space inevitably ended up interfering with initial intentions. Despite this, it was clear that while some preferred machine guns, others favoured German paperwork, medals or military badges, and these are often displayed in an artistic

[107] Interview between author and Martin Walton, 31 August 2009.

[108] Interview between author and Peter Le Vesconte, 6 April 2010.

[109] Interview between author and Graeme Delanoe, 25 May 2010.

[110] Interview between author and Damien Horn, 11 May 2010.

manner rather than entirely haphazardly. The style in which these items were mounted on the wall differs between museums. Some favoured grouping all items of a certain type (such as pistols or medical equipment) in one display case or wall, and others clearly delight in creating scenes with mannequins. Graeme Delanoe remembers the island Fortress Occupation Museum in St Helier in its heyday. '*This was the time when the MG34 machine guns and flak guns from Portugal had just started to be put onto the open market … so [the owner] had this 2 cm flak gun with all the associated equipment and kit you could imagine … and he'd made it into a working diorama … you could walk around and touch as you went into the room*'.[111]

To be able to touch a collection on display was an early prerequisite for Occupation museums that was much valued by collectors; this sensory engagement with the objects was and is highly important. This was contrasted by Graeme Delanoe with museums with more modern modes of display. '*Unfortunately … with certain museums where it's just a computer screen and you press a button and it tells you the information, they're not interested in the original equipment. They've put that in a little cupboard somewhere … but to me history is hands-on and being able to see something for yourself*'.[112]

La Hougue Bie Occupation Museum in Jersey is one that is often recalled with fondness. '*It was a hands-on museum … I remember going in there and you could actually cock the rifles … they just had a barrier … you could touch them, and a lot of people used to pinch them*'.[113] The danger of theft inevitably led to the increased use of glass display cases, but collectors without museums, who display their collection in their own houses, also emphasise the importance of sensory engagement. '*I want to see a big room full of all the equipment and I want people to come in and actually see it there, and smell it … pick up a helmet and actually see inside it*'.[114] Once again, we can see notions of 'closeness to the Occupation' coming to the fore in systems of value. To be able to touch, feel, use and smell an object handled by a German soldier during the Occupation is clearly closer to actual event than an interpretative display, a computer screen or even glass case that prohibits touching.

It is pertinent here to consider the concept of authenticity in museum display. For our collectors, this is achieved by the use of large numbers of artefacts which originated from the Occupation, preferably acquired first hand and chosen from the best of a collection (as opposed to reproductions). Objects originating from another formerly occupied country in Western Europe or (even worse) from Eastern Europe after the fall of the Berlin Wall are not valued as highly. Chronological and geographical distances both conspire to lessen the perceived value of an object or display.

---

[111] Interview between author and Graeme Delanoe, 25 May 2010.

[112] Interview between author and Graeme Delanoe, 8 April 2010.

[113] Interview with author, Graeme Delanoe and Damien Horn, 8 April 2010.

[114] Interview between author and Graeme Delanoe, 25 May 2010.

Authenticity is achieved and perceived in different ways by museums not owned by collectors. At Jersey War Tunnels, for example, while the use of militaria or items dating from the Occupation are useful, and authenticity is certainly the goal, whether the objects on display are reproduction or not is perhaps not as important, as most visitors to the facility are unlikely to be specialist collectors. Kjeldbæk (2009b: 30) argues that the problem of authenticity is seldom about whether an object is a fake or not, but rather in what condition it should be exhibited, because 'objects have a history in terms of use and physical decay apart from when they were freshly made and apart from the historical moment you want them to bear witness to'. At the point at which it was used—the period that the item is illustrating in the museum—what was its condition then? Was it mud-spattered, dirty and rusty or was it highly polished daily? If an item is kept on display in the open air, to what extent should it be preserved or allowed to weather?

Holtorf (2008: 126) argues that it can empirically be shown that visitors to museums experience authenticity and aura to the same extent whether they are looking at originals or copies, as long as they do not believe them to be copies. As Sharon Macdonald found in her study of a heritage centre on the Isle of Skye, the provenance does not particularly matter when it comes to authenticity; 'what matters is that they convey the right kind of picture … authenticity lies not in the aura of the artefacts, but in the "story" which gets told' (1997: 170). While this would apply to Jersey War Tunnels, almost the opposite would be true for the collector-owner for the Channel Islands Military Museum in Jersey.

Because German tunnels, such as the one in which Jersey War Tunnels is situated, are prone to dampness, it can be detrimental to leave genuine objects, especially paperwork, textiles and photos, on display. Such items are also at risk of fading under electric light. This means that while a good number of selected and well-spaced, original objects are on display, inherited or purchased from other collectors, authenticity it sought and achieved in other ways. This is done through videos of interviews with witnesses of the Occupation; the use of original film; interactive and thought-provoking displays which present ethical dilemmas to the visitor; appropriate background sounds or commentary; hands-on exhibits; and art installations which intend to convey or invoke appropriate emotions and atmosphere (see Addy (2009) for further information). While such displays are very effective, intelligent, well thought out and are inclusive of (and indeed focus on) victims of Nazism, they are often not to the taste of collectors, who have different systems of value and are more likely to perceive such displays as inauthentic or staged for tourist consumption.

We might contrast the two approaches to authenticity as a 'grass-roots' approach from the collectors, an approach that operates from the 'ground up', versus one that operates from the 'top down' and is controlled by larger groups. Neither is more 'authentic' than the other; they simply have different values. In her study of maritime heritage in Bermuda, Andrews (2009: 143) emphasised that grass-roots heritage is not more 'authentic' than that produced by 'top-down' heritage professionals, and nor is the latter's approach more 'tainted' or 'ideologically driven'; both are integrated. As she states, 'any claim to certify heritage

"100 percent organic" is patently untrue and denies the constructed nature of all heritage, no matter its orientation or scale'.

Ideas relating to authenticity are beginning to be questioned and supplemented by concepts such as the 'vividness' of the experience (e.g. Holtorf 2008: 112). As Mary-Catherine Garden has argued with reference to heritage sites, 'the way in which the site (and the "past") is being conveyed and the resonance of the experience of the heritage site that ultimately will determine the strength of the sense of the place'; she argues that it is more useful to consider how a site creates a distinct 'place of the past' rather than how 'real' that version of the past is (2009: 273 and 288).

Typology

We can see that, broadly speaking, there are two main types of Occupation Museum in the Channel Islands and they have different aims to each other. One of the aims of the modern, professional museum such as Jersey War Tunnels is to educate the public and to give a fuller picture of the whole of the Occupation. The smaller, old-fashioned Occupation Museum seeks to display and show off a personal collection which is often built around esteem for particular types of equipment and their features, such as engineering, workmanship or style. German equipment plays a different role in the two museum types and is treated differently according to how it is valued for the role that it plays. The professional museum uses military equipment in an illustrative role, for the creation of context for daily life or particular events of the Occupation; it is not the focus of attention and need not be kept in full working order. While not ideal, it is not a matter of great concern whether the pair of binoculars or the gun or the military radio on display is broken or not. The aim is not to use them as functioning objects, nor to return them to the marketplace; their financial value is, to a certain extent, immaterial. Such a system of value and display is entirely dissonant to the active collector or owner of the small Occupation Museum, for whom condition and working order are paramount to their systems of value; these aspects of their equipment also reflect well or badly upon the owner/collector, who derives prestige and status from his collection and how it is perceived by others. Items on display in these museums are not necessarily permanently removed from the marketplace. Most objects are deemed to have a price and can be purchased or swapped for the right price or item. It can thus be seen that there are two different trajectories for German equipment, depending on to whom they belong.

The two types of Occupation Museum in the Channel Islands are difficult to label or even to classify as falling into only two types, although two extremes are possible to discern within the wider range (see Table 2.7) While size could be used to distinguish between them, this is not enough; there is also the issue of function. Of the two roles of museums I have listed above, the 'display of the collection' and the 'educational' roles clearly overlap. Some museums which started their life as small displays of a personal collection have grown to become

Table 2.7 The two extremes of Occupation Museum types in the Channel Islands

Size	Small	Large
Budget	Low	High
Primary use of museum	Display of private collection	Education/entertainment
Function of militaria	Prime focus, 'auratic'	Illustration/creation of context
Density of objects	High	Low
Importance of perfection of condition of objects	High	Low
Type of presentation	'Old-fashioned'	'Modern'
Aim of mode of display	Original, authentic, 'atmospheric', not artificial	Recreation of atmosphere through modern interpretation
Status of owners/curators	Amateur	Professional
Owners	Collectors	Landowners/private companies
Status of objects	Potentially for sale	Not (officially) for sale

large, educational displays. Among these, we might list the German Occupation Museum in Guernsey. Both also have the function of entertainment, of satisfying the curiosity of a particular type visitor and of, perhaps, showing off the darker side of the islands' heritage. Occupation museums are thus a destination of 'dark tourism'—sites or attractions that are 'linked in one way or another, with death, suffering, violence or disaster' (Sharpley and Stone 2009: 4), something that is compounded in Occupation museums located inside German fortifications built by forced and slave labour. This added dimension means that some of the museums also function as or contain memorials to these groups or others that suffered during the Occupation. Among these, we might include the German Underground Hospital in Guernsey and Jersey War Tunnels.

It is also possible to classify Occupation Museum types according to budget. Jersey War Tunnels has a larger budget than the others and has thus been able to afford in the past many staff, cutting-edge technology and modes of display, and impressive new exhibitions. Other museums are funded by the collector alone, who often has to run all aspects of the museum personally. Some of these museums are heavily constrained by space and budget, and simply heating, lighting and ventilating museums can stretch the finances to breaking point especially now that the tourist industry in the Channel Islands is perceived to be in decline.

Probably allied to budget is also an acknowledgement of the contrast between 'old-fashioned' and 'modern' Occupation museums and the greater value placed upon the former by collectors. In recalling St Peter's Bunker War Museum, for example, Graeme Delanoe described it as '*the best there was*'.[115] In describing his own museum, Damien Horn told me that '*maybe my way of doing the display [in my museum] is old-fashioned, but there is no other way of showing kit*'.[116] This belief that there is 'no other way' of doing things is actually an expression of value. It was a

[115] Interview between author and Graeme Delanoe, 25 May 2010.

[116] Interview between author and Damien Horn, 8 April 2010.

Fig. 2.9 Occupation kitchen scene, German Occupation Museum, Guernsey (© Gilly Carr)

matter of pride among collectors that their museums, and those of others, did not have computers (their expression of the ultimate in undesirability in a museum) and used old-fashioned modes of display. Several collectors expressed appreciation for museums which retained the atmosphere of the Occupation and had not sanitised or destroyed it with modern displays. Once again we are reminded that artefacts, bunkers, displays and museums which are somehow 'closer to the Occupation' have a higher value among collectors. This has led to great cultural conservatism in Occupation museums in the islands, where the key difference between them is in the poetry of the display or the predominance of particular types of military equipment, depending on the preferences of the collector.

The desire to be 'closer to the Occupation' has also led to a tendency to favour displays which recreate scenes from the Occupation using mannequins. The German Occupation Museum in Guernsey, for example, has a scene showing a kitchen, complete with ersatz food, make-do-and-mend kitchen equipment, and a man illicitly listening to the radio, while his wife looks anxiously out of the window (Fig. 2.9). In another part of the museum, an old 'Occupation street' is reconstructed, complete with old shopfronts and queues of islanders. More common in other museums are scenes of soldiers at work. In the Valette Military Museum in Guernsey, for example, soldiers operate a military radio. In the Channel Islands Military Museum in Jersey, displays feature soldiers operating an Enigma machine, manning a gun emplacement or maintaining the air-conditioning system in the bunker. When he displayed some of his collections in the island Fortress Museum in St Helier, Martin Walton explained that he liked to '*collect with a diorama in mind—a sort of recreation of a scene from history being reinterpreted by myself*'.[117]

Several museums, including the German Occupation Museum, the German Underground Hospital and the Valette Military Museum, all in Guernsey, have

[117] Email to author from Martin Walton, 25 July 2011.

Fig. 2.10 Slave worker in unfinished tunnel, La Valette Military Museum, Guernsey, © Gilly Carr

mannequins dressed as slave workers, digging into the granite to make tunnels. In the latter two examples, the mannequins are placed in unfinished tunnels for added realism, adding to the sense that the Germans are still around and have merely left the scene for a few seconds (Fig. 2.10).

While a desire to recreate the atmosphere of the Occupation using authentic means is valued among collectors, professional museums aim to achieve this using different methods of interpretation and display. This leads us to another potential way to differentiate between museum types, but this is rejected by some collectors. We could describe Jersey War Tunnels as the only 'professional' Occupation Museum in the Channel Islands, with displays designed in the past by trained heritage professionals, categorising all other Occupation museums as 'amateur'. Such labels can be offensive to the owners of the latter type of museums. For men who have devoted a lifetime to collecting militaria and building up extensive, even unrivalled, knowledge about the artefacts of the German Occupation, it is insulting to be given an apparently lower status or classification than someone with a university degree who '*does not know one end of a German helmet from another*', as one collector puts it to me. '*Unfortunately I don't qualify for letters after my name, but I have served my time … my two aims when I was at school were to own a wartime German vehicle and have a museum … I have the car which cost me five years of*

Table 2.8 Second World War museums organised according to the generation that produced them (Kjeldbæk 2009a: 384–385)

	First generation	Second generation	Third generation
Displays	Symmetric/chaotic	Planned route	Scenographic
Texts	Who/what/when/why (short)	Why (long)	Videos, sound
Role of objects	Proof/documentation	Information	Fascination
Funding	Money for things	Money for staff	Money for events
Perspective	Rights of group	Rights of society	Rights of the individual
Function	A monument	Official opinion	Current trends

work in restoration … and I got the museum when I was 25. I think either of those is more worthy than letters after my name'.[118] If we do not wish to insult, we must be wary of differentiating between museums based on the methods of training of the owners or curators. These people have very different knowledge bases, interests and priorities. Although there are bonds of acquaintance and regard between the 'amateur' and 'professional' groups, built through working together on projects, they move in different circles and have different values, as we have seen.

Esben Kjeldbæk, head of the museum of Danish Resistance, suggests a different way to overcome the minefield of ways to differentiate between museum types, categorising them instead in terms of the generation that produced them (2009a) (Table 2.8).

To what extent do the Occupation museums of the Channel Islands lend themselves to such analysis? Do those owned by the war-youth, first and second generations of islanders follow Kjeldbæk's trend? For him, the first-generation museums are made up of collections which have become museums because 'there is a collective will, a driving force, that claims them to be socially and morally important enough to merit public display' (ibid.: 364). Such museums were grass-roots initiatives which aimed to 'celebrate a victory won, a success achieved or wealth acquired by a person or by a class' (ibid.: 365). Using this rationale, one might imagine that Occupation museums might be celebrations of victory, liberation or resistance, but this Kjeldbæk's theory holds only if one perceives collections of German militaria as battle trophies. We must not forget that museums are not static and a long-running museum can evolve from one type to another. Today, for example, the German Occupation Museum in Guernsey has evolved to typify many elements of Kjeldbæk's second-generation museum and espouses an official or mainstream opinion that held for generations but is now beginning to change—and new extensions to the museum reflect this change.

Members of the Channel Islands Occupation Society (CIOS), of which many collectors were founder members, were perceived to be the guardians of Occupation knowledge and memory, and their opinion became official opinion and shaped cultural memory. Thus, as time progressed, museums no longer needed to be monuments to victory with their associated display of trophies; they were free

[118] Email to author from Damien Horn, 8 April 2010.

to express their official narrative of the Occupation. The longevity of this narrative has meant that only one museum in the Channel Islands can now legitimately claim to be a third-generation museum, and that is Jersey War Tunnels. The cultural conservatism already noted among collectors and their museums has meant that a number of Occupation museums opened by later generations have still followed the first-generation model, indicating that the age of the owner or the collector whose material is displayed does not necessarily dictate which form the museum will take.

In summary then, the Occupation museums of the Channel Islands reflect a range of approaches from different generations, while acknowledging the very strong influence of the model of those from the first generation. This museum type, and the collectors who remember it, valued what are now seen as traditional and old-fashioned displays. This has led to few collector-owner museums radically changing or evolving with time, or embracing new ideas in display. Because almost all Occupation museums (with the lone exception of Jersey War Tunnels) are in the hands of collector-owners, the greatest difference in style can still be detected between the collector-owner museum and those belonging to non-collectors rather than solely the generation into which they were born.

Morality, Ethics and the Collection and Display of German Militaria

Now that the systems of value, authenticity and typology among collectors and museums have been established, we must now consider the difficult issue of the morality of collecting objects of German or Nazi militaria. All collectors in the Channel Islands are aware of how their collections might be perceived in a negative way by those who do not understand what they do, but they firmly reject such perceptions.

To be explicit about how such collections are seen, we must turn to Susan Pearce's seminal study which investigates the history of European collecting. In this volume, Pearce (1995: 194–195) has labelled such collections of Nazi militaria as 'deviant and sinister'. She writes that 'A Nazi memorabilia collector is unlikely to concern himself with moral issues at all, in any other than a lip-serving way. For him, the issue appears as one not of ethics but of personal identity; his relationship to his material is that of worshipper to relic … We have to conclude that most of those who collect Nazi material now would have actually been Nazis then. Ethics and identity come together because the collector (blind to the significantly appalling bad taste of Nazi material culture) sees glamour in evil and wishes to identify with it through its relics'.

While Pearce's analysis might be correct for some collectors of Nazi memorabilia, it fails to take into account the context of collecting. I have clearly demonstrated in this chapter that the historical context of the Occupation and growing up in the decades immediately afterwards has had a very direct impact on the imagination and hobbies of boys and men of that era. They have not collected German equipment because of any neo-Nazi sympathies or 'deviant' tastes. Rather, it has been my intention here—and in the volume as a whole—to demonstrate that the population of the Channel Islands as a whole has, to a greater or lesser extent as the years have passed, grown up surrounded by the debris of war. It was almost inevitable that this would affect what some of them chose to collect.

We must also bear in mind that the Channel Islands have a strong shooting tradition because of the presence of the garrisons of the Royal Guernsey and Jersey Militias in the islands for hundreds of years.[119] The college cadet forces (CCFs) at Elizabeth College in St Peter Port and Victoria College in St Helier, the two top private schools for boys in the islands, have also had an influence on the desire of young boys to collect militaria.[120] These two features of male life in the islands sparked an interest in military history in some of the collectors interviewed. Pearce (1995: 197) notes that collecting is shot through with emotions about sexuality and gender, and we can see how concepts of shooting, militaria and masculinity will have been reinforced in generations of schoolboys through their participation in CCFs or that of their fathers or grandfathers in the militia.

It is important to examine motivation in the words of the collectors. Each person I interviewed was asked precisely why they chose to collect such objects, given that these actions could be misconstrued by others. Damien Horn, for example, said '*I always collected German kit, stuff, memorabilia. It's never Nazi. It's never been Nazi. It's just German. It's German military, it's not a political thing. It's just German kit. They were Germans and they were here and that's what they had*'.[121] Graeme Delanoe added to this. '*I had no interest in the political side and I certainly don't have now. This is the awkward thing about it … that anyone who collects German equipment is deemed to be a Nazi, and it's something that is very frustrating because it couldn't be more opposite … it's history, because it was Jersey [that was occupied] and this is what was here. Nothing political, and I've got to keep stressing this. Nothing can be further from the truth*'.[122] Ian Channing, on the other hand, accepted that such an all-encompassing hobby was liable to be misconstrued. '*There are always the nutters who, for one reason or another, don't see it for what it is … they glorify it … but if you're interested in German stuff you tend to be branded a bit of a nutter anyway*'.[123]

Many collectors emphasised a strong link between the history of their island and what they chose to collect. As Damien Horn explained, '*I do it because it is part of me, part of my island's history …*'[124] This quote is particularly insightful,

---

119 I thank Martin Walton for reminding me of the importance of this tradition.

120 I thank Richard Heaume for making this link.

121 Interview between author and Damien Horn, 8 April 2010.

122 Interview between author and Graeme Delanoe, 25 May 2010.

123 Interview between author and Ian Channing, 22 May 2010.

124 Email from Damien Horn to author, 8 April 2010.

because it emphasises the very strong link between people, objects, their identity and their history. Belk (1988: 149) has explored this link, arguing that the acquisition and retention of memorabilia, antiques and objects from past are part of the desire to know one's past, a nostalgic 'desire to identify with an era, place, or person … a desire to bask in the glory of the past in the hope that some of it will magically rub off …' He also argues that possessions have a function in creating, enhancing and preserving a sense of identity (ibid.: 150). While most collectors would reject that their collection enables them to 'bask in the glory' of the Third Reich (as some might perceive it), most would accept that it enables them to come closer to the Occupation and that some of that period might 'magically rub off' on them through possession of these objects.

At its most superficial level, however, it seems that boys and young men chose to collect militaria simply because it was plentiful around the islands. One collector emphasised this link, saying that '*you can't go anywhere, particularly here in Guernsey, without seeing something that the Germans left behind. It's a presence all the time, it's always there … I reckon that there must be a memento of the Occupation in every house in the island*'.[125]

Belk (2006: 540) emphasises the importance of the 'seed gift' from a friend or family which starts off the interest in collecting, and it seems that a souvenired German helmet, bayonet or military badge was deemed to be an appropriate gift for boys for several decades after the Occupation. Peter Le Vesconte, who was given a bayonet by his father, confirmed the importance of the seed gift. '*My collection seemed to just stem from liking old things. If someone had brought me something that was very, very old, it could have set me off on another course. For me, bayonets were at a price I could afford, so from that point of view I could get a number*'. The first object for one Guernsey collector was a German helmet, a gift from his grandfather. He particularly valued it because he associated it with his grandfather's stories of the Occupation. The importance of the link between objects and Occupation-related stories has already been made earlier in this chapter. It is also clear that the adventure involved in acquiring German militaria, most especially in breaking into German tunnels, and the fun involved in playing soldiers with real equipment, was also a huge draw to the collectors in their youth. These objects were also free or very cheap in the decades after the war, and this would have appealed to the young. Price is certainly a factor which prevents young people in the islands from becoming involved today.

Some collectors valued or expressed a subjective appreciation for the mechanics, the engineering, the development or the style of the items of German militaria. Peter Le Vesconte, for example, was impressed by the German uniforms. '*Well, be honest—look at a German uniform and look at a British uniform. Which is the smartest? It'd be by a mile the Germans*'.[126] Not all collectors have the same appreciation; Damien Horn, for example, who has been involved in re-enactment

---

[125] Interview with author, name withheld, 14 July 2011.

[126] Interview between author and Peter Le Vesconte, 6 April 2010.

in the past, thought that the German uniform was '*not very flattering if you're the wrong size and shape, and it itches and it's hot and it's nasty*'.[127]

It also cannot be denied that there was also a status and respect which went along with the knowledge acquired about military equipment among men of a certain generation; this was also hugely valued in a place where such equipment and military souvenirs were ubiquitous. As Ian Channing put it, '*It fires the imagination. You're always trying to find out more and more*'.[128] It is also likely that items of military equipment, especially the iconic German helmet, played the role of a battle trophy, especially when put on display. The Germans were a notoriously strong enemy, and there was much kudos in defeating them and inviting tourists to the islands to see the spoils of war.

This brings us to the subject of the ethical issues involved in displaying swastikas, pictures of Hitler and German paraphernalia in the old-fashioned, collector-owner Occupation museums. As I have already discussed, such a display is valued among collectors because it is deemed to be more authentic and 'closer to the Occupation'. Also, because these museums have a primary focus on German militaria because this is what was collected (and it will not have escaped the reader that half of the Occupation museums listed in Table 2.6 have a military or war-related focus in their title), one should not be surprised that these museums focus on 'the perpetrators of Nazism' rather than the victims (e.g. Vitaliev 1998: 4).

Lowenthal (1998: 102) tells us that 'history is the past that actually happened, heritage a partisan perversion, the past manipulated for some present aim'. How appropriate is this when applied to collector-owner Occupation museums? Do they 'manipulate the past' any more or less than the modern museum? Is it ethical to present a partial rather than a holistic vision of the past? We have already noted that the primary aim of collector-owner museums is not to present a holistic vision of the past; rather, it is to display a prize collection of militaria, thus testifying to the reality of the German Occupation.

That collector-owner Occupation museums should be criticised for unethical display is rejected among collectors. As Damien Horn says of his museum, '*The museum reflects* my *interest and* my *collection*'.[129] Thus, to accuse these museums of not displaying the material culture of victims of Nazism would be to misunderstand the aims and functions which many of these museums have had historically. In speaking about his father's museum, the St Peter's Bunker War Museum, the son of this collector explained that it was important for low-budget museums to take a commercial point of view. '*People who go into these museums are interested in things like daggers and flags and Lugers and flak guns. They're not interested in a set of wooden clogs [belonging to slave workers] … I think it's more a reflection on the business side of things … Any museum's going to have an eye on attracting people in through the obvious … and that's going to be lots of*

[127] Interview between author and Damien Horn, 8 April 2010.

[128] Interview between author and Ian Channing, 2 May 2010.

[129] Interview between author and Damien Horn, 11 May 2010.

German flags and swastikas and things like that; that's what really gets people, attracts their attention'.[130] The first Occupation museums to open in the Channel Islands, the Jersey Underground Hospital and La Hougue Bie, were geared towards tourists as a way of garnering revenue to help the islanders recover after the Occupation. These venues set the trend for what was to follow and, more importantly, what was later valued by collectors who remembered their childhoods with nostalgia. I have already noted the cultural conservatism of collectors and collector-owners of museums. The museums of this type still open today all owe something to their earliest progenitors, which also had a narrow focus on militaria.

Because there are Occupation museums and memorials in the Channel Islands which tell the story of victims of Nazi persecution, one of the collectors I spoke to felt no compunction to do the same in his museum. '*I can only collect what's out there. I can't show things I haven't got. If I haven't got anything Jewish or if I haven't got anything from a political prisoner that's because there were so few of them, and what they had, they've either got or got rid of … My interest is reflected in the museum. If it isn't the full story, well, things change … if I happen to pick up a sack full of stuff relating to the Jews on the island or the political prisoners then it may go into the museum. But I feel that that's covered; you've got other places that will show that*'. For those who might be offended by the contents of his museum for reasons of political incorrectness, the same collector asked, '*If people find it politically incorrect then what are they doing going into a German bunker? … They've got a free choice to either pay and go in or walk away*'.[131]

Perhaps the real question is not just concerned with partial or holistic views of history, but rather the display of what Kjeldbæk (2009b) calls 'dangerous objects'. For the Channel Islands, such objects are swastikas and portraits of Hitler. Kjeldbæk suggests that the dilemma for the curator is not between showing or not showing such objects, but 'how to show it and … how much controversy he wishes to generate' (2009b: 50). Objects are powerful, subversive things. Do you lessen the impact of a swastika flag by folding it and showing only part of it? Is there a 'safe' or even uncontroversial way to display a portrait of Hitler, such as the nine-foot-high painting that was on display at the Hougue Bie Occupation Museum until 1963? Perhaps the consideration of 'appropriateness' in artefacts is more pertinent than concepts of those which are 'dangerous' or 'safe', as this changes through time, and those who own or curate museums—even the self-taught—should be sensitive to such changes. The problem with all museums of the Second World War is where to draw the line, and that is something which can only be decided locally unless the museum has an eye on a wider audience.

---

[130] Interview with author, name withheld, 26 August 2009.

[131] Interview between author and Damien Horn, 11 May 2010.

Museums as Sites and Creations of Nostalgic Memory

The overwhelming impression gained from the study of collector-owner/first post-war generation Occupation museums is that they are sites where very particular nostalgic memories (a nostalgia that is sometimes inherited) of the Occupation are played out. Pierre Nora argues that there are *lieux de mémoire* in places where there are no longer *milieux de mémoire*, real environments of memory (1989). Thus, for our collectors, because the Occupation (a *milieu de mémoire)* is over and there are no more Germans occupying the Channel Islands, the memory of them is bound up in the equipment and fortifications that they left behind.

Objects (military equipment) and places (fortifications) associated with Germans are bound up so intimately in the Channel Islands that the two are frequently combined together. German bunkers and tunnels have been chosen as the natural home for seven of the ten current and former Occupation museums in the islands. Here, we encounter a potential contradiction in the expression of nostalgia among collectors. I have argued above that Svetlana Boym's concept of restorative nostalgia is dominant among adult collectors and that they prefer their artefacts (and, indeed, their German fortifications) to be restored, rather than revelling in the decay, the cracks and the rust of age. We must couple this with the collectors' system of value, which attaches importance to the concept of 'closeness to the event'. Thus, a bunker or museum which gives the impression that its former inhabitants have only just left is preferable to one which has been over-restored, modernised and 'sanitised'. Graeme Delanoe describes the German Underground Hospital Occupation Museum in Jersey in the early 1970s, contrasting it with its more modern incarnation as Jersey War Tunnels: '*That was probably the best it's ever been ... basically it was walking through a very damp, eerie tunnel ... it was almost as it was when the Germans had left. ... Today it's a little bit modern, It's gone the way everything has, it's got to be done for today's tourist. But we weren't tourists in those days; we were looking at it as our heritage and what was left behind*'.

The contradiction is not real. What is valued is an artefact (or bunker) which appears in the same state that it was during the Occupation, when the Germans were using it or 'as it was when the Germans had left'. To be restored or maintained is one thing; this maintains the value and aesthetic appeal. To over-restore or to modernise a bunker is seen as too much and diminishes its value. This is why the restoration of military items is also something which requires great skill and care so that the item does not end up looking fake or obviously inauthentic.

While the particular phenomenon of the Occupation Museum in the Channel Islands has a long pedigree and can be readily understood by reference to the specific historical context in which it came about, it cannot be disputed that some present—or have in the past presented—a very particular and narrow picture or individual memory of the Occupation, i.e. a memory where the experience and possessions of German soldiers predominate. It is a memory that most collectors share, and although their number has never been vast (even though it seems that the collection of militaria was a passing craze at school for many more male islanders than are discussed here), the resulting collected memories of our collectors have had a disproportionate influence on the Occupation heritage of the Channel Islands through the medium of the Occupation museum.

Olick (1999: 338) defines 'collected memory' as 'the aggregated individual memories of members of a group', where 'the memories of some command more attention than those of others'. For our collectors, the nostalgic memories of the older members of the group carry more weight and are valued more highly as they were closer to the Occupation. As the older modes of display in Occupation museums focused heavily on the German experience, by putting this on display the collected memories of this small group have, over time, unduly contributed to or shaped the popular collective memory of many of the rest of the population of the Channel Islands. As Boym (2001: 54) has observed, nostalgia can act as an intermediary between individual and collective memory.

In his discussion of remnants of the past, historian James Young warns us that such remnants or relics in museums 'have long come to stand for the whole of events' and are too often 'mistaken for the events from which they have been torn … authentic historical artifacts are used not only to gesture toward the past, to move us toward its examination, but also to naturalise particular versions of the past' (1993: 127). Applied to the Channel Islands, this means that visions of the past presented in Occupation museums, where Jews, political prisoners, forced and slave labourers and other victims of Nazism are largely absent, give the impression that these people were not present or not persecuted during the Occupation. It is too easy to confuse proof that something existed (i.e. the German Occupation) with proof that it existed in a particular way.

I noted earlier that as the collectors were the first to shape Occupation heritage, they were perceived as the authorities and the guardians of Occupation-related knowledge for many decades. The partial version of the past on display in their museums attained the status of 'official memory', that is, the memory of cultural leaders or authorities, which can be contrasted with the 'popular memory' of ordinary people (Bodnar 1992).

This memory was not necessarily dissonant to the popular memory of 'ordinary people', the non-collectors in the population; after all, the Channel Islands were densely occupied with a ratio of one soldier for every three civilians at the height of the garrison, a number that compares to a ratio of one to 100 in France, after the occupation of the Occupied Zone (Sanders 2004: 128). The very real experience of Occupation in the islands was a German-dominated one.

People in the Channel Islands have now become normalised to prominent images of German soldiers in a way that can be shocking to those from other countries.[132] These images were at the forefront of people's consciousness during the years of Occupation and have been kept in that position in the post-war decades through Occupation heritage, especially through the very museums that I discuss here, and particularly through the use of uniformed mannequins.

132 My thanks to Jon Carter, Director of Jersey Museum, for this observation.

That German soldiers are prominent in the psyche of islanders can be seen in a number of commemorative tapestries throughout the islands. In Jersey, the twelve-panel Occupation tapestry, unveiled by Prince Charles in 1995 at the fiftieth anniversary of liberation, features outsize German soldiers in eleven of the panels. In a tapestry made by children on display in the German Occupation Museum in Guernsey, the head and shoulders of a helmeted German soldier takes a central position in the canvas. The twentieth-century panel of the Guernsey Millennium Tapestry also features a helmeted soldier, as does a tapestry embroidered in the late 1970s on display in Sark's Church. Here, the panel representing the war years shows a soldier slightly larger than the map of the island next to which he stands.

In their study of memory in post-war Europe, historians Fogu and Kansteiner suggest that low-intensity collective memories (which, for our collectors and many islanders, might feature a soldier-heavy vision of the past) focus on 'representations of the past that are produced and consumed routinely without causing much disagreement. Most groups settle on such collective memories and reproduce them for years and decades until they are questioned and overturned, often in the wake of generational turnover' (2006: 292). As we will see in nearly every chapter of this volume, generational turnover has been responsible for changes in the way that the Occupation is perceived in the Channel Islands. Slowly, most Occupation museums in the Channel Islands have become more inclusive of the previously marginalised or absent voices of the victims of Nazism.

In 2001, for example, the German Occupation Museum in Guernsey was extended to include a 'memorial room'. In this room, the plight of the three Jewish women deported from Guernsey to Auschwitz is highlighted. The accounts of many political prisoners have also been added, with a particular focus on those who died in continental prisons and camps. The death roll of forced and slave workers has also been listed, and museum cases in that room include the uniform of the Organisation Todt overseers and a pair of striped pyjamas from the concentration camp of Sylt in Alderney.

In the same year, Jersey War Tunnels unveiled its new permanent exhibition, 'Captive Island', which aimed 'to tell the whole story of the German Occupation of Jersey in the words and phrases of the people who were there … it serves as both a memorial to those who suffered and a vibrant expression of life during those five years'.[133] That both of the main Occupation museums in Guernsey and Jersey incorporated these narratives at the turn of the twenty-first century speaks to the wider changes that were in evidence elsewhere in the Occupation heritage of the islands, echoed in the changing narratives of Liberation Day and in the inclusion of minority groups in memorialisation of the Occupation years.

Just as Kevin Walsh observed that the large number of museums in France dedicated to the topics of resistance and deportation 'reflects a need to mediate this difficult period in French history' (2001: 87), so we might observe that the number of Occupation museums and exhibitions in the Channel Islands, opened in the

[133] Jersey War Tunnels guidebook, p. 8.

1940s, 1960s, 1980s and 2000s, reflects an equal and ongoing need or desire to discuss and represent this subject over several generations up until the present day. We have noted, however, how the image of the past and, thus, the memory transmitted, has changed during this period.

It is also worth noting that, just as in the French examples, the earliest museums were owned or curated by those who had lived through the Occupation and had a vested interest in presenting their version of the past. A good example of this is Joe Mière, a former curator of the Jersey Underground Hospital, who nurtured and expanded his display of political prisoners, in whose ranks he stood, during his period of guardianship.

National memory and the vision of Occupation for the French revolve around the twin themes of resistance and deportation. Although the Channel Islanders experienced both phenomena, this neither frames their memory nor (unlike the French) influences the title of their museums. We have already noted that the years 1940–1945 are perceived in the islands through the lens of military occupation and that this influences the location of most museums of this type (i.e. inside fortifications) and historically has left little room for other perspectives.

Through examining WWII museums, Walsh has observed how the category of hero varies from country to country and how the popularity of these figures has changed through time (2001: 97). While the prime subject of Occupation museums in the islands is the German soldier, this character type can more accurately be described as an anti-hero. Although he is not described locally in these terms, this is the way that he is treated. The soldier's possessions and instruments of war are fetishised, his clothes (uniform) are carefully curated, and scenes or dioramas are constructed in which he, as a mannequin, can 'live'. Although not exactly glorified, this anti-hero is housed, dressed and armed and kept in good working order; at the same time, he is safely contained in static displays inside his steel-reinforced bunker. Although his dominance is now challenged by mannequins and other representations of forced and slave labourers, deportees, Jews and those who committed acts of resistance, he has not yet been moth-balled.

The collector-owned Occupation Museum in the Channel Islands represents a very specific local or regional identity: one that has maintained its partial vision of the past until relatively recent years—a vision that is still maintained in some museums. While they have been subject to criticism in the past, both locally (*sotto voce*) and in the UK press for their neglect of the full story of Occupation, they should be seen for what they are: the product of a very particular historical experience.

Conclusion

Several key themes have run through this chapter. Chief among them has been the role of nostalgic memory for the Occupation or immediate post-Occupation period for our collectors, and the impact that this has had on concepts of value and authenticity for items of German militaria. This in turn has shaped the contents and design of Occupation museums, which traditionally have also been vehicles for nostalgic memory. In their turn, museums and the vision of the past that they displayed affected the collective memory of most Channel Islanders until the mid-1990s or early twenty-first century.

My aim in this chapter has been to reveal the dominating historical influences that have motivated and inspired generations of children and, later, men to create such particular visions of the past. It is my hope that this will go some way to shedding light on a practice which is often misunderstood by outsiders and, indeed, some other islanders.

Nostalgic memory with regard to the Occupation has played a large role in cultural conservatism in heritage in the Channel Islands. People have been reluctant to let go of the experiences of youth or of the cherished experiences of their parents and grandparents. Theirs are the memories which are still recited today, and the story is rare that does not contain a German soldier lurking in the background. Such experiences of Occupation are hard to shift; they formed the memories of the majority. Only the few were victims of Nazism, and so their stories were marginalised. Because the forced and slave workers, Jews and political prisoners had little in the way of representative material culture, the sheer volume of the materiality of the occupier dominated. As this is what the post-war tourists came to the Channel Islands to see and to souvenir, this helped to stimulate and encourage collectors during the 1960s and 1970s, during the heyday of tourism. Today, however, with the tourism industry reputed to be in decline and the mass of material in the hands of only a few, the end of the phenomenon of militaria collecting in the islands is in sight. It is my hope that this chapter has faithfully documented and interpreted this particular legacy of the Occupation using the words of those who were involved in its creation from the beginning.

References

Addy, C. (2009). Jersey war tunnels. In E. Kjeldbæk (Ed.), *The power of the object: Museums and World War II* (pp. 200–231). Edinburgh: MuseumsEtc.

Andrews, C. (2009). Heritage ethnography as a specialised craft: Grasping maritime heritage in Bermuda. In M. L. Stig Sørensen & J. Carman (Eds.), *Heritage studies: Methods and approaches* (pp. 140–163). London and New York: Routledge.

Appadurai, A. (1986). Introduction: Commodities and the politics of value. In A. Appadurai (Ed.), *The social life of things: Commodities in cultural perspective* (pp. 3–63). Cambridge: Cambridge University Press.

Baekeland, F. (1994). Psychological aspects of art collecting. In S. M. Pearce (Ed.), *Interpreting objects and collections* (pp. 205–219). London and New York: Routledge.

Belk, R. (1988). Possessions and the extended self. *Journal of Consumer Research, 15*, 139–168.

Belk, R. (1994). Collectors and collecting. In S. M. Pearce (Ed.), *Interpreting objects and collections* (pp. 317–326). London and New York: Routledge.

Belk, R. (2006). Collectors and collecting. In C. Tilley, W. Keane, S. Küchler, M. Rowlands, & P. Spyer (Eds.), *Handbook of material culture* (pp. 534–545). London and New Delhi: Sage Publications.

Belk, R. W., & Wallendorf, M. (1994). Of mice and men: Gender identity in collecting. In S. M. Pearce (Ed.), *Interpreting objects and collections* (pp. 240–253). London and New York: Routledge.

Bodnar, J. (1992). *Remaking America: Public memory, commemoration and patriotism in the twentieth century*. Princeton: Princeton University Press.

Boym, S. (2001). *The future of nostalgia*. New York: Basic Books.

Fogu, C., & Kansteiner, W. (2006). The politics of memory and the poetics of history. In R. N. Lebow, W. Kansteiner, & C. Fogu (Eds.), *The politics of memory in postwar Europe* (pp. 284–310). Durham and London: Duke University Press.

Garden, M. E. (2009). The heritage scape: looking at heritage sites. In M. L. Stig Sørensen & J. Carman (Eds.), *Heritage studies: Methods and approaches*, (pp. 270–291). London and New York: Routledge.

Ginns, M. (1978). *German fortifications in Jersey*. Jersey: Meadowbank Trading Co. Ltd.

Ginns, M. (1985). Operation 'Nest Egg' and Task Force 135. *Channel Islands Occupation Society Review, 10*, 19–49.

Ginns, M. (1993). *German tunnels in the Channel Islands*. Jersey: Channel Islands Occupation Society.

Gosden, C., & Marshall, Y. (1999). The cultural biography of objects. *World Archaeology, 31*(2), 169–178.

Harris, L. (2000). *A boy remembers*. Jersey: Channel Island Publishing.

Harris, L. (2002). *A boy remembers more*. Jersey: Apache Guides Limited.

Hirsch, M. (1996). Past lives: Postmemories in exile. *Poetics Today, 17*, 659–686.

Hirsch, M. (1997). *Family frames: Photography, narrative and postmemory*. Cambridge Mass and London: Harvard University Press.

Hirsch, M. (1999). Projected memory: Holocaust photographs in personal and public fantasy. In M. Bal, J. Crewe, & L. Spitzer (Eds.), *Acts of memory: Cultural recall in the present* (pp. 2–14). Hanover and London: University Press of New England.

Holtorf, C. (2008). Is the past a non-renewable resource? In G. Fairclough, R. Harrison, J. H. Jameson, & J. Schofield (Eds.), *The heritage reader* (pp. 125–133). London and New York: Routledge.

Hoskins, J. (1998). *Biographical objects: How things tell the stories of people's lives*. New York and London: Routledge.

King, P. (1991). *The Channel Islands War 1940–1945*. London: Robert Hale.

Kjeldbæk, E. (2009a). How museums speak. In E. Kjeldbæk (Ed.), *The power of the object: Museums and World War II* (pp. 362–392). Edinburgh: MuseumsEtc.

Kjeldbæk, E. (2009b). What is the power of the object? In E. Kjeldbæk (Ed.), *The power of the object: Museums and World War II* (pp. 22–51). Edinburgh: MuseumsEtc.

Kopytoff, I. (1986). The cultural biography of things: Commoditization as process. In A. Appadurai (Ed.), *The social life of things: Commodities in cultural perspective* (pp. 64–91). Cambridge: Cambridge University Press.

Lowenthal, D. (1998). *The heritage crusade and the spoils of history*. Cambridge: Cambridge University Press.

Macdonald, S. (1997). 'A people's story: Heritage, identity and authenticity. In C. Rojek & J. Urry (Eds.), *Touring cultures: Transformations of travel and theory* (pp. 155–175). London and New York: Routledge.

Marshall, M. (1957). *The small army*. London: Constable.

Morin, V. (1969). L'objet biographique. *Communications, 13*, 131–139.

Moshenska, G. (2008). A hard rain: Children's shrapnel collections in the Second World War. *Journal of Material Culture, 13*(1), 107–125.

Nadkarni, M. (2003). The death of socialism and the afterlife of its monuments: Making and marketing the past in Budapest's statue park museum. In K. Hodgkin & S. Radstone (Eds.), *Contested pasts: The politics of memory* (pp. 193–207). London and New York: Routledge.

Nora, P. (1989). Between memory and history: *Les Lieux de Mémoire*. *Representations, 26*, 7–25.

Olick, J. (1999). Collective memory: The two cultures. *Sociological Theory, 17*(3), 333–348.

Pearce, S. M. (1994a). The urge to collect. In S. M. Pearce (Ed.), *Interpreting objects and collections* (pp. 157–159). London and New York: Routledge.
Pearce, S. M. (1994b). Collecting reconsidered. In S. M. Pearce (Ed.), *Interpreting objects and collections* (pp. 193–204). London and New York: Routledge.
Pearce, S. M. (1995). *On collecting: An investigation into collecting in the European tradition*. London and New York: Routledge.
Pels, P. (1998). The spirit of matter: On fetish, rarity, fact, and fancy. In P. Spyer (Ed.), *Border fetishisms: Material objects in unstable spaces* (pp. 91–92). New York and London: Routledge.
Sanders, P. (2004). *The ultimate sacrifice*. Jersey: Jersey Heritage Trust.
Saunders, N. (2003). *Trench art: Materialities and memories of war*. Oxford and New York: Berg.
Sharpley, R., & Stone, P. R. (2009). *The darker side of travel: The theory and practice of dark tourism*. Bristol: Channel View Publications.
Stewart, S. (1984). *On Longing: Narratives of the miniature, the gigantic, the souvenir and the collection*. Baltimore and London: The Johns Hopkins University Press.
Sturken, M. (2007). *Tourists of history: Memory, kitsch and consumerism from Oklahoma City to ground zero*. Durham and London: Duke University Press.
Suleiman, S. R. (2006). *Crises of memory and the Second World War*. London and Cambridge: Harvard University Press.
Vitaliev, V. (1998). Showing off the sites of shame. *The Guardian, 10*, 4.
Walsh, K. (2001). Collective amnesia and the mediation of painful pasts: The representation of France in the Second World War. *International Journal of Heritage Studies, 7*(1), 83–98.
Walters, I. (1997). Vietnam Zippos. *Journal of Material Culture, 2*(1), 61–75.
Weiner, A. B. (1985). Inalienable wealth. *American Ethnologist, 12*(2), 210–227.
Willmot, L. (2000). The Channel Islands. In B. Moore (Ed.), *Resistance in Western Europe* (pp. 65–91). Oxford and New York: Berg.
Winterflood, H. (1980, May 9). Stole a German soldier's cap, collected leaflets, shrapnel. Guernsey Evening Press, p. 12.
Young, J. (1993). *The texture of memory: Holocaust memorials and meanings*. New Haven and London: Yale University Press.

Chapter 3
Bunkers: Edifices of Abomination or Heritage Sites?

Changing Perceptions of German Bunkers

In January 2009 I showed my partner around the many varied German fortifications at Noirmont Point in Jersey. This headland is filled with gun emplacements and bunkers in various stages of preservation. While some are still buried beneath the earth, having been sealed in 1948, others are present as empty shells, still in the state they were left after liberating soldiers, souvenir hunters and scrap dealers had stripped them of anything of any value after the war.

The command bunker at Noirmont has now been fully restored. The interior has been refitted to look as it did during the Occupation. Soldiers are represented by uniformed mannequins; swastikas and guns are on display; and information is provided on the original role of the battery, the soldiers who worked there, and the capability of the weaponry. Such displays can now be seen in other countries which hosted the Atlantic Wall, but these countries also have their share of overgrown or neglected bunkers and fortifications reused for other purposes.

Jon and I soon began to discuss what the best thing was to do with a bunker. Are these neutral spaces with which one can do anything? Is there a strategy that should be applied to all of them? Should they all have been destroyed after the war? Are they best neglected, forgotten or reused? What message does this give, if any? Are there any ethical implications for restoring bunkers? Because they were built on the orders of an enemy, using slave and forced labour, but also locally-employed people, they are structures which are redolent with difficult issues regarding whose story one should tell when turning them into tourist or heritage sites. Is it appropriate to ignore one group (i.e. those who built the structure) at the expense of others (i.e. the occupiers)? Should we be open about those who voluntarily worked for the enemy and tackle allegations of collaboration? Is this fair? Who should have the final say in the way bunkers are used today? Is there a compromise position to be found? Will any decision made now be irrevocable or will it be just another transitionary phase for these fortifications? And are there differences between German bunkers and older military structures from earlier centuries?.

G. Carr, *Legacies of Occupation*, Contributions To Global Historical Archaeology 40, DOI: 10.1007/978-3-319-03407-2_3,

Fig. 3.1 A bunker on the south coast of Guernsey (© Gilly Carr)

Introduction: The Atlantic Wall

A decade ago, John Schofield argued that representative examples of defences, fortifications and other military sites from the Second World War should be protected or retained because of their value as surviving monuments or 'living memorials' which can provide a focus for commemorative events and remembrance. He described them as providing a 'touchstone to the past', as 'sacred sites' which should 'engage the visitor', 'provoke emotions which bring the events of 60 years ago into sharp focus', and as providing 'the best opportunities for engaging the events of the Second World War' (Schofield 2002: 156–7).

Schofield was, however, writing in such positive terms about military sites in England—sites built by the inhabitants to protect their own island. His attitudes towards these sites were not fraught with the array of negative emotions which Paul Virilio encountered when he examined the German bunkers of the Atlantic Wall along the French coast in the late 1950s. These bunkers were vandalised by 'hostile graffiti' and 'insults'; they had been destroyed by 'iconoclastic vengeance when the territory had been liberated … the explosion of the solid concrete mass had overjoyed the countryside's inhabitants, as in a summary execution'. He found that the bunkers 'frightened' the local people and 'called back too many bad memories'; they were the 'symbols of soldiery' and 'bought upon themselves the hatred of passers-by' (1994: 13); they were 'edifices of abomination' (ibid: 45). Local people told Virilio that time needed to pass before they would be able to 'consider anew these military monuments'. In the meantime, bunkers were being covered in posters and filling both with litter and 'less ideologically inclined vagabonds' (ibid: 14).

Fast forward more than 50 years after Virilio walked along the beaches of Brittany and nearly 70 years after it was built, the seven European countries[1]

[1] Norway, Denmark, France, Belgium, the Netherlands, Germany and the Channel Islands.

which played host to the Atlantic Wall are still finding ways to deal with their concrete legacy of occupation and war; still going through phases of destruction and preservation, neglect, conservation, reuse and restoration.

Today, in all of these countries, there are associations which devote themselves to the care of these structures, and while some fortifications are looked after in one manner or another by local government, heritage, or tourist authorities, there are also a number of local voluntary organisations who have made it their business to preserve and restore fortifications. In Norway, for example, groups of 'friends' have emerged to look after individual fortifications, such as the *Kvalviks Fort Venner* or 'Friends of Kvalviks Fort'.[2] In Holland, there are many *Bunkerclubs* or *Bunker Liefhebbers* (bunker clubs or bunker lovers).[3] In Germany, which has a particularly difficult relationship with its Nazi past, those who are interested in bunkers call themselves *Bunkerforscher* (bunker explorers or bunker researchers), but they are referred to by others as *Bunkerküsser* or 'bunker kissers' (a term derived from *Pufferküsser* or trainspotter)—a pejorative term.[4] These groups seem to be a distinct and recognisable phenomenon in Europe.

In the Channel Islands, the local voluntary organisation is the Channel Islands Occupation Society (CIOS), founded in 1961 in Guernsey; a separate Jersey branch emerged 10 years later. The CIOS is dedicated to the 'preservation and recording of all aspects of the German Occupation', and although its membership comprises various sub-groups which have an interest in different parts of the Occupation, bunker preservation, recording and restoration is today very much a major part of the society's remit.

Although the CIOS were one of the very earliest groups to begin their restoration work, this is now quite a popular endeavour throughout Europe, and the bunkers of the Maginot Line and the Siegfried Line or *Westwall* are also being rehabilitated and opened to the public (e.g. Smart 1996). Prominent examples of restored German fortifications include the Silkeborg Bunkermuseum,[5] and the Hanstholm Bunkermuseum in Denmark[6]; the Batterie Todt museum[7] and the sites of the V1 and V2 rocket launchers at Eperlecques and La Coupole in the Pas-de-Calais region of France[8]; and the Westwall museums in Germany.[9] These are just a very small selection of the very many that can be found along the Atlantic coast of northern Europe today.

---

2 My thanks to Professor Marek Jasinski at the Norwegian University of Science and Technology for this information.

3 My thanks to Rose Tzalmona at VU University Amsterdam and the Technical University in Delft for this information.

4 My thanks to Niko Rollmann, Robert-Tillmanns-Haus, Berlin, for this information.

5 http://www.wartourist.eu/places_overview_gb.htm

6 http://www.museumscenterhanstholm.dk/

7 http://www.batterietodt.com/

8 http://www.lacoupole-france.com/en/default.asp

9 http://www.westwallmuseen-saar-mosel.eu/

Typically, different countries and communities took several decades before they were ready to intervene in this particular debris of occupation, and to reuse or rehabilitate the structures. The decision to re-engage in their concrete legacies was not without problems. These fortifications were not entirely neutral spaces, even though most had been wholly neglected for years. Their prior associations have still not faded, yet have weakened a little with time. Not only were fortifications manned within living memory by a once-hated enemy, but these structures were imposed on occupied landscapes against the wishes of the local people. As most bunkers were along coastal areas that had been previously valued for their natural beauty or scenic vistas, the positioning of concrete structures jarred with the wildlife and environment that surrounded or were choked by them. Further, substantial areas of residential housing in villages, towns and cities were often demolished so that bunkers could be built; such demolition in The Hague in the Netherlands is one such example. Bad memories of the 'collateral damage'[10] associated with the building of the Atlantic Wall are another reason why people had no desire to revisit this particular past for many years.

There are yet other troubling issues. Not only were there bad memories of occupiers to contend with, but also the memory of those who built the fortifications. While German engineers of the Organisation Todt (OT) were responsible for some, the OT also hired local occupied peoples, often on good rates of pay. These people were sometimes perceived to be collaborating with the enemy, and they and their families were in no rush after the war to remind people that they volunteered for such work, such was the stigma that it carried. Further, the OT used conscripted, forced and slave labour all along the Atlantic Wall, and the sight of these people and the way that many were treated horrified and shocked local people. It was a matter of shame that people had been brought from all over occupied Europe and were, in many cases, abused, with local people prohibited and prevented from helping them by German orders, which threatened severe penalties.

In September 2011, the subject of the bunkers of the Atlantic Wall hit the European headlines. French enthusiasts from *Gramasa*, a group of amateur archaeologists dedicated to safeguarding portions of the Atlantic Wall, had started to clear and restore the bunkers around the bay of Arcachon (Schofield 2011). For the French, German bunkers are seen as emblems of national humiliation and dishonour and as symbols of defeat and collaboration, especially as many French construction companies grew rich building the Wall. Many thousands of Frenchmen were forced to work on the Atlantic Wall as part of an arrangement between the Vichy government and the OT. The founder of *Gramasa*, Marc Mentel, was quoted as saying that restoration work has only been possible in the last three or four years, now that time has moved on and his grandfather's generations have passed away (ibid). It would have been too disrespectful and painful to those who participated in building the Wall as forced labour to do the restoration work earlier.

[10] I credit Professor Koos Bosma, VU University Amsterdam, for the use of the term 'collateral damage' in this context.

In the Channel Islands, the local population were very rarely used as forced labour in this way and the fortifications of the Atlantic Wall today have a very different meaning to them. Rather than being symbols of humiliation and defeat as they are for the French, they are perceived as prime symbols of local heritage and as proud battle scars. How have they made this transition? To what extent are these perceptions contingent on the experience of occupation in the Channel Islands and to what extent have islanders intervened in their legacy of occupation to enforce this interpretation?

In some countries in which the Atlantic Wall was built, after the passage of some decades when the shame and humiliation of occupation had faded a little and the post-war generation grew curious about these neglected structures, the investigation of bunkers provided just one way of understanding and re-experiencing the war, but such investigations took longer in some countries than in others. It seems that the worse and more destructive the occupation or the greater the humiliation endured, the longer it took to begin to delve into an aspect of war that epitomised all that was worst about the experience: potential collaboration, human rights abuses, destruction of landscape, and the location and presence of the enemy. Yet, despite—and perhaps because of—these memories and associations, the three most popular reactions to bunkers today predominate all over Europe: complete neglect; reuse in another guise; or rehabilitation and restoration as a tourist or heritage destination in a manner which ignores or lightly skims over all of the problematic associations and focuses only on the military context. Only a very few have become memorials. This is equally true in the Channel Islands.

To ignore the difficult history associated with the Atlantic Wall and to write those who suffered out of the tourist or heritage presentation of the bunkers is to disinherit these people. This kind of heritage has been called 'dissonant heritage' by John Tunbridge and Gregory Ashworth (1996), and lying at its heart are issues of the discord that disinheritance can cause. They were prompted to state at the outset of their volume that they would never again look at a monument or exhibit without posing not only the 'whose heritage is it?' question but also the insistent 'who is disinherited here and what are the consequences of such dispossession?' (ibid: xi).

Implicit in their work is a call for all those who manage their heritage, whether local volunteers or trained professionals, to make sure that their presentation is honest, ethical and inclusive, and minimises dissonance. But what, precisely, does this mean in practice? While professionally trained heritage practitioners are aware of these issues and trained in ethical and inclusive presentation strategies, local volunteers do not necessarily have the same agenda or interests. Instead, such groups—whether Norwegian 'friends', Dutch bunker club members, or Channel Island bunker enthusiasts—are often deeply committed and interested volunteers who have made it their life's work over decades to conserve and look after the structures that they have personally rescued and turned into their heritage. Sometimes, these groups are not particularly interested in, or are even actively resistant to, issues that concern the trained professionals. And if this is the case, what is the solution? To what extent should heritage professionals intervene, or should they mind their own business? Is it the concern of anyone else if those who have spent their free time over many years maintaining bunkers choose to present them in the way that pleases themselves and a good number of interested tourists? Is it possible for both groups to work together in the presentation of the past, and what are the difficulties that might stand in the way? What is wrong with focusing on the experience of the German soldier and the military and architectural details of the bunker when this represents an accurate depiction of what these bunkers looked like when in use, and when this represents 'real history'? This chapter explores these issues within the context of the Channel Islands, where the German fortifications—or 'bunkers' as they are more popularly collectively known—represent the most visible heritage of the Occupation (Fig. 3.1).

It would seem that throughout Europe, bunkers have become symbolic space of a very particular kind, where memories, identities, and attitudes towards, and perceptions and narratives of, occupation can be expressed by specific groups. The precise narratives are variously dictated by the group who controls the bunker, the country or region in which the bunker is located, and the experience of occupation of the local people. Thus, where trained heritage professionals or local government have ownership of the bunker, the narratives expressed will differ, sometimes dramatically, to that espoused by bunker enthusiasts. While one group will emphasise official histories, others may focus on traumatic, dark or hidden histories, or on the experience of German military personnel. As Barbara Bender (1993: 3) has observed, 'the landscape is never inert; people engage with it, rework it, appropriate and contest it. It is part of the way in which identities are created and disputed, whether as individual, group, or nation-state'.

This contested aspect of landscapes and bunkers is certainly true in the Channel Islands, where the tussle for control since the occupiers left has been ongoing between different generations, different social groups, and between heritage professionals and bunker enthusiasts. Like the communist-era bunkers in Albania, they have been and are symbols of domination and control (Galaty et al. 1999: 198), are 'around every corner' (ibid: 202) and have an impact on landscapes and psyches alike. This impact or 'agency' will be discussed later.

Bunkers in the Channel Islands

Elsewhere in this volume I discuss how, although the Channel Islands shared many of the experiences of occupation with their continental cousins (such as deportations, anti-Jewish legislation, food shortages, confiscation of property, and increasingly restrictive orders), their identity and self-esteem is tied to that of the victorious British. Thus, they have seemingly had no option other than to identify with the Churchillian paradigm, namely that the British were not a nation of victims, but of victors (Sanders 2005: 256). Herein lies the uniqueness of the Channel Islands and their special status within European history and formerly occupied Western Europe: their wartime experience was directly analogous to the other occupied countries, yet their war memory is tied to that of the British as a nation, who had a very different war experience. The British were still fighting and were never conquered or occupied in the Second World War—except in the Channel Islands. The occupied islanders were victims in war, yet out of victimhood had to be carved a sense of heroism, bravery, and stoicism in suffering until eventual victory, which they were able to share with the British.

This victorious identity has, in turn, lead to the marginalisation of the experience of the victims of Nazism in the Channel Islands. While the real story of the Occupation is dissonant to the self-image that the British have nurtured since the end of the war, the renovation of sites of war memory such as bunkers, which marginalise the experience of the victims of Nazism, has, in turn, caused further dissonance. The bunkers have unintentionally become breeding grounds of dissonant heritage because they are devoted not to islanders, nor to the collateral damage that bunker building caused, nor even to those who built them, but instead to the German experience of occupation.

In the Channel Islands, the CIOS, Festung Guernsey, and Guernsey Armouries are all volunteer groups who have custodianship or control of the vast majority of the bunkers that are excavated, preserved or restored. They are primarily responsible for their ongoing maintenance and have amassed detailed records and knowledge of these structures. They are seen as the local experts in this domain. They refer to themselves as 'bunkerologists', 'professionals' and 'experts in the field of bunker excavation',[11] 'bunker archaeologists',[12] Atlantic Wall historians',[13] and 'bunker enthusiasts'.[14] Because in this chapter I compare and contrast these volunteers with paid and trained professional heritage practitioners, for these purposes I will refer to them here as 'bunker enthusiasts'. The choice of a term which apparently denies professional status is not meant to denigrate; neither is it used to criticise the quality of their preservation and restoration work. I have seen for myself the effort that goes into maintaining bunkers during the winter season and the time given freely in opening bunkers to the public (and curious researchers) during the tourist season. The dedication and commitment of the volunteers and enthusiasts is absolutely not in doubt. Rather, my reason for distinguishing the two groups in this manner is to emphasise just one thing: the differences in interpretation and presentation espoused by each group, and which form the nucleus of this chapter.

While I discussed the displays in bunkers which have been turned into Occupation museums in the last chapter, here, I will be discussing in detail a further seven bunker sites, all of them restored: the Command Bunker at Noirmont Point; the M19 bunkers at La Corbière; the anti-tank gun casemate at Millbrook, St Lawrence; and Batterie Moltke at Les Landes, all of which are in Jersey

---

[11] Interview between Paul Burnal and the author, Jersey, 15 August 2010.

[12] Email from Jeremy Hamon to author, 25 August 2011.

[13] Email from Paul Burnal to author, 25 August 2011.

[14] Email from Matthew Costard to author, 25 August 2011.

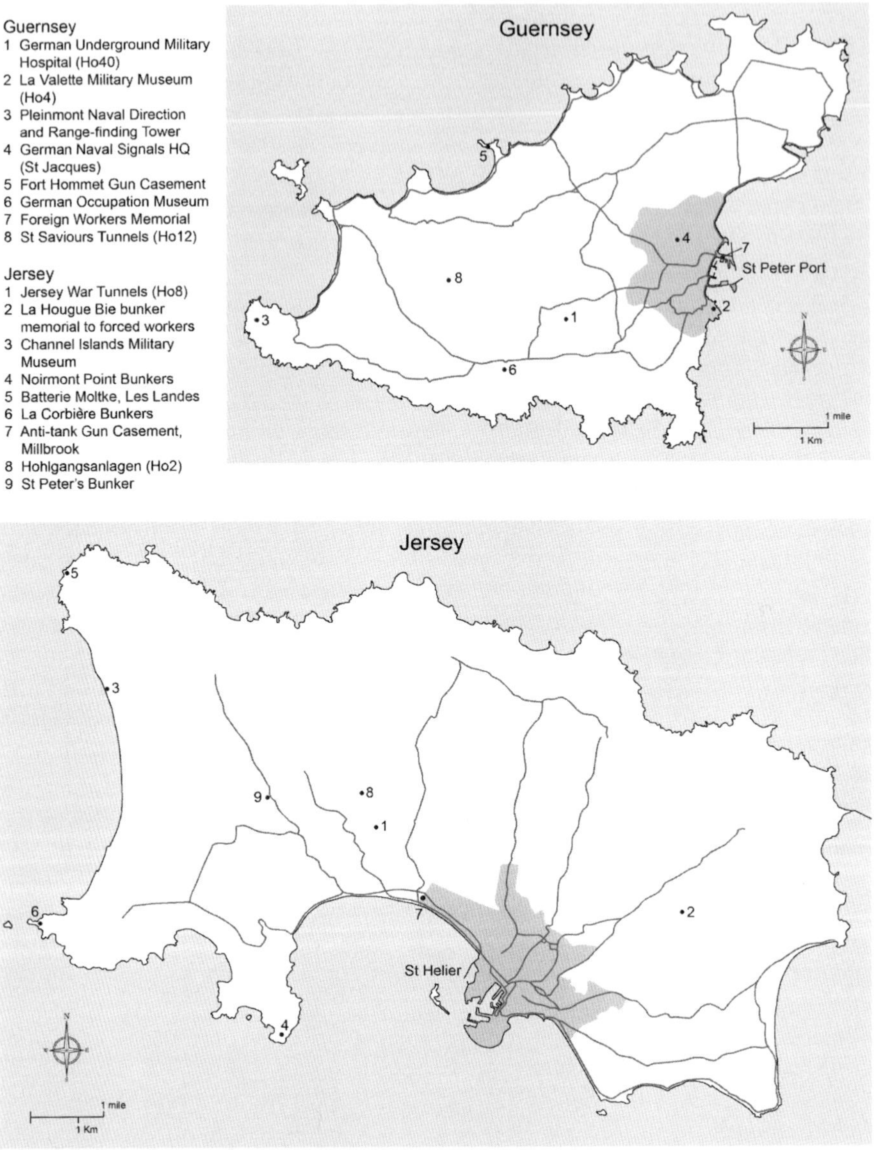

Fig. 3.2 Map of key fortifications and museums mentioned in the text (© and courtesy Ian Taylor)

(noting that there are also other restored bunkers within the island); and the Naval Observation Tower and the associated Battery Dollmann at Pleinmont, the Naval Headquarters at St Jacques, and the Fort Hommet Gun Casement Bunker, all three of which are in Guernsey (Fig. 3.2).

Guernsey and Jersey have been particularly active in re-engaging with bunkers, and I discuss the many ways in which these structures have been used to preserve and convey Occupation history. These seven sites and others have been restored, renovated and opened to tourists. They are recognised within the islands as tourist sites and are advertised and marketed as such. Like the French bunkers of the Maginot Line, they have not, however, been restored purely for the tourist market; rather, there is a strong element of bunkers as 'a place where middle-aged men with an engineering or electrical bent indulge their hobby of restoring, renovating and maintaining' (Smart 1996: 231). Those who restore bunkers (and own Occupation museums in bunkers) often do so just as much for their own interest. This is clearly demonstrated by the continuation of the phenomena described in this chapter long after the decline of the tourist industry in the Channel Islands.

Akin to those who work on the bunkers of the Maginot Line, it is doubtful whether some German bunker restorers stop to consider the important heritage issues inherent in the structures. As Smart puts it, 'the question of whether military historians should revise their views … is not one that seems to generate much excitement. Instead, they have engineering problems to solve … Seeing the work of these engineering archaeologists, the tourist witnesses something very technical and intimate which is difficult to place within the concept of heritage' (ibid: 233).

The methodology upon which my observations were based involved an investigation into (1) which aspects of the Occupation are conveyed in restored bunkers; (2) how the information is conveyed; (3) when the restoration work took place; (4) whose experiences are portrayed and (5) why each of these choices were made. All of these are discussed below in the biography of the bunkers in the Channel Islands. My principal concern in this chapter is the question of *why* these bunkers have been restored in the manner in which they have, i.e. why a certain version of war memory has predominated over others, and how this has been achieved.

It is worth stating at the outset that, despite bunkers being a non-neutral arena in which to dabble because of their association with the German occupiers and also because they were built by a range of workers which included slave and forced labourers, they can be seen as sites of both victimhood and perpetration. In fact, they might also be candidates for sites of collaboration if one considers that local people on good rates of pay also helped in their construction. This alone should make them extremely controversial structures. One might imagine that they have surely been the focus of prolonged and heated debate over decades, of the kind faced by the city of Nuremberg over the Nazi party rally grounds (Macdonald 2009a), about the modes of restoration and reuse that have taken place inside them. This has not been the case. In fact, bunkers have only infrequently caused controversy in the Channel Islands: at the time of their first restoration in the 1970s and 1980s in both Jersey and Guernsey, and only a few times in the last 15 years in Jersey. On the face of it, this is surprising, and I discuss this lack of controversy and reasons for it in more detail later in this chapter.

The Atlantic Wall in the Channel Islands, 1941 to Present

In the next chapter, I describe how a workforce of thousands was brought to the Channel Islands in order to build fortifications for the Germans. These structures comprised ammunition stores, observation towers, personnel shelters and gun emplacements (among others) and were built as part of Hitler's defensive 'Atlantic Wall', the 'wall of concrete and steel' which was to stretch from Norway in the north to the Spanish border in the south and was also built along the coasts of Denmark, France, Belgium and the Netherlands. Bunkers were also built in Germany itself. It is said that in the Channel Islands, there are more defences per square mile than at any other point along the main Atlantic Wall (Ginns 1999a: 3); indeed, the Royal Engineers carried out a survey of all fortifications after the war and discovered 1,623 concrete defences of one sort or another throughout the Channel Islands as a whole (Ginns 1985: 38). This was in accordance with Hitler's edict of October 1941 that the islands were to be converted into an 'impregnable fortress' so that they could not be recaptured or easily liberated by the Allies. In fact, Turner (2010: 157) has argued that it was Hitler's paranoia in wanting to keep hold of the islands, coupled with the 'exertions of the Organization Todt', that induced a fear of failure in Mountbatten, and which thus saved the islands from being heavily bombed like St Malo and Caen and recaptured by force.

The makeup of the OT workforce is noted in the next chapter. I emphasise the importance of acknowledging that, while a range of labourers of different nationalities working under different conditions built the fortifications, it cannot be denied that slave labour contributed to their construction. Because of this, bunkers can be seen by many (such as the descendents of former OT workers, or islanders who saw the mistreatment of workers at these sites), as haunted sites (Till 2005), places that have become imbued with negative memories and the 'ghosts of place' (Bell 1997: 831).

During the Occupation, islanders were not allowed to approach or enter the fortifications.[15] After the Germans left the islands, the population was curious to see inside these structures, although the first forays were filled with nerves and excitement in case they had been booby-trapped. Over the last 70 years, islanders have reacted and interacted with bunkers in a variety of ways. I describe and categorise these into four chronologically consecutive phases: *erasure*, *amnesia* (a category which also includes disguise), *rehabilitation* and *memorialisation*. These characterise the emerging and dominant themes that can be teased out of the data. While islanders have never been emotionally neutral towards bunkers, those emotions have changed through time. Today, bunkers have become important symbols of heritage and identity, but this not always how they have been perceived.

One of the ways in which we can understand how people's perceptions towards bunkers have changed is through the metaphor of the scar. Along with the German helmet, the bunker stands as a prime symbol of occupation and as a trace of both

[15] *Jersey Evening Post*, 11 June 1945: 1; *Guernsey Evening Press*, 8 August 1945: 1.

the physical and emotional scars that have been wrought upon the landscape and the people of the Channel Islands. For some people—and here we might cite the younger generation whose parents and grandparents did not live through the Occupation—these scars have not yet become incorporated upon young bodies in the peculiar form of deliberate, historical self-harm that might be said to characterise the practice of excavating and restoring bunkers, a practice which keeps the old scars open. Yet for others, these scars are still in the process of healing or have remained red and inflamed.

But what of the healing process itself? What methods have been employed, consciously or unconsciously, and have these have been successful in allowing islanders to 'work through' their past trauma in a therapeutic way? How has the trauma of occupation been passed down through the generations? Has this yet played out, or is it being deliberately or inadvertently prolonged by certain members of society? I will return to these questions later, after we have examined the phases through which bunkers have passed over the last 70 years.

Phase 1: Erasure: 1945–1953

Immediately after the war, the bunkers were comprehensively looted and their contents salvaged by islanders. At the same time, the British army, using German POWs as labourers, set about removing the 'taint' of the occupying forces (Ginns 1985: 38), which involved dumping war materiel at sea, sealing it in tunnels, or throwing it off the cliffs (Ginns 1978: 73), as discussed in Chap. 7. The fortifications themselves were perceived as the detested 'mark of the beast',[16] fit only to be destroyed by whatever means possible.

One of the first priorities for the British liberating troops was to survey all the German building work. It was soon realised that it would be exceedingly difficult and expensive to blow up steel-reinforced concrete up to several feet thick, so they agreed instead to demolish structures only where practicable (such as gun emplacements in previously agricultural fields) and where they protruded into roads. This happened on both Guernsey and Jersey. Other bunkers were covered in soil and thus made almost undistinguishable from prehistoric burial mounds.

The question of what to do with the bunkers was one that taxed the local population, even before the war was over. In the pages of the *Channel Islands Monthly Review*, the journal compiled by Channel Islands refugees who evacuated to Britain just before the Occupation began, the subject was debated in November and December 1944. While it was acknowledged by a correspondent in the November issue (Anon 1944: 1) that that evidence of occupation should be removed as soon as possible after liberation, and that the sight of them would otherwise 'keep alive unhappy memories', it was also pointed out that they would

[16] *Guernsey Evening Press*, 6 May 1947, 1.

have attraction for tourists for generations and would prove an asset that could not be duplicated anywhere else in Britain. With remarkable foresight, the correspondent remarked that 'what is a disfigurement of the landscape today will be a historic monument tomorrow'.

The following month, another correspondent wrote in, stating that 'German fortifications in the Channel Islands should be removed as soon as possible. The sight of them will always bring heart-twisting memories to those who have endured the miseries of the occupation ... We shall have to possess better attractions that concrete ruins to entice holiday makers' (Coysh 1944). This was certainly a popular post-war sentiment.

The future value of the bunkers to the tourist industry thus came onto the agenda in the islands soon after liberation. Having been heavily damaged economically by the Occupation, making money was vital. An article in the *Guernsey Evening Press*[17] supported the idea that the military strongholds should be 'turned into show places' or 'war museum exhibits' for 'the English, who will turn with very real interest to the Channel Islands in order to see for themselves where the enemy was in power for a period', but expressed the hope that the sites would never be displayed in the 'flamboyant guise' of circus exhibits.[18]

A few days later, the Lieutenant-Governor of Guernsey, Sir Philip Neame, wrote to the War Office to suggest that the 'island authorities might be agreeable to having some of the interesting German gun emplacements, control towers, etc., left intact for publicity purposes and as historical relics to be shown to tourists' (Ginns 1985: 38; PRO WO 106/3013). No similar suggestions or schemes for bunkers were entertained in Jersey (ibid.), although examples of German weaponry and the machinery of war were quietly put aside by the authorities for a future museum.

By February 1946, the policy being followed in Jersey was that bunkers were to be left intact but that all woodwork and camouflage netting was to be removed to leave the concrete structures to weather in the hope that, in the years to come, they would not prove to be such eyesores to people and would be no worse than the Napoleonic Martello towers that ringed the coastline.[19]

By April 1946, the States of Guernsey publicity committee met to discuss once again the desirability of the retention of a number of fortifications as 'relics of lasting interest and historic value'. While it was accepted that some should be retained, it was believed that not all gun sites should be kept, as some were duplications of others, and they felt it likely that they would not be of lasting interest to the public and should perhaps be kept for only three to 5 years. In addition, they felt that the purchase of private land on which some fortifications

---

[17] The local newspaper in Guernsey, the *Guernsey Evening Press*, merged with *The Star* newspaper in November 1965. In September 1999, it became renamed as the *Guernsey Press and Star*.

[18] *Guernsey Evening Press*, 17 September 1945.

[19] *Jersey Evening Post*, 23 February 1946.

stood, and the cost of maintenance and staff to run them, could not be justified under the post-war austerity conditions.[20]

Any fear that visiting tourists would not be interested was quickly dismissed during the 1946 tourist season. Articles in the *Jersey Evening Post* for this year record the traffic congestion and crowds at the site of what was then the German Underground Hospital (and is now the Jersey War Tunnels) at the time of its opening on the first anniversary of liberation. British soldiers still in the island took people on guided tours around the structure.[21]

By 1947, the UK was in a financial crisis and implemented a scrap-metal drive, and so from 1947 to 1950 in Guernsey, the weapons that had been left in position earlier were removed, as were many of the tanks, field guns, helmets and ammunition cases, etc., that had been previously sealed up in numerous German tunnels by the British Army. Armour plate and steel bunker fittings were removed and cut up for scrap and, once stripped, many bunkers in both islands were buried in soil to remove them from view or to enable the resumption of agricultural work above them, or were sealed with concrete for reasons of safety. Others were left as open, empty shells. The scrap merchants visited Jersey in 1953, and various enterprising individuals were able to make a fair amount of money (Wood and Wood 1955: 231). As far as the general population was concerned, the bunkers were hideous and ruined their beautiful islands; the fewer that existed, and the more that were destroyed or covered in soil, the better. The first decade after the Occupation, when memories were still fresh and raw, was thus marked by a period of *erasure* and a desire to return the islands to their former condition as if the Germans had never been there. If the bunkers could not be destroyed, then they had to be stripped of any useful features and then covered in soil to render them invisible.

Phase 2: Amnesia and Disguise: 1950s–1970s

After the fortifications had been stripped of scrap metal and their contents, they were buried, sealed, locked or just abandoned. Adults wanted nothing to do with the structures that reminded them of war or of the occupiers. The bunkers formed no part of their post-war lives and this was the way they wanted it. They turned their backs on them, tried to forget about them and entered a period of voluntary and apparent amnesia about their original context of use. Bunkers became a shunned and rejected space, the debris of war that nobody wanted to face or, as far as possible, see. They were hated and seen as 'eyesores' and 'blots on the landscape'.[22] If they were used at all, then it was as impromptu public toilets, as rubbish dumps, or as changing rooms when going for a sea swim.

[20] Guernsey *Billets d'Etat*, 3 April 1946.

[21] *Jersey Evening Post*, 10 May 1946.

[22] Richard Heaume personal communication 2009.

Young people took advantage of the absence of adult ownership of this space and began to use bunkers as childhood dens and, later, places for illicit drinking or parties; in fact, 'bunker parties' are still a well-known phenomenon in the Channel Islands and generally held in abandoned bunkers or hosted by people with bunkers on their property. One Guernseyman told me that bunkers had played an important part of his childhood:

> I would cycle out to the cliffs with my friends and explore the undergrowth, occasionally finding some hidden structures that had become overgrown with brambles. We would take the time to clear them out and make them our own for a couple of weeks before we would move on and search for somewhere else to play. Many of them go unvisited for weeks, months, years, and so lend themselves perfectly to children's playgrounds. We could play for weeks without being disturbed … as most of them are left to decay you assume no-one else cares and so you claim ownership to them easily.

As he got older, into his teenage years, he recalled that,

> Several people had bunkers on private property that we decked out with generators, we fitted lockable doors and built bars where the minimum age to drink didn't apply. We would fill them with sofas, lighting and a stereo and use them as places to socialise. We would throw parties and make as much noise as we liked until whenever we wanted … The bunkers we occupied were places we could call our own where no-one would come and disturb us … [23]

We can see the importance here of bunkers as abandoned or empty structures where young people could play or have fun without being disturbed by anyone; places where they could go to get away from adults. Over 6 years of fieldwork, I learned how popular bunker parties had been and were, although some people claimed never to have attended one because their parents forbade it, or because such parties were associated only with the 'rougher kids'.

Because of their rejection as usable space by adults, bunkers began to acquire a reputation as places for secluded, seedy or illicit activities. In fact, by the 1960s, the bad reputation of bunkers was so great that even prisoners who escaped from Jersey prison are alleged to have hidden in them.[24] One of the German tunnels in Jersey was turned into an illegal gambling den. Although long since damaged by waterlogging, the green baize tables painted with hearts and diamonds can still be seen today.[25] It is alleged that one bunker was even used as a location for abusing children.[26] In Guernsey, by the mid-1980s, it was found that some young people were sleeping in the bunkers at night and using them for solvent abuse (Fooks 1985: 20).

---

[23] Email to author from AS, 17 September 2007.

[24] Interview between author and Michael Ginns, 9 February 2009.

[25] Conversation between author and Chris Addy, Jersey War Tunnels, 19 August 2008.

[26] In the summer of 2008, Jersey was the focus of media attention over the child abuse scandal at the former childrens' home of Haut de la Garenne. On 24 July 2008, the *Jersey Evening Post* carried a report on the excavation of a nearby network of bunkers which had apparently been the location of child abuse in the 1970s and 1980s.

Fig. 3.3 Sealed bunker entrance in Guernsey (© Gilly Carr)

Although some of the bunkers and tunnels had been sealed after the war by pouring soil and rock down into the entrances, the Public Works Committee (who looked after historic monuments) continued to seal more in Jersey in the 1960s and the early and mid-1970s, mostly in an effort to stop children and teenagers breaking into them in their search for items of militaria for their collections. More were sealed in Guernsey in the mid-1980s (Fig. 3.3). Sealing bunkers and tunnels effectively also prevented them from being used as public toilets and places to dump litter, but some bunkers remained open, especially those on private land. These second and third phases of sealing represent steps taken by adults to reclaim the bunkers from children and young people. Despite being marginal, derelict or unwanted spaces, some bunkers have also been a locus of private (and sometimes public) generational and community tensions over the years, with adults attempting to wrest control from teenagers, or from other adults, for their use.[27] The ongoing battle for their control is one of several ways in which power and authority manifests itself in the islands, and the case study presented in this chapter is just one example of this and gives an insight into the authority that the CIOS has acquired, as Occupation specialists, in the islands.

Although we cannot say precisely when the process began, adults started to reclaim and 'tame' the bunkers for their own use. This happened first of all with

[27] In 2007, a local art group in Guernsey known as the 'Readerswives Collective', and made up of disaffected youths, petitioned to cover a bunker in graffiti or 'street art', as they preferred to call it. This grossly offended members of the CIOS, who saw such an act as vandalism. Permission was not granted.

bunkers on private land, where they were used as garden sheds or workshops for storage or as a place to keep tools, but one by one, others were brought back into use as well. To be sure, many remained as neglected dumping grounds for old tyres, or as a convenient place on the coast for fishermen to leave their equipment. Others were simply vandalised. But people were beginning to find another use for them. This did not signal an end to the era of amnesia; in fact, it was only another phase of this period because very few bunkers were reused within their original context. In fact, only two fulfilled this criterion and both were in Jersey. The bunker built into the side of La Hougue Bie Neolithic chambered tomb was turned into an Occupation museum in 1947 and St Peter's Bunker war museum opened in 1965, both capitalising on the tourist industry by displaying the spoils of war. Neither was restored in the manner undertaken in Jersey in the late 1970s.

Although I suggest that the dominant era of amnesia continued into the 1970s, this did not mark the end point; in fact, many islanders today continue to use bunkers on their properties for purposes which have no relation to the Occupation. However, for these people, I do not believe that deliberate amnesia is in play in quite the same way that it was at the time of the first reuse of bunkers. I also believe that this amnesia did not signal a real or actual forgetting. Of course people remembered and knew what the bunkers symbolised; they just chose to deliberately ignore it. This deliberate 'amnesia' carried an inherent form of remembering-through-deliberate-ignoring; remembering and doing anything with a bunker, as long as it had nothing at all to do with its original use. In this, there appeared to be almost (but not entirely) universal tacit agreement across the Channel Islands.

More fully, I characterise this period as *amnesia and disguise*, because reuse took place as long as the Occupation was not invoked and bunkers were 'disguised' and used as other kinds of buildings. As the 1960s and 1970s marked the heyday of the tourist industry in the islands, some of the 'disguises' in this period catered for the hospitality industry, including the examples in Jersey of the Gunsite Café in St Aubin, or the planned 'Bunkerbar Last Chance' at L'Etacquerel, the designs for which were submitted in 1978 but never realised. Other such past and present uses for disguised bunkers in the Channel Islands include a mushroom farm in Jersey; a bird hide in Guernsey; a Catholic shrine built in 1963 in Fort Hommet in Guernsey; a fishery established in 1980 at L'Etacq in Jersey; a diving school in St Helier, Jersey; a club house for a motorcycle group in Guernsey; and more recently, 'Battletec', a war gaming company in Guernsey, who operate out of one of the gun sites of the Mirus battery. The list was and is seemingly endless and continues to grow.

As well as being reused, from the 1980s onwards a minority of bunkers began to be 'domesticated'. Some were used as wine cellars for hotels and one or two were converted into tourist accommodation such as the observation tower overlooking the Corbière lighthouse in Jersey. Such was the public acceptance of these structures that a small number of people were prepared to turn them into extensions for their houses. One man in Guernsey, a member of the CIOS, has even cut his garden hedge into the shape of the lookout platform of an observation tower.

Although all of these examples of reuse of bunkers constitute an intervention in the legacy of the Occupation, they do not class as 'heritage'; none of the sites is being reclaimed as part of local identity or collective memory; in fact, quite the opposite. By disguising the bunkers, they have denied the original meaning of these structures and excluded them from memory.

Phase 3: Rehabilitation and Restoration: 1977 to Present

A survey of back issues of the CIOS *Review* shows that, by the 1970s, its members were already developing an interest in recording, protecting and preserving the German fortifications of the islands. This marked the beginning of an era of rehabilitation and restoration of bunkers, a phase which continues to the present day. For the first time, islanders were beginning to perceive these fortifications as heritage and began to take active steps to reclaim them, pull back the brambles and strip away the disguises.

In the early 1970s, the CIOS battled with bureaucracy and the older 'establishment' politicians who had lived through the Occupation and who believed that bunkers were 'scars on the landscape'.[28] In a general atmosphere of official indifference and suspicion, it was hard to convince those in authority that the bunkers were worth saving (Costard 1991: 4). For good or ill, the CIOS was, at the time, out of step with the prevailing attitude among the general public in the 1970s, who seemed in agreement with those in authority. Bunkers were 'violently' contrasted with the Martello towers that merged with the landscape 'admirably'. The 'German towers' were seen as ugly structures, 'as alien in appearance as they were in the making' (Coysh 1975: 9).

In 1975, CIOS member and occupation veteran Michael Ginns wrote a guide to the fortifications in Jersey, arguing that such a publication was necessary because interest was growing among the younger generation; because other guidebooks on the fortifications of other eras 'either choose to ignore the German constructions altogether or refer to them in a manner which is at once both oblique and embarrassed'; and because 'it is important for posterity that the German fortifications should be recorded while there are those still alive who can remember their purpose, so that future generations will not have to indulge in guesswork' (Ginns 1978: iv).

A year later, while secretary of the Jersey branch of the CIOS after 2 years as president, Ginns had what he later referred to as a 'eureka' moment.

> By 1976 things were slowing down and the CIOS looked as if it might settle into a rut with nothing more exciting than meetings and rambles', he wrote. 'In the bath one day, the restoration/preservation thing came to me and, like Archimedes, I jumped out of the bath

---

[28] Michael Ginns personal communication 2011; this perception gave rise to a film of the same name, made by the CIOS in 1976.

> … shouting 'Eureka!' … My initial thought was that Public Works should run Noirmont[29] as they did Gorey Castle at that time. So imagine my surprise when they suggested that the CIOS look after the place after it had been made secure.[30]

As there were already a few bunkers being used as Occupation museums, Ginns had the idea that some could be used as tourist attractions and shown off as historical fortifications like those of other periods in the island, under the control of the States of Jersey Department for Public Works. However, after reviewing the idea, the Public Works committee told Ginns that it would be costly to run, but if they were to make the command bunker (Batterie Lothringen) at Noirmont secure, then the CIOS could become the custodians.[31]

This was quite a sensitive area of the island because in 1947, the headland, which was riddled with a network of buried major bunkers, had been bought as a memorial to the men and women of Jersey who died in the Second World War. The land had thus been 'pacified' and 'liberated', and yet to excavate and restore bunkers in this area was a form of reversal of that liberation.

In February 1977, the Department of Public Works excavated the entrance of the bunker so that CIOS members could get in, and the rubbish and rubble inside was emptied by members into skips. The chance of seeing inside an underground bunker for the first time since it was sealed drew a large number of volunteers.

In June 1977, the bunker was open to the public for the first time, and people had to climb down a ladder to get inside. It proved to be an immensely popular tourist attraction. As Ginns put it later, 'We boomed! … We could only open it alternate Sundays, because you had to have some time off, and Thursday evenings, and at nine o'clock at night you could still have a queue outside the door nearly 200 strong'.[32] Many of those who came to see inside the bunker were curious local people who remembered visiting the bunker after the war, before it was sealed.

Although the opening of the command bunker at Noirmont proved to be a popular enterprise, supported by a new and younger President of Public Works who was more open-minded about opening up bunkers than his older predecessor, not everyone approved of bunker restoration. Ginns recalled that there were some 'rumblings in the paper' and that some people complained that it was 'too soon after the Occupation', but that his position was that 'if it's ignored, it's forgotten. People have got to know what happened without being vindictive about it … a thousand years from now it'll just be another little speck of history, won't it?'[33]

In 1976, just 1 year earlier, Ginns had joined the local camera club, where his friend David Bishop was already a member. The club had recently made a number of films which used a method of dual projection where alternating images could be

---

29 Noirmont Point is a headland in the south-west of Jersey known today for its concentration of bunkers.

30 Letter to author from Michael Ginns, 11 March 2009.

31 Interview between author and Michael Ginns, 11 September 2011.

32 Interview between author and Michael Ginns, 11 September 2011.

33 Interview between author and Michael Ginns, 11 September 2011.

faded in and out. Ginns became inspired to make a 40 minute film with Bishop called *Scars on the Landscape*, where images of bunkers, both during the Occupation and in their present state (or 'wartime and peacetime bunkers', as Ginns put it),[34] could be shown side by side.

While copies of the original ciné film are now difficult to find, a shorter version was made on video in 1984, the script of which Ginns wrote. Ginns described the commentary of this to me as a 'party political broadcast'[35]; it was made to persuade the general public that 'bunker restoration has nothing whatsoever to do with admiration of the Third Reich and has all to do with historical relics. Otherwise, we might as well tear down the castles, forts, etc., of the wars against France'.[36] The commentary of the 1984 film gives an insight into the attitudes that had to be overcome at that time and is worth quoting at length:

> They are described as being 'grim reminders of World War Two', 'concrete monstrosities' or 'scars on the landscape'. Many people would be only too happy to see all the German fortifications demolished or buried. Why would this be? Is it because they are a reminder of war? If this is the case then surely all Jersey's fortifications should be demolished for, make no mistake, no matter how attractive it looks in its surroundings, and whether built of stark granite or concrete, a fortification is a fortification, and they were all built with one purpose in mind: to repel an invader. Why, for example, should this one be called a monstrosity [camera points to German observation tower] but this one be cherished as part of the island's heritage? [camera points to Martello tower].

Accompanied by background German military marching music, the film compares historic castles and towers of earlier centuries to the German bunkers, arguing that they should be seen as the same thing.

> Citing those, and in answer to those who would call for the demolition of every German bunker, the CIOS would argue that every fortification in Jersey of whatever age has played its part in the island's history and should be preserved according to its merits. This is not to say that every piece of concrete erected in World War Two should be put under a glass case, but that the best examples of each type should be refurbished and preserved for posterity.

The film then goes on to argue that 'something must be left for our descendants' and that the destruction of bunkers after the war (referred to as the 'mistakes of 1945 and 1946') must 'on no account' be repeated. In 1953, a massive scrap drive took place which removed all surviving tank turrets and coastal guns. The film argues that:

> The same must not happen to the surviving fortifications of the period. We repeat that not every piece of concrete should be placed under a glass case, but that the best examples of each type should be refurbished and preserved ...
>
> For, while it is a view that is not popularly held at the moment, the German fortifications have all played their part in Jersey's continuing history and will one day take their place alongside the granite towers and castles which have guarded the island for centuries.

---

34 Interview between author and Michael Ginns, 11 September 2011.

35 Michael Ginns Personal communication 2009.

36 Letter to author from Michael Ginns, 11 March 2009.

> It is realised that as long as there remains alive more than one person who can recall the Second World War, there will always be someone who will detest the constructions and all that they stood for, but rest assured, when the last person who lived through the Occupation has passed on, the German fortifications of Jersey will have truly passed into history. They will cease to be scars on the landscape and become respectable ...[37]

The film was shown at the reception after the official opening of the command bunker at Noirmont,[38] where the audience was no doubt appreciative, but even by 1985, when the population had had a few years to get used to the restoration of bunkers, the film received some boos when it was shown a few days before Liberation Day.[39]

At the time that the command bunker was first opened, the CIOS announced that it was now in a position to accept from the public military items on permanent loan for display at Noirmont. During the winter of 1977–1978, the CIOS began to scrape the rust off the doors and steel plates and repaint the interior of the bunker. A display case was erected inside and, two years later, the first of the large coastal artillery guns was winched back up the cliff it had been pushed off after the war and was replaced on one of the gun platforms at Noirmont. By that time, the bunker had been more or less restored internally to how it would have looked when operational.

In 1980, the Planning Department in Jersey paid for one of each type of bunker to be excavated,[40] and from around the same date, the CIOS Review started a regular feature which kept their readership up to date on the excavation and preservation of bunkers. Michael Ginns suggests that at that time, apart from the example of the Batterie Todt in the Pas-de-Calais region of France, the CIOS in Jersey were the only group in Europe who restored and preserved bunkers. 'The original idea came from me and the concept has blossomed, not only in Jersey but in other islands as well, to say nothing of the Atlantic Wall sites along the coast of Europe. And all because of the CIOS in Jersey'.[41]

As part of the wider move to preserve bunkers, the CIOS knew that the work of their volunteers would or could be undone if the local government did not continue to back them. Thus, they fought for the official preservation and scheduling of the bunkers. In Guernsey, the CIOS wrote a report in 1979 called the *Survey and Classification of German Military Structures and Sites in Guernsey, 1945–1945* (Kreckeler and Partridge 1979), which listed structures 'suitable for preservation/ restoration' according to their perceived historic importance (Grade A) or architectural interest (Grade B). While five were subsequently put on the protected monuments list in 1982, more were recommended for listing in 1990,[42] some of which were successfully registered soon after. It was noted in 1990 by the author

[37] Scars on the Landscape; script by Michael Ginns. Jersey Heritage L/D/25/J2/1.

[38] *Jersey Evening Post*, 24 June 1977: 11.

[39] Michael Ginns personal communication 2009.

[40] Michael Ginns personal communication 2009.

[41] Letter to author from Michael Ginns, 19 February 2009.

[42] Letter to the President of the Ancient Monuments Committee from Colin Partridge, 4 May 1990.

of the report that 'it would not be ... politic to recommend listing in one step', with the implied recognition that such an action might draw too much negative attention to itself.

In Jersey, Michael Ginns was once again at the heart of the bid for heritage protection and in 1986 wrote a 72-page report arguing for the official preservation and designation of 15 German fortifications in the island as Sites of Special Interest (SSI). This followed a report written earlier that was used to get permission to restore the command bunker at Noirmont (Ginns 1986: 3).

The 1986 report gave five reasons why bunkers should be preserved: they were part of the island's history; several were unique to the Channel Islands; after demolition and neglect, some surviving fortifications were unique to Jersey; they had an educational value; and, uniquely among other European countries, official preservation of bunkers had taken place only in Jersey and that it was important that it should continue. The criteria selected for preservation was that the site in question should be on public land and the bunker in the care of the CIOS; the structure should have architectural value; it should have military value; and it should be unique (Ginns 1986: 3–4). This report became the basis for current proposed Site of Special Interest (pSSI) listings and many other Occupation structures have since been given a 'default' status of Building of Local Interest (BLI).

By 1991, the twentieth anniversary of the Jersey branch of the CIOS, nine bunkers (a figure which included several individual bunkers at Noirmont) were described as being 'in the Society's care' (Costard 1991: 4). Although the Society's aims were to 'actively promote reconciliation between former enemies'; to 'present a non-partisan, non-political interpretation of historical fact' in order to 'stress the folly of war'; and to 'recreate the past on an authentic basis ... placed in an enlightened perspective' (ibid.), the actual restorations were focused almost entirely on German soldiers and the capability of their weaponry to the marginalisation and (in most fortifications) complete exclusion of those who built the bunkers and those who the Germans were occupying. It was thus hard to see precisely how the restoration of bunkers fulfilled any of the society's aims; it was and remains unclear how the restocking of bunkers with weapons, ammunition and soldiers 'stresses the folly of war'.

Restoration, then as now, involved turning the concrete shells of bunkers into a close approximation of how they would have looked during the Occupation, complete with original fixtures and fittings where possible, new wood panelling, mannequins in replica uniforms, swastika flags hanging on the walls (at Noirmont Point) and repainted murals (Fig. 3.4).

The OT and its workers are mentioned in two locations in Jersey's restored bunkers. At the Command Bunker at Noirmont, the Germans are present in full force in the main rooms of the bunker in the first underground level that one arrives at as one descends the stairs (Fig. 3.5). In the level below, the main room is unpopulated by mannequins, flags, artefacts or display cases. Instead, a small number of information boards are placed on the wall in an otherwise empty room. One of these boards tells the visitor about the OT in Jersey. Another reproduces

Fig. 3.4 Restored interior of a bunker at Noirmont, Jersey (© Gilly Carr)

Fig. 3.5 Michael Ginns (*right*) and Paul Burnal (current President of the Jersey branch of the CIOS, *left*) at the entrance to the command bunker at Noirmont Point, Jersey (© Gilly Carr)

newspaper articles on escaped Russian slave workers who stole food from local farms. A third lists the command structure of the OT. Information is not presented in a way that deliberately seeks to sympathise or empathise with the foreign workers.

At the two linked Corbière bunkers, similarly packed with mannequins and furniture, the sole small information board on the OT describes the nationalities of the workers, describing how they came to be in the island. It also includes the following paragraph: 'Gangs of marauding Russians would not think twice about killing a Jerseyman in the hunt for food! In St Peter, one shop keeper was stabbed nine times by escaped Russians; the man's sister was seriously wounded in the same attack. Two incidents occurred in St Mary where one farmer was badly beaten and another wounded with a pitchfork'.

What is striking about this, apart from its tone (which accords with the message that German-controlled newspapers issued during the Occupation) is its lack of sympathy and understanding towards 'gangs of Russians'; their exaggerated threat to Jerseymen is exactly what the occupiers wished to emphasise so as to prevent islanders from offering them aid. Although the information panel explains that Russians were 'treated very badly' and as 'beasts of burden', it does not explain to the reader why a small number escaped from their camps and needed to scavenge for food.

In Guernsey, the restoration situation did not and does not differ greatly to Jersey although it initially took place a little later and, to date, the workers of the OT are excluded from presentation. Guernsey does not have a policy of including reference to the OT or slave workers on interpretation boards. I was told by the director of Guernsey museum that 'it would be mentioned where relevant, but not on a prescriptive basis'.[43] The current problem is that it is not mentioned at all in any restored bunkers in the island.

The 1980s and 1990s were characterised by increasing restoration and refitting of bunkers in both islands, and such work became increasingly mainstream and less contentious. The CIOS soon became seen as the authority on the fortifications and, rather than being overruled by politicians, they became the institution whose opinion and advice was sought by all.

In Guernsey, preservation and restoration went in two directions: in addition to bunker restoration, a further project was launched. In 1991, 'Fortress Guernsey' was established, with the tripartite aim of emphasising the value of the island's fortifications of *all* eras, their role as a vital part of the island's social history, and their value as tourist assets. The eventual aim was to build a fortifications interpretation centre of international stature in the island, although this did not happen. Some monuments, including bunkers, became protected through this project, and a comprehensive programme of conservation and full restoration of selected sites was planned. This restoration would return selected bunkers to their original condition complete with installation of 'appropriate ordinance', the exact shade of paint, and faithfully reproduced lighting. The bunker restoration plan in Jersey was held up as an ideal to aim for, and described as 'a model of military archaeological excellence' (Mahy 1992: 17).

Fortress Guernsey had to break down the old taboos in the island, just as the CIOS had done in Jersey over a decade earlier. A member of the CIOS fortifications sub-committee wrote to the *Guernsey Evening Press and Star* to tackle and debate publically the contentious issues head on. He acknowledged that when it would be realised that Fortress Guernsey would focus with equal intensity on the German bunkers and older fortifications, 'many will become outraged and opposed to the idea … [as] this traumatic period remains well within living memory … however, German bunkers are not living war criminals and it is surely time to look at these structures in a fresh light' (ibid).

Having been convincing enough to get permission to go ahead, much of the restoration was carried out, especially on bunkers, although Fortress Guernsey lost

---

[43] Email from Jason Monaghan to author, 13 March 2009.

Fig. 3.6 Excavation of a bunker at Noirmont Point in 2010 by members of the CIOS Jersey (© and courtesy Tony Pike and Jersey Evening Post)

its financial backing from the island's Heritage Committee in 2003. A sub-committee of the CIOS, Festung Guernsey, succeeded it in 2005, but without any kind of financial backing. This was a similar initiative with similar aims, but with a focus purely on the German fortifications. Because many structures were gradually degrading, with internal fittings suffering from vandalism, it was felt that work was still needed and a large number of bunkers remained in the island that had not yet been preserved or restored.

Thus, amateur enthusiasts are still extremely active in both islands (Fig. 3.6). They have replaced as much of the missing original fabric of selected bunkers as possible to restore them, complete with light switches, period wiring, stoves, periscopes, tables, bunk beds and guns. Where the equipment and original fittings have not been available locally, the bunkers of the neighbouring island or of France have been scoured for spare parts. New wood panelling has been put up inside some, and ceilings have been whitewashed.

In summary, the 'flagship' bunkers of the CIOS have been lovingly restored, such as those at Noirmont Point, Les Landes and La Corbière in Jersey; and at Pleinmont, St Jacques and Fort Hommet in Guernsey. They represent countless hours of work, costs borne mostly by members themselves, and many hours of volunteers' time over the years in keeping the bunkers open to the public. The CIOS is tremendously proud and protective of bunkers under their custodianship, and have put up information panels on the inside and outside for visitors. These panels focus on the military capabilities of the structures and their guns, the daily lives of the personnel who manned them, and the restoration work. We have seen how information on those who built the structures, i.e. the foreign workers of the OT, is (most often) either absent, (rarely) summarised in a sentence on outside information panels, or else (where it exists) physically marginalised within the bunker. The mannequins inside the bunkers show German soldiers at work, but never the OT workers in the act of construction. Restored rooms show the living quarters of the German soldiers, but the former camps of OT workers remain unrestored and unmarked as discussed in the next chapter; these are now unsuitable for such restoration.

Videoed interviews with former soldiers are shown, but no testimony from OT workers is presented. The displays are certainly occupier-heavy. The photographs of the workers that were shown are taken by the occupiers, and are thus as viewed by their masters and overseers. They are photographed working or posing as a group for the camera. They are also represented or replaced on information boards by images of the fruit of their labours (the bunkers) or by their OT overseers. No photographs exist, and no accounts are displayed of torture and ill treatment (although these accounts exist; see e.g. Bunting 1995, Chap. 5). The images on display are the most sanitised of all photographs of OT workers and were probably staged for the camera for propaganda purposes (for a discussion of staged war photographs, see Sontag 2003: 41–52). Photographs of these of ill-clad or starved figures are missing both from restored bunkers and from most published books on the Occupation—even those that specialise on the OT or bunkers (e.g. Gavey 1997; Ginns 1999a, 2006).

Phase 4: Contestation and Memorialisation: 1998 to Present

In 1998, a controversy began in Jersey, the repercussions of which are still being felt today. The dissonance in the way that bunkers were presented to the public, and the disinheritance of those who built them, was criticised in the national press (Vitaliev 1998). The image of the Channel Islands was being tarnished on a national stage for ignoring their past rather than publically acknowledging it.

Channel Islanders are known for their dislike of outside criticism and interference (c.f. Bunting 1995: 4–5, 2004), and so this created a furore in the local press. Vitaliev, a Guardian journalist, reported that 'Occupation sites' (i.e. bunkers) were unwillingly promoting 'elements of Nazi ideology' in Jersey (and, by implication, the Channel Islands as a whole), a place that was reported as having a 'peculiar pride … about the fact that they were occupied by the Nazis'. The article implied that only the perpetrators and not the victims of the crimes of Nazism were being commemorated (Vitaliev 1998: 4). Vitaliev also criticised the amount of German- and Nazi-oriented souvenirs for sale in the Channel Islands, ranging from the music of the Third Reich and facsimile copies of wartime German newspapers to Occupation postcards featuring marching German soldiers—all of which can still be found for sale today.

While much research and memorialisation (in Jersey at least) has since recognised the suffering of victims of Nazi persecution, this implied accusation levelled against the CIOS and bunker restorers came as a surprise to the local population, who were (and are) still reeling from the blow dealt by journalist Madeleine Bunting and her accusations of wartime collaboration of 3 years earlier (1995).

Vitaliev's newspaper article was followed a few days later by furious correspondence in the *Jersey Evening Post*. Not only were people incensed by Vitaliev's article, but it also coincided with the advance publication of Jersey's tourist authority's intended campaign for 1999. This carried the slogan 'Jersey. Where there's something to keep everyone occupied', showing an image of tourists taking photographs at the restored gun emplacements at Noirmont Point.[44] Complaints were made that not only was the slogan extremely offensive, but that the headland was being 'desecrated' and turned into 'Hitlerworld', by the 'concrete edifices' (Dryden 1998). Michael Day, Jersey Museum's director at the time, was then interviewed and called for the island to rethink the way it treated the Occupation. He believed that there had been too much emphasis on the technical aspects of sites like gun emplacements for too long, and not enough about the human side of the story, such as the slave workers who died building them, and the evil regime that the bunkers were designed to sustain. He called for a broader interpretation of the sites, of their significance, and what they symbolised; in short, for more sensitive interpretation at bunker sites (Lewis 1998a: 3, b: 8–9), something that, 15 years later, is still unfortunately lacking at many sites.

Michael Ginns, the acknowledged expert and founding father of bunker restoration, replied to Day's comments, stating that information panels had to be filled with technical details of weaponry, and that 'it wouldn't be done if it wasn't necessary—the public want to know and will go away disappointed if all the information is not on display' (1999b).

With regards to deaths of OT workers during bunker construction, Ginns has argued that 'it is not possible to say for certain how many did die building a particular bunker, because nobody knows'. Also, because some bunkers were built by German construction troops, local workers and conscientious objectors from the UK on good rates of pay, he believed that this was not the kind of human story that people would want on information plaques. He preferred the (then) current methodology of the CIOS, in which the story of the slave workers was provided to visitors to Noirmont by means of written text, photographs and guided tours.

[44] Although this was in poor taste, Channel Islanders have a sense of humour about the Occupation. Above the bar in a pub in Alderney hangs a sign saying 'Don't mention the war!' (a quote from the popular 1970s television programme, *Faulty Towers*). At a bicycle hire shop in Sark, a photograph of a platoon of German soldiers on bicycle is accompanied by the caption 'rare photograph of the 1940 Tour de France.'

Today, the casual visitor is left to his or her own devices to wander round the bunkers, reading the information provided.

Many members of the CIOS subsequently contributed to the debate in the press, encouraged by Michael Ginns,[45] both complimenting the CIOS on their restoration work and pointing out what a boon the bunkers were to the tourist economy of the islands. Others felt that sensitive aspects of the Occupation should neither be exploited by tourism, nor 'brought into line with what is currently politically acceptable' (Walton 1999).

Although existing information plaques at bunkers did not change in Jersey, the work of Bunting, Vitaliev and Jersey Tourism's misplaced advertising prompted Michael Day to change the way one particular bunker was read by tourists. In 2001, to commemorate the first Holocaust Memorial Day, the Forced Workers Memorial (a memorial-museum and sculpture dedicated to forced labourers and their experiences) was constructed at the former Occupation museum at the Hougue Bie bunker, also now a Jersey Heritage (JH) site. La Hougue Bie and Jersey War Tunnels are currently the only German fortifications in the Channel Island to highlight the plight of those who built them. The transformation of the bunker at La Hougue Bie from a museum to a memorial was controversial due to the associated removal of original fixtures and fittings. The author has heard several bunker enthusiasts describe it as 'a waste of a good bunker', 'desecrated', and 'ruined'.

One of the intentions of the Hougue Bie bunker memorial is to make people question the appropriateness of refurbishment with its associated sole focus on the military context, but it stands alone. The restoration work of JH and the CIOS stand ideologically opposed to each other in this respect; one performed by heritage professionals and the other by local enthusiasts; one focusing on the victims of Nazism and the other, it would seem, on the perpetrators (although not the OT overseers). Islanders will often state that not all German soldiers in the islands were dyed-in-the-wool Nazis, and showed acts of kindness and humanity towards islanders (e.g. Bunting 1995: 53–55). We should remember, however, that they were all, collectively, occupiers and oppressors who could and did back up their authority with force, and were actively involved in deporting islanders to concentration, prison and internment camps in France and Germany. Unsurprisingly, this role of the occupiers is rarely, if ever, highlighted and a more nostalgic and innocuous image of the German soldier is presented.

In 2008, the CIOS in Jersey encountered opposition in their programme of restoration of another Noirmont fortification from the former Environment Minister, Senator Freddie Cohen. Cohen was at that time in charge of planning applications in the island and has written a book on the fate of the Jews (including the Jewish slave workers) in the Channel Islands (Cohen 2000). Cohen refused to process a planning application sent in by the CIOS for a final piece of bunker restoration work at Noirmont Point because he was 'deeply concerned about the

[45] Michael Ginns personal communication.

moral issues surrounding the aggrandisement of Nazi structures' (Hutchison 2008: 7).[46] He believed that if one was going to do anything to a bunker, it should be primarily based on the memorial and not the military context.[47]

He, instead, delegated the request to his Assistant Minister because he felt that he could not give the request a fair hearing. Planning permission was eventually granted in August 2008 with several conditions, one of which was that a plaque acknowledging the use of forced slave labour in the island be erected.[48] This was eventually erected in 2010 and placed at the bottom of a stairwell leading to the underground bunker.

When faced with these accusations of 'aggrandising Nazi structures', perhaps implying some admiration of the Third Reich, we have seen already how Ginns had replied that bunkers were simply part of the island's military history and no different to the other castles and forts. However, as Michael Day argued in 1998, bunkers are significantly different from other fortifications in the island. First, the earlier fortifications were built with the support of Jersey people to protect themselves from oppressors, and second, the Third Reich could not 'be judged against any other regime' because 'it was manifestly corrupt and evil' (Day quoted in Lewis 1998b: 9).

So used are they to images and mannequins of German soldiers, the general population of the Channel Islands has little problem, it seems, with bunker restoration. The opinion of JH and Senator Cohen appear not to be typical of the rest of the island, although their views are becoming better known. Jersey Tourism, for example, recently commissioned an 'Occupation Trail' map of Jersey in consultation with the CIOS, JH and JWT. The map places the sole focus, perhaps unsurprisingly, on the most evident German fortifications and concrete structures that abound in the island's landscape. Although initially it made only passing mention of the forced and slave labourers, this has been enhanced since the involvement of JWT by introductory information clarifying their plight. Tellingly, the Occupation trail does not list the Forced Worker Bunker Memorial at La Hougue Bie, although it does include fortifications which have been turned into a café, a cycle-hire premises, a turbot farm, tourist accommodation and, of course, those which have been refurbished and restored. Nowhere does it invite or encourage tourists to question the use to which these structures have now been put.

On the reverse is a map of Occupation memorials in the town centre of St Helier, which inexplicably misses out a few key memorials, such as the Lighthouse Memorial to the 'Jersey 22', political prisoners who did not survive their incarceration. Because the map covers only the town centre, it also misses the memorial to slave and forced workers at the crematorium on the edge of town, and the memorial to workers, entitled 'Silence', at JWT on the other side of the island.

---

[46] See also SSI/2007/0835.

[47] Interview between author and Freddie Cohen, 26 January 2009.

[48] Planning permit, planning application number SSI/2007/0835.

Despite Jersey's media interest in Vitaliev's article and the tourism slogan of 1999, and the ripples caused by Cohen's refusal to process the CIOS's planning application in 2008, Guernsey's bunker restorations have remained almost completely unaffected by the same ethical issues. In 1993, during the initial discussions of funding to develop the Fortress Guernsey project, Guernsey politician Deputy Len Corbin complained that the enhancement of fortifications would 'glorify the Nazi regime'. At the same meeting, Deputy Pat Mellor said that a plaque should be put on certain fortifications reminding people that workers had died during their construction (Ogier 1993). Neither call was heeded.

In Guernsey today, there is no policy on bunker restoration, and the island's museum service has an informal arrangement of working closely with Festung Guernsey. The island's Environment Department have more formal agreements with the group, and bunkers in the Department's care have been signed over to them.[49] The OT workers are currently absent from all information panels in restored Guernsey bunkers. The deaths and ill treatment of the forced and slave workers of the OT would appear currently to be a non-issue among heritage professionals in Guernsey, although their plight is recognised in two private Occupation museums in the island.

In 2001, a new playground/peace garden was built for La Houguette Primary school in Guernsey in the gun pit of one of the massive Mirus batteries, on whose land it stands. A panel was erected on the side of the gun pit with the words 'Out of hostility comes tranquillity'. With the exception to the private memorial plaque erected in the German Underground Hospital in the 1960s, this is the closest that Guernsey has come to a memorial at the site of a German fortification in over 50 years.

It is worth noting that in Alderney, despite the active interest in and mapping of fortifications by a couple of local historians (e.g. Partridge and Davenport 1993; Davenport 2003), almost every fortification is neglected or in a state of dereliction (Fig. 3.7). Only a couple appear not to be in this category: the Alderney Wildlife Trust bunker and the Alderney Civil Defence bunker (also called the 'Hospital bunker' which is used by army cadets), although this latter structure currently looks derelict. Between 1945 and 2002, there was no serious attempt to clear out, renovate or preserve any bunker on Alderney; for 50 years, the great majority were vandalised or stripped of their fittings (Davenport 2006: 51).

Bunker restoration is something that uses volunteers, and if they are not forthcoming in Alderney, then this in itself speaks volumes. Most bunker preservation or clearance in the island has been done with volunteers from Guernsey (ibid). Davenport comments that most of those in the small population of Alderney who are willing and able to carry out such preservation work have already been snapped up by the Alderney Wildlife Trust. We might draw from this the observation that the people of Alderney would prefer to support their wildlife than their Occupation legacy. This is backed up by a glance at the island's 52-page tourist

[49] Email to author from HC, Guernsey, 5 March 2009.

Fig. 3.7 Neglected bunker in Alderney, 2010 (© Gilly Carr)

brochure, which heavily promotes the wildlife, devotes around four or five sentences to the Occupation, and includes a map of the island which is remarkably shy in promoting German sites.[50] It is fairly easy to see how the people of Alderney wish to be perceived and how their current identity is constructed.

Generally speaking, the island has a very different attitude to its Occupation heritage compared to its sister islands of Jersey and Guernsey. In order to understand the attitude of Alderney people towards German bunkers, I was recommended to talk to one man who, along with almost the entire population of the island, was evacuated to the UK for the length of the war. He explained his position to me in the following terms:

> We returned to Alderney on 20 January 1946 to the utter devastation of our homes and landscapes by the hateful German army. All the big guns were still a terrifying presence everywhere, hundreds of bunkers, gun emplacements, shelters, trenches and miles of … barbed wire. It was not a pleasant site and one that I can never forget. All this desecration done by the illustrious German army … landowners worked hard for years to try to get their island back into some sort of respectable order. A lot of the smaller fortifications and barbed wire has been removed over the years, but alas the eyesore bunkers are immovable and here to stay. But we do not have to glorify the illustrious German army for the desecration of our home land.
>
> … My feelings about the unsightly monstrosities [the bunkers] has developed over the years, brought on by Guernsey's love attitude towards anything to do with the occupation … Guernsey makes a lot of money from visiting Germans wanting to see what their illustrious ancestors had done to our beautiful islands; bunkers and gun emplacements that had been filled in and obliterated are being excavated and restocked … I was proud of the Alderney people not getting involved in this form of worship of the illustrious German army for financial gain.
>
> I have several bunkers on my land; there is nothing we can do to remove them completely and they are here to stay as a constant reminder of the German occupation and

[50] Observations made from the 2011 tourist 'ebrochure', http://ebrochure.submarine.gg/alderney/.

> what the Alderney people lost, but they should not be used as places of worship for the illustrious German army. Leave them to get overgrown, let them decay, try to forget about their existence if possible.[51]

While it is hard to know how representative this opinion is of other islanders, or even of people from this age group, Davenport writes that 'anything German was anathema to the people of Alderney … only in very recent years has this attitude begun to change' (2006: 51). This suggests that the attitudes of one man towards the bunkers on his property might well be fairly widely shared.

If the chronological phases through which bunkers have passed in Guernsey and Jersey apply to Alderney, then it seems that the latter island is much further behind Guernsey. Given that the island's bunkers are mostly still in the process of being 'erased' by undergrowth and that it took Jersey 50 years to get from that point to begin to enter a phase of memorialisation, we should not expect the island to adopt this focus any time soon without some radical intervention on behalf of local government or heritage professionals in either Alderney or Guernsey.[52] The perceived Occupation-related sensitivities in both islands have so far prevented such intervention, and the restoration work of Festung Guernsey and Guernsey Armouries continues apace. However, as Alderney has followed an entirely different trajectory to Jersey and Guernsey in terms of its attitude towards it legacies of occupation, it is likely that it cannot be compared directly to its sister islands. Because the vast majority of the population did not stay in Alderney to witness the Occupation, their relationship to their island, and thus their identity, is quite radically different.

The attitudes of the Bailiffs[53] of Guernsey and Jersey are reflective of the prevailing attitudes of the heritage professionals in each island. When interviewed in 2009, the then-Bailiff of Guernsey, Sir Geoffrey Rowland, believed that, with regards to restoration, 'the island's environment is adversely affected by the sheer volume of German fortifications. It would not be feasible or sensible to restore them all, but as they are part of our heritage it must be right that some of them are preserved … how many you need is a different matter… A balance must be struck so that an important but awful period of our history is not neglected whilst at the same time taking cognisance of local sensitivities'.[54] Former Bailiff of Jersey, Sir Philip Bailhache, interviewed in the same year, told me that he was 'slightly uncomfortable about the enthusiasm for renovating bunkers and concrete outposts and putting guns in them and restoring them to the way in which they were during the Occupation as if this is an end in itself. I think that the trouble with that is that

---

[51] Letter to author from JM, Alderney, 9 February 2009.

[52] Alderney is part of the Bailiwick of Guernsey and thus falls under its jurisdiction.

[53] The position of Bailiff in the Channel Islands is that of chief justice; he (there has never yet been a female Bailiff) presides over the Royal Court. He also serves as president of the legislature and has ceremonial and executive functions. Bailiffs are Crown appointments.

[54] Interview with Sir Geoffrey Rowland, 16 February 2009; comments added by email 19 February 2013. My thanks to Sir Geoffrey for permission to quote him.

you do then risk glorifying the nastiness of the Occupation—and I don't have any particular difficulties about having a small number of outposts and bunkers restored to the condition in which they were during the Occupation, but I'd like to see at least one which acknowledges the blood and the suffering and the misery and the death that accompanied the construction of these concrete fortifications'.[55] But even these ambivalent attitudes display what Macdonald (2009: 85) describes as the 'oscillation between preserving or neglecting Nazi heritage … which could take place within individuals as well as between them'.

The nub of the situation would seem to be this: Jersey has gone through a phase of openness and debate about the Occupation during the period of office of Bailhache, during which time vocal debate took place in the local press between the heritage professionals and the CIOS over bunker restoration. This was followed by the heritage professionals presenting their own vision of bunker restoration-as-memorialisation at the site of La Hougue Bie. Ten years later, the political climate was then such that the Planning Minister was able to turn down a request to excavate and renovate another bunker at Noirmont. Guernsey, on the other hand, has not yet had a period of openness about its potential role in the darker events of 1940–1945, and heritage professionals and local government still shy away from it in deference to 'local sensitivities', preferring instead (it would seem) to wait until the Occupation generation have departed the stage. While this day is sadly not too far off, the children of this generation are still very sensitive to Occupation-related topics. Quite how long the island is prepared to wait without intervention by heritage mangers or local government, or how long it will take until the political climate is right, will be interesting to observe.

Generations of People, Biographies of Bunkers

I have detailed above how, since 1945, German fortifications (or attitudes towards them) have gone through a series of changes (Table 3.1). Immediately after the war, the population and local authorities wished to be rid of them through whatever means possible. When it was found that such desires were almost impossible to fulfil, many on public land were sealed and buried. Slowly, and after a passage of time, they began to be reused, but only in ways that entirely disguised their original function and use. 30 years after the war, when the first post-war generation had reached maturity, the process of rehabilitation of bunkers began in Jersey, something which gathered momentum and popularity in Guernsey a little later and was not without controversy in both islands. Alderney has either not yet fully reached this stage or, more likely, is following a different trajectory. Finally, a generation later, the way in which Occupation history in bunkers was presented

[55] Interview with Sir Philip Bailhache, Jersey, 22 June 2009. My thanks to Sir Philip for permission to quote him.

Table 3.1 Summary of phases of attitudes towards bunkers in Guernsey and Jersey

Phase 1: 1945–1953	Erasure
Phase 2: 1950s–1970s	Amnesia and disguise
Phase 3: 1976 to present	Rehabilitation and restoration
Phase 4: 1998 to present	Contestation and memorialisation

was questioned. This was not an intergenerational clash like those which surfaced earlier; rather, it was an ideological collision between two groups interested in Occupation heritage. On the one side were the professionally trained heritage managers and on the other were the local, self-taught enthusiasts who had picked up their knowledge through experience and also saw themselves as professionals in their field.

The resulting transformation of a bunker from an Occupation museum into a memorial was a controversial act in Jersey, and one which still draws comment; this was no doubt part of its original aim. Although another high-profile German fortification in the island also promotes the memorial context (JWT), such interpretations have yet to become mainstream and have not reached Guernsey or Alderney. The addition of an information plaque acknowledging forced and slave labour at the Noirmont complex of bunkers in Jersey is too small and hidden to make any impact on the wider landscape. However, comparisons with changes in interpretation on Liberation Day and in memorial practices in the Channel Islands suggest that this may just be the first green shoots indicative of a new beginning in bunker interpretation. There is still a very long way to go before it becomes mainstream.

The range of responses to sites which have had an uncomfortable history has been studied by others. In his examination of 'sites of sorrow', i.e. places that had witnessed traumatic or unpleasant events, David Lowenthal (2003) outlined five tactics that have been employed to cope with 'heritage that hurts': ignoring; erasing (a response that includes sanitisation, hiding or renaming); celebration (a redemptive and triumphal response); mutation (rehabilitation using tactics such as remorse and atonement); and commemoration (a response that includes memorialisation). These tactics were not necessarily to be seen as end points, nor as a series of phases through which places with traumatic pasts must pass. Rather, they were observations that, as time passes since a traumatic event, generations become increasingly detached and so try to preserve the event in various different ways in collective memory.

While Lowenthal was basing his analysis on sites in different islands throughout the world, Kenneth Foote examined sites of violence and tragedy in America and the range of responses to these (Foote 2003). He observed four different categories which resulted in major modifications to the landscape, and which could be seen as falling along a continuum. The first response was sanctification, where a memorial or monument is erected, indicating that the site holds a lasting positive and even sacred meaning for the community. This type of site is usually consecrated with a ceremony, can become a site of pilgrimage, and can involve a change from private to public stewardship. It can also become a contested site when tensions arise over whether the individual(s) deserve commemoration. The second category, designation, indicates that something important happened at the site, but omits rituals of consecration. It is often a transitional phase and is thus best seen as 'in process'. There is little disagreement about the significance of such sites. The third, rectification, is where signs of violence and tragedy are removed so that a site can return to its former use implying no lasting positive or negative meaning; it frequently produces little activity at the site and the site itself is seen as exonerated of involvement in the tragedy, failing to gain any sense of significance. The fourth response, obliteration, is where all evidence of the event is removed; the site is scoured and rarely returned to use. If it is ever occupied again, it is usually after a long period of use. Consecration never takes place; rather, the site is stigmatised, scarred and forgotten. Such sites can often become the subjects of stories, oral tradition and legends (ibid: 7–26).

Although it is possible to compare responses in the Channel Islands to those in other islands or in America, an exact correlation becomes more difficult if we try to fit bunkers and OT work camps into such pre-existing typologies. Their identification as 'sites of sorrow', 'heritage that hurts' or part of a 'landscape of violence and tragedy' is not in doubt. It has been suggested, for example, that as much as 90 % of the workforce who built the German fortifications were slave, forced or conscripted labourers[56]; we know that many of these workers were also treated with violence or died or were injured through negligent working conditions and rock falls during the construction of tunnels.

According to official narratives embraced by islanders, their occupation was marked by correct relations between islanders and occupiers, where the local authorities did the 'right thing'. Because the presence of sites of forced and slave labour runs counter to this narrative, they were sites of shame and were thus obliterated, erased, ignored or just swallowed by the undergrowth. Although bunkers were originally in the same category, their very size and strength protected them from a similar fate. Thus, any attempted erasure was temporary and, in the end, proved impossible for the vast majority of structures.

Their size and number prevented them from being ignored for long; after 30 years, by the time the post-war generation reached maturity and grew curious about the Occupation, their attention was directed to these ubiquitous, semi-mysterious, empty or sealed structures. After being surveyed and categorised, the next stage was their excavation, preservation and restoration.

The difficulty in a direct comparison with Lowenthal and Foote's categories comes with the rehabilitation and restoration of bunkers. Does this constitute Lowenthal's 'celebration' and Foote's 'sanctification' and, if so, was this an appropriate way for bunkers to be treated either in the 1970s or today? Interpretation at these sites is currently almost exclusively focused upon the occupier and his weaponry. Although the CIOS deny that their interpretation glorifies Nazism, it

[56] Statistics presented at Jersey War Tunnels.

Fig. 3.8 Restored casemate bunker at Millbrook, Jersey (© Gilly Carr)

does appear to glorify the occupiers (a subtle but important difference). As in many Occupation museums, the occupier is present in mannequin form in his uniform. The symbol of his allegiance and ideology, the swastika, is often in evidence (e.g. at Noirmont); the image of his Führer is sometimes framed on the wall (e.g. at the gun casemate bunker at Millbrook in Jersey, Fig. 3.8). His weapons are in place, details about his daily life abound, and he is often even provided with a bunk bed and plastic food. All his needs are catered for and all the instruments of war that he might need to oppress the local people are on hand. He is, however, safely contained inside the bunker. Only at a time when the Germans were safely vanquished and their memory had had a generation to fade was it safe to reawaken their ghosts and display them in a static, plastic and unthreatening form. At a period when the narrative of a 'correct' occupation was being commemorated in an annual ceremony which allowed remembrance and a reliving of the 'safer' aspects of the Occupation, the time was then right for the second generation to carry out their restorative work. The era had not yet arrived when this perspective began to be questioned.

Although members of the CIOS deny vehemently that bunker displays constitute any kind of 'glorification' or 'celebration' of the occupier, it is hard to pinpoint what aspects of display might counter such an impression, or how they might highlight the folly of war. If the aim *was* to glorify or celebrate war, it is even harder to imagine what aspects of display would need to be changed. For example, the German soldier is not presented in these displays in any way as a villain. And while it would be denied by bunker restorers that he is presented as a hero (and, indeed, perhaps this is the wrong word given the local context), he is, arguably, an anti-hero. We might also pause to consider how a Nazi sympathiser would view the bunker restorations and representations of German soldiers. My fear is that, because of the swastikas, pictures of Hitler, and the weaponry, they would find approval, even if they might prefer to see the soldiers in action and carrying out Nazi policy rather than at rest in a bunker.

One could argue that the German soldier is presented in a celebratory way, in Lowenthal's sense—he appears to have been redeemed and is certainly not condemned. Bunkers are also now sanctified, in Foote's sense. There are memorials inside and outside those at the prime bunker site at Noirmont, either to Allied servicemen or members of the CIOS (in fact, the whole Noirmont headland is supposed to be a war memorial); the command bunker was 'consecrated' with an opening ceremony and became a site of pilgrimage for many members of the community. The very sanctification of these bunkers is what causes contestation and anger when heritage professionals and others criticise the mode of presentation. Such is the power, authority and respect garnered by the CIOS today that bunker restoration is beyond reproach. Restoration has led to a 'heritage effect', where preservation and display has conferred a legitimacy upon bunkers, made them 'worthy of preservation and attention … and [given them] a symbolic value' which demands 'particular ways of treating and viewing' them (Macdonald 2009a: 87).

Lest it be argued that bunkers are not sanctified in the Channel Islands, it is worth noting that over the last few years, members of the Council for the Protection of Jersey's Heritage and the Société Jersiaise have taken the lead in seeking official financial backing for an application to be on the UK's list of sites bidding for World Heritage status. The fortifications of the Channel Islands are the focus of the application, based upon the fortifications of all eras, and German bunkers are an important part of this.

In her report on the heritage of the Channel Islands, commissioned by Jersey Heritage to assess the islands for World Heritage status, Kate Clark's observed that 'the fortifications of the Channel Islands as a whole represent a very significant group, and … there may be some potential in putting them forward for inclusion on the UK Tentative List, as and when it is revised' (2008: 7), further noting that 'the fortifications as a group, including the Second World War remains, have the potential [to demonstrate Outstanding Universal Value] in terms of the density of remains, the diversity of different military site types and the long time span that they represent' (ibid: 9).

Even if their stories are not narrated in the vast majority of restored bunkers, it is interesting that Clark felt it important to comment that 'as well as being of technological significance, the sites [German bunkers] are an important testament to the suffering of the local population and of the labourers from across Europe brought here to construct them' (ibid: 45). In flagging up the importance for World Heritage listing of 'appropriate management' at fortifications, Clark also stressed the 'strong risk that these sites could also become the focus of inappropriate political activity' (ibid: 48). It is unknown whether Clark was moved to write this based on the swastikas on display in several bunkers, or on the glorification of occupation which is currently, albeit unintentionally, emphasised. Nonetheless, the strong inclusion of bunkers within the report communicated high-level approval for the perception of German fortifications as important heritage worthy of that ultimate celebrated and sanctified accolade: World Heritage status.

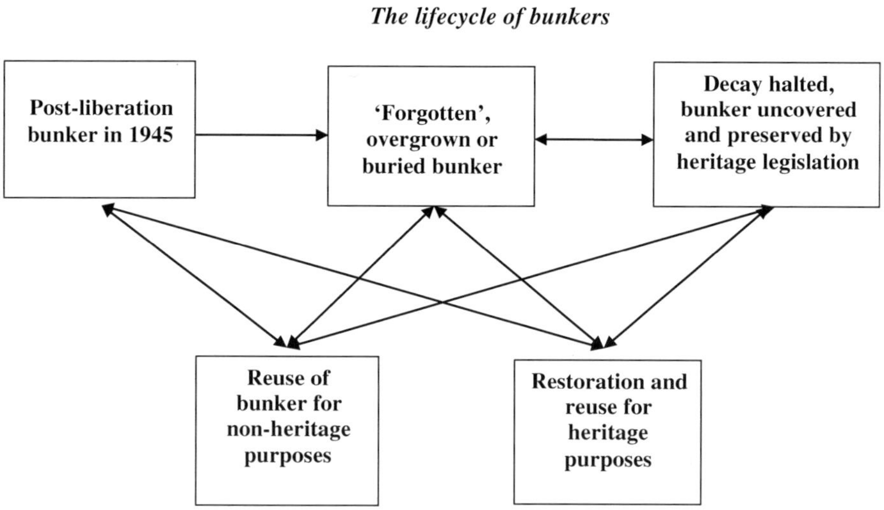

Fig. 3.9 Potential stages in the life cycle or biography of bunkers

The Life Cycle of Bunkers

Figure 3.9 shows the number of stages through which bunkers can pass during their life cycle, and this applies to bunkers throughout Europe. They also represent the several states in which bunkers currently exist in the Channel Islands. There are two things to note: first, because many of the stages are reversible, they are not necessarily consecutive, i.e. while weeds and rubbish can be removed to halt decay and leave the bunker as an empty shell, these can soon return. Once a bunker has been listed, preserved or scheduled, it can then go on to be restored or reused for heritage or non-heritage purposes. While it would not be allowed (in theory) to return to a state in which weeds and rubbish would be allowed to colonise the structure, in practice this could happen in remote bunkers.

The second observation to note is that every stage (a) is potentially open or subject to interpretation and criticism by others and (b) can be seen as either a passive or active intervention in the life cycle of the bunker. This is troubling for the heritage professional or guardian of a bunker, because if they own a bunker which has become overgrown then they could, in theory, be accused of repressing or attempting to cover up an ugly past. If they intervene to the extent of removing the undergrowth and rubbish, then they could be accused of exposing, showing off and attempting to turn into heritage a shameful or unwanted legacy. There is more controversial territory: the attempt to preserve, protect or schedule bunkers as 'heritage' makes a statement about what a society values. Is it appropriate or desirable to talk of 'valuing' Nazi architecture? To reuse a bunker as something which has no connection to heritage is to risk being accused of being in denial; to restore one for heritage purposes, to make a statement and construct a narrative for display to the public, is perhaps the most risky of all strategies, because then the statement is more deliberate, unambiguous and openly invites critique. This is why to do *anything* with a bunker is to enter an ethical arena and those who do so should be aware of this.

While these stages can be interpreted in a number of ways, in order to understand Channel Island bunkers contextually we need to examine more closely the real motivations behind the interventions in this particular legacy of the Occupation.

Bunkers have been rehabilitated and restored for over 35 years and now appear as uncontroversial fixtures in the landscape. Brave is the person who would suggest that this is but a transitionary period. Those who restore bunkers would be extremely angry if it were suggested that bunker restoration was but a 'phase' and that some of their hard work may potentially be undone in the future.

It is clear, as Foote also observed (2003: 27 and 214), that a site's treatment and interpretation may change through time and pass through several stages during its lifetime. As social, political and cultural attitudes and values change, so does the way that the past is perceived. As memory of the Occupation in the Channel Islands increasingly embraces victims of Nazism, so interpretation may follow suit, although it is clear that there is reluctance to admit that this may be necessary or desirable. Paul Sanders has astutely observed that 'attacking or even questioning any of these building blocks [of official occupation history] has been next to impossible, as over the years traditionalists have feared that even minute changes would lead to a collapse of the entire structure' (Sanders 2005: 235). In the case of bunker enthusiasts, the fear is that any criticism at all will result in the closure of all restored bunkers and the waste of 30 years of restoration efforts.[57] If bunker enthusiasts have been allowed to intervene in the legacy of occupation from the late 1970s onwards, why should they be the only ones allowed to do so? Bunker interpretation is set to become a more greatly contested heritage; why should the CIOS be the only guardians of Occupation heritage? Presumably there is room for two or more sets of interpretation in Guernsey, Jersey and Alderney, but the CIOS have a 35 year head start in acquiring bunkers, and the professional heritage managers are severely financially constrained and have many other historic structures from all eras to safeguard.

In reality, all that is desired by some heritage professionals is a change of focus in interpretation and display, and bunker restoration could become an excellent space for the two groups to work together to achieve this end. Instead, they have become battle grounds, firstly between generations and increasingly between the trained heritage professionals and the self-taught bunker enthusiasts. While both groups have knowledge to share with each other, neither is happy with the approaches of the other. In recent years, both sides have retreated to their corners rather than face another stand-off, although both sides will come together on other Occupation-related tourist projects or will offer advice on issues (such as conservation) which dance around the central problems of interpretation.

[57] Letters to author from Michael Ginns, 19 February 2009 and 23 February 2009.

Let us now turn to examine some of the details regarding bunker restoration in the Channel Islands to see where the dissonance lies.

Explaining the Oddities of Bunker Restoration in the Channel Islands

I noted above how, in 2008, Jersey's planning minister stated that bunker restoration was related to the aggrandisement of Nazi structures and admiration of the Third Reich. If this explanation is to be rejected, as it is by those who restore bunkers, what, then, lies at its core instead? Why has bunker restoration become so popular in the Channel Islands, and why did it begin when it did? Uzzell (1989: 44) suggests that the kind of men (and the vast majority of bunker enthusiasts are male) who get involved in war-related re-enactment and restoration simply graduate from playing soldiers to being them, or in this case, from playing in bunkers to restoring them. However, it is likely that this only partly explains the fascination of this pursuit in the Channel Islands.

There are many reasons, conscious and subconscious, why bunker restoration has appealed to so many, and I outline some of them here. While these are speculative suggestions, they have been informed by ongoing conversations with bunker restorers and observation of their work over several years of fieldwork.

Restoration as a Symbol of Pride

While in France bunkers are unmistakably symbols of shame and dishonour, in the Channel Islands they have become symbols of pride. Restorers are very proud of the displays that they have created, the books that they have written about German fortifications, and the respect that they have subsequently received from other islanders because of their work. But their pride is more deeply rooted.

Later in this volume, I discuss how Channel Islanders have a pride in having endured the hardship of occupation, in their moral fortitude, and in having survived until liberation. As symbols of occupation, bunkers have also come to symbolise these very things. *Despite* the occupiers and *despite* the strength of the garrison and their fortifications, islanders survived. The bunkers are thus testimony to all that was endured. To prioritise the German experience of the Occupation at the expense of marginalised others inside bunkers is to highlight what is seen as the 'reality' of occupation by a strong and ubiquitous enemy. One senses that to have arrived in 1945 on the side of the victors made Channel Islanders feel like David after the defeat of Goliath. To restore bunkers and fill them with mannequins and swastikas is, in some small sense, akin to displaying the dead body of the overthrown giant. By displaying the strength of the enemy, they are making a statement about how much stronger they were, morally if not physically, to have overcome such a fearsome foe. Bunkers are thus also battle trophies. Like German militaria, they are the spoils of war claimed by the victor. Islanders know that they earned the right to do with these structures as they saw fit and no-one, especially not outsiders or those who did not live through the Occupation, have the right of censure.

This is one side of the coin. In the next chapter, which examines OT camps, I explore how islanders' self-perception and identity as or with victors has led to a rejection or non-association with victims and their legacy, who and which for many years—at least until the mid-1990s—were perceived as 'other' and marginalised. If islanders associated themselves with victors and embraced the legacies of victory, then we might ask what this says about the uncritical acceptance of, association with, or heritagisation of the German experience and legacy of occupation. I would suggest that, as a strong army of occupation who were victorious in Europe for most of the war, the Germans were not in any sense perceived as victims; nor are they seen that way today. One might speculate on the extent to which a subconscious perception of Germans as 'co-victors'—or at least as non-victims—exists among bunker restorers.

Restoration as Intervention in Forgetting

Restoration can be a means of remembrance: by restoring a bunker to its original condition, the post-Occupation generation could experience a period that their parents and grandparents lived through, and thereby honour and remember them—although, as bunker sites were always strictly out of bounds to the civilian population, perhaps their interest is down to simple curiosity about what could never be observed by islanders during the Occupation.

For those who lived through the Occupation and restore bunkers, I believe that another motive can be brought into play. Bunkers began to be restored over 30 years after the end of the Occupation, at a time when memories of the period were fading and those in authority or at the peak of adulthood during the Occupation were reaching the end of their lives. This was also a time when Liberation Day celebrations had fizzled out to little more than a church service and was before the period of monumental memorialisation of the Occupation years. I believe that, for this generation, bunker restoration was an attempt to prevent people from forgetting the Occupation, the occupiers, and the suffering of those wartime years. This idea was suggested by conversations with Michael Ginns, and it is important to emphasise strongly that his original idea was *not* to restore the bunker as a museum with display cases, but to make the bunker look as it was during the Occupation.[58] There was no discussion in 1977 of how the display was going to be constructed or whose story was going to be told. Conversations with Michael Ginns suggest that it was natural to present the bunker in an occupier-heavy way

[58] Interview with Michael Ginns, 11 September 2011.

Fig. 3.10 The interior of the restored M19 bunker at La Corbière, Jersey (© Gilly Carr)

because that was the way that Occupation museums were done in the island—'it always has been from the early days; it's always this emphasis on the Germans', 'it was what was expected … it's in answer to the many questions we get asked [about the Occupation]'.[59] Those who collected German militaria in the Occupation and immediate post-Occupation era set the tone and the trend for all those who followed them. Because of them and their museums, this is the way that Occupation heritage has—almost unthinkingly—been displayed and, perhaps, stereotyped in the Channel Islands from the very earliest days.

The motivation to restore a bunker to how it would have looked when operational is still very much a guiding ethos in the Channel Islands today. CIOS member Malcolm Amy, who has restored the M19 bunker at La Corbière in Jersey since 1994 (Fig. 3.10), explained to me that he has portrayed the bunker 'exactly as it was, [I've] told the stories that the people who were actually there [told me] so it's recorded for the future, because if I don't do it today it's going to get lost; you won't have the first-hand information you can get off soldiers who were there, and then it's just lost, so someone really needs to do it'. Malcolm was inspired by the restorations already completed at Noirmont Point, but he recognised that 'they weren't done exact. I'm a huge perfectionist; if it's not right I'll rip it out and do it again, I saw some of the way some of the things were done weren't quite right; I'm not happy with having artefacts, just walls with cases along the walls … the whole bunker here at Corbière, it's restored how it would have looked when it was operational … it's put back exactly as it was if you walked in here in 1944–1945, that's my view. I personally don't like display cases as it distracts from the original feel. You see from going in, it's as if it's operational now and you expect to see a soldier when you walk round the corner…'.[60] Malcolm's stated desire to restore a bunker so that it appears as it did during the Occupation, as if a German soldier

[59] Interview with Michael Ginns, 11 September 2011.

[60] Interview with Michael Ginns, 11 September 2011.

was about to walk in, resonates with the nostalgic vision valued by collectors for their museums, as discussed in the previous chapter.

Restoration as Nostalgia

I suggested earlier in this volume that the first and second post-war generations of collectors of German militaria had a nostalgic longing for the period before they were born; the time spoken about by those around them as they were growing up; that most 'exciting' of periods that they had missed. Just as Marianne Hirsch suggests that the connection of this generation to the event is 'mediated not through recollection but through imaginative investment and creation' (1996: 662), so we can understand the important role that bunker restoration also plays in this mediation for the postmemory generation.

I have also explored how nostalgia allowed collectors to encounter the Occupation at one remove, and how their systems of value placed great importance upon objects and museum displays that are perceived to be 'closer to the Occupation', as if the Germans had just left the room and were due back at any minute. It is important to note that most collectors and bunker restorers are members of the CIOS and are overlapping constituencies with the same interests and values. Thus, it comes as no surprise to discover that there is an overlap in the kind and content of display in Occupation museums and in restored bunkers. If anything, the focus upon the occupier and his weaponry are far greater in the bunkers.

Like the collectors, the bunker restorers exhibit a tendency towards Svetlana Boym's 'restorative nostalgia', the form of nostalgia which 'manifests itself in total reconstructions of monuments of the past' and has 'no use for the signs of historical time—patina, ruins, cracks imperfections'. Moreover, 'the past is not supposed to reveal any signs of decay; it has to be freshly painted in its 'original image' and remain eternally young' (Boym 2001: 41, 45 and 49). This desire for 'fresh paint' can be literal. Michael Ginns was at great pains to emphasise to me that restored bunkers should not look too glossy or 'antiseptic and sterile', despite the preference of many restorers for keeping paintwork new and clean. Restoration should not necessarily imply cleanliness, believes Ginns, because when in use, bunkers could be quite grubby and messy.[61]

Over the last 30 years, the CIOS *Review* has been dominated by articles which detail precisely how such reconstructions and restorations have taken place. In most cases, once clearance had taken place, the restorers were faced with an empty shell of a bunker and wanted to go beyond this stage as part of their presentation.

It is interesting to observe how, when faced with a bunker which had remained sealed for over 60 years, the discussion of what to do with it did not result in

[61] Interview with Michael Ginns, 11 September 2011.

restoration. When the CIOS finally received permission to excavate another bunker at Noirmont Point in 2009, a job that took two months, they found that it was entirely sealed and had been since 1948. Around thirty members of the CIOS gathered for the moment at which the bunker was to be breached for the first time in over 60 years, and they were thrilled to find that many original features and artefacts were still preserved inside, such as the armoured doors, stencils on the wall, red linoleum on the floor, ventilation piping, a chimney pipe and a bath tub. Although these had decayed, faded and rusted, the CIOS intend to keep this bunker in its present condition. As the president of the society said 'we thought with this one, we thought because there's so much that's intact and in situ ... we thought it best to actually leave it in its 'as found' state, so that's what we did ... if it's been like this since 1948 ... we'll just leave it'.[62]

Because this bunker was *authentically* 'closer to the Occupation' and thus accorded with the systems of value upheld by collectors and bunker restorers, there was no need to do a thing to it. As nobody had touched this bunker since 1948, it was almost sacred space in the eyes of bunker restorers.

One might perceive this bunker to be interpretation free. It has been opened up but then left alone. The only information panel is the new one placed outside its doorway, which emphases the role of slave and forced workers. We might argue that at last this is a balanced interpretation. No attempt has been made to turn the clock back to the Occupation and there are no mannequins of soldiers emphasising the military context. However, the fact that this bunker has been opened up represents an intervention in the legacy of war. Now that the intervention has taken place, the bunker excavated, cleaned up and the rubble removed, and the few artefacts recovered (the chimney and the bath tub) placed on display on a table, a statement has been made about what is valued in island heritage. Inside, attention is drawn to the remains of the *German* presence. When the bunker was buried (itself an earlier intervention), it represented another statement of what was not valued. It is difficult to suggest what should be done in the future with other bunkers. Is it possible to find a neutral way of treating them and, if so, what would this look like? Even an empty bunker—a bunker-as-empty-shell—makes a statement. While there are those who suggest that the bunkers themselves are memorials to OT labourers simply by virtue of their existence (e.g. Ginns 2006: 157), this seems unsatisfactory and unrealistic. Can a bunker be a memorial without an intervention that makes it such? Rather than trying to find a value-free way to present a bunker, I would argue that it is better to find a balanced method of presentation, as discussed below. While it is important to recognise the historical context in which current restorations took place, this does not mean that we cannot continue to improve and change what has been done, and keep apace of modern demands of ethical heritage presentation.

---

[62] Interview between PB and the author, Jersey, 15 August 2010.

Restoration as Therapeutic Healing

Another interpretation worth exploring is the observation that there may be a therapeutic or healing element to bunker restoration in that it provides a particular way of 'working through' the inherited trauma of occupation, albeit one that appears partially blind to the full meaning of coming to terms with the past.

As part of this, bunkers have, in the past, occasionally provided a locus of reconciliation and friendship between islanders and former occupying soldiers. This can be seen a form of what Lehrer (2010: 269) calls 'conciliatory heritage'; a grass-roots public space where former geographically dissociated opponents can encounter one another in everyday interactions to meaningfully engage with difficult histories. When these old soldiers have taken holidays in the islands where they spent their war years, they have been feted by members of the CIOS and taken to their old personnel bunkers to recall memories and have their photographs taken. Their visits (and photographs at the bunkers) are recorded in a regular feature in the CIOS Review, entitled 'Do they ever come back?' (e.g. Aubin 2009; Amy 2007; Bourgaize 2004). But what of the reconciliation needed between occupiers and their victims, especially those forced to build the bunkers? This is one area that has never been catered for as the legacy of victims has never been turned into heritage.

Continuing with the possibilities of bunker restoration as a healing strategy, I noted above that their presence did not invoke happy memories for local people who saw them being built, nor for those who were involved in the construction. It was thus easier to ignore the bunkers and to let them become an old scar concealed in soil or the undergrowth.

To uncover and restore bunkers was to pick open and inflame old scars and memories, but to a certain extent I believe that this was a positive thing to do as people began to face the Occupation after a long period of determined looking to the future. We can see bunkers and the associated memories of occupation as a metaphorical long-lived infection that lay dormant, just under the skin, flaring up now and then when provoked, but something that could not begin to heal until it was opened up and drained of its poison. To many ordinary islanders, the legacy of occupation was simply a splinter under the skin—visible, uncomfortable at times, but mostly just a part of the body that could be safely ignored. To what extent the splinter will ever be purged from the body—and to what extent this is locally desired—is an interesting question and perhaps gives us an insight into why restoration is done in a way that I believe prevents this. Healing carries with it implications of forgetting, and the Occupation has become such an integral part of identity in the Channel Islands that forgetting is not, at present, a desirable option.

During fieldwork in 2009, the author observed the excavation, by Festung Guernsey, of *Batterie Scharnhorst* (Fig. 3.11). The majority of this extensive structure was fully overgrown, covered in thick undergrowth, forgotten and entirely invisible from the road, yet was being revealed and re-exposed by the excavators. Such work is no longer controversial in the Channel Islands as the vast

Fig. 3.11 Excavation of *Batterie Scharnhorst* in Guernsey (© Gilly Carr)

majority of the population today have no first-hand bitter memories associated with these structures to interfere with their vision.

I suggest here that although Occupation heritage and its reworking can reawaken traumatic memories, it can also have therapeutic healing value. For some of the Occupation generation, hiding bunkers and OT camps from view ameliorated the trauma associated with them. This, however, did not *deal* with the residual mental suffering and anguish experienced during the Occupation years, but just avoided it. To deal with it has inevitably, in the Channel Islands, meant re-engaging with it, and this has mostly (but not exclusively) been carried out by the post-Occupation generation.

To re-engage with bunkers was, in the 1970s, to pick at old wounds and memories. However, this has had a therapeutic effect as it encouraged people to talk about experiences of the Occupation years. While the passage of time was necessary to turn a scar on the landscape into a potential site of heritage, this transformation was only brought about through human action; where it happened, it often led to a partial healing of the relationship between the population and this particular legacy of the Occupation.

I do not believe that this healing process is complete. While the Occupation is spoken about daily and it is no longer taboo to invoke the occupiers (in mannequin form), some subjects have still not been faced or openly discussed in a public forum. There is still more poison to be drained from the bunker-as-scar, namely the shame associated with those islanders who helped to build them, or the shame felt by those who did not do more to help foreign workers. I believe that once these groups and their actions are fully discussed and included in heritage presentation in bunkers, then a second stage of healing will have had a chance to progress and the islands will have had a chance to attain a new level of maturity in dealing with their difficult past.

Meskell and Scheermeyer rightly call upon us to 'expand the category of 'heritage' beyond the confines of traditional understanding, and to see heritage as a form of therapy' (2008: 156). This is certainly an appropriate way to see heritage in the Channel Islands, but usually only where the scars of occupation have been reworked, uncovered and openly discussed. The full implications of reworking many heritage sites have, however, yet to be felt or ethically presented in many places in the islands.

Seventy years after the start of the Occupation, bunkers have become historic monuments and integral parts of the islands' heritage and identity. This has only been achieved by the next generation opening and reworking old wounds, letting healing occur in a way that the passage of time alone could not have achieved. Where bunkers remain covered in brambles, as in Alderney, these sites also remain metaphorically 'concealed in the undergrowth', festering and not dealt with.

Restoration as Marginalisation of Victims

The key issue at present in the Channel Islands is that bunker restoration and the resulting displays are seen as nothing to do with those who built them. They are not seen as relevant and so are not included. One of the reasons for this is that the bunkers in the Channel Islands are complete and not half built. As restorer Malcolm Amy put it to me (recalling that his aim was to recreate his bunker as it was in 1944), 'the idea is, this is a very specific time period; the bunkers are [already] constructed, they're here, they're operational and they're here for a reason, to stop the Allies invading, so are restored at that point. If there was on this headland a half-constructed bunker they never finished, then it would be ideal to have a display there and maybe a set-up of how they were constructed'.[63]

This explanation should not be dismissed. As Malcolm was inspired by the restoration at Noirmont, as were all restorers in the Channel Islands as the command bunker at Noirmont was the first to be restored, and Michael Ginns who led the restoration was in turn inspired by the displays in Occupation museums, we can perfectly easily understand the historic sequence of events which led to bunker restoration taking the form it currently does.

The truth is that, for all the many reasons why the dominance of the German wartime experience inside the bunker has been seen as 'right' or the only way to restore bunkers, until it was pointed out in the late 1990s that the slave labour involved in building them had been excluded, nobody had thought to include them. They were simply not part of the picture of a complete bunker. In any case, they were easily dismissed because they were seen as 'only a minority' of the workforce. As bunkers were designed by 'skilled German engineers', they were the architects to be admired. The study and appreciation of bunkers seemed to cause blinkered vision. It is now the case that, because Jersey Heritage has restored the bunker at La Hougue Bie as a memorial for forced and slave workers, bunker restorers feel no obligation to do the same thing at their bunkers. This kind of display is perceived as having already been done for those who want to see it.

---

[63] Interview with Malcolm Amy, 11 September 2011.

But for some CIOS members, La Hougue Bie still represents a 'perfectly authentic bunker that has been badly damaged'.

One of the difficulties in displaying the OT worker experience is that these people were materially poor, lessening the potential for the visual display of their possessions and equipment and thus lessening the perceived potential draw for tourists. Bunkers began to be restored during the height of the tourism industry and many of the same arguments apply about pandering to what tourists were and are perceived to want.

Rather than identifying with victims of Nazism, islanders seem to have identified, instead, with the strong occupying German forces. Because much of the true story of the Occupation is also a story of victimhood, it was anathema to the British war memory to embrace it with pride. This led to certain aspects of those five years being blanked out in public discourse, and best forgotten or repressed. Sanders argues that what emerged was a 'sanitised occupation memory focusing on fortifications' (Sanders 2005: 257), which were perceived as 'safe' and uncontroversial. Because islanders would rather avoid the perceived sensitivities of some Occupation-related issues, it is easier to withdraw from and ignore such debates rather than to take part and risk facing the removal or change of displays that have been carefully put together and created using volunteer labour over more than three decades.

Dealing with Difficult Heritage

Over the last few years of fieldwork, I have observed how Channel Islanders, especially those involved in heritage management in Guernsey, have shied away from courting controversy, those in Jersey only rarely poking their heads above the parapet to speak their minds and then facing a backlash from supporters of bunker restoration for doing so. With regard to bunker restoration, heritage professionals are very aware of the perceived local sensitivities relating to the darker side of the Occupation, in other words, to subjects such as collaboration, the victims of Nazism, or atrocities. Because the darker side of the Occupation has remained unspoken, undiscussed and under-researched (although known about locally) for generations, national newspapers and sensationalist authors have, from time to time, visited the islands and published headlines and superficially researched books that have drawn adverse attention and publicity to the islands. Islanders and heritage professionals alike have not welcomed this kind of exposure and so it has remained safer to avoid drawing further press or TV coverage by not awakening sleeping dogs. While this more properly characterises attitudes in Guernsey and certainly Alderney, Jersey has been proactive in discussing victims of Nazism and issues of collaboration since the fiftieth anniversary of liberation. The events that took place during this period are now referred to as the result of the 'Bailhache effect' because Sir Philip Bailhache's period of office espoused openness, debate and memorialisation of many minority victim groups, as discussed later in this volume.

Because bunker restoration has not been an area for *continuous* debate, most islanders have no problem with it at all and see it as a considerable tourist asset; something of which they can be justifiably proud. The CIOS is a trusted and respected organisation and is usually beyond criticism. Past sparring, which has taken place only in Jersey, has resulted in entrenched views, competing modes of bunker restoration (i.e. the memorial versus the military context) followed by a retreat to separate corners of the boxing ring for prolonged periods. Compromise positions have not yet been reached.

Yet why has difficult heritage in the Channel Islands not been the subject of the kind of discussion, ongoing debate and self-critical examination as we see in other examples of difficult heritage elsewhere in Europe?

Difficult heritage has been defined by Sharon Macdonald as 'a past that is recognised as meaningful in the present but that is also contested and awkward for public reconciliation with a positive self-affirming contemporary identity' (Macdonald, 2009a: 1). Macdonald used this term in her examination of changing approaches to a different example of Nazi architecture: the Nazi party rally grounds at Nuremberg. She found that, over time, different parts of the site were negotiated using different strategies, such as 'demolition, amputation, profanation, reconstruction, looking elsewhere, commemoration, art, education and moral witnessing' (ibid: 186) as local people made the long and difficult journey of confronting the history of their town. The Nazi party rally grounds faced many of the same issues as bunkers. They were built using slave and forced labour and they were tainted by association with Nazism. They were also a site of perpetration, and while bunkers *could* be similarly categorised in this way in the Channel Islands, they seldom *are*.

There are also important differences between Channel Island bunkers and the buildings of the rally grounds. Bunkers did not witness mass spectacles of Nazi rallies; they are also much smaller structures. The rally buildings were built on a massive scale, created in order to have a certain social and physical effect upon those who saw them; they were intended to impress and to inspire awe, thus giving them a form of agency. The landscape was fashioned to 'generate senses of identity and feelings of enthusiasm' which, as Macdonald puts it, 'have since come to be widely regarded as problematic or reprehensible, and this poses problems over what to do with it' (2006a: 106).

While Channel Island bunkers do not generate the same feelings, perhaps because of their much smaller size, their architecture certainly draws admiration among members of the CIOS, thus showing how bunkers can exhibit agency of a similar kind. However, as Macdonald (ibid: 110) reminds us, Nazi architecture can be seen as 'part of the distributed Nazi 'person' or 'mind', as Gell (1998) might have put it, which renders it potentially 'tainted' and difficult to deal with in the present.

Fig. 3.12 The Catholic shrine inside the bunker at Fort Hommet, Guernsey (© Jon Bartlett)

After the war, various attempts were made to 'cleanse' both bunkers and the buildings of the rally grounds by removing symbols of Nazism, an attempt to also remove their agency and power. Over the generations, they were used for a variety of purposes which attempted to disguise or 'profane' their original use. While such profanation was a deliberate strategy in Nuremburg, in the Channel Islands, one senses that the reuse of the bunkers in a different guise was not, on the whole, symptomatic of a conscious desire to deliberately rob them of their power, although an exception might be made in the case of the Catholic shrine built into a room of the bunker at Fort Hommet in Guernsey (Fig. 3.12).

Unlike bunkers, the rally grounds have never been restored to their wartime greatness; such restoration would be unthinkable in modern Germany and would be seen as imbuing the buildings once again with the agency with which they had been originally invested and encouraging neo-Nazism, i.e. triggering the 'wrong' kind of reaction and risking a problematic identification (Macdonald 2006b: 18–19), but such considerations seem not to trouble Channel Islanders. Like bunkers, various displays or past phases of reuse of the rally ground structures were silent on the subject of who constructed the site and the original purpose for which it was intended, but today this message is not hidden or marginalised—unlike in bunkers.

Macdonald has described how the value-according 'heritage effect' of the documentation centre, housed in one of the original Nazi buildings in the rally grounds, has been 'negated' or 'neutralised' by its newly acquired architecture: the modern glass façade incorporated a glass and steel 'stake' which penetrated the heart of the building. Similarly, the exhibition inside aimed to avoid contributing to the allure or fascination of the subject matter by not displaying uniforms or insignia. Again, apart from the single example of the memorial to forced workers in the bunker at La Hougue Bie in Jersey, no such attempt has been made in the Channel Islands to restore a bunker in such a way that deliberately attempts to negate or neutralise the potential 'allure' of the Nazi regime expressed through the power and might of its bunkers or through its symbols. Quite the opposite: it has been a deliberate decision to restore bunkers to include all of these things as accurately and fully as possible, regardless of the consequences, which are not perceived to exist.

Lest it be thought that there are no consequences to such restoration and the familiarity with swastikas and symbols of the Nazi regime that it has provided to the local population for decades, a recent event in Guernsey which garnered a great deal of press attention provides evidence to the contrary.

In September 2011, a 24-year-old Guernseyman, Darren Salituri, was caught flying from his fishing boat a flag featuring the swastika and SS symbols. Other fishermen were reported to have climbed aboard and tied the flag in a knot so that the symbols could not be seen (Pouteaux 2011a: 1). Salituri, who had a swastika and BNP (British National Party) tattoos but who somewhat unconvincingly claimed not to be racist or a neo-Nazi, was reported to be unrepentant, saying that it was a 'Guernseyman's right to fly any flag he wants', and if people didn't like it, they shouldn't look at it. He also added 'I understand about the Occupation, but this is nothing to do with that' (Heath 2011: 12).

It then transpired that Salituri had purchased the flag from a local fancy-dress shop in the island which hired out, among other costumes, Nazi and SS uniforms. The owner of the shop said that if demand continued, she would get in another order of flags (Pouteaux 2011a: 1); she subsequently received hate messages. The president of Jersey's Jewish Congregation said he would be writing to the Bailiff of Guernsey to express the community's outrage (Heath 2011). He also said that neither Salituri nor the fancy-dress shop 'do the Channel Islands a lot of credit' (Pouteaux 2011b: 3).

This event suggests that, for some people in the Channel Islands, images such as the swastika have lost their ability to shock because of their ubiquity in Occupation heritage sites in the islands. The owner of the fancy-dress shop was quoted in the *Jewish Chronicle* as saying that she didn't find the display of Nazi flags or swastikas offensive and that they didn't bother her (Eglot 2011). She defended herself by saying that museums in the islands sold the flag[64] and that many people in the island collected German helmets and Nazi militaria (Pouteaux 2011b: 1).

As I have discussed in the last chapter, this hobby is very much historically contingent and should be understood within the post-war context in which it began. But for those who restore bunkers or own Occupation museums and hang up swastikas inside, whether or not it accurately recreates life inside the bunker during the Occupation, such symbols are not neutral and we should question whether the aim of achieving historical accuracy is enough to excuse the impact that that these symbols have on members of the local population who are growing up desensitised to such imagery.

---

[64] In six years of fieldwork and extensive visits to all Occupation museums in the Islands, the author did not witness this.

Given that the CIOS is a powerful lobbying force in the Channel Islands, and given that bunker restoration retains much public support, how might one go about 'neutralising' or changing the current military context? How might difficult heritage be 'unsettled' and the 'heritage effect' countered?

Macdonald (2009a: 191–192) suggests that, rather than finding or fixing on a single solution to the problem of difficult heritage, we might, instead, acknowledge the 'continuing oscillation' of temporary solutions and allow them to flourish. However, she does not advocate that this should happen in a *laissez-faire* manner; rather, she suggests instead a 'structured oscillation' with the means for 'accompanied witnessing' to help open up reflection and understanding. Moreover, she suggests that we try to enable awareness of the post-1945 history of the site 'in ways that recognise ongoing change and developments, rather than reaching closure'. What this means for bunker restoration is to give adequate space for acknowledging both the controversies that restoration has provoked since the 1970s and the periodic 'resolutions' that have been sought in memorialisation. At present, displays which acknowledge the post-1945 biography of bunkers end with the triumphal story of their restoration and presentation to the public.

Rather than settling for one comfortable heritage solution, Macdonald (ibid: 192) calls for 'continued unsettlement' by opening up heritage with the 'palimpsest effect'; allowing different layers of the past to appear and, in doing so, to 'disturb, prod and raise questions'. If the results of this in the Channel Islands are anything like that at Nuremberg, then this, in turn, will raise questions among visitors about how bunkers have been negotiated since 1945, which will in turn prompt what Macdonald sees as 'wider moral reflection and commentary' (ibid). This, she argues, is the basis for providing accompanied witnessing to help visitors reflect further.

Conclusion: Acknowledging an Uncomfortable Past

Occupation heritage in the Channel Islands, whether in bunkers, Occupation museums or represented by memorials, has historically been reticent in acknowledging that the occupiers were perpetrators who colluded or were active in deportations of islanders, the islands' Jews and political prisoners, in mistreating OT workers, and in generally oppressing the population. Instead, and for the historically and locally specific reasons explored in this volume, the occupiers have become lauded as anti-heroes; the victims of Nazism were, for the first 50 years after occupation, ignored or marginalised. It was easier to focus on survival, liberation, and what amounted to glorification of a strong enemy and his very visible works (i.e. the bunkers).

Since the fiftieth anniversary of liberation in 1995, those who suffered most during the Occupation have begun to be acknowledged and memorialised, but bunkers have stood as bastions to the pre-1995 narrative. Despite criticism, the military context of interpretation has endured to the virtual exclusion—or at least marginalisation—of other narratives.

Questions and debate relating to the appropriate way to treat bunkers have emerged at moments of change and intervention since 1945, but have been firmly and quickly rejected or ignored by the restorers. We have seen this at the first opening of bunkers (e.g. at Noirmont in 1977), at the launch of a new project (Fortress Guernsey in 1991), in outside criticism (e.g. by Vitaliev in 1998), in a new advertising campaign (in Jersey in 1999) and even in the planning application to excavate a new bunker (in Jersey in 2008). It is likely that the publication of this book will also provoke similar debate, but bunker restoration focusing on the military context may continue to survive, just as it has before. The memorial bunker at La Hougue Bie in Jersey and the heritage presentation at Jersey War Tunnels remain as the only fortifications with alternative or rival narratives in the Channel Islands.

The existence of these few structures, and of memorials to OT workers, is given as an excuse for other bunkers to continue being restored and maintained without adequate reference or due consideration to the role of slave and forced workers or local labour. Additionally, the CIOS claim that some bunkers were built only by German engineers and so it would be historically incorrect to discuss slave and forced workers in these places. Does this mean that there are no problems in presenting only the military context of such structures?

To refrain from acknowledging the potential problems inherent in a solely military interpretation has, however inadvertently, glorified the Occupation and given the impression of hero-worshipping the occupiers, providing their *doppelgängers* (in the form of mannequins) with everything that they might need—uniform, weapons, machinery, beds and food—for continued existence. Paul Virilio's observation of bunkers as 'funeral ceremony' and 'religious space' (1994: 11) were not wide of the mark here.

While the first green shoots of a turn towards memorialisation at bunkers have been in evidence in Jersey in the last decade, these have yet to appear in Guernsey. And while a couple of restored bunkers do provide some information on OT workers, this information is either physically marginalised within or entirely absent outside the bunker. The problem is not just a question of balance in the heritage presentation of OT workers and German occupying soldiers, but also one of the recognition that current interpretations are problematic. Instead, those who restore bunkers strongly believe that they are simply displaying the military history of the Occupation, no different to that which is displayed at castles and towers from earlier periods in the islands. They have emphasised to detractors that their removal would aid in denying that the Occupation took place.

While there are many narratives that could be given about the Occupation, the only acceptable and appropriate one is deemed to be that which records daily life inside the bunkers, and this is presented through mannequins performing inoffensive acts such as operating a radio, playing chess, eating a meal, manning a gun post, reading a newspaper or displaying the uniform (Fig. 3.13). The soldier is not

Fig. 3.13 Inside the restored bunker at Fort Hommet, Guernsey (© Gilly Carr)

shown in a controversial or negative light and his misdeeds during the Occupation and role as perpetrator are not mentioned. Colin Long and Keir Reeves have no difficulty in stating that 'if the purpose of heritage preservation in places of 'pain and shame' [a category for which bunkers qualify] is to commemorate the victims, then there is little role for the preservation of perpetrator sites' (2009: 78). However, because bunkers are sites of both perpetration and victimhood, there is a role for bunkers if they acknowledge both these roles—which they currently do not.

To an outsider, but perhaps not to many islanders, current presentations are highly dissonant and show inadequate signs of openness or honesty about the past or, indeed, in the present. There is little willingness to be self-critical about these restorations. But what strategies can be employed in future to minimise heritage dissonance in bunkers and increase openness? What would be the ideal response to a bunker?

The addition of memorial or information plaques at every major German fortification or group of fortifications throughout the islands would be beneficial as a form of 'accompanied witnessing' of the sort advocated by Macdonald (2009a, b). These could explain not only the role of slave and forced workers generally in bunker construction, but also could denounce the OT (i.e. drawing attention to the forced labour conscription that existed in occupied countries, and the employment of slave labour) and the way they (mis)treated sections of their workforce. The contravention of human rights in bunker construction generally could be acknowledged. In the interest of an open and honest approach in heritage presentation, the role of conscientious objectors and voluntary local labour in bunker construction should also be acknowledged and discussed.

Such plurality of presentation in other aspects of Occupation heritage could be of benefit. As noted earlier, although the Jersey Occupation Trail map available to tourists comprises only German fortifications and some memorial sites, other sites involving slave and forced OT workers could and should be included, such as the bunker memorial at La Hougue Bie and the commemorative plaque on the house of Louisa Gould, who gave shelter to a Russian slave worker; the Westmount slave worker memorial; and the sites of former OT camps.

The problem, however, with introducing shared heritage presentation and in seeking balance in interpretation through plurality is, as Tunbridge and Ashworth ask (1996: 190), how do you know what balance to strive for and when it has been attained? And while a balance may involve the addition of substantially more information on OT workers (whether inside bunkers or at other sites such as museums), it is also likely to involve the continuation of dissonant heritage in the form of restored bunkers in the military context unless these bunkers are stripped or greatly modified. Such actions would be locally unacceptable and undesirable and would cause a great deal of distress to the CIOS and its associated restoration groups, effectively disinheriting them from over 30 years of involvement with this heritage, denying their role in their restoration, and creating a different sort of heritage dissonance.

Bunkers are heritage sites with which require sensitive management strategies. While, like OT labour camp sites, they are 'orphan heritage' with no clear successor or community to argue for their significance (Price 2005), unlike OT camps there are many who would seek to claim them for their own and who have turned them into an owned and used 'living heritage'. Only those in Alderney are rejected and for the most part unused.

One way that heritage interpretation could be modified in bunkers is through the use of 'hot interpretation' of the kind advocated by Uzzell (1989) and Uzzell and Ballantyne (2008). For them, hot interpretation embraces the emotional arousal that some sites engender, especially sites relating to war. It questions the desirability and achievability of cool objectivity, advocating instead the capture of 'what the conflict meant at a human level for those involved so the story told is as complete and 'truthful' as possible' rather than presenting a 'sanitised form of the truth which will not upset, offend or challenge' (Uzzell and Ballantyne 2008: 509). Hot interpretation should encourage visitors to question and explore different understandings, values and viewpoints—for example, in this context, viewpoints other than those of the occupiers. Uzzell and Ballantyne believe that we should not ignore human suffering at the expense of the 'sartorial elegance of the soldiery and the impressiveness of the instruments of war' (ibid, 504) and further suggest that interpretation that arouses the emotions will 'more adequately convey the meaning and significance of the heritage of the people, places, events and artefacts' (ibid, 510). Emotional arousal may be important, but anything which stirs up old hatreds should certainly be avoided.

It is entirely possible for OT workers to be given a bigger profile within the bunker, perhaps most appropriately in the bunker-as-Occupation-museum, but also in the restored bunkers, and coupled with direct testimony from former workers which still survive in a number of books, archives and interviews in the islands and in the UK. This kind of shocking and moving eyewitness testimony would make excellent 'hot interpretation' and has been used in two other locations in Jersey to excellent effect (the Occupation generation quotes engraved into pavement slabs at Charing Cross in St Helier discussed later, and at the Hougue Bie bunker memorial).

Uzzell (1989: 40) asks whether we have the courage to interpret the past like this and whether we are prepared to risk losing some of our market share if we do so. Perhaps, in a time of global recession and a dying tourist economy, the Channel Islands cannot afford to lose the tourists who come to learn about uniforms, bunker architecture and heavy guns. However, if interpretation does not become more sensitive, the negative publicity that travel articles like Vitaliev's cause, and the continued marginalisation of these victims of Nazism, will surely bring more condemnation, fewer tourists, and even a continued underlying outside belief in wartime collaboration, as promulgated in popular literature.

Coupled with plural, balanced and ethical interpretations which espouse the aims of hot interpretation, restoration could move away from stating military facts and figures and towards the kind of openness that Macdonald advocates, where the post-1945 history of bunkers and the controversy that restoration has provoked is presented in order to engender debate, reflection and discussion, and to 'unsettle' previously 'fixed' heritage.

Macdonald (2009b: 102–103) observes the beginning of a worldwide trend towards incorporating 'unsettling' and 'awkward memories' and a 'more disturbing vision of the past' into public contexts. She follows Peckham (2003: 207) in advocating 'ethico-political interventions', where 'memories of trauma are taking the place of an increasingly discredited heritage'. This has made heritage more available as an ethical space in which values can be explored and debated, and German bunkers are ideal spaces for such values and disturbing visions of the past to be explored. However, as Peckham (ibid: 214) has observed, 'histories of suffering throw into relief the lack of consensus over interpretations of the past', a consequence of which can be 'multiple local pasts, where ghettoised and antagonistic styles of remembrance, reflecting different group interests, compete'. This has resonance in Jersey, which is slowly learning to embrace its history of suffering.

In order to emphasise the lack of consensus, increase dialogue, and to lessen the feeling of finger-pointing, it would be useful to include space in bunkers—or perhaps whole bunkers—devoted to how other European countries and groups have treated their bunkers. These could emphasise the variety of ways in which it is possible to restore or treat a difficult legacy and invite visitors to debate and critique the different approaches and discuss how 'successful' they are in their aims, perhaps including space within the bunkers for visitors to leave their thoughts and comments.

Such setting of bunkers within a wider European context would also be useful in widening the perspective of current inward-looking presentations which give the impression that the Channel Islands were the only places to be occupied during the war. A European perspective would also be vital in highlighting the country of origin of most of the labour force who built the bunkers.

Blessed as they are with such substantial Occupation heritage concentrated within small areas, the Channel Islands have the potential to one day become market leaders in ethical and sensitive interpretation of difficult heritage, but one senses that this day is still a long way off. Perhaps a good starting place for the present is education among school children about what to do with their occupation inheritance and the difficulties associated with current strategies. Although it has not yet proved possible, perhaps face-to-face discussion, dialogue, consultation and cooperation among all current and potential stakeholders will soon be an option so that the divisions in occupation heritage interpretation are not passed on to the next generation of islanders.

References

Amy, M. (2007). Do they ever come back? Engelbert Hoppe—return of the reluctant soldier. *Channel Islands Occupation Review, 35*, 47–80.

Anon. (1944). Retain the fortifications. *Channel Islands Monthly Review: Journal of Channel Islands Refugees in Great Britain, 7*(5), 1.

Aubin, H. (2009). Do they ever come back? *Channel Islands Occupation Review, 37*, 102–104.

Bell, M. M. (1997). The ghosts of place. *Theory and Society, 26*, 813–836.

Bender, B. (1993). Introduction: Landscape—meaning and action. In B. Bender (Ed.), *Landscape: Politics and perspectives* (pp. 1–17). Providence: Berg.

Bourgaize, P. (2004). Do they ever come back?—Paul Sommerfeld. *Channel Islands Occupation Review, 32*, 56–61.

Boym, S. (2001). *The future of Nostalgia*. New York: Basic Books.

Bunting, M. (1995). *The model occupation*. London: BCA.

Bunting, M. (2004, January 24). Our part in the Holocaust. One Channel Island at least is owning up to its wartime shame. *The Guardian*.

Clark, K. (2008). *Valuing the Heritage of the Channel Islands: An initial assessment against world heritage site criteria and public value criteria*. Jersey: Jersey Heritage. http://www.gov.je/SiteCollectionDocuments/Government%20and%20administration/R%20ValuingHeritageofC.I%2020080801%20KCA.pdf.

Cohen, F. (2000). *The Jews in the Channel Islands during the German Occupation 1940–1945*. Jersey Heritage Trust: Jersey, in association with The Institute of Contemporary History and Wiener Library Ltd: London.

Costard, M. (1991). Editorial. *Channel Islands Occupation Review, 19*, 4–5.

Coysh, V. (1944). Those fortifications: letter to the editor. Channel Islands monthly review. Journal of Channel Islands Refugees in Great Britain, *7*, 6.

Coysh, V. (1975, November 25). Martello towers—part of the local scene! *Guernsey Evening Press*, p. 9.

Davenport, T. (2003). *Festung Alderney: The German defences of Alderney*. The Alderney Society: CIOS (Guernsey)/Barnes Publishing Ltd.

Davenport, T. (2006). Alderney preservation progress. *Channel Islands Occupation Society Review, 34*, 51–57.

Dryden, M. (1998, December 17). Welcome to Hitlerworld. *Jersey Evening Post*.
Eglot, J. (2011). Swastikas fly high in Guernsey. *Jewish Chronicle Online*, 8 September 2011. http://www.thejc.com/news/uk-news/54326/swastikas-fly-high-guernsey.
Fooks, M. (1985, May 3). Seal old German bunkers to stop missing youngsters hiding. *Guernsey Evening Press*, p. 20.
Foote, K. E. (2003) [1997]. *Shadowed ground: America's landscapes of violence and tragedy*. Austin: University of Texas Press.
Galaty, M., Stocker, S. R., & Watkinson, C. (1999). Beyond bunkers: domination, resistance and change in an Albanian regional landscape. *Journal of Mediterranean Archaeology, 12*(2), 197–214.
Gavey, E. (1997). *A guide to German fortifications on Guernsey*. Guernsey: Guernsey Armouries.
Gell, A. (1998). *Art and agency: an anthropological theory*. Oxford: Oxford University Press.
Ginns, M. (1978) [1975]. *German fortifications in Jersey*. Jersey: Meadowbank Trading Co. Ltd.
Ginns, M. (1985). Operation 'Nest Egg' and Task Force 135. *Channel Islands Occupation Society Review, 10*, 19–49.
Ginns, M. (1986) *Sites of Special Interest. German Fortifications: Report on sites of German defensive structures in Jersey of military and architectural importance*. Unpublished report.
Ginns, M. (1999a) *Jersey's German Bunkers*. Channel Islands Occupation Society Archive Book no. 9, Jersey.
Ginns, M. (1999b January 5). Publicity shot for castle of the future. *Jersey Evening Post*.
Ginns, M. (2006) [1994]. *The organisation Todt and the fortress engineers in the Channel Islands*. Channel Islands Occupation Society Archive Book no. 8, Jersey.
Heath, R. (2011, September 10). Boat owner flies flag—for the Nazis. *Jersey Evening Post*, p. 12.
Hirsch, M. (1996). Past lives: Postmemories in Exile. *Poetics Today, 17*, 659–686.
Hutchison, J. (2008, August 7). Cohen abstains from decision over Occupation bunker move. *Jersey Evening Post*, p. 7.
Kreckeler, D., Partridge, C.W. (1979). *Survey and Classification of German Military Structures and Sites in Guernsey, 1940–1945*. Unpublished report.
Lagrou, P. (2000). *The legacy of the Nazi occupation: Patriotic memory and national recovery in Western Europe, 1945–1965*. Cambridge: Cambridge University Press.
Lehrer, E. (2010). Can there be a conciliatory heritage? *International Journal of Heritage Studies, 16*(4–5), 269–288.
Lewis, A. (1998a December 22). Call for 'more human' history. *Jersey Evening Post*, p.3.
Lewis, A. (1998b, December 23). In the wake of that tourism picture and the controversy it caused … is it time to rethink our bunker mentality? *Jersey Evening Post*, pp. 8–9.
Long, C., & Reeves, K. (2009). 'Dig a hole and bury the past in it': reconciliation and the heritage of genocide in Cambodia. In W. Logan & K. Reeves (Eds.), *Places of pain and shame: Dealing with difficult heritage* (pp. 68–81). London: Routledge.
Lowenthal, D. (2003). Tragic traces on the Rhodian shore. *Historic Environment, 17*(1), 3–7.
Macdonald, S. (2006a). Words in stone? Agency and identity in a Nazi landscape. *Journal of Material Culture 11*(1/2), 105–126.
Macdonald, S. (2006b). Undesirable heritage: Fascist material culture and historical consciousness in Nuremberg. *International Journal of Heritage Studies, 12*(1), 9–28.
Macdonald, S. (2009a). *Difficult Heritage: negotiating the Nazi past in Nuremberg and beyond*. Abingdon: Routledge.
Macdonald, S. (2009b). Unsettling memories: intervention and controversy over difficult public heritage. In M. Anico & E. Peralta (Eds.), *Heritage and identity: Engagement and demission in the contemporary world* (pp. 93–104). London: Routledge.
Mahy, E. (1992, June 16). Enchanted places full of dark secrets. *Guernsey Evening Press*, p. 17.
Meskell, L., & Scheermeyer, C. (2008). Heritage as therapy: Set pieces from the new South Africa. *Journal of Material Culture, 13*(2), 153–173.
Ogier, M. (1993, October 28). Fortress plan stands firm against attack. *Guernsey Evening Press*.
Partridge, C., & Davenport, T. (1993). *The fortifications of Alderney*. Alderney: Alderney Publishers.

Peckham, R. S. (2003). Mourning heritage: memory, trauma and restitution. In R. S. Peckham (Ed.), *Rethinking Heritage: Cultures and politics in Europe* (pp. 205–214). London: I.B. Tauris.

Pouteaux, J. (2011a, September 7). Demand for Nazi items 'too strong' to ignore. *Guernsey Evening Press*, p. 1.

Pouteaux, J. (2011b, September, 9). Swastika flag shop boss 'in fear' after hate calls. *Guernsey Evening Press*, p. 1.

Sanders, P. (2005). *The British Channel Islands under German Occupation 1940–1945*. Jersey: Jersey Heritage Trust and Société Jersiaise.

Schofield, J. (2002). Monuments and the memories of war: motivations for preserving military sites in England. In J. Schofield, W. G. Johnson, & C. M. Beck (Eds.), *Matériel culture: The archaeology of twentieth century conflict* (pp. 143–158). London: Routledge.

Schofield, H. (2011, September 13). Hitler's Atlantic Wall: Should France preserve it? *BBC News Magazine,* http://www.bbc.co.uk/news/world-europe-10632543.

Smart, N. (1996). The Maginot Line: an indestructible inheritance. *International Journal of Heritage Studies,* 2(4), 222–233.

Sontag, S. (2003). *Regarding the pain of others*. London: Penguin Books.

Till, K. (2005). *The New Berlin: Memory, politics, place*. Minneapolis: University of Minnesota Press.

Tunbridge, J. E., & Ashworth, G. J. (Eds.). (1996). *Dissonant Heritage: The management of the past as a resource in conflict*. Chichester: John Wiley and Sons.

Turner, B. (2010). *Outpost of Occupation: How the Channel Islands survived Nazi rule 1940–1945*. London: Aurum Press.

Uzzell, D. L. (1989). The hot interpretation of war and conflict. In D. L. Uzzell (Ed.), *Heritage interpretation volume I: The natural and built environment* (pp. 33–47). London: Belhaven Press.

Uzzell, D., Ballantyne, R. (2008). Heritage that hurts: interpretation in a postmodern world. In G. Fairclough, R. Harrison, J.H. Jameson Jnr, J. Schofield (Eds.), *The Heritage Reader* (pp. 502–513). London: Routledge.

Virilio, P. (1994). *Bunker archaeology*. New York: Princeton Architectural Press.

Vitaliev, V. (1998, December 10). Showing off the sites of shame. *The Guardian*, p. 4.

Walton, M. (1999, January 2). Keep bureaucracy away from the Occupation Society's restorations. *Jersey Evening Post*.

Wood, A., & Wood, M. (1955). *Islands in danger*. New York: MacMillan.

Chapter 4
Labour Camps: Forgotten Sites or Sites of Deliberate Amnesia?

The Legacy of the Workers of the Organisation Todt

In the summer of 2006 *I was shown round the sites of OT camps in Alderney by a local historian and was surprised to find that none of them was, at that time, recognised as a heritage site; they were either thoroughly overgrown or built upon. Nothing marked the spot. No commemorative plaques, no information boards, nothing. Three years later I drove around Jersey with two members of the Occupation generation, Bob Le Sueur and Michael Ginns, trying to identify more of these sites. Bob had helped to house escaped OT workers during the Occupation and Michael is a local historian who has written books on German fortifications and the OT. Once again, the sites where camps once stood were not marked or recognised in any way at all. There was no sign that anything worth remembering had ever been there. Although here and there small traces remained such as part of a concrete hut platform or a pair of entrance posts, these sites were very definitely not considered part of the island's heritage. Later that year, I saw exactly the same thing in Guernsey as I was shown round the sites by a local historian. In one field I was shown the utterly overgrown and ruined shell of a building from one of the camps, but such was the degree of undergrowth that, once outside the tangled roots and branches of the bushes and trees that had totally swallowed the structure, there was no sign that there was anything to be seen within.*

Why was this? In islands where anything to do with the Occupation is highly valued, why were these sites excluded? What made them different? Why had they been allowed to fade from memory and why were they not considered as 'heritage'?

Introduction

Seaton (2001: 117) writes that 'one of the sinister and poignant features of slavery is that it is a phantom industry that leaves scant traces; its capital lies in people, long since dead, not machinery'. Although writing about the transatlantic slave trade, his comments are just as appropriate to the vestiges of the practice of

G. Carr, *Legacies of Occupation*, Contributions To Global Historical Archaeology 40, DOI: 10.1007/978-3-319-03407-2_4, © Springer International Publishing Switzerland 2014

modern slave labour carried out by the Organisation Todt (OT). The remnants that remain in the Channel Islands and which have undergone the process of heritagisation amount to very little. A greater amount yet remains to be uncovered by archaeological excavation, but this has never taken place and, in most cases, is unlikely ever to, due to the presence of residential housing on top of key sites. For the small number of sites which are potentially available to be turned into heritage but which have not, whether through accident or deliberate intent, we must ask why this has not happened, and I explore this crucial question here. Such ‘potential heritage’, which I describe here as still at the status of a legacy, is in a state of pre-heritagisation[1]; it is also ‘uninherited heritage’ as Grydehøj (2010) calls it and is a resource which remains to be tapped. For reasons which I explore here, excavation of sites of slavery and forced labour in the Channel Islands is something which might trigger unease because of what might be exposed. Drawing attention to dark histories is never a comfortable thing for any community, especially as such narratives, for a long time, hovered on the edges of most accounts of occupation.

The established narrative of occupation in the Channel Islands fears accusations of collaboration above all else, and this has led to a lack of local questioning of, or research into, potentially sensitive subjects for the first 50 years after liberation. Sites of slavery thus became *lieux d’oubli* or sites of forgetting. This chapter examines the processes through which this took place, the reasons for the selective presentation, absence or marginalisation of forced and slave labour in island museums and, finally, suggests strategies for change.

Foreign voluntary, forced and slave labour was used all over German-occupied Europe, including the Channel Islands, for building projects. The most well known of these projects was the Atlantic Wall, which employed people in a variety of worker categories and through a variety of measures, often abusing their basic human rights in the process. These people worked for the OT, and this chapter explores the varying commitment to their memory in various spheres in the Channel Islands today. Although some islanders volunteered (or were forced) to work for the OT, the majority of the workforce was made up of foreign labourers who were brought to the islands.

After the war, most of the labourers who survived left the islands, although a very small number married local women and decided to stay. The people in these categories were not the Eastern European slave workers; rather, they were those who were treated better and received pay, such as the volunteer and forced labourers from the Netherlands, Belgium and Spain. It was these people who were later to petition for recognition, in the form of memorials, of their treatment at the hands of the occupiers.

The camp sites where many (although not all) OT workers lived when they were not out working on German fortifications are, for the most part, entirely

[1] Although such a term implies an eventual trajectory into the heritage state, which is not assured.

Fig. 4.1 The latrines—all that remains of Lager Ehrenbreitstein, St Helier, Jersey (© Gilly Carr)

unmarked and invisible in the landscape today. While most have been built upon, others are on empty or neglected ground. The best preserved, if one can describe them as such, are overgrown and choked by brambles and dense foliage. While the wooden barrack huts have long since been removed, reused or burnt down, the few signs of structures that still exist include concrete hut platforms, entrance posts, latrines or parts of other unidentifiable concrete structures (Fig. 4.1).

In this chapter, I will be exploring the extent to which and the way that the workers of the OT and their surviving physical legacy has been remembered or forgotten over the last 70 years in the Channel Islands. While it is impossible to talk about the memory of the OT workers and the heritage associated with them without discussing the German fortifications, memorials and Occupation museums, I touch upon these subjects lightly so as not to repeat or pre-empt discussions which are explored in more depth in other chapters. Instead, the focus here will be the OT camps, their memory, and the consideration of what kind of heritage or non-heritage they represent today. As part of this, I will explore why their memory and their legacy have been forgotten, and what features of the camps could potentially be salvaged or turned into heritage in the future.

The OT in the Channel Islands

The treatment of the Atlantic Wall and its associated memory presents something of a paradox in the Channel Islands today. On the one hand, the concrete fortifications that litter their scenic coasts and turquoise bays are perceived as historic monuments. For the last 35 years, some of what are seen as the best examples of their type have been cleaned up, restored and turned into various kinds of museum which recall the German occupation in different ways, as discussed in Chaps. 2 and 3. For all of this devotion to the memory of occupation, which for the most part involves the display of the material culture of the occupiers, there is little information about the people who actually built the structures.

The OT, named after civil engineer and chief of construction in the occupied territories, Fritz Todt, was the military engineering auxiliary of the German armed forces. The manual labourers of the OT were a workforce which reached a height of around 16,000 in May 1943 (Cruickshank 1975: 204). They comprised voluntary, conscripted and forced workers, but also slave labourers. Among these were heterogeneous groups that included Jews who had been rounded up in occupied Europe. Those sent to the Channel Islands included Poles, Czechs, Belarusians, Ukrainians, Russians, Belgians, French, North Africans, Dutch, Spanish Republicans, and also German 'criminals' and political prisoners (Cohen 2000: 122 and 130). Even local Channel Islanders attracted by the high rates of pay worked for the OT as cooks, interpreters, drivers and skilled labour (Ginns 2006: 64–67; Bunting 1995: 94–95). While various nationalities and groups of the labour force were treated better than others, and some even paid and given time off, the Russians, Ukrainians and people considered by the Nazis to be of 'Slavic origin' were categorised as *Untermenschen* or sub-human, treated appallingly and often brutally, and given very little food. The number of deaths of slave workers in the islands is disputed and will probably never be known with any accuracy, although has been discussed and estimated in a variety of sources (e.g. Bunting 1995: 293; Cruickshank 1975: 213–214; Cohen 2000: 147–152; Ginns 2006: 115–125; Knowles Smith 2007: 209–130; Pantcheff 1981: 64–749; Sanders 2005). These sources and others also record the testimony of a number of former slave workers, and the extreme suffering of these people is beyond doubt. Although a summary of this is outside the scope of this chapter, it will suffice to record that the unremitting hard labour involved in building bunkers, coupled with the starvation rations given to many workers, poor living and sanitary conditions, negligent working conditions, overseer violence and lack of medical attention directly contributed to or caused most of the deaths.

OT Heritage in the Channel Islands

In order to consider what might constitute an 'OT heritage' in the twenty-first century, it is necessary to define what I mean here by 'heritage'. In this volume, I argue that the debris or legacy of war only becomes 'heritage' when members of the population turn it into such because they value it. In other words, when people directly intervene in aspects of the past which survive into or can be recreated in the present and claim or reclaim it as part of their identity and/or collective memory (broadly defined). This is done by active processes which include excavation, restoration, curation, reuse, recall and memorialisation. According to this definition, if no such direct intervention is made, can we legitimately refer to such aspects of the past which survive into the present as 'heritage'? I suggest here that, instead, they remain at the status of a 'legacy': something that may or may not be transformed into heritage status at a later date.

In addition to the OT camps in Alderney, Jersey and Guernsey, the other aspects of the legacy of the OT workers that remained in the islands at the end of the Occupation include the bunkers that they helped to build, their material culture in the form of their tools of work and the objects which they sometimes made as gifts for islanders who gave them food or humanitarian aid. While the bunkers have been restored and turned into heritage sites from the late 1970s onwards as discussed in the previous chapter, the OT workers have been mostly disinherited from this aspect of their heritage. Some of their material culture has now been recognised as heritage and given to island museums, and it is likely that there is also a range of other small, personal items that may have been accidentally left behind or lost in the camps or other accommodation where workers lived, but archaeological excavation would be needed to retrieve these items where they still survive. To date, no such excavation has been conducted.

My definition of heritage in this volume is very specific to occupation-related data and is more widely applicable to other conflict-related or occupation-related legacies. I do not claim to provide a one-size-fits-all definition. Heritage is a concept that can be interpreted in a number of ways by different people with different aims, which has led Sørensen and Carman (2009: 3) to describe it as an 'object of study', a 'means of generating income', 'part of political action or sustainable development to engender community spirit and involvement', an 'inalienable right', a 'construct' or as 'timeless and belonging to all'; in fact, all of these could be applied to some extent to the elements of occupation-related heritage that I discuss in this volume. Insisting on clear-cut definitions of the term, argue Carman and Sørensen (2009: 12), 'risks constraining and delimiting both analytical efforts and the recognition of particular social scenarios'.

My aim in defining the kind of heritage discussed in this volume is not to constrain the kind of data or analyses that can be included—indeed, I throw the net wide in my consideration of the multiple legacies of occupation. I also include intangible heritage within my definition. Intangible heritage, as defined by UNESCO, is 'not limited to monuments and objects' but 'encompasses living expressions and the traditions that countless groups and communities worldwide have inherited from their ancestors and transmit to their descendants, in most cases orally'.[2]

For the Channel Islands, such a definition would include the oral testimony and memories of the Occupation that are inherited and passed down through the generations. We might consider the intangible heritage of OT workers to comprise their own personal stories of war: narratives of how they came to the islands; how they were treated by their overseers; their experiences of building fortifications;

[2] http://portal.unesco.org/culture/en/ev.phpURL_ID=34325&URL_DO=DO_TOPIC&URL_SECTION=201.html, Accessed 31 July 2011.

and their memories of help given by islanders. Islanders themselves could also contribute to such an oral record.

Smith and Akagawa (2009: 6) question the usefulness of drawing a distinction between tangible and intangible heritage. Instead, they argue that 'heritage only becomes "heritage" when it becomes recognisable within a particular set of social or cultural values, which are themselves "intangible"'. They argue instead that heritage should be retheorised as a cultural practice rather than just a site, place, performance or event. Although this volume carries discussions of sites as heritage, to a greater degree, it emphasises the cultural practices and processes that create heritage such as the acts of excavation, restoration, curation, reuse, recall and memorialisation that I list above.

In this volume, I argue that, by various means, heritage is claimed or reclaimed as part of identity or collective memory in the Channel Islands. The link between these three terms is now well established (e.g. Anheier and Isar 2011). While for Lowenthal (1994: 41), heritage and identity 'swim in a self-congratulatory swamp of collective memory', Isar et al. (2011: 2) are only a little more specific. For them, 'as different human groups define certain objects and practices as "heritage"; as they envision heritage to reflect some form of collective memory, either lived or imagined; and as they combine to construct composite cultural identities, the potency of the triad becomes evident'. But what happens when elements of this triad are missing? In this chapter, it will become apparent that, just as the OT labourers form little or no part of collective memory for most islanders, and just as they are not embraced as part of Channel Island identity except by a few who will be discussed later, similarly their heritage—or aspects of their legacy which have become heritage—are marginalised more than might otherwise be the case had their memory been embraced as part of collective memory.

In this chapter, I will explore the legacy—the proto-heritage—of OT camps in the Channel Islands. While the term 'proto-heritage' may imply that they will become accepted as heritage at some point in the future, I do not make any assumptions about this transition. I will examine the fate of the camp sites and how they are treated today and will question why they have been excluded from heritage status and whether this will be the final position in their post-war trajectory. Before considering the camps, I will first touch lightly on other aspects of the legacy of OT workers which have become heritage, such as the fortifications, museums, memorials and artefacts, to see whether this can shed any light on the attitudes towards camp sites. Although separating out the heritage into categories of sites in this way is helpful, it should be noted that they are overlapping as, for example, some fortifications are also museums and memorials. In order to discuss the legacy of OT workers, I have examined all memorials to this group, and exhibits presented in all Occupation museums and restored bunkers, in the Channel Islands.

Restored Fortifications

In the previous chapter, I have highlighted the marginalisation of information about the OT workers in the bunkers which have been restored by local enthusiasts. I have discussed how it is typically the case that in these structures in Guernsey and in Jersey, the presentation of the occupiers is given prime position and their narratives prioritised. Alderney's bunkers have not been restored in this way. There is one exception: the interior of what is now the 'Countryside Interpretation Centre' has been cleaned up and repainted in 2003. It remains largely unfurnished except for some lockers. It belongs to the Alderney Wildlife Trust and is used as a venue for showcasing Alderney's natural and military history. The military history showcased in the bunker, comprising only a series of laminated information posters fixed to the walls, shows the German strongholds, resistance nests, bunkers, artillery and batteries in the island. Just two paragraphs on basic information about the OT camps are given, and visitors are referred elsewhere if they want to learn more.

The priority given to the occupiers and their material culture is also the case in most occupation museums in Guernsey and Jersey (many of which are located in bunkers). There are many reasons why this should be the case, but I argue in Chap. 2 that this is due to the combined factors of the collecting choices of museum owners (something dictated by the historical context of their childhoods) and the specific nostalgic vision of the past recreated by these collectors in their museums. The OT labourers play no part in either of these as the abuse of human rights has found no place in nostalgic views of the past.

In Chap. 3, I discussed how, where they are mentioned on information boards, the OT labourers are presented through the eyes of the overseers or the occupiers. This is done through the use of staged photographs, or images of labourers at work, often with German soldiers standing around, watching, and through articles from the German-controlled newspapers which record their escape from camps and their thefts of food from farms. While undetailed maps of the islands are included in such information panels, showing the position of the camps, the workers are often presented as an anonymous and/or homogeneous male mass of alive (or dead) workers differentiated only by country. The exception to this rule of thumb is the display at Jersey War Tunnels (JWT).

JWT is a subterranean network of tunnels constructed from 1941 to 1942 by French North Africans, Spanish Republicans, political prisoners from various occupied countries and local labour. Later on, Russian and Ukrainian slave workers also carried out work on the site (Ginns 1993: 26). While this fortification was once an amateur Occupation museum, it is now a private, professional venture which highlights many of the victims of Nazism, including OT workers. The museum provides information about the many nationalities and worker types who helped to build the German fortifications, helping to dispel the myth of the 'Russian slave worker'. Four life-size, white plaster casts of typical workers from each category are displayed, complete with what is deemed to be a representative piece of material culture for each (e.g. a spade for a slave worker and an axe for a conscripted worker). However, the myth is also reinforced by the display of newspaper articles of the time about escaped Russians or Russians begging for food. Anonymous quotes from two former workers are included in the display. While not perfect, it is an improvement on other restored fortifications because it 'personifies' the worker types by making them life-size and 'up close' rather than presenting them at a physical distance. More could still be done, perhaps by modelling them on actual individuals and their experiences and putting more emphasis on human rights abuses and the corrupt recruitment practices of the OT. Elsewhere in the museum, in a new exhibition on resistance in occupied Jersey which opened in 2010, a panel on those who gave shelter to Russian slave workers is included. More of this information could profitably be included in the OT display.

Museums

As discussed in the last chapter, bunkers and fortifications which have been claimed as heritage sites include those which have been restored and those which have been turned into Occupation museums. As both of these types are controlled by members of the same group, namely the CIOS, the information that they present on the OT is similar—and similarly impersonal. My interpretations for both are thus nearly identical, but I discuss the information presented in museums in more detail here.

While the OT workers are unrepresented at the Channel Islands Military Museum in Jersey because the owner does not have any of their material culture in his collection, there are three private collector museums in Guernsey which record their presence. At the Valette Military Museum in St Peter Port (housed in a former German fuel store tunnel), the accoutrements of the OT overseer are on display, complete with swastika arm band, whip and truncheon. Other aspects of OT life are represented by a pair of blue striped pyjamas from *SS Lager* Sylt concentration camp in Alderney; a photo of half a dozen 'slave workers' at work, with a dozen German officers looking on; and a picture of an OT labourer, painted in pastels by a German soldier. At one end of the museum is an unfinished tunnel. A mannequin of a labourer at work has been placed half way down the tunnel and a spotlight shines upon him.

These aspects of the OT worker are presented with minimal labelling and no background information providing context. The labourers are anonymous; the visitors are left to make their own interpretation and infer information about them from a distance. This was the experience of many islanders during the occupation, and so we are left to learn about the workers in the same way as they did. Ill-treatment is hinted at through the display of the truncheon and whip; the familiar blue striped pyjamas of the concentration camp inmate are left to speak for themselves.

Fig. 4.2 Display relating to the OT, German Occupation Museum, Guernsey (© Gilly Carr)

The German Underground Hospital presents its information in much the same way, although this series of largely empty subterranean tunnels is vast, dark, damp, rather frightening and uncomfortable for the visitor. Only as one heads towards the exit are the now-rusty and mouldy exhibits shown. These include the work tools used by 'slave workers' and the obligatory slave worker mannequins excavating an unfinished tunnel. Again, the foreign labourers are experienced at one remove.

At Guernsey's German Occupation Museum, the visitor is brought a little closer to the workers in an extension opened in 2001. No longer entirely anonymous, those who died and were buried in Guernsey and Alderney are listed by name and nationality in an information panel. The locations of the camp sites are shown, along with the usual photos and a mannequin of a labourer at work. Continuing with the now-familiar formula, an OT overseer's uniform and instruments of punishment, such as whips, leg manacles and truncheons, are displayed in a cabinet, along with workers' shovels and spades (Fig. 4.2). Next to it is another cabinet displaying a pair of blue striped pyjamas and wooden clogs from the concentration camp in Alderney. Two original headstones from the exhumed graves of OT workers are displayed. Poignantly, and somewhat fittingly for the style of display of OT heritage in the Channel Islands, in place of the name of one of the deceased is engraved, in inaccurate German, 'unbokannter OT arbeiter' (unknown OT worker). This Occupation museum, however, breaks with the formula by providing three extra

Fig. 4.3 Display relating to the OT in Alderney Museum (© Gilly Carr)

exhibits, although none of these are in a prominent place. The first is a pen and ink sketch by the well-known Jersey artist Edmund Blampied, of an OT overseer kicking a prostrate Russian slave worker. The second is the photo and associated story of Jerseywoman Louisa Gould, who died in Ravensbrück after being caught sheltering a Russian slave worker. Both of these are framed and hung on the side of a museum case which displays striped pyjamas from Sylt. The third item is a small rubber figurine of policeman which hung over the doorway of the island's OT prison; inmates had to bow to it when passing. It is on the floor of the case which displays the overseer's uniform. While none of these exhibits tell us much about individual OT workers, they depart from the established formula by giving us an insight into their plight. We see them not just as anonymous workers at a distance but as victims who were seen, by islanders, being abused; as people with agency who could escape; and as people who suffered indignities and daily humiliations in their status as captive or imprisoned people.

The display relating to the occupation period in Alderney's small museum has recently been reworked. The emphasis is on the soldiers, but half of one glass cabinet (i.e. one information panel) deals with 'forced and volunteer labour', citing the 5,000 workers who were brought to the island and the several hundred who died of overwork, starvation and brutality. Human rights abuses are briefly listed in the 360 word panel (a figure that includes picture captions). The cruelty and working conditions are described, and the display shows images of labourers at work, the OT overseers and the concentration camp at Sylt. Artefacts include a weighted club and a whip, sandals worn by an inmate of Sylt, and an old bronze plaque commemorating the dead Russian prisoners, erected after the war and now removed from its original location (Fig. 4.3).

Clearly, there is a long-standing formula for the representation of OT labourers in the occupation museums of the Channel Islands, although this is supplemented here and there with more recent attempts to communicate their suffering to the museum visitor. In the main, despite the images of their faces in photographs, items of their clothing and their tools of work, they are a silent, collective and anonymous mass, known not in life but only in death by the names of some of them in registers or on (no longer in situ) gravestones. Their overseers are also anonymous, but we get the measure of them by their associated instruments of cruelty and oppression. Factual information is provided about the location of camps and the working hours of the workforce, but they are rarely given a voice or a personal identity. Anecdotes of cruel and barbaric treatment by overseers in the words of local eyewitnesses or fellow workers are rarely given. Similarly, accounts of islanders who helped them or who sheltered them is either absent or marginalised in the many of museums. JWT is the only exception to the formula of overseer-as-focus, OT-worker-as-anonymous-victim and islander-as-absent/passive-observer.

As argued in Chap. 2, modes of display in Occupation museums are part of a long tradition in the Channel Islands and the earliest museums are held up as an ideal to which to aspire. The original rationale for such presentations is likely to be that OT workers were only known from such observation at a distance for most islanders; there was, at that time, no other way to portray them in the early post-war years. Descriptions of witnessed acts of cruelty in private memoirs and diaries were as yet unpublished or unknown, and post-war interviews with surviving workers were still classified. Interviews with workers who settled in the islands had yet to be undertaken. Most locally well-known books which testified to the experience of workers were not published until much later (e.g. Pantcheff 1981; Steckoll 1982; Bonnard 1991). In any case, such accounts are likely to have been deemed unsuitable in family museums, especially when most people wanted to put the horrors of war behind them.

The more modern museums with displays designed by trained heritage/museum professionals are more likely to be attuned to the need for ethical presentation, which involves giving the OT workers a voice and an identity and highlighting the role of the many islanders who gave them food, clothes and shelter. The neglect until very recently of this aspect of the OT worker story is curious and can probably be explained only by the lack of knowledge of those involved. In fact, the first collection of names of families and individuals who helped workers is only now being made (Willmot 2014). Those few who were known about in the past came to public attention because they had been sent to concentration camps where they had suffered and/or died.

Memorials

Memorials to OT workers who suffered or died in the Channel Islands offer us what is probably the most useful litmus test of attitudes of islanders towards OT workers. A number of memorial plaques have been erected over the years, usually at the behest of former workers themselves. As I discuss the remains of former OT labour and prison camps below, and the extent to which their locations are remembered today, my discussion of memorials in this section excludes those

Fig. 4.4 Sculpture at JWT (© Gilly Carr)

associated directly with or next to camps, of which only one exists: that erected in 2008 at *SS Lager* Sylt in Alderney. I also approach the history and current use of the other memorials with a light touch here, preferring to save in-depth discussion until the later chapter on memorialisation of the Occupation years.

Of the seven other memorials erected to OT workers since the end of the occupation, three are associated with museums or former museums (of which, all are at bunker sites); two, with former burial places of OT workers; and two are in areas of other memorials in the capitals of Guernsey and Jersey.

Jersey is alone in the Channel Islands in having any German fortifications, and exhibitions inside these structures, dedicated to OT workers. There are two sites which fit this description, and both exhibitions and memorials were designed by heritage professionals. The bunker at La Hougue Bie in the east of the island was once the site of an Occupation museum, but it is now a memorial dedicated to forced workers transported to the Channel Islands from all over Europe. Despite the tendency elsewhere to perceive the foreign labourers in a collective shorthand as anonymous 'Russian slave workers' (see Ginns 2006: 59 and 61; Sanders 2005: 193, n6), at La Hougue Bie, the story of a few individual men is told in their own words, giving a face to the thousands who worked in the islands. Jerseywoman Louisa Gould is also included in the exhibition. A memorial sculpture of a slave worker emerging from the ground was also commissioned to mark the 2001 renovation of the site.

To mark the bicentenary of the abolition of slavery in 2007, a new sculpture was commissioned at JWT (Fig. 4.4). The chosen design took its inspiration from the metal 'prop dog', an invaluable tool used by the OT workers to bind wooden beams together as temporary roof supports when excavating into the granite to make tunnels. The sculpture is titled 'Silence', a reference to the description of the slave workers' midday break in Auschwitz by Primo Levi (Levi 1987: 77).

The third memorial at a museum is in the German Underground Hospital in Guernsey. This was erected just inside the exit of the tunnels at some time in the 1950s and is dedicated to 'the slave workers who died in Guernsey for Hitler's OT'. As can be seen, this older memorial follows the more traditional notion of the anonymous 'slave worker'.

Of those memorials at former cemeteries of OT workers, it should be remembered that the bodies of all workers were removed by the German War Graves Commission (*Volksbund Deutsche Kriegsgräberfürsorge*) in 1961, and taken, along with the bodies of most German military personnel buried in the islands, to the German military cemetery of Mont-de-Huisnes in Normandy. It is ironic that, even in death, the OT workers were still under the control of the Germans.

Memorials which today display plaques representing various nationalities were erected at, or overlooking, OT burial sites at Longis Common in Alderney and at Westmount in St Helier. The circumstance of their initial erection, their subsequent biographies and the details of how they are used today are provided later in this volume. It will suffice here to note that the first memorial stone at Alderney's memorial was erected in memory of French workers in 1951 by local government. In 1966, a government member, Herbert Hammond, erected a small walled memorial garden structure at his own expense, complete with a bench, a flagpole, many flowering plants, the cremated ashes of his own family and an associated large plaque recording them. Over the years, additional plaques have been added to Polish, Jewish, Soviet and Spanish workers, and the memorial is now called the Hammond Memorial.

Jersey's memorial on the site of the former burial place of OT workers (the Strangers Cemetery at Westmount) was initiated by the crew of a passing Soviet timber ship in 1960, who collected money for a plaque. They were taken to the spot by Norman Le Brocq from the Jersey Communist Party. In 1971, former Spanish Republican forced workers still living in Jersey, along with members of the Jersey Communist Party, worked together to get a suitable permanent memorial erected in the cemetery. The two groups had known each other since the Occupation, when members of the Communist Party had given aid to OT workers. Over the years, additional plaques have been attached to the memorial site, so that French, Spanish Republican, Polish, Jewish, Belgian, French North African and Byelorussian workers are now remembered alongside those from Russia.

Quotes from former OT workers are also included in an 'Occupation pavement' in the Charing Cross area of St Helier. This piece of street art was erected in 2005 to mark the sixtieth anniversary of liberation and includes quotes from a number of members of the Occupation generation inscribed into the pavement. Each of the quotes is moving and gives an insight into the experiences and suffering of the OT workers.

In 1999 in Guernsey, a memorial was erected to 'foreign civilians who lost their lives while working as forced labour under the German occupying forces'. The original granite plaque had the merit of listing the names of all those who had

Table 4.1 Dates of erection of memorials to OT workers

Name of site	Date of erection of plaque
German Underground Hospital, Guernsey	1960s
Foreign Labourers Memorial, St Peter Port, Guernsey	1999 (2001)
Forced Worker Memorial, La Hougue Bie, Jersey	2001
Jersey War Tunnels Slavery Memorial	2007
Westmount Slave Worker Memorial, St Helier, Jersey	1960 (1971)
'Occupation Pavement', St Helier, Jersey	2005
Hammond Memorial, Alderney	1951 (1966)
Children's Peace Garden, Alderney	2010
Alderney Museum	Unknown

died in the island, but quickly became controversial when it was pointed out that the names of some of the dead OT overseers had inadvertently been included (a fact that was disputed at the time). A second simpler plaque went up in 2001, but this once again reduced OT workers to an anonymous mass. Although it was originally erected after petitioning by a former forced worker who stayed in the island, it is not visited on Liberation Day or Holocaust Memorial Day, although a wreath is laid on Armistice Day by the CIOS and the Bailiff. Due to its location (in a recess in the harbour wall and at a distance from the Liberation Monument which forms the main point of focus for this part of the town), it is neglected or ignored at all other times of the year. Thus, the wreaths of Armistice Day give the impression of being a tokenistic 'discharge of obligation', classifying this particular memorial as the kind of 'wreath drop zone' discussed by Geyer (1997: 37).

In Alderney, there are two further memorial plaques which refer to OT camps. The first is a brass plaque recently attached to the wall of Alderney Museum, showing the site of the camps. It records that the thousands of workers transported to the island were from many countries and 'were treated with great cruelty and brutality'. The second, a ceramic plaque, was made by children in 2010 and is placed in a peace garden. The plaque shows the location of the camps on a map of Alderney and depicts a broken chain stretching across the island. The caption, split above and below the map, reads 'Face the future. Never forget the past' and is flanked by a sea of ceramic faces made by the children.

The children have painted and carved words on other ceramic plaques elsewhere in the garden (e.g. 'Alderney is small, but not too small to forget, by Rachel, aged 11'), making it clear that the more disturbing history of the island is being taught at school. The next generation, here at least, is being encouraged to be active in their commitment to remembering.

As Table 4.1 shows, the date of erection of memorials to OT workers broadly clusters in two decades: the 1960s and the last 10 years. The more recent memorials have been attempts (mostly by heritage professionals) to rectify either a long silence or the perception of OT workers as an anonymous mass. They have also occurred at a time that Geyer (1997: 6) refers to as the 'return of memory' which he sees as an 'unmistakable sign of the mortality of the surviving witnesses to mass murder and annihilation'. Memorials have been erected in an attempt to preserve memory in order to counteract the anxiety that when these witnesses die, the memory itself will also pass on.

With regards to the *first* initiation of the older memorials, a cynic might attribute them to the effect of tourism (Guernsey), political manoeuvring and family memory (Alderney) and, in the case of the plaque at the slave worker memorial in St Helier, outsiders (i.e. the visiting Russians who first left a memorial plaque at this site). However, memorials do not tell the whole story and do not represent the full and only expression of remembrance. With regards to the Strangers' Cemetery in St Helier, the States of Jersey erected a large Russian Orthodox cross on the site after the war, and this was still there when the Russians visited the island in 1960. It should also be noted that members of the Spanish Republican community and the Jersey Communist Party used to make an annual pilgrimage to the German Underground Hospital (today, JWT) in St Lawrence, built by forced and slave labour, to pay their respects to deceased workers.[3] So even when a memorial is apparently 'missing', this does not always indicate a lack of respect for the memory of the deceased group. Today, the Hammond memorial in Alderney and the Westmount memorial in St Helier play an important and popular role in annual ceremonies and are well respected.

The erection of the initial stone in 1951 at what was later to become the Hammond Memorial and the plaque at the German Underground Hospital in Guernsey in the early 1960s both signal the readiness of local communities (or sections of them) to come to terms with the darker aspects of occupation for the first time. It is interesting to note that these first memorials were not inclusive of all OT worker categories or nationalities, but remembered just one sub-section of the workforce: the slave workers (Guernsey), the Russians (Jersey) and the French (Alderney). This is likely to be because less information was available then and so the memorial played upon popular perceptions.

It is pertinent here to reflect upon the latest memorial (or rather, information plaque erected in memory) to forced and slave workers erected in the Channel Islands. Unlike the others of recent years, this was not erected by heritage professionals, but rather by the Channel Islands Occupation Society at the behest of local government as a condition of granting permission for the excavation of the bunker. This plaque is not in a prominent position; rather, it is attached to a wall at bottom of the original stairwell which leads down to a newly excavated underground bunker.

All previous information panels in or outside bunkers at Noirmont Point are either silent on the subject of the OT labourers, or else marginalise them or depict them through a German lens, so it might have been anticipated that the new panel would be more outspoken in its condemnation of the OT, its recruitment practices, its corruption or the way it treated its workforce. While the panel was titled 'In memory to all those forced and slave labourers who died constructing the Atlantic

[3] Email from Gary Font, 15 August 2012.

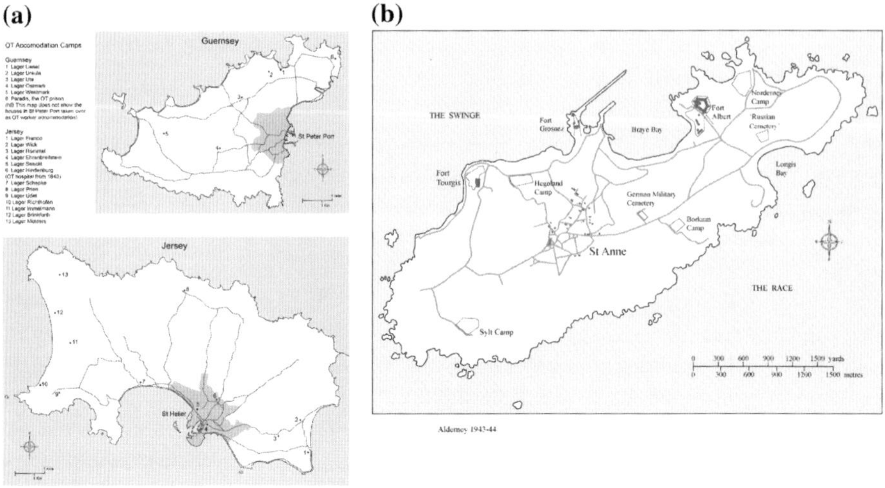

Fig. 4.5 **a**, **b** Maps of OT camps in Guernsey, Jersey and Alderney (© and courtesy Ian Taylor)

Wall fortifications in the Channel Islands', the text was matter of fact, objective and detached in style, provoking little emotional response—a clear example of what Uzzell (1989) calls 'cold interpretation'.

OT Camp Sites

The final aspect of OT heritage, and the most neglected, is the sites of the work camps where once foreign workers were accommodated (Fig. 4.5). These camps comprised mostly barrack-style wooden huts but occasionally also reused existing buildings. Those in the latter category included sites such as *Paradis*, the OT prison set up in the barn of a farmhouse in the north of Guernsey in the Vale parish and *Lager* Hindenburg, the OT hospital which took over the Jersey College for Girls in St Helier. Generally speaking, the labour camps were set up close to the fortifications on which members of the OT worked. Table 4.2 below shows the current uses of these camp sites today. It is likely that other temporary and unnamed work camps once existed which are not listed here.

As in some other formerly occupied countries, such as France and Norway, there is now little public awareness or knowledge about the inhabitants or the locations of the camps (Roberts 2010; Jasinski and Stenvik 2010: 206). The information we have today comes mostly from diaries or from eyewitness accounts, and this latter resource is fast becoming scarce. In the Channel Islands, as in Norway, the first post-occupation generation did their best to remove traces of the camps from their land (Jasinski and Stenvik 2010), and this has contributed to the lack of visibility in the landscape of these structures today. In Jersey, for example, Ginns has described

Table 4.2 Current uses of OT camp sites in the Channel Islands

Name of camp	Category of worker/site	Location	Current use of site
Lager Franco	Forced labourers	Jersey	Housing estate
Lager Wick	Forced labourers	Jersey	Nature reserve
Lager Hindenburg	OT hospital	Jersey	Girls' college (abandoned)
Lager Ehrenbreitstein	Political prisoners and forced labourers	Jersey	Electricity sub-station
Lager Seeckt	Forced labourers	Jersey	Luxury apartments
Lager Schepke	Forced and slave labourers	Jersey	Jersey steel company
Lager Udet	Forced and slave labourers	Jersey	Housing
Lager Richthofen	Forced labourers	Jersey	Hotel
Lager Immelmann	Slave labourers	Jersey	Agriculture
Lager Brinkforth	Forced and slave labourers	Jersey	Unused land
Lager Mölders	Forced and slave labourers	Jersey	Housing estate
Lager Prien	Forced, then slave labourers	Jersey	Hotel
Lager Rommel	Slave labourers	Jersey	Housing estate
Lager Hühnlein	HQ of NSKK (worked for OT)	Jersey	Private land
Lager Westmark	Forced labourers	Guernsey	Housing estate
Lager Ostmark	?	Guernsey	Housing estate
Lager Ursula	Forced and slave labourers	Guernsey	Housing estate
Lager Liesel	?	Guernsey	Housing estate
Lager Ute	Forced labourers	Guernsey	Playing fields
Lager Helgoland	Forced labourers/Soviet camp	Alderney	Bungalows
Lager Norderney	SS camp?/Jewish camp and resistance workers	Alderney	Camping grounds
Lager Borkum	Specialist workers	Alderney	Road to rubbish dump
Lager Sylt	SS concentration camp	Alderney	Empty/overgrown land
Citadella	POW or temporary camp	Alderney	Lumber yard

Sources Ginns 2006 and personal communication; Sanders 2005: 194
NB list incomplete

how, after it was abandoned, *Lager* Wick was dismantled for firewood in the winter of 1944; the barracks of *Lager* Udet were taken apart by the Germans and reused to camouflage tank pens; and every piece of concrete foundation and hoggin track that had been laid at *Lager* Immelmann was 'literally grubbed up by hand' by those who rented the land after the war (2006: 76–80).

Out of all camps listed above, and as noted earlier, only one, *SS Lager* Sylt, has received any kind of memorial plaque. This was erected in 2008 by a former inmate of the camp and not at the request of islanders or the States of Alderney (Fig. 4.6). Although the entrance pillars of the camp, like those of *Lager* Borkum in Alderney and *Lager* Wick in Jersey, still stand, they are the only parts of the camp still easily recognisable today. Although some concrete bases of the hut platforms at Sylt and Borkum are still discernable, these are thoroughly overgrown. Vegetation has been an active agent in promoting the forgetting of these sites, and no one has deemed it prudent or desirable to check their growth.

Fig. 4.6 Entrance posts of Lager Sylt in Alderney (© Gilly Carr)

While this studied neglect is painfully obvious at the site of the only concentration camp on British soil (Sylt), it is even more actively encouraged at *Lager* Wick in Jersey, which is now a nature reserve on Crown land, to which access is forbidden.

I noted above that many of the camp sites in the Channel Islands were dug up, burned or otherwise destroyed during and after the occupation. Local people also took away and reused some of the barrack huts as workshops or sheds. The fact that almost every site has been built upon or otherwise reused signals that, far from being *lieux de memoire*, they have now become *lieux d'oubli*. Like the Norwegian camps, the memory of them is painful and unwanted and so has become 'neglected or wiped out from the collective memory both by society and the heritage management systems' (Jasinski and Stenvik 2010: 207–208). The almost total reuse or abandonment of these sites indicates that the commitment to remembering OT workers, extended to memorials, some museum displays and fewer restored bunkers, only stretches so far.

Such treatment and active or passive forgetting of this painful legacy of conflict is neither unique to British sites of slavery (e.g. Seaton 2001), nor to formerly occupied countries, nor to camps used by the OT. Such a phenomenon has been recognised at twentieth century POW camps (e.g. Thomas 2011; Seitsonen and Herva 2011); internment camps in Francoist Spain (González-Ruibal 2011); so-called 'wild' concentration camps and *Folterkeller* or torture chambers in Berlin (Jordan 2006: 153); camps of exile on Greek islands (Pantzou 2011); Swedish military labour-company camps (Landzelius 2003); and detention and torture camps in Argentina (Zarankin and Salerno 2011). All such sites are witness to a less than glorious part of recent history in these countries. and there has been little desire by governments to memorialise or remember the victims or their experiences, or the role of those same governments either as bystanders or as active persecutors or agents of internment. The sites are not sources of national pride, even when those interned have had the status of national enemies in war time.

Because all such sites are bearers of traumatic memories, they constitute examples of what Meskell (2002: 558) has termed 'negative heritage', a concept which includes sites such as Auschwitz, Hiroshima and the site of the World Trade Centre in New York. Such a site 'becomes the repository of negative memory in the collective imaginary' and occupies a dual role, where it can be 'mobilised for positive didactic purposes' or 'erased if such places cannot be culturally rehabilitated and thus resist incorporation into the national imaginary'. While there is great potential for all such internment camp types listed above to play a positive, didactic 'never again' role, it seems apparent that most countries have found it easier for such sites to be forgotten and erased. Because most camp sites (and certainly those associated with the OT discussed here) rarely currently play a positive role, the dual role or ambiguity of this kind of negative heritage has been redesignated by Pantzou (2011: 192) as 'traumatic heritage'. This more inclusive term carries implications of the potential gradual healing of social or political traumas. Thus, the position of OT camp sites as neglected legacies need not represent their final status or position in national memory; archaeologists have been active in the rediscovery and rehabilitation of traumatic sites, turning them into positive heritage (e.g. Farrell and Burton 2011). The passage of time is necessary and, indeed, crucial for communities to be able to accept such transformations in their landscape and of their legacies of war. The pain of occupation lessens with time, and although memories are passed down through the generations, the children or grandchildren of those affected are less often held back by their inherited memories; this is why it is often they who are active in turning their history into heritage.

It is not a quick procedure to transform a long-neglected site and its associated hidden histories into a heritage or tourist site. It is important to first record oral testimony, material culture and all physical remains of the camps in question. By securing this information and by working, where possible, with those who have taken it upon themselves to be the guardians of memory of the experiences of OT workers, a solid foundation can be built to raise awareness and to emphasise the potential of such sites for education. But none of this can take place until a community is ready to accept it. People will be unwilling to speak and unwilling to help; permission will not be granted for surveying or excavation on private or public land; and local museums may not wish to grant space or time for exhibitions which are likely to be deeply locally controversial or offensive.

Why are OT Camps *Still* Neglected?

Given that heritage can be 'what contemporary society chooses to inherit and to pass on' (Tunbridge and Ashworth 1996: 6), why have the ordinary people of the Channel Islands chosen not to inherit this particular legacy of the OT workers? While they have chosen to represent workers in museums in a certain way and to memorialise them in a selective form for many years now, why are camps uniquely and almost completely disregarded? Given the absence of former OT workers in the islands today to tell their story at a time when people might be more ready to hear them, the sites of the camps themselves have the capability to testify to the realities of internment, to the living conditions in which workers were kept and to some of the human rights abuses to which many workers were subjected. While the truth of oral testimony may be questioned, physical remains provide their own 'truth' and their own evidence. Yet why has it been convenient or useful for the camp sites to remain overgrown and for them not to have been uncovered or lauded in earlier generations? Or is this simply 'the way that things turned out', and that no thought has been given to the matter, especially in recent years? There are many factors which can shed light on this state of affairs. While it would be highly instructive to approach this subject from a biographical perspective and to untangle what actions of destruction or construction were undertaken at each site and in each island over the last 70 years, such information is no longer readily available and only fragments of information remain. This means that we are reduced to putting forward a number of hypotheses for discussion about what might have happened, when and why, comparing these hypotheses and analyses with the situation in other countries which were forced to play host to the Atlantic Wall. Although not ideal, this is now the only avenue left open.

A fruitful clue to the long neglect of OT camp sites comes from the immediate post-war treatment of these places. As the vast majority were dismantled or destroyed and the structures removed or burnt down very soon after the end of the war, long before any such thoughts of turning the debris of occupation into heritage, there *was* very little in the way of physical structures that could be resurrected for heritage purposes, especially by the time that post-war generations came of age and developed an interest in their past. Besides, what and who, precisely, was supposed to be remembered by the preservation of the camps?

A good illustration of what I mean is provided in the description of camp and worker types by Jerseyman Bob Le Sueur who, during the Occupation, was friendly with Spanish Republicans in the island and helped escaped Russians to move between safe houses. He described the Spanish camps to me as follows:

> Army-type wooden huts, heated by wood stoves in the winter, bunk beds, lockers for personal belongings. Anyone could walk into these camps and I did frequently to see people I knew … These chaps were paid, and much more than the German-controlled maximum wage for Jersey residents on non-German work. This spending power made the forced foreign workers, most of whom were Spaniards, privileged buyers on the local black market and in the second-hand shops. One Spaniard whom I got to know particularly well … was housed with three others in a pleasantly furnished detached house whose owners had left in 1940 … In St Peter Port, I saw many Spaniards walking about and was told that most were in houses that had been abandoned in 1940.[4]
>
> … Their barracks were not guarded by soldiers, nor were the other non-Slav people like the French, Belgians and Dutch. And, yes, these latter were paid. They all did whatever labouring was required. They earned more than local people not working from the Germans and therefore had first pickings on black market food, could out-price locals on

[4] Letter from Bob Le Sueur to author, 25 May 2010.

> second-hand clothes [and] footwear … There was no comparison between the working conditions of the 'forced workers' who were non-Slav and those of the slaves.[5]

If Le Sueur's perceptions of OT workers are typical of others of his generation, then OT camps of forced workers were not perceived in a negative way at all; this was not a potential 'victim heritage' where islanders and tourists could gather to remember the 'poor' forced workers who were paid a superior wage, lived in relative comfort (if lacking in privacy) and who had access to more food than islanders. Why commemorate these people and their camps if this is how they were perceived? The Russian camps, on the other hand, were a different matter. Le Sueur described these in the following way:

> The Russians were in various camps, mostly in the south-west and west of the island in reasonably close walking distances from the work sites. The huts were similar to those put up for the Spaniards and other 'forced' but paid workers, but the camps surrounded by barbed wire fencing which was increased to minimise escapes. There were also armed OT guards. They really were prisoners in a way in which most other groups were not. They were not paid … Those who did escape usually did so either from columns on their way to or from the work sites or else at the place of work itself. Conditions in these camps varied, often because of the personalities of those in charge of them … All they received in their bowls was watery vegetable soup and, in many cases, one slice of rye bread a day.[6]

Given that Le Sueur was probably fairly unusual in entering forced worker camps and islanders were not allowed to approach or enter slave worker camps, it is likely that both types soon became associated in the minds of islanders after the Occupation, especially as most OT workers were perceived as 'Russians', regardless of their real status, and especially as thousands of islanders either spent the war years as evacuees in the UK or were deported to Germany soon after the arrival of the OT. Rumour and a lack of real knowledge have often proved fertile breeding grounds for occupation myths.

There are other reasons why camp sites may have been overlooked as heritage. First of all, we have already noted that very few former workers remained behind in the islands after the war to campaign for any recognition. Whatever their experiences and for a number of obvious reasons, the population of the Channel Islands simply wanted to put the war years behind them. It was important for all Europeans to build a heroic memory of occupation that was fundamental to national recovery and to create and sustain national identity at this time and to avoid any moral responsibility for their roles as Holocaust perpetrators, bystanders and collaborators (Confino 2005).

It was also important for islanders not to dwell on a traumatic past but, rather, to rebuild their lives and islands instead. This sentiment was echoed by all those interviewed over six years of fieldwork. Because of the lack or very small number of former foreign workers remaining in the Channel Islands after the Occupation, the OT camp sites (and, indeed, the German fortifications) in the Channel Islands

---

[5] Letter from Bob Le Sueur to author, 8 June 2010.

[6] Letter from Bob Le Sueur to author, 25 May 2010.

became 'orphan heritage' (Price 2005), a heritage with no clear successor or community who wanted to argue for its significance. While, after 30 years, fortifications were claimed by local people, the sites of the camps were not, most probably because there was little left to see by this date.[7]

I have also noted that the foreign workers were just that—foreign—and thus 'not us'. The OT workers have been 'othered' and contrasted with the Channel Islander 'self'. They were marginalised in national war memory and commemoration, although lurked shadow-like in the background of memoirs, diaries and locally published popular accounts of the Occupation. I note elsewhere in this volume how war memory in the Channel Islands has been intrinsically linked with that of the UK and is one in which Britons are perceived as victors ('self') and not victims ('other'). Thus, while other occupied countries built their war myths on narratives of victimhood, martyrdom or resistance, the islanders celebrated stoic endurance until liberation and eventual victory over the Germans. Victims of Nazism, whether Jews, OT workers, political prisoners or deportees, were marginalised or absented from this version of events for the first 50 years after liberation. This 'othering' of their narratives has also led to an 'othering' of their legacy and, thus, potential heritage. While islanders have been active in turning what they perceive to be their own legacies into heritage, there has been less political or public support or interest for the legacies of these multiple 'others'; in fact, such legacies have sometimes been actively rejected as they are felt not to represent the Channel Islander experience. There has also been an associated lack of interest in exploring whether the boundaries of the Channel Islander 'self' and victim 'other' might actually have been blurred during the Occupation, especially with regards to the OT worker.

Light (2007) has observed that, as part of the cultural politics of tourism development, tourism may be exploited to affirm, emphasise or enhance cultural identity and values. By the same token, tourism at certain sites may remain unexploited in order to deny, marginalise or prevent certain voices from being embraced as an equal part of identity. Similarly, certain parts of the heritage of a group might be portrayed in a certain way in order to put a certain acceptable gloss on those involved.

The experiences of OT workers, especially slave workers, were rarely shared by Channel Islanders. Those who voluntarily worked for the OT for extra pay kept quiet about it because of the ambiguities of whether this constituted collaboration. Thus, islanders did not identify with the foreign workers. While many may have pitied them or given them food, clothing or shelter (see Wood and Wood 1955: 126; Sanders 2005: 105–109; Willmot 2000: 73–74; Willmot 2014), it was very rare that Channel Islanders were subject to human rights abuses at the hands of the OT overseers.[8]

---

[7] Michael Ginns personal communication, 11 September 2011.

[8] Gordon Pringent and Walter Gallichan are perhaps the best-known Jerseymen who found themselves in the same plight as other foreign labourers. Pringent's testimony can be found at http://www.jerseyheritage.org/media/PDFs/prigent.pdf. See also Sanders (2005, 201–204).

The difficulty of some islanders in identifying with foreign workers is perhaps expressed most clearly by Wyatt (1945 [1985]: 41), who wrote that 'we ought, perhaps, to have been more deeply moved than we were by the horrible plights of the Russian prisoners—some fifteen hundred men, women and children—who were dumped far from home on Jersey and, half-clothed and less than half-fed, set to forced labour, or—to be candid—slavery. But this did not affect most of us *personally*. In fact, we have heard or seen little of the Russians except occasionally when, desperate with starvation, a few have escaped from their 'pen' and subsisted by petty thefts from fields, larders and chicken runs. It needed a glimpse of the possibility of finding *ourselves* in somewhat similar case, to make us realise what that would mean', which he wrote with reference to the deportations of much of the English-born sector of the population in September 1942. Wyatt's views may not have been typical as we know that some islanders stood up for OT workers or interposed themselves between the workers and overseers (Sanders 2005: 228–229).

This confirms the earlier observation that most workers were seen at a distance and not often encountered by islanders, a view endorsed by the Woods (1955: 124), although this would very much have depended on which part of the island one lived; for some, they were a common sight (Willmot 2000: 74; Sanders 2005: 226). Wyatt also raises the issue of the escapes and the 'petty thefts', and this also acted to further distance foreign workers from their would-be helpers. Mollet, secretary to the Bailiff of Jersey during the Occupation, wrote about these thefts too, referring to them as a 'Reign of Terror' (1945: 64–65). 'From the day of their arrival they were constantly escaping from their camps in the country parishes', he wrote. 'During the daytime they begged and robbed, and at night they attacked the houses in order to steal food and clothing. The local police were powerless ... On one occasion a Jersey farmer was killed by a Russian'. Mollet also refers to islanders who were prosecuted for aiding workers: 'When these workers were taken back to the Continent to work, it was found that a considerable number were still at large on the island, many being sheltered and fed by farmers. This led to prosecutions by the German Field Court, and the local inhabitants concerned were fined and some sentenced to imprisonment and transported to the Continent for sheltering them' (ibid.: 65).

We cannot know whether Mollet's detached and matter-of-fact attitude towards both the plight of the workers, and those who were imprisoned for sheltering them was shared by those in positions of authority in the islands' government, or whether it was just a personal reaction. Not everyone kept diaries that allow us such insights. Sympathetic comments about OT workers are present, however, in the memoirs of some, such as Senator Edward Le Quesne in Jersey, who witnessed an atrocity committed against a Russian (Le Quesne 1999: 182). Le Quesne was not alone. In his memoirs, compiled by H.R.S. Pocock 30 years after the Occupation, Bailiff Coutanche of Jersey relates how he had witnessed 'some horrible incidents' regarding 'Russian prisoners of war' and went to see von Schmettow, Commander-in-Chief of the Channel Islands. 'He appeared to be as shocked as I was when I told him how I had seen these wretched prisoners being driven to work by their guards when their feet were so sore that they were wrapped up in sacks' (Pocock 1975: 34). As Sanders (2005: 228) notes, we cannot rule out whether Coutanche's intervention on the shift in German attitude and treatment in 1943, when conditions improved for workers.

Later on, after the war, at a period when more sympathy could have been retrospectively given, the growing Cold War acted to distance islanders from the 'Russian slave workers'. It was hardly fashionable or politically desirable or correct to have any sympathy for Communists or Russians in this period. Clearly, such sentiments were not shared by those who once sheltered escaped workers, or who were related to forced labourers who stayed behind in the islands; such people regularly attended annual ceremonies of remembrance at memorials.

In their discussion of dissonant heritage, Tunbridge and Ashworth cite the case study of the Channel Islands, where (as they put it) 'foreign conscript labour was employed with the knowledge and connivance of the local authorities and population' and where 'collaborating officials' were 'not blamed for conniving at atrocity' after the war (1996: 109). This black-and-white assessment rather oversimplifies the situation, overlooks attempts by island officials such as Coutanche to complain to the occupiers about the way that workers were treated and entirely ignores those who helped the workers. The use of the emotive and polarised term 'collaboration' is also problematic in this context. In his assessment of the Occupation, Sanders (2005: 97–98) considered that the Channel Islands were a 'haven of sanity' compared to the 'delirious heights' to which collaboration rose in other parts of Europe; in his judgement, 'comparison fades when we look at the enormity of European collaboration'. For him, the dominating influence in the islands was 'submission on the grounds of superior force'. While such an assessment does not fully excuse island leaders from not doing more, it does highlight the need for an in-depth understanding of the particular circumstances of the Occupation in the Channel Islands, where the ratio of soldiers to islanders was suffocatingly high and where increasingly severe penalties (imprisonment with hard labour, fines and deportation) were variously in force for giving aid to OT workers. Without a discussion of these factors, any assessment of a 'conniving' and 'collaborating' population or authorities lacks balance and context.

This assessment does not brush away all accusations of collaboration (in whatever form) or feelings that, although the authorities of the Channel Islands did what they could, they could still have done even more to defy the occupiers. In terms of what might be called 'collaboration', let us briefly detail the two other acts relevant to the case of the OT workers that might be classed in this way. The Woods note that the Guernsey police cooperated with the Germans in catching escaped foreign workers, but only on the grounds that the workers could only live by stealing from local people (Wood and Wood 1955: 126). This must have proved a dilemma for the local police force; as islanders, Germans and OT workers were all starving or at least facing great problems in procuring food, their loyalty must have been primarily to the local population. We have no record of policemen turning a blind eye to escaped foreign workers, but this is not confirmation that it did not take place.

We also know that some Channel Islanders voluntarily worked for the OT because of the high wages that were on offer (Ginns 2006: 64–68), although research related to this group has not yet been fully conducted. Ginns suggests that other categories of local men who worked for the OT were either Irish (i.e. not local at all), conscientious objectors who had come to Jersey to help with the potato harvest (not local either), or forced to work after offending the German authorities in some way, but who then took the opportunity to carry out acts of sabotage or resistance. It will not escape the notice of the reader that all of these (quite legitimate) explanations exonerate Channel Islanders from any wrongdoing by working for the OT. Occupation veteran Bob Le Sueur also has something to say about local men who worked for the OT:

> Yes, some workers chose to work for the OT, in some cases bare-facedly because of the money, in some cases, particularly married men with children, shame-facedly but in order to be able to compete on the black market for extra food, children's clothes. I personally sympathised with these men, despised single men—that was probably general. That kind of 'collaboration' was pretty common and what was surprising, perhaps, was the very large number of married working men who did not submit to the temptation and which must have been with them all the time. If it was a conflict between the very real needs of your children, not just desires but needs, or your national honour I think I might well have seen the former as a priority. I was able to smugly retain my honour because I had no dependents. It is so easy to sit on the moral high ground when you can economically afford to do so. When married men succumbed to the temptation I should say that most people deplored the virtual necessity which had driven them to it rather than deplore the act in itself or those perpetuating it.[9] [Original emphases preserved]

Despite Le Sueur's balanced view of the situation, there is still, perhaps, a feeling of unease that working for the OT voluntarily was not something to be admitted publically. Indeed, any description of local employment by the OT is missing from official histories (e.g. Cruickshank 2004: 210–215). Using the case study of what Tunbridge and Ashworth saw as Channel Islander collaboration, they argue that an obvious and defensive group strategy for such 'perpetrator heritage' is deliberate collective amnesia. Under such an attack of amnesia, the 'events are ignored in official taught histories and public commemoration and a popular consensus is encouraged that regards the events as too distant and too irrelevant to more pressing concerns to be worth further consideration' (1996: 108).

OT camps can be seen as either a victim or a perpetrator legacy and, perhaps, are both simultaneously. However, they are also an orphan legacy, meaning that they do not *belong* to islanders—or at least, islanders have not yet laid claim to them in the way that they have with German bunkers. Their *continued* lack of ownership or involvement in this legacy of occupation is likely to be at the heart of what has led to its continued neglect, and the more time that passes, the less will remain to be one day claimed.

Tunbridge and Ashworth suggest that the success of policies of deliberate amnesia 'become less likely in second and subsequent generations who have less

[9] Letter from Bob Le Sueur to author, 18 June 2010.

personal reasons for concealment and more potential curiosity about gaps in the historical record' (1996: 109). It seems apparent that the *continued* lack of curiosity among subsequent generations and the continuation of deliberate or accidental amnesia in the islands today suggest that Tunbridge and Ashworth's assessment needs refinement. One wonders what the situation would be today if the camps had been built of concrete and survived in the same condition as the fortifications.

OT camps today are simply non-heritage in Jersey and Guernsey. They appear not to prick anybody's conscience in the way that is more subtly apparent in Alderney. They seem not to be worth preserving, not worth commemorating and nothing to do with the Channel Islanders' experience of occupation. Such similar disownership of a legacy of war that was not their experience is very apparent elsewhere in Alderney today, where the Occupation and most of its associated debris are rejected, save for a few items put on display in the small island museum. If a time comes when collective amnesia fails and any degree of complicity in atrocity must be confronted, Tunbridge and Ashworth (ibid.: 109–110) have identified two management strategies that can emerge. The first seeks to mitigate blame by extending it as widely as possible: if everyone is guilty (in this instance, for not doing more to help the foreign labourers), then no one can really be blamed. Alternatively, if blame is limited to certain specific groups (e.g. the OT overseers or the authorities), then everyone else is exonerated. Unfortunately, the well-documented lack of post-war trials and purges in the Channel Islands after the Occupation (e.g. Sanders 2005, Chap. 7; Turner 2010: 261–266) meant that nobody would ever be convicted of any wrongdoing, and precisely, what constituted 'wrongdoing' would never be established in a court of law. This has led to a semi-official position of 'letting sleeping dogs lie' among many in the islands today; research projects on any potentially revealing topics are heavily criticised in articles and letters to the editor of the local press.

If deliberate and sustained collective amnesia is, to any degree, responsible for the neglect of OT camp sites, and I suggest that this was probably the case for a period after the Occupation when the remains of the camps were apparent to all, then we can understand such amnesia or disinheritance on the grounds of this being an unwanted memory, perhaps something that pricked consciences as an event that islanders and officials were relatively powerless to confront or prevent. It was a dark aspect of the past that was better eradicated. I want to explore further this notion of 'darkness', as it is likely that this played a part in absenting OT camps in local collective memory.

OT Camps as a Dark Legacy

OT camp sites are potential sites of dark memory and dark heritage, and I would suggest that this may have led to them being tabooed places to be removed or covered up and, later, simply forgotten. I use the term 'dark heritage' as an

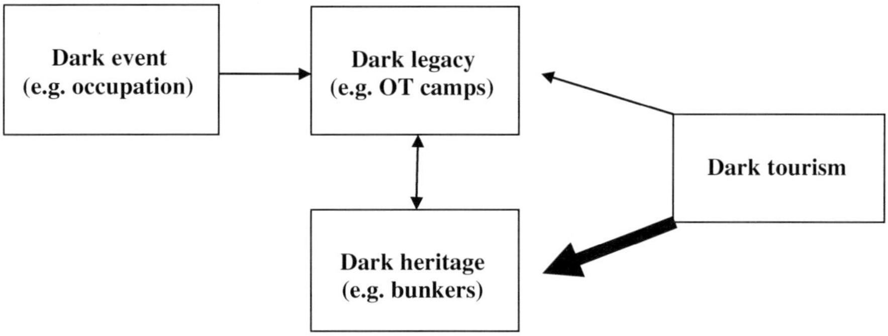

Fig. 4.7 The relationship between event, legacy, heritage and tourism

extension (or rather, contraction) of the concept of dark tourism, defined by Sharpley (2009a: 9) as 'travel to places associated with death, disaster and destruction' and by Stone (2006: 146) as 'the act of travel to sites associated with death, suffering and the seemingly macabre'. It should however be noted that dark tourists do not always visit such sites because of a fascination with death or suffering (Biran et al. 2011); other reasons for visits to such sites include a desire for an educational or an emotional heritage experience. While these sites are arguably dark, we cannot refer to them as sites of dark tourism when they are not presented as tourist destinations or commoditised in any way; nonetheless, the theoretical literature in this field is pertinent to this case study. It is perhaps equally inappropriate to refer to OT camps as dark heritage when, as I have already established, they have not been turned into heritage sites either. They are thus better described as a dark legacy, in a similar category of darkness to other kinds of camps such as concentration camps, but different in degree.

Below, I outline a way in which dark events, dark legacies, dark heritage and dark tourism are interlinked. The disjunction caused by the nonlinear representation of the connections between these terms indicates that the links are not preordained, necessary or automatic. While a dark event will nearly always leave a legacy, whether tangible or intangible, that legacy can only be turned into heritage (whether at the site of the event or not) through intervention of some kind. Similarly, a neglect or lack of intervention will turn heritage back into a legacy or prevent a legacy from gaining heritage status. While dark tourists are more likely to visit a site of dark heritage (indicated by a thicker arrow), there will still be some (such as researchers or victims of the event) who visit sites with a dark legacy (Fig. 4.7).

Is it correct to categorise these features as 'dark'? In the parlance of Stone (2006), who proposed a spectrum of dark tourism in order to typologise the supply of dark sites into various 'shades of darkness', there is a difference between sites *associated with* death and suffering (such as the Holocaust memorial museum in Washington DC) and the sites *of* death and suffering (such as Auschwitz), where the latter constitute a 'darker' tourism (Miles 2002). According to this categorisation, OT camp sites are darker than museum exhibitions on OT workers in Channel

Island museums, although of course many of these exhibitions are inside German bunkers or tunnels which were built using forced and slave labour, which also classes these locations as a darker heritage. Typically, sites of darker tourism are close in space and time to the event in question, are in an authentic location and are focused on education and commemoration rather than commerciality or entertainment. Walter (2009: 52) factors in another aspect which can conspire to darken sites of death, such as deaths which 'challenge the collective narratives of a nation'; OT camp sites have the power to do just this.

However, if the site in question is not intended as a dark tourism site (much like OT camps, which are not intended as tourist sites at all), then Sharpley (2009a: 20) demotes them to a paler or grey form of tourism—or, in this case, legacy. This implies that just as there are factors of time frame, location and event which can conspire to make a site dark, there are also factors such as whether or not a site is exposed or exploited for tourism or heritage that can 'lighten' its classification, and this is backed up by the apparent indifference of those that are happy to live on top of such sites today, as discussed below. This does not mean that these sites do not have the power to grow darker if ever they are uncovered and draw an audience.

Because of what happened at concentration camps, just as some people are drawn to such places (i.e. dark tourists), others shy away from facing the reality of such horrors. To uncover or excavate sites such as these is to open Pandora's box and risks revealing something which one may not yet be prepared to face. It is known, for example, that Jews were among those brought to the Channel Islands to work for the OT (e.g. Cohen 2000: 121–154; Sanders 2005: Chap. 6), and this adds to the feelings of anxiety about what could yet be revealed.

While OT camps are not presented as tourist sites, it is not entirely true to say that they are not visited. While local historians or researchers visit these sites, former OT workers have also made the pilgrimage back to the sites of their suffering. Photographic evidence exists of this in Jersey in around 1970, when resident Spanish Republicans visited the sites of camps in the island.[10] A similar event also took place when the memorial plaque was attached to the gate post of the concentration camp of Sylt in Alderney in 2008. On another occasion, when Russian slave worker Georgi Kondakov revisited Alderney, it was important for him to revisit the locations of his mental torment (Bonnard 1991). What comes across clearly is that not only did his return to Alderney have a profound effect on him and help him to make sense of and come to terms with his past, but it was in particular the remains of the buildings and specifically their locations which acted as a trigger to his memories and associated emotions. We should not underestimate the power or importance of the remains of former camps to those who once lived there.

If the attitudes to those who were in Auschwitz are anything to go by, we could do worse than to listen to the words of Levi (1986: 185), who wrote:

[10] Jersey Heritage reference L/F/64/B/1.

> If, at the time of liberation, we had been asked: 'What would you like to do with these infected barracks, these wire fences, these rows of toilets, these ovens, these gallows?" I think that most of us would have answered: 'Get rid of everything, raze it to the ground along with Nazism and everything German." We would have said this (and many have by tearing down the barbed wire, and setting fire to the barracks), and we would have been wrong. These are not mistakes to efface. With the passing of years and decades, their remains do not lose any of their significance as a Warning Monument; rather they gain in meaning.

Should we, then, preserve OT camps for both their value in warning us against the evils of slave and forced labour and for their meaning to former workers? It would be interesting to gather the opinions of former workers on this subject. Unfortunately, very few are still alive or accessible today. Gary Font, son of Francisco Font, a Spanish Republican slave worker in Alderney and forced worker in Jersey, believes that a simple plaque on the site of the camps would be appropriate.[11] This view is shared by Jean-Louis Vigla, the son of a volunteer worker in Alderney. However, Vigla also suggests that a small visitor information centre should be set up in the island, located in a former prisoner barrack hut, where a plan of all the camps, prison houses, cabins and huts which housed workers during the war, could be identified and shown in relief in a map of the island.[12] Memorialisation, raising awareness and education are clearly important values held by the sons of those involved.

Many sites of dark tourism are perceived as sacred spaces, places with an 'auratic' quality, although this aura can sometimes be more unholy than sacred (Seaton 2009: 85). This negative aura is likely to come from the knowledge, memory or perception of what occurred at such sites (i.e. a dark intangible heritage) rather than emanating in some mysterious fashion from the site itself. It is likely to be in the eye of the beholder. If this knowledge or memory is lost or marginalised, perhaps by the death or departure either of those who experienced violence or atrocity at such sites or of those who have taken it upon themselves to safeguard and preserve such knowledge, or else simply marginalised by other narratives or by the passage of time, then the perception by others of dark sites can change. This means that, over time, any such aura can be lost or dwindle sharply. Given that many former OT camp sites in Guernsey and Jersey are now residential housing estates (see Table 4.2), we can probably safely assume that any former aura has either dissipated or else those who live in such places are ignorant or indifferent to what once occurred there. As Seaton reminds us, narratives told about dark spaces can be 'reverentially accepted, ignored, resisted or flatly denied' (ibid.: 97).

Some of the most extraordinary examples of this are the bungalows built on top of *Lager* Helgoland and the holiday camp site built on top of *Lager* Norderney, both in Alderney. At Helgoland, the former entrance posts to the camp are used as the entrance posts to the driveway of the bungalow (Fig. 4.8); at Norderney, various concrete structures are still visible in the long grass. Local people here are aware of what they live and camp on top of. It is apparent that the OT camps in the Channel

[11] Email from Gary Font to author, 11 September 2006.

[12] Emails from Jean-Louis Vigla, 18 and 27 October 2006.

Fig. 4.8 The disguised entrance posts of Lager Helgoland, Alderney (© Gilly Carr)

Islands (especially in Guernsey and Jersey) have lost much of their aura and darkness, although the avoidance and neglect of Sylt and Borkum especially suggest that, perhaps, local people still avoid these sites for a reason. By not confronting what happened at these sites, local people are able to continue ignoring them. Only a forced confrontation has the power to change local perceptions.

It is difficult to tell whether the general dissipation of the aura of OT camps in Guernsey and Jersey especially happened slowly over several generations or, as is more likely, whether the real neutering of the camps took place quite early on, when they were destroyed or dismantled by the Germans and locals alike. It is not known whether the motivation for the destruction or removal of any of the camps stemmed from a desire to cover up the evidence of their crimes (in the case of the Germans) or not to be reminded of the crimes that took place on their soil (in the case of the islanders). It was probably a combination of both.

While we may wonder at the lack of anxiety of islanders over the role of their islands in the Holocaust, we should remember that it was not until the early 1970s, after the Eichmann trial of 1961, the 1967 Arab–Israeli war and the 1968 student protests, that the Holocaust began to assume centre stage in the consciousness of Western Europeans (Koonz 1994: 269). By this time, the state of preservation of most OT camp sites in the Channel Islands may not have been too different to their status today, as the photos taken around this time by Spanish Republicans in the island attest.

Should we be concerned that most of these sites have apparently lost their power to disturb? Is it sometimes a good thing for dark sites to lose their darkness? On the one hand, it means that communities can reclaim the land for the living, let go of the past and move forwards, ridding themselves of the burden of war, all of which might be perceived as a thoroughly healthy and positive thing several generations after the original conflict. On the other hand, there are ethical ramifications to ignoring such sites. Even the apparently innocuous camps of forced labourers described above housed people who were taken against their will or who had little choice but to agree to work for the OT rather than face an unknown fate in Germany (Sanders 2005: 205). Human rights abuses within a corrupt system were endemic inside the OT, and to separate out some camp types as an unproblematic heritage, or to ignore the camp sites in general, is to turn one's back on past suffering.

The current neglect of OT camps does not necessarily indicate their terminal position. The debris of war does not have a preordained trajectory or life cycle; something that is covered in the undergrowth or long forgotten does not have to stay in this state. Interventions by archaeologists or any other stakeholder to uncover and preserve the camps are possible, but the success of these efforts will be dictated either by the local community or by those in positions of authority who have the power to sanction or loudly welcome such interventions. However, as Geyer (1997: 7) wisely points out, 'no preservation, however perfect, can save these traces for the present unless they are accepted in the present'. An uncovered site imposed upon the local community as 'heritage' can return to its previously neglected state if locally rejected or disliked. The converse is also true.

The question, then, is this: if members of the local community show no sign of wanting to change the status quo, do outside or even local heritage practitioners have any right to intervene and engineer or impose a change of any kind? And, if so, on what grounds and using what methods? Are ethical and educational reasons and a desire to show respect to victims of Nazism enough to claim the moral high ground? Or will any such heritage that results be the outcome of power imbalances between professionals and communities in relation to the control of the site of the camps and the narratives that they provide? We must also not lose sight of *why* members of the community have not turned the camps into heritage. Such a decision makes a statement about what Channel Islands identity does and does not embrace, with the associated implications that to force a change is an attempt to manipulate or misrepresent locally held concepts of identity and even collective memory. Arguably, however, the decision to ignore this legacy of occupation was taken many decades ago, and the subject has never rearisen for debate. Since the fiftieth anniversary of liberation, islanders are more open to embracing and remembering victims of Nazism, especially in Jersey. If this subject were discussed again today, it is possible that the outcome could be different.

I would suggest that, in Guernsey and Jersey especially, most people today have no idea about the location of the camps or why or whether they should be remembered. They may not even care. This suggests that the best place to start is with education and awareness-raising to see how and whether this inspires local people to change the status quo and reclaim ownership of the camps without the strong-arm intervention of heritage practitioners, which by itself could be potentially ethically and professionally questionable.

In Alderney, one senses that, rather than a lack of knowledge, there is a lack of a desire to know or be told about the OT camps. In fact, their one-time presence and general (but perhaps not specific) location on the island are fairly well known among the population. Such a state of accidental or deliberate ignorance is likely to continue in all islands for the foreseeable future unless some intervention is made which actively turns this legacy of occupation into heritage, and I believe that there is still a long way to go before this would be welcomed by the local community who has to live with these sites under their property or in their back yard. Koonz (1994: 270), for example, records that the Germans living near Dachau, Neuengamme and Bergen-Belsen concentration camps 'hated the camps that blemished the reputation of their communities'.

Such negative feelings towards 'theatres of death' in one's back yard is likely to be especially intense among residents if the historical legacies in question are from a past that they did not play any part in (Seaton 2009: 100). Elsewhere (Carr 2007), I argue that such feelings are particularly strong in Alderney, where most of the population spent the war years in England. For similar reasons, it is not difficult to see why it might be controversial to suggest the future excavation, opening up, display or commodification of OT camps for tourists.

One might, instead, suggest the presence of memorials at the site of all former OT camps as part of a process of heritagisation and as part of the solution to the problem of neglect. This is likely to be controversial for the same reasons as excavation. Sometimes a 'solution' should not be sought at all, as this implies that the case (and the opportunities for debate) can be closed and that people can go back to the more comfortable state of forgetting. Judt (2005) suggests that to memorialise the past is also a way to contain and even neglect it, leaving the responsibility of memory to others. Judt is also a partial advocate for neglect, suggesting that some measure of neglect and even forgetting are necessary conditions for civic health, although first a nation must remember, acknowledge, discuss and digest something before it can forget it. It is debateable whether all of the Channel Islands have yet done this sufficiently, and this is one of the key problems.

Education, awareness-raising, information panels, excavation and memorialisation are all possible steps or consecutive intervention strategies for the future of the OT camps. To what extent should we be deterred if any of them, especially the latter two, prove to be deeply controversial or unsettling to local communities? What can excavation and memorialisation achieve? Given the modern trend for heritage practitioners to work alongside communities and local stakeholders as part of good practice, who are the stakeholder groups and should they be granted any power of veto if they prefer OT camps to stay hidden in the undergrowth? What compromise positions, if any, can be reached and what wider benefits are there for the community if these sites become heritage? What narratives could or should be produced? And what strategies can be suggested for the future care of these sites?

Strategies for the Future of OT Camps

The Power of Controversial Strategies

Let us first consider the desirability of controversial or unsettling heritage strategies by considering 'settled' heritage. As discussed in the last chapter with reference to future bunker presentation, Macdonald (2009b: 93 and 103) suggests that this is the 'sedimented, publically established and valued distillation of history'. She argues that by incorporating minority or previously excluded voices into official discourse (or by including the OT camps into established Occupation heritage), existing accounts of the past—and even the traditional view of heritage itself—can be unsettled and disrupted, making it more likely to be regarded as contestable and contingent, and as an ethical space in which values can be explored and debated. This is precisely the kind of outcome which is desirable if neglected legacies are to be incorporated into the pantheon of accepted and acceptable heritage. To provoke a debate on OT camps, their role as potential heritage, and what they might represent to the islands today, would provide a very useful opportunity for ethical debate on unethical practices during the Occupation, what more could have been done to prevent them, and what we can do to prevent such practices happening again.

Opportunities and spaces for ethical debate on Occupation issues (and here, I include public art projects, memorial erection and the transformation of a couple of German fortifications into overtly victim heritage) have been slowly growing in Jersey for the past decade, although they remain a minority phenomenon. Guernsey lags behind, and while memorialisation in this island has embraced the victims of Nazism over the last 10 years, these do not appear to interfere or unsettle existing narratives, as discussed later.

Spaces for ethical debates exist elsewhere in Europe and further afield in the form of 'Sites of Conscience'. Such sites include museums and other heritage spaces that have made three commitments to achieving 'Never Again': to interpret history through a site (believing in the power of place to inspire a culture of human rights); to engage in programmes that stimulate dialogue on pressing social issues today and to promote democratic and humanitarian values; and to share opportunities for public involvement in those issues (Ševčenko 2011). Sites of Conscience need to 'shape a heritage of *doing* rather than of *being*. Not who we were in the past and who we are today, but what we did do in the past and what we want to do today' (ibid.: 115, original emphases preserved).

It seems to me that OT camps and associated museum exhibitions would make excellent potential sites of conscience that could pledge a desire to 'never again' let such abuse of human rights take place in the Channel Islands; to 'never again' let such abuses happen without the intervention of authorities and the general population; and to 'never again' let humanitarian aid be illegal or carry penalties. An associated museum exhibition could include a series of workshops, lectures and open debates for school children, island lawyers, local government and members of the public on these subjects and on the subject of modern slave labour in the British Isles.[13] An exhibition could also call upon the public to help shape

[13] In September 2011, a case of modern slave labour emerged, where 24 slaves were found living in a caravan in the town of Leighton Buzzard, recruited from homeless shelters and dole queues for labouring jobs (http://www.guardian.co.uk/world/2011/sep/11/leighton-buzzard-slaves-released).

content through dialogue and debate and through sharing memories of OT workers which still exist among some members of the population.

Without an opportunity for open and ongoing discussion about the legacy of the Occupation, Ševčenko argues that 'sites risk becoming divisive lightning rods that can exacerbate underlying social conflicts'; thus, funding and planning for this kind of heritage need to factor in time and space for this kind of discussion 'as a fundamental and ongoing part of heritage management' (ibid.: 121).

Intervention through provocation and asking uncomfortable questions is needed to initiate and encourage debate on Occupation heritage. Such an approach is advocated by Moshenska (2008b: 168) in his discussion of ethical critique in the archaeology of modern conflict. He suggests that 'a critical, niggling, troublesome ethical discourse asking rude and awkward questions at inopportune moments' will keep heritage practitioners on their toes and outside their comfort zones (ibid.: 172) and argues in favour of a place for 'ethically challenging and potentially transgressive research that pushes against the comfortable boundaries of the discipline' (ibid.: 173).

Moshenska and Macdonald are not the only practitioners who advocate deliberately provocative heritage strategies in order to cause discontent. Geographer Michael Landzelius, too, makes similarly challenging suggestions about the way to change the non-representation, non-display and general amnesia surrounding Swedish military labour company camps of the 1930s, which were built far from centres of power and invisible to most Swedish citizens. These sites have also been omitted from museum publications, exhibitions, and critical enquiry, and as almost nothing remains from these structures, this has been used as a convenient excuse for heritage bodies to ignore them (2003).

Landzelius suggests that these camps should be mobilised and relocated 'for critical and subversive purposes in order to make the past implode into the present in ways that unsettle' (ibid.: 215). He provocatively suggests that a reconstructed camp could be erected in the courtyard of the Royal Palace in Stockholm, where 'the Nazi sympathiser King Gustav V (1858–1950) resided during the war. In this way the marginalised past would be critically relocated to the centre …'. He also suggests that 'such disinherited assemblages could, as part of a politico-spatial struggle for the advancement of democratic principles and accountability, be made into 'touring exhibitions' resituated into centres of power and abjection' (ibid.: 216).

While I am not suggesting anything of this kind for the Channel Islands (although Landzelius suggests that any resulting discontent indicates the importance of this kind of project for issues of memorialisation and public political deliberation), there is certainly potential for critical, unsettling and thought-provoking exhibitions in the islands' capitals, in Jersey Museum in St Helier and Guernsey Museum in St Peter Port.

The Value of Excavation and Memorialisation

In 2010, the British archaeology television programme *Time Team* came to Jersey to excavate a German anti-aircraft site, a project with which I was involved. In the planning stages, I suggested that it would be more interesting to excavate an OT camp site, although this was deemed by the producers to be too controversial and generally unsuitable for a family audience. A Jersey heritage practitioner asked me what I would hope to find by conducting such a dig.

There is a danger, as Seitsonen and Herva point out, that the archaeology of the recent past can all too easily serve to simply illustrate and reiterate pre-existing historical narratives, revealing nothing new (2011: 179). They argue that a more useful approach is to focus on and explore the relationship between the interned and their material culture (which they take to include the structures in which they lived and the architecture of confinement) and the wider world of the historical context in which they once lived. By revealing such relationships, they argue, we can get a new perspective on the past. Spatial organisation of OT camp huts, for example, would give us an insight into German attitudes, thought and behaviour towards OT workers, and into their way of life in the camp. Such physical arrangements of the camp are likely to have 'mediated and manipulated particular sets of thought and behaviour' of the overseers and workers (ibid.: 183).

Camps such as those used by the OT are not always built according to purely pragmatic considerations. Like the military buildings described by Schofield (2005: 51–53), they can be used to give an indication of the conditions under which people lived and operated, the patterns of use of the structures, and can give an insight into the way that space is 'controlled and demarcated by convention, order and discipline' and used to 'reflect social structure and social relations'.

Archaeologist Gonzalo Compañy and his colleagues, who worked with former clandestine detention centres in Latin America, are strong advocates of a political, ethical and non-neutral archaeology; they argue that in their work they are forced to take such a position because of the horror of the events they worked with (2011: 243). They attempted an archaeology that could rethink and reconnect the traumatic past with the present by recovering not just the traces of horror, but 'the sense of the humane'. 'With a political archaeology', they write, 'one starts by asking ourselves what we investigate for, where we begin, who we dig for, and who we dig against'. For them, the recovery of historical memory has 'less to do with the establishment of answers, than with enabling the questioning' (ibid.). Their focus was 'those processes that conditioned, favoured, and enabled the creation of those places and their latter silencing and negation' (ibid.: 244).

The humanitarian and non-neutral stance advocated by Compañy and his colleagues accords with the kind of ethical position taken at the Sites of Conscience discussed above. The excavation of an OT camp is not (just) about finding the odd personal possession of an OT guard or a foreign worker, although such finds could benefit from proper contextualisation; it is about revealing the circumstances in which people were forced to live, the inequality of power relations in the past, and the perceptions and attitudes of the OT towards its workers. By systematically recording the evidence of 'horrible living conditions', archaeology provides a testimony of the very physical and historical existence of the past (Casella 2011: 290). Such a record would also allow us to instigate dialogue and debate about the past and about the processes that resulted in the establishment of these sites.

The excavation of an OT camp has the power and potential to cause a considerable impact in the Channel Islands, especially if coupled with an exhibition and public debate to prolong and deepen that impact. It would have the potential to register as a 'memory event'. Etkind defines this concept as a 'rediscovery of the past that creates a rupture with its accepted cultural meaning'. They are 'secondary to the historical events that they interpret, usually taking place many years or decades later', and their cultural genres include revelations, historical debates, museum openings, and the erection or destruction of memorials (to give a small selection). They 'circulate in cultural space and reverberate in time' and 'produce volatile effects that generate secondary waves and aftershocks' (2010: 4–5). While many memory events can occur accidentally, I suggest that they can also be potentially manipulated and engineered, although the success of such endeavours cannot be predicted in advance.

Archaeology can certainly be a powerful tool. Moshenska (2008b: 170–171) reminds us of the power that archaeologists can wield when working with modern conflict and memory; a power 'that can rewrite history on the ground and embed itself deeply in popular consciousness. *By engaging with the ethical questions raised by our work we can begin to exercise this power with considered responsibility*' [emphases added]. Again, ethics and the opportunity and space for debate are emphasised as an important part of any excavation.

By securing information about OT camps through excavation and survey and through raising awareness about this legacy of war currently exiled from public space and memory, we can lay emphases about the importance of these sites in their own right and their importance in education and ethical debate. They can be used to reinforce memory of a history that is neglected, subject to amnesia and marginalised in official narratives. In short, through excavation, archaeologists can make a contribution to justice. To hide a disturbing past is, to a certain extent, to collude with the perpetrators and so an intervention can be seen as an act of social responsibility. Turning this legacy of the Occupation into heritage is part of the commitment to the memory of former OT workers and increases and facilitates the opportunities for their voices to be heard.

Memorialisation, too, can share many of the same aims of excavation in terms of prompting debate and a questioning of the accepted historical record. A memorial could act as a pledge that we would do things differently now: that we would defend and aid OT workers. It could act as a tangible way of seeking forgiveness for not doing enough in the past. We must, however, be careful that any memorial does not divest us of the obligation to remember (Young 2000: 94 and 194).

What form of memorial are we talking about? Non-controversial memorials become invisible and ignored very quickly, especially ones which recite received and uncontroversial history. But how does one make a memorial controversial? Rice (2009: 240) recommends the use of the 'guerrilla memorial' at sites of slavery, which provide the names of perpetrators and their deeds and acts of atrocity. A number of the names of overseers and their personal acts can be recovered today (e.g. Sanders 2005: 195–200), and the surviving testimony given by former OT workers could be harnessed for such a project as part of our duty to remember the perpetrators and their crimes.

Another memorial form, the 'counter-monument', was developed in Germany as a way of keeping the memory of the Holocaust alive and visible. These are memorial spaces which push the duty of remembering back on to the viewer; they are 'ethically certain of their duty to remember, but aesthetically sceptical of the assumptions underpinning traditional memorial forms' (Young 1993: 27). They aim to 'jar viewers from complacency, to challenge and denaturalise the viewers' assumptions' (ibid.: 28). Like an excavation, such a memorial can be used to disturb and unsettle those who see it. In fact, a counter-monument does not have to be a monument or memorial at all; an excavation can act as a temporary counter-monument. If that site becomes opened up as heritage, accepted and safeguarded by local people, it can become more permanent, acting as a site of 'counter-memory', a site which people refuse to forget and which struggle and compete for remembrance against dominant sites and interpretations of the past (Legg 2005: 181). There is also the potential for such sites to one day become mainstream sites of memory of the Occupation.

Controversial excavation and memorialisation, then, can act as powerful strategies to bring neglected histories and marginalised voices to the fore and to challenge and question established perceptions of the forced, slave and voluntary labour, and the attitudes of islanders towards these groups. It can provoke and encourage debate and a re-evaluation of official history. An ethical and non-neutral stance and the support of local heritage practitioners would be important for such a project in order to get permission to survey and dig and to gain access to museum space. But the archaeologist and other heritage practitioners do not work in a vacuum. It is important to identify other stakeholders and interest groups within the community, as any heritage project cannot thrive or achieve lasting success without local support.

Identifying Communities and Stakeholders

Who are the different interest groups or stakeholders who might be given a say in a heritage project of this type? Should they all have an equal say in what happens? Do they have the right to veto any such project? Can heritage practitioners overrule them? There are no set answers to such questions, but they should be open to debate. In the past, stakeholders and interest groups in the community have been overlooked, subordinated or impeded because they are not 'heritage experts' and therefore are 'potentially "lacking" a particular vision or understanding of heritage and the accepted values that underpin this vision' (Waterton and Smith 2010: 10). It is thus important for all interest groups to be recognised and heard, although

Waterton and Smith note the reluctance of professionals in the heritage sector to give up some of their power in order to allow other groups the status to participate as equals (ibid.: 11). A better role for heritage professionals is, perhaps, as facilitators rather than as 'heritage police' (Emerick 2009) in order to accomplish results of mutual benefit to all concerned. If all groups are not listened to or felt that they have not been heard, then engagement with the community may not succeed long term or even at all. Compromise and negotiation are clearly needed on all sides.

In seeking to turn sites of the camps into heritage, who are the many groups who would have an interest in this project—who are the stakeholders? Sharpley divides stakeholders at dark heritage sites into victims, perpetrators and contemporary independent visitors to such sites who identify with neither of the former groups (2009b: 150). I would be surprised if, especially at sites of recent dark heritage, 'independent visitors' did not identify, whether through empathy or bonds of kinship or nationality, with one or the other and mostly, one would assume, with the victims. Such a narrow definition of stakeholders would also be insufficient in the Channel Islands.

In any case, to follow through with this line of thought, in the Channel Islands, the victim group would include former OT workers themselves and their descendents, most especially those still living locally today. In terms of perpetrators, we can divide this group into the 'actual' and the 'perceived'. While the *actual* includes the former OT overseers and the soldiers of occupation, the *perceived* perpetrators might stretch to include visiting German tourists; there are those in the Channel Islands from the Occupation generation who have yet to forgive old foes. The perception of perpetrators can also be considered from two perspectives, both emic (inside looking out) and etic (outside looking in). While Tunbridge and Ashworth (1996: 109), taking an etic viewpoint, place the wartime local government in the position of, at best, bystanders; this would be firmly rejected locally.

I would argue that the different and wider stakeholders in any OT-related project in the Channel Islands would or should include the following, in no particular order:

- The surviving former OT workers, their children and grandchildren. While those who live locally can be readily consulted, this is more difficult for those in other European countries. The views and needs of those in the Channel Islands should be given priority to those who live elsewhere, as they have to live with the heritage and may be called upon to speak about it. The small Spanish Republican community in Jersey is a good example of this group;
- Islanders who once fed, sheltered or gave aid to former OT workers;
- Those who live on top of or near the sites of OT camps. Any memorial or excavation and the ensuing exposure and debate that it would generate are likely to be conducted in their back yard or under their noses; they would face more disturbance than islanders who live at a distance from such sites. If this group were not amenable to the placement of memorials at every camp site, for example, then it is likely that any such memorials would be removed by such

residents within a short space of time. There is a slim chance, and one that may grow with time, especially if the project were successful, that there will be a perceived caché attached to living on top of 'Occupation heritage' (albeit a dark one) given the value that islanders attach to other parts of this heritage;
- Landowners on which OT sites are situated;
- Local heritage practitioners (e.g. those who work for Jersey Heritage or the Department of Culture and Leisure in Guernsey) who would be involved in putting the project into practice and helping to create museum displays;
- Local archaeology societies, including the archaeology sub-section of the Société Jersiaise and the Société Guernesiaise;
- Tourism professionals (whose job would be to make the best use of these sites for the tourist market);
- Local Occupation enthusiasts and local historians and their societies. Most notably, this would include members or representatives of the CIOS. Since its foundation, this group has become the guardians of memory of the Occupation and is seen by many locally as the experts when it comes to Occupation heritage of all kinds;
- The scholars or researchers behind the project.

Clearly, the negotiating table will be a busy one, hence the need for heritage practitioners to act as facilitators. But with such a large number of stakeholders, none of whom are likely to have a disinterested, unbiased or entirely independent point of view, how can a resolution be reached? Baillie (2011: 527–529) suggests a way forward by dividing stakeholders into three: primary stakeholders, heritage managers and secondary stakeholders, each with an internally elected representative whose task would be to collect the views of individuals within the group. Each representative would be given one-third of the voting power, and a two-thirds majority would be necessary for any decision to be followed through.

In practice, Baillie's model might be difficult to implement in the Channel Islands, as the model was designed to cope with 'living heritage', i.e. heritage sites (such as churches) that are used and legally or culturally owned. As established earlier, OT camp sites are disused and disowned; they are orphan heritage with no clear successor community, although the children or former OT workers in the Channel Islands might have some claim in this regard.

Baillie defines primary stakeholders as the users or owners of a site, and in this case, the landowners would be either private individuals who happened to have a camp built on their property during the Occupation or who have subsequently purchased the land, or else live in houses built on top of camp sites. The landowners may also be the Crown or the local government. Baillie (2011: 528) suggests that secondary stakeholders are 'groups or organisations outside of the primary stakeholder group who have a direct or indirect stake' in a site because 'said stakeholder can affect or be affected by the actions, objectives, and policies within which the heritage in question is managed'. The secondary stakeholders in the Channel Islands are likely to be the largest group, made up of individuals and several formal and informal groups, such as children of OT workers; the CIOS and other local history societies; those who once gave assistance to workers and those who live near the site. It is likely that the choice of representative for this group will be difficult.

This is an emotive topic, redolent with issues of ethics and morality. Moshenska (2008: 173) argues that 'a concern with ethics need not and must not imply a cold or apparently impartial or disinterested viewpoint'. I have already suggested that this is a project that would require a non-neutral stance because of the nature of the evidence. If one of the *aims* is to disturb, question, challenge and unsettle existing narratives, can this be achieved without an agenda which seeks justice for the victims? It possibly could, but then, in whose memory should one carry out the project? Why argue in favour of intervention and heritagisation of this legacy? Why seek to challenge and unsettle local people?

A non-neutral position is not without its problems. Sharpley (2009b: 150) suggests that while any potential interpretation of the past (created at the site of OT camps or in museum exhibitions) can create an 'inheritance' for one group of stakeholders (i.e. the victims), it can create a 'disinheritance' for others. This may be a way of rebalancing the current mode of interpretation at most German fortifications in the Channel Islands, where those who built them are most definitely disinherited in favour of the German occupiers.

If a project's aims are non-neutral and seek justice for, and acknowledgement of, a victim group, it does not mean that interpretation cannot also be ethical, sensitive, honest and balanced (in the sense of hiding nothing and not shying away from giving the whole picture), and inclusive of all stakeholders, and surely, this is to be desired. It should be noted, however, that perpetrators are omitted from the list of interest groups listed above. Indeed, it is unlikely that any would come forward, especially as very few former OT overseers returned to the islands to settle there after the war.[14] Why would we want a heritage that caters for a perpetrators-as-stakeholders or one with which they may identify, unless we are seeking to name and shame and to point out evil crimes so that they are not covered up in perpetuity? Presumably, such stakeholders would only be welcomed if they approached the site in question as an act of contrition, reconciliation or memorialisation. However, in the interests of moving beyond polarised positions of 'victim' and 'perpetrator' in order to facilitate reconciliation and avoid the perpetuation of hate, it may be best to include multiple voices in any heritage interpretation at the site of an OT camp.

Ultimately, we cannot control who visits a site and with what intentions. If we choose to take the perspective of Tunbridge and Ashworth and perceive local government officials as 'bystanders' or worse, then there is no reason why someone from local government, or a representative from the children of members of the Occupation period government, should not also be invited to join the debate. Their perspective and opinions should be seen as equally welcome and interesting to record, even if they reject the reasons for being included among the stakeholders.

---

[14] The author knows of one such case in Jersey, where an OT overseer married a local woman, much to the disapproval of the rest of the family.

Benefits and Compromise Positions

Challenging official histories and narratives of the Occupation need not be to the complete disadvantage of Channel Islanders. There are opportunities to draw attention to positive acts among the negative by focusing on those who provided humanitarian assistance to foreign workers. The number of people who did this is much larger than is previously thought, and research on this subject is still ongoing (Willmot 2014). While the names of one or two are relatively well known because they paid for their humanitarian acts with their lives, such as Louisa Gould in Jersey and Marie Ozanne in Guernsey, there are many others who could and should be acknowledged.

Conversely, being ready to face the past, to own up to, examine, and debate any wrongdoing and to have an attitude of openness and honesty about the sins (perceived or actual) of one's parents and grandparents is the sign of a mature society and is a process that many other formerly occupied European countries went through between the late 1960s and the 1980s. Elsewhere in this volume and using the evidence of Occupation heritage, I discuss how the Channel Islands have not yet fully arrived at this position, although Jersey has made significantly more progress than any other island. The excavation and/or memorialisation of selected OT camps and an associated museum exhibition and public debate would be a very visible and important step towards achieving and signalling this maturity. However, if any project involving survey, excavation, memorialisation or exhibition was given little local or vocal support or publicity, if all interest groups except the researchers, archaeologists and heritage practitioners directly involved were excluded in order to keep the project low-key, and if the opportunity was not seized to encourage debate, then some of the key aims of the project would not be realised. While some 'memory events' are spontaneous or happen accidentally, others can be engineered to create publicity and impact. This does not have to be a bad thing if the cause is publically agreed to be a good one. The motives behind the project should be declared at the outset and should be transparent and subject to scrutiny. The project should be discussed and negotiated openly among all interest groups and if necessary, compromise positions can be sought. As Moshenska (2008: 165) argues, the values and risks must be weighed up with a careful and critical eye.

We might suggest that, rather than memorialise or excavate the site of every single OT camp in the Channel Islands, regardless of what the site is being used for today, a more sensitive or productive approach might be to choose, say, one site per Channel Island, perhaps one that is not next to a residential area (despite the desire of the project to unsettle), and to let those represent the others as a compromise position. Because of the degree to which the camp sites have been put to other uses, the number of camps left that could be turned into heritage sites is now very small in Guernsey and Jersey especially. It is likely that good choices would include *Lagers* Wick (a nature reserve; Fig. 4.9) or Brinkforth (unused land next to houses, but probably an unsuitable option due to its proximity to housing) in

Fig. 4.9 Part of the hidden entrance post of Lager Wick, Jersey (© Gilly Carr)

Fig. 4.10 Part of Lager Ostmark, Guernsey (© Gilly Carr)

Jersey; part of *Lager* Ostmark in Guernsey (today represented by a ruined wash-house in a field; Fig. 4.10) and *Lagers* Norderney, Borkum or Sylt in Alderney. Given the stated intention to unsettle existing narratives, Sylt would be the best option in Alderney given its status as the only concentration camp on British soil.

The interest groups listed above are people who do not normally work together in the Channel Islands. When it comes to Occupation heritage, there has been disagreement in the past between heritage professionals and enthusiasts, especially in the realm of bunker restoration in Jersey, as discussed in the last chapter. Such disagreement has caused divisions between these communities, and a new project in which both have an interest would be a good opportunity for everyone to work together as a community and to build bridges and heal divisions. Any excavation could function as a community dig where members of the CIOS could work alongside archaeologists as voluntary labour; in fact, the theme of 'labour'—especially local labour—would be a most pertinent one for the project and could form part of on-site discussion and debate. Where labour was once used in the past in the Channel Islands to produce sites of negative heritage (i.e. the fortifications), a positively produced heritage (i.e. the camps) could emerge from excavation in the present.

The Production of Narratives

What is the best way of going about producing the set of balanced, honest and ethical narratives recommended above? Who decides? Can and should this be negotiated and compromised through discussion? If we accept that the aim is to challenge and unsettle, then nothing should be covered up or marginalised in order to please a stakeholder. Interpretation should be honest and open. The results of excavation and survey, conducted along lines which follow far-reaching and revealing research questions, should by themselves produce new and uncomfortable narratives.

A useful way to proceed is suggested by Sharpley (2009b), who advocates a combination of Seaton's (2001) model of the 'heritage force field' and Poria's (2001, 2007) concept of stakeholder histories. In Seaton's model, four main stakeholders are identified (the owners and controllers of the site, who normally supply the management; the subjects of dark tourism and/or their spokespersons; the host communities who live around the site; and the audience or visitors), although I list many more above who would be pertinent to this particular case study. Poria (2007: 51–52) identifies four different histories of each of these stakeholders: bad active (i.e. 'actions taken by my social group, to which are assigned feelings of shame'); bad passive (i.e. 'actions not taken by someone in my social group but rather perpetrated on my group and to which are assigned feelings of sadness and revenge'); good active (i.e. 'actions taken by my social group to which are assigned positive feelings such as pride'); and good passive (i.e. 'actions not performed by my social group but from which they have derived benefit, including feelings of thankfulness').

The histories of most local stakeholders listed above might be characterised in the following way:

- *Good active history*: islanders who fed, clothed or sheltered slave or forced workers and who stood up to the overseers; alternatively, islanders who worked for the OT but carried out sabotage or theft, or else who worked for the OT to earn money to feed their families, but who 'went slow' on the job (a form of economic resistance);
- *Good passive history*: islanders who did not volunteer for the OT and thus avoided accusations of collaboration;
- *Bad active history*: encouragement by the local authorities to follow German orders in order to avoid reprisals; voluntary employment for the OT;
- *Bad passive history*: avoidance of OT workers and their camps in order to avoid German penalties.

Non-local tourists, or those related to the perpetrators or victims, would have somewhat different histories and perspectives. There is a tendency for bad active histories to be excluded from heritage presentation, resulting in dissonant heritage or 'collective amnesia' (Timothy and Boyd 2003), and this has certainly been the case in the Channel Islands. Bad passive history, which might also be labelled 'bystander history', has also been avoided in much heritage interpretation presented by local enthusiasts such as the CIOS.

Sharpley (2009b: 163) suggests that new narratives should be created, embracing all four histories within a more cooperative and negotiated approach to interpretation. Recognition should be given to all the relevant histories, good and bad, of all stakeholders as a 'basis for encouraging harmony, reconciliation, understanding or learning' through a more inclusive memorialisation and interpretation of dark pasts. I would endorse such a position, on the understanding that a 'negotiated approach' does not involve hiding or marginalising uncomfortable narratives. On the contrary, these are the very stories which should be placed centre stage in order to encourage debate and open discussion.

The Future for OT Camp Sites

There are four issues which must be considered for the future of OT camp sites as legacy (i.e. those which continue in their current overgrown/hidden state) and OT camp sites as heritage (i.e. the sites that could be excavated, memorialised or otherwise turned into heritage): recording, preservation, presentation and commodification.

OT camp sites today in Guernsey and Jersey are largely unrecorded (although see Ginns (2006: 74–87) for a brief description of the location and inmates of each camp). More work has been done in Alderney (Davenport 2003: 26, 50, 66, 106), but this should not be considered the final work on the matter; more structures remain to be uncovered, recorded and interpreted (Sturdy Colls 2011) in order to reinvest structures with value and meanings. It is important to conduct a programme of research, using both available aerial photographs and geophysical surveying and recording on the ground, before more sites are lost. Depending on what such a programme reveals, it would be desirable for remaining structures at any sites to be preserved rather than used as foundations for new building work. These sites may be useful for future excavation or heritagisation; Occupation historians in the islands often bemoan the fate of wartime structures that were destroyed before the days when such sites were considered heritage, and this perspective is useful to bear in mind.

Presentation of the sites can occur online as well as in museums or in the field. Recognising the need to 'engender a degree of empathy between the sightseer and the past victim' as well as the need to provide historical knowledge, Miles (2002: 1176) suggests different ways in which dark sites can be presented to the public. He proposes the use of websites, loaded with video footage and online survivor testimony, which would connect young people to the disappearing eyewitnesses.

In terms of the presentation of the sites on the ground, should excavation trenches remain (and be kept) open? Should the undergrowth be pulled back to reveal all extant structures? What strategy would provide the lowest-cost and most practical solution? Charlesworth and Addis (2002) have discussed similar issues in their assessment of the overgrown landscape of the former concentration camp site of Płaszów in a suburb of Kraków, Poland, and they considered how the site could be managed in order to influence or enhance the experience of visitors to the site. They suggest that, while controlled burning of the undergrowth would not be appropriate given the proximity of housing and grazing would not be practical given that the site is both a former Jewish cemetery as well as a place of death and cremation, creating mown pathways among the remaining building foundations plus the use of orientation boards for visitors would then 'open up a landscape which had previously been hidden' and could all be achieved at low cost (ibid.: 238). To provide *something* to see is important in a heritage site; as Charlesworth and Addis remind us, 'heritage sites where there is apparently little or nothing to see do not thrive' (ibid.: 240). However, land ownership problems and the potential of the land for development have caused problems at Płaszów and are likely to be issues in the Channel Islands as well.

While their suggestions for the presentation of Płaszów are very useful, issues of the potential commodification of OT camps must also be considered if these sites are to be included in tourist literature or promoted on the tourist circuit as part of raising awareness. The original 'stakeholder team' should consider from the outset the following question, proposed by Sharpley (2009a: 8) and Stone (2009: 60), of whether it is ethical to develop, promote or offer dark sites for touristic consumption and to capitalise upon tragedy. Are ethics compromised only if money changes hands? While commerce and commoditisation can taint a site, is this ameliorated or lessened if revenues are used to maintain it or employ local people, thus benefitting the community (Seaton 2009: 87)? Would it make a difference if these sites were free to visitors? As we have already noted, dark sites are spaces which both provide and are provided with many potential moral meanings and are places for a society's morality to be questioned in all sorts of ways (Stone 2009: 71).

Whatever strategies are considered for the future of OT camp sites, it is important to consider whether this should be a deliberately open-ended project; memory work of this kind should ideally remain ongoing in order to keep interpretation contested, exciting and fresh and able to be reinterpreted for each generation. The resolutions that are reached today are contingent on the particular time and place where and when they were constructed. Interpretations that challenge today can bore or become stale tomorrow.

Conclusion: Intervention, Activism and Provocative Heritage

OT heritage in the Channel Islands is not completely ignored. Memorials and museum exhibits exist in several locations throughout the islands. However, I have argued here that both the heritage and the interpretation have had a strong tendency in the past to be selective. Museum exhibitions have tended to be formulaic, depicting OT workers as seen through German eyes. Workers are portrayed as helpless (foreign) victims, and islanders are seen as absent or passive observers, even though documentary evidence exists which undermines both narratives. Older memorials have been partial, anonymising or homogenising, although the more recent have been more inclusive.

As I discussed in the last chapter, in current presentations, OT workers have been marginalised or absented from the fortifications which they helped to build. The camps in which they lived, which have been the focus of this chapter, are not treated as heritage at all. They remain as a legacy of the Occupation, part of the debris of war that was first deliberately and then later, probably accidentally, overlooked because there was nothing left to see. Because of this, they were excluded from heritage strategies.

In a group of islands that values traces of the Occupation highly, this deliberate or accidental amnesia is superficially puzzling, but soon readily understandable for a cumulative number of reasons, including the othering narratives of the OT workers as ‘Russians’, ‘communists’ and ‘foreigners’ (a narrative that conveniently forgot that islanders also worked for the OT) and the associated othering of their legacies; the building of a war narrative which glorified liberation and victory to the exclusion of victims of Nazism; and the focus on building a future which ignored the dark foundations upon which that construction sometimes stood.

In this chapter, I have also highlighted the potential role of heritage practitioners and archaeologists as activists with the power of turning war legacies into a very visible and high-impact heritage. I have outlined a number of ways in which this might be carried out, and all of these set out to be deliberately provocative and challenging yet conducted with a team of local stakeholders in order to ensure proper locally relevant ethical debate and transparency.

Following Moshenska (2008), I have noted that the archaeology of modern military conflict is nearly always emotive and controversial and that it can impact upon and change pre-existing memory narratives. However, because such intervention can also cause distress to traumatised individuals who were directly involved in the events discussed here and because the power that excavation can wield can be misused, a set of appropriate methodological, theoretical and ethical frameworks must be in place (ibid.).

Given these frameworks, archaeologists and other heritage practitioners should not shy away from getting involved, in intervening in unethical or neglected heritage or from producing deliberately provocative heritage when the context demands it.

In this particular case, archaeological evidence for slavery and forced labour is still awaiting discovery. The tangible remains of the poor living conditions and the use of space which could give insight into unequal power relations and the attitudes of overseers to the workers, are, in some locations, lying undisturbed. Such an archaeological project would be non-neutral, ethical and even political. It could also be subversive. However, it could harness members of the local community and bring together competing interest groups. It could use the opportunity to gather oral testimony, to remember and commemorate, and to provoke public debate and openness about aspects of the past that have remained largely undiscussed for three generations. Through these processes, negative heritage could at least partially be rehabilitated and resurrected as positive narratives and heritage practices, such as by centring neglected but positive aspects of a negative history, and through the ethically positive work of the community of stakeholders.

The Channel Islands are not alone in neglecting their sites of forced and slave labour resulting from the construction of the Atlantic Wall, as Jasinski and Stenvik (2010) and Roberts (2010) attest for Norway and France respectively. If the wide-ranging discussion in the recent volume by Myers and Moshenska (2011) is any indication, conflict-related internment camps of various kinds worldwide have for many years been neglected and subject to amnesia, erasure and oblivion.

I am not alone in calling for an ethically motivated archaeological intervention into sites of slave and forced labour. Roberts has argued that 'the greatest imperative in the interpretation of these sites is an ethical one. Not to remember and to attempt to tell this story is a moral acquiescence to Nazi crimes and criminals and a denigration of the victims. The act of memory itself provides the victims of the Nazis with an existence and a past: all too often the victims of the Holocaust are extinguished from history itself' (2010: 99).

While not adopting such an overtly activist tone, Jasinski and Stenvik nonetheless emphasize the importance of building a heritage management system for the Norwegian 'landscape of evil' (the name of their project). They have an objective similar to that which I outline here, namely to understand the life of prisoners through the physical structures of their camps as these were 'their personal and collective arena for fear, hope, concern and prayers—in other words—their painful landscape of evil' (2010: 215). They also argue that archaeological research is a necessary part of 'satisfactory management' of cultural heritage and an 'important tool' for bringing the 'material culture of the darker sides of human history into the light and into common knowledge' (ibid.: 221).

This chapter has argued for a new (provocative) heritage strategy for the legacy of the OT in the Channel Islands; one that uses a high-visibility, high-impact, vocal archaeological project as one of its key methodological tools. Such a method would allow the darker recesses of the islands' landscapes of memory to be better understood and illuminated as part of a commitment to coming to terms with the past and the commitment to the memory of OT workers.

With such a rich resource of OT heritage—possibly the richest per square mile in formerly occupied Europe—if properly uncovered, highlighted, interpreted and debated, the Channel Islands *could* set a new standard for research and heritage management for the Atlantic Wall. Without any intervention, OT camp sites are destined for further erasure from the landscape. Perhaps, in another generation or two, when the Occupation has passed beyond living memory and the children of Occupation veterans have also left the stage, interest and the courage to investigate may once again grow. The disapprobation of those with a direct connection to the events of the Occupation is still a powerful and sanctionary force in the Channel Islands. When the time is right, whenever that may be, to accept this heritage strategy and to turn this legacy of war into heritage is to risk nothing less than the rewriting of history.

References

Anheier, H., & Isar, Y. R. (2011). *Heritage, memory and identity*. Los Angeles and London: Sage.

Baillie, B. (2011). *The Wounded Church: War, destruction and reconstruction of Vukovar's religious heritage*. Unpublished PhD thesis, University of Cambridge.

Baillie, B. (2013). Memorialising the 'Martyred City': Negotiating Vukovar's wartime past. In W. Pullan & B. Baillie (Eds.), *Locating urban conflicts: Ethnicity, nationalism, religion* (pp. 115–131). London: Palgrave MacMillan.

Bartov, O. (2004). The holocaust as 'Leitmotif' of the twentieth century. *Zeitgeschichte, 5*, 315–327.

Biran, A., Poria, Y., & Oren, G. (2011). Sought experiences and (dark) heritage sites. *Annals of Tourism Research, 38*(3), 820–841.

Bonnard, B. (1991). *The island of dread in the Channel: The story of Georgi Ivanovitch Kondakov*. Stroud: Alan Sutton Publishing.

Bunting, M. (1995). *The model occupation*. London: BCA.

Carman, J., & Sørensen, M. L. S. (2009). Heritage studies: An outline. In M. L. S. Sørensen & J. Carman (Eds.), *Heritage studies: Methods and approaches* (pp. 11–28). London and New York: Routledge.

Carr, G. (2007). The politics of forgetting on the island of Alderney. *Archaeological Review from Cambridge, 22*(2), 89–112.

Carr, G. (2010). Shining a light on dark tourism: German bunkers in the British Channel Islands. *Public Archaeology, 9*(2), 64–84.

Casella, E. C. (2011). Lockdown: on the materiality of confinement. In A. Myers & G. Moshenska (Eds.), *Archaeologies of internment* (pp. 285–295). New York: Springer.

Charlesworth, A., & Addis, M. (2002). Memorialisation and the ecological landscapes of Holocaust sites: The case of Płaszow and Auschwitz-Birkenau. *Landscape Research, 27*(3), 229–251.

Cohen, F. (2000). *The Jews in the Channel Islands during the German occupation 1940–1945*. London: Jersey Heritage Trust/The Institute of Contemporary History and Wiener Library Ltd.

Compañy, G., González, G., Ovando, L., & Rossetto, D. (2011). A political archaeology of Latin America's recent past: A bride towards our history. In A. Myers & G. Moshenska (Eds.), *Archaeologies of internment* (pp. 229–244). New York: Springer.

Confino, A. (2005). Remembering the Second World War, 1945–1965: Narratives of victimhood and genocide. *Cultural Analysis, 4*, 46–75.

Cruickshank, C. (2004) [1975] *The German occupation of the Channel Islands*. London: Oxford University Press/Channel Islands: Guernsey Press.

Davenport, T. (2003). *Festung Alderney: The German defences of Alderney*. Guernsey: The Alderney Society and the Channel Islands Occupation Society.

Emerick, K. (2009). Archaeology and the cultural heritage management 'toolkit': The example of a community heritage project at Cawood, North Yorkshire. In E. Waterton & L. Smith (Eds.), *Taking Archaeology out of Heritage* (pp. 91–116). Newcastle-upon-Tyne: Cambridge Scholars Press.

Etkind, A. (2010). Mapping memory events in the East European space. *East European Memory Studies, 1*, 4–5.

Farrell, M., & Burton, J. (2011). Gordon Hirabayashi, the Tucsonians, and the U.S. constitution: Negotiating reconciliation in a landscape of exile. In A. Myers & G. Moshenska (Eds.), *Archaeologies of internment* (pp. 89–110). New York: Springer.

Foote, K. E. (1997). *Shadowed ground: America's landscapes of violence and tragedy*. Austin: University of Texas Press.

Fraser, D. (2000). *The Jews of the Channel Islands and the rule of Law 1940–1945: Quite contrary to the principles of British Justice*. Brighton: Portland.

Geyer, M. (1997). The place of the Second World War in German memory and history. *New German Critique, 71*, 5–40.

Ginns, M. (1993). *German Tunnels in the Channel Islands* (p. 7). Jersey: Channel Islands Occupation Society Archive Book No.

Ginns, M. (2006) [1994] *The Organisation Todt and the fortress engineers in the Channel Islands*. Jersey: Channel Islands Occupation Society Archive Book No. 8.

González-Ruibal, (2011). The Archaeology of internment in Francoist Spain (1936–1952). In A. Myers & G. Moshenska (Eds.), *Archaeologies of internment* (pp. 53–74). New York: Springer.

Grydehøj, A. (2010). Uninherited heritage: Tradition and heritage production in Shetland, Åland and Svalbard. *International Journal of Heritage Studies, 16*(1–2), 77–89.

Isar, Y. R., Viejo-Rose, D., & Anheier, H. K. (2011). Introduction. In H. Anheier & Y. R. Isar (Eds.), *Heritage, memory and identity* (pp. 1–20). Los Angeles and London: Sage.

Jasinski, M., & Stenvik, L. F. (2010). Landscape of evil—archaeology and Nazi POW camps in Norway: A new approach. In M. Neerland Soleim (Ed.), *Prisoners of war and forced labour: Histories of war and occupation* (pp. 205–223). Newcastle: Cambridge Scholars Publishing.

Jordan, J. A. (2006). *Structures of memory: Understanding urban change in Berlin and beyond*. Stanford: Stanford University Press.

Judt, T. (2005). From the house of the dead: On modern European memory. *New York Review of Books, 52*(15), 6.

Knowles Smith, H. R. (2007). *The changing face of the Channel Islands Occupation: Record, Memory and Myth*. Basingstoke: Palgrave Macmillan.

Koonz, C. (1994). Between memory and oblivion: Concentration camps in German memory. In J. R. Gillis (Ed.), *Memory and identity: The history of a relationship* (pp. 258–280). Princeton: Princeton University Press.

Landzelius, M. (2003). Commemorative dis(re)membering: Erasing heritage, spatializing disinheritance. *Environment and Planning D: Society and Space, 21*, 195–221.

Le Quesne, E. (1999). *The Occupation of Jersey day by day: The personal diary of Deputy Edward Le Quesne*. Jersey: La Haule Books.

Legg, S. (2005). Sites of counter-memory: The refusal to forget and the nationalist struggle in colonial Delhi. *Historical Geography, 33*, 180–201.

Levi, P. (1986). Revisiting the camps. In J. E. Young (Ed.), *The art of memory: Holocaust memorials in history* (pp. 198–204). Washington: Prestel.

Levi, P. (1987). *If this is a man*. London: Abacus Books.

Light, D. (2007). Dracula tourism in Romania: Cultural identity and the state. *Annals of Tourism Research, 34*(3), 746–765.

Lowenthal, D. (1975). Past time, present place: landscape and memory. *The Geographical Review, 65*(1), 1–36.

Lowenthal, D. (1994). Identity, heritage and history. In J. R. Gillis (Ed.), *Commemorations: The politics of national identity* (pp. 41–57). Princeton: Princeton University Press.

Lowenthal, D. (2003). Tragic traces on the Rhodian shore. *Historic Environment, 17*(1), 3–7.

Macdonald, S. (2009a). *Difficult Heritage: Negotiating the Nazi past in Nuremberg and beyond*. Abingdon: Routledge.

Macdonald, S. (2009b). Unsettling memories: Intervention and controversy over difficult public heritage. In M. Anico & E. Peralta (Eds.), *Heritage and identity: Engagement and demission in the contemporary world* (pp. 93–104). London and New York: Routledge.

Meskell, L. (2002). Negative heritage and past mastering in archaeology. *Anthropological Quarterly, 75*(3), 557–574.

Miles, W. F. S. (2002). Auschwitz: Museum interpretation and darker tourism. *Annals of Tourism Research, 29*(4), 1175–1178.

Mollet, R. (1945). *Jersey under the Swastika*. London: The Hyperion Press Ltd.

Moshenska, G. (2008). Ethics and ethical critique in the archaeology of modern conflict. *Norwegian Archaeological Review, 41*(2), 159–175.

Myers, A., & Moshenska, G. (eds), (2011). *Archaeologies of Internment*. New York: Springer.

Nora, P. (1989). Between memory and history: Les lieux de mémoire. *Representations, 26*, 7–25.

Pantcheff, T. X. H. (1981). *Alderney: Fortress Island*. Chichester: Phillimore and Co. Ltd.

Pantzou, N. (2011). Materialities and traumatic memories of a twentieth century Greek exile island. In A. Myers & G. Moshenska (Eds.), *Archaeologies of internment* (pp. 91–206). New York: Springer.

Perkin, C. (2010). Beyond the rhetoric: Negotiating the politics and realising the potential of community-driven heritage engagement. *International Journal of Heritage Studies, 16*(1–2), 107–122.

Pocock, H. R. S. (1975). *The memoirs of Lord Coutanche: A Jerseyman looks back*. London and Chichester: Phillimore and Co. Ltd.

Poria, Y. (2001). The show must not go on. *Tourism and Hospitality Research, 3*(2), 115–119.

Poria, Y. (2007). Establishing cooperation between Israel and Poland to save Auschwitz concentration camp: Globalising the responsibility for the massacre. *International Journal of Tourism Policy, 1*(1), 45–57.

Price, J. (2005). Orphan heritage: Issues in managing the heritage of the Great War in Northern France and Belgium. *Journal of Conflict Archaeology, 1*(1), 181–196.

Rice, A. (2009). Museums, memorials and plantation houses in the Black Atlantic: Slavery and the development of dark tourism. In R. Sharpley & P. R. Stone (Eds.), *The darker side of travel: The theory and practice of dark tourism* (pp. 224–246). Bristol: Channel View Publications.

Roberts, M. R. (2010). 'Footprints in the concrete': A study of the Chemin des Juifs (Jews' Road), Jewish slave labour camps, and related sites, in the Nord-Pas-de-Calais, France. *The Historic Environment, 1*(1), 70–102.

Sanders, P. (2004). *The ultimate sacrifice*. Jersey: Jersey Heritage Trust.

Sanders, P. (2005). *The British Channel Islands under German Occupation 1940–1945*. Jersey: Jersey Heritage Trust and Société Jersiaise.

Schofield, J. (2005). *Combat archaeology: Material culture and modern conflict*. London: Duckworth.

Seaton, A. (2001). Sources of slavery—destinations of slavery: The silences and disclosures of slavery heritage in the UK and US. In G. Dann & A. Seaton (Eds.), *Slavery, contested heritage and thanatourism* (pp. 107–129). Binghampton: Haworth.

Seaton, A. (2009). Purposeful otherness: Approaches to the management of thanotourism. In R. Sharpley & P. R. Stone (Eds.), *The darker side of travel: The theory and practice of dark tourism* (pp. 75–108). Bristol: Channel View Publications.

Seitsonen, O., & Herva, V.-P. (2011). Forgotten in the wilderness: WWII German POW camps in Finnish Lapland. In A. Myers & G. Moshenska (Eds.), *Archaeologies of internment* (pp. 171–190). New York: Springer.

Ševčenko, L. (2011). Sites of conscience: Heritage of and for human rights. In H. Anheier & Y. R. Isar (Eds.), *Heritage, memory and identity* (pp. 114–123). London: Sage.

Sharpley, R. (2009a). Shedding light on dark tourism: An introduction. In R. Sharpley & P. R. Stone (Eds.), *The darker side of travel: The theory and practice of dark tourism* (pp. 3–22). Bristol: Channel View Publications.

Sharpley, R. (2009b). Dark tourism and political ideology: Towards a governance model. In R. Sharpley & P. R. Stone (Eds.), *The darker side of travel: The theory and practice of dark tourism* (pp. 145–163). Bristol: Channel View Publications.

Smith, L., & Akagawa, N. (2009). Introduction. In L. Smith & N. Akagawa (Eds.), *Intangible Heritage* (pp. 1–9). London and New York: Routledge.

Sørensen, M. L. S., & Carman, J. (2009). Introduction: Making the means transparent: Reasons and reflections. In M. L. S. Sørensen & J. Carman (Eds.), *Heritage studies: Methods and approaches* (pp. 3–10). London and New York: Routledge.

Steckoll, S. (1982). *The Alderney death camp*. St Albans and London: Granada Publishing Ltd.

Stone, P. (2006). A dark tourism spectrum: Towards a typology of death and macabre related tourist sites, attractions and exhibitions. *Tourism, 54*(2), 145–160.

Stone, P. (2009). Dark tourism: Morality and new moral spaces. In R. Sharpley & P. R. Stone (Eds.), *The darker side of travel: The theory and practice of dark tourism* (pp. 56–72). Bristol: Channel View Publications.

Sturdy Colls, C. (2011, 3–5 August). *The past is history? The archaeology of occupation and persecution*. Paper presented at the Heritage of the Atlantic Wall: Seeking a Common European Response. European Workshop, University of Cambridge.

Thomas, J. (2011). Archaeological investigations of Second World War prisoner of war camps at Fort Hood, Texas. In A. Myers & G. Moshenska (Eds.), *Archaeologies of internment* (pp. 147–170). New York: Springer.

Timothy, D., & Boyd, S. (2003). *Heritage tourism*. Harlow: Prentice Hall.

Tunbridge, J. E., & Ashworth, G. J. (1996). *Dissonant heritage: The management of the past as a resource in conflict*. Chichester: Wiley.

Turner, B. (2010). *Outpost of occupation: How the Channel Islands survived Nazi rule 1940–45*. London: Aurum Press.

Uzzell, D. (1989). The hot interpretation of war and conflict. In D. L. Uzzell (Ed.), *Heritage interpretation volume I: The natural and built environment* (pp. 33–47). London and New York: Belhaven Press.

Walter, T. (2009). Dark tourism: Mediating between the dead and the living. In R. Sharpley & P. R. Stone (Eds.), *The darker side of travel: The theory and practice of dark tourism* (pp. 39–55). Bristol: Channel View Publications.

Waterton, E., & Smith, L. (2010). The recognition and misrecognition of community heritage. *International Journal of Heritage Studies, 16*(1–2), 4–15.

Willmot, L. (2000). The Channel Islands. In B. Moore (Ed.), *Resistance in Western Europe* (pp. 65–91). Oxford and New York: Berg.

Willmot, L. (2014). Humanitarian assistance: Help to Jews and OT workers during the occupation. In G. Carr, P. Sanders, & L. Willmot (Eds.), *Protest, defiance and resistance in the Channel Islands* (pp. 1940–1945). London: Bloomsbury Academic.

Wood, N. (1999). *Vectors of memory: Legacies of trauma in postwar Europe*. Oxford and New York: Berg.

Wood, A., & Wood, M. (1955). *Islands in danger*. New York: MacMillan.

Wyatt, H. (1945) [1985]. *Jersey in jail*. Jersey: Ernest Huelin (La Haule Books Ltd).

Young, J. E. (1993). *The texture of memory: Holocaust memorials and meaning*. New Haven and London: Yale University Press.

Young, J. E. (2000). *At memory's edge: After-images of the Holocaust in contemporary art and architecture*. New Haven and London: Yale University Press.

Zarankin, A., & Salerno, M. (2011). The engineering of genocide: An archaeology of dictatorship in Argentina. In A. Myers & G. Moshenska (Eds.), *Archaeologies of internment* (pp. 207–228). New York: Springer.

Chapter 5
The Politics of Memory on Liberation Day

My first Liberation Day in Jersey, in 2007, was an exciting experience. The day began with a champagne breakfast with members of the Occupation generation at Jersey War Tunnels. Later I joined the crowds in Liberation Square in St Helier for the open air church service and the singing of local patriotic songs such as Beautiful Jersey *and* Ma Normandie. *I glimpsed, over the heads of others, the re-enactment of the events of Liberation Day 1945, as men dressed as British Tommies found a path through the throngs of people to the Pomme D'Or Hotel, and went on to the balcony to re-enact the raising of the Union Jack, much to the delight of the crowds. Shortly afterwards I joined the parade of military and vintage vehicles as a friend gave me a ride in his German Stoewer, the last German vehicle from the Occupation still in the Channel Islands. We did a lap around the town, past the shop windows decorated with liberation themes and bunting, and past the platform on which the visiting Duke of Kent and the island's dignitaries stood. Afterwards we drove to the bunker-filled landscape of Noirmont Point.*

Later in the day I was back in St Helier, in the People's Park, for the Liberation Day concert. With a pint of Jersey cider in one hand and my camera in the other, I photographed the flag-waving crowds who had come to watch the premiere of Jersey composer Gerard Le Feuvre's Island Home, *later to become Jersey's new anthem. The lyrics, which contained many elements of Jersey's history and identity, seemed to me to be redolent with themes so appropriate for Liberation Day: the memory of loss and sacrifice of earlier generations; the island's loyalty to the monarchy; its pride in its history; its faith in God; and its prayer for endurance. I didn't realise it then, but what I had witnessed that day was a palimpsest of Liberation Day themes from 1946 to the present day.*

Introduction: Commemoration and Memory in the Channel Islands

Liberation Day, 9 May, is locally considered to be the most important and eagerly anticipated day in the Channel Islands' commemorative calendar and has been subject to major annual celebrations since 1946. It is a true *lieux de mémoire*

G. Carr, *Legacies of Occupation*, Contributions To Global Historical Archaeology 40,
DOI: 10.1007/978-3-319-03407-2_5,

within the occupationscape. While different groups are remembered on other commemorative days, such as Armistice Day, Holocaust Memorial Day, Homecoming Day (Alderney) and Charybdis Day (Guernsey), these days combine to give an overview of the collective memory of war: who is included, who is marginalised and whose memory is not admitted into the pantheon of heroes or victims (Carr 2012). While we might once have categorised heroes as those whose memory evokes pride, and victims as those whose memory evokes feelings of discomfort, shame or guilt, the various groups of victims of Nazism in the Channel Islands have, since the mid-1990s, been treading a long path towards official recognition and incorporation into collective memory.

Collective memory can be understood, at its broadest definition, as the widely shared perceptions of a group about the past, a past that they need not necessarily have experienced themselves. The concept was developed by Maurice Halbwachs, who argued that collective memory is a socially constructed notion, i.e. that it is a reconstruction of the past in the present (Coser 1992: 22). As the past can never be reconstructed in its entirety, and arguably such a reconstruction is rarely socially or politically desirable, certain elements—certain collective memories—have to be selected. In this way, collective memories of nations (or islands) are 'made' and not just owned. Sontag (2003: 76) has argued that this selective aspect of collective memory is more about stipulating rather than remembering: stipulating that '*this* is important, and this is the story about how it happened'.

Halbwachs suggested that the selected elements of collective memory need a collective social context or framework for reconstruction and display. In the Channel Islands, Liberation Day acts as just such a framework or vehicle for memory narration. Through the rituals of annual commemoration, islanders have been able to create, express and negotiate their shared and inherited memories of the Occupation.

Liberation Day celebrations were and are, of course, an entirely invented tradition. Hobsbawm and Ranger (1983: 4) have observed how such invented traditions occur more frequently when a rapid transformation of society takes place; the Channel Islands went through such transformations and modernisations in their traditional systems of government immediately after the war after the much pressure.

Paul Connerton (1989: 65) has discussed how, generally speaking, elites have been particularly active in the performance of traditions. Such performances often include calendrical, verbal and gestural re-enactments. Together, these repeated liturgies or speeches and gestures or movements combine to form what he calls a 'rhetoric of re-enactment'. This rhetoric of re-enactment by island elites is visible every Liberation Day, in Guernsey's church parade and cavalcade, and in Jersey's speeches and re-enactment of liberation. At these ceremonies, islanders are reminded of their identity as represented by and told in a commemorative master narrative.

Connerton argues that if there is any such thing as collective or social memory, then it resides particularly and especially in commemorative ceremonies (1989: 70–71). Memories are not just stories to be told; they are sustained and enacted by performance. People remember them by being habituated bodily to the performance of them. Thus, memory resides very specifically in the performance of the body itself rather than in the mind. Nancy Woods, too, believes that collective memory is performative, coming into existence at a given time and place through specific forms of memorial activities or 'vectors' (1999: 2).

The performance of the collective framework of Liberation Day can be observed, as Halbwachs suggested, to 'reconstruct an image of the past which is in accord, *in each epoch*, with the predominant thoughts of the society' (Halbwachs 1992: 40, emphasis added). This acknowledgement that images of the past change through time is the impetus in this chapter for analysing the changes in Liberation Day commemorations since 1946, and what this can tell us about Channel Islanders' changing collective memory of (and relationship with) the Occupation. Although the ceremonies have followed broadly similar basic patterns since the end of the war, each time they have been enacted subtle changes have entered the script. Certain narratives and groups of people have been emphasised at the expense of others. Specific historical events have been called into play at particular times; others are rarely, if ever, invoked. As Zerubavel has observed in his study of the performance of commemorative rituals in Israel, people can 'revive and affirm older memories of the past but also modify them ... each act of commemoration makes it possible to introduce new interpretations of the past, yet the recurrence of commemorative performances contributes to an overall sense of continuity of collective memory' (1995: 6). This has strong resonances with the celebrations of Liberation Day.

The concept of a collective memory is problematic (e.g. Olick 1999; Kansteiner 2002; Assmann 2008); it has been criticised for its vagueness and its neglect of both the individual and the interaction and communication between those who contribute to it. It is not a straightforward concept and neither is it politically neutral. It can be contested by various sources and it can be continually renegotiated through time, often with generational shifts, according to social, intellectual and political agendas emanating from different directions. It can also be perceived as an umbrella term for different types of memory (Assmann 2008: 55).

In acknowledgement of this, and drawing from his study of American commemorations, Bodnar (1992: 13–16 and 20) has contrasted the 'official memory' of cultural leaders or authorities with the 'vernacular memory' (sometimes also termed 'popular memory') of the ordinary people, seeing 'public memory' emerging from the intersection of these. Public memory is thus a more nuanced and politically aware way of understanding the collective memory of a society. Because it is subject to both elite manipulation and popular contestation, to study public memory is to explore the tension that emerges between official and popular memory. As Koonz (1994: 261) puts it, 'public memory is the battlefield on which these two compete for hegemony'. Therefore, it is fair to say that Liberation Day can be seen as a battlefield on which official and popular memory compete or bargain to produce a resulting public memory. As Pakier and Stråth (2010b: 13) observe, such bargaining can rarely be integrated into one cohesive narrative. As we shall see, in Jersey two narratives have operated in parallel; one articulated in the centre of St Helier by elites and the other, on a hill above St Helier, at a memorial to forced and slave workers, expressing a very particular aspect of memory of a minority group.

It is worth noting two further considerations. First, in small societies where most people seem to know each other, one rarely operates at the level of an amorphous or anonymous popular or elite 'group'; rather, any such contestation is between individuals whose interests are both often known to one another in advance, and who have an opinion (and make demands) on the memory of the Occupation. Second, the Channel Islands are culturally conservative and have a great affection for tradition. This combination has lead to a tendency to dislike or avoid radical change. This has, to a large extent, lead only to subtle annual changes in Liberation Day ceremonies and a disgruntlement among the population whenever any large change has been mooted, as we shall see. Added to this, Occupation heritage and memory are extremely precious in the islands and any attempt to interfere with or change the status quo can cause considerable upset (e.g. Carr 2010: 259–263). Thus, to analyse memory politics in the islands is often to talk about the memories of very specific individuals or small groups.

In addition to being a display of memory, Liberation Day is also a display of identity. I have often thought that if one wants to understand what it means to be a Channel Islander; what it means to have been occupied—and I believe that these two aspects of identity are interlinked—then the best place to start is to visit the islands on Liberation Day. It is on this occasion that multiple narratives and memories manifest themselves for all to see; it is on this day that Channel Islanders seem to proclaim that *this* is who they are. At this time of year more than any other, islanders visit occupation museums and bunkers, recite family stories and generally celebrate the memory of freedom from German rule. It is, today, an immensely patriotic and proud day, where only positive memories (or negative memories with a positive spin) are invoked.

To give an idea of how the Occupation is perceived today, I recall an incident that took place right at the beginning of my research. I had been invited to dinner at a Cambridge college by a friend and one of the other guests was a historian of the Second World War. 'Of course', he told me, 'occupation is a terribly humiliating experience, and this is the key thing to remember in your work'. I remember being quite startled by this, but not necessarily because I disagreed with his statement. What took me by surprise was that this is not how it is ever talked about or presented in the Channel Islands, and especially not on Liberation Day. I had never heard anyone talk about 'humiliation' in connection with the Occupation.

As I discussed earlier in this volume, when journalist Vitali Vitaliev wrote a critical article in *The Guardian* about the Channel Islands, he was clearly disconcerted by (and uncomprehending of) what he observed during his brief trip. He accused the islanders of having a 'peculiar pride' in having been occupied (Vitaliev 1998: 4). While his observation was superficial, it is partially accurate. Islanders are indeed proud of their wartime experience, but not in the way Vitaliev understood it. While he believed that this was a badly misplaced pride in the perpetrators of Nazism at the expense of victims of Nazi persecution, it is, as

I argue here, about something else entirely. It is a pride in having endured the hardship of occupation; in having survived until liberation at the hands of the British and on the side of victory; and it is especially a pride in moral fortitude. This is nowhere more apparent than on Liberation Day, where pride is part of a master commemorative narrative that has been encouraged since the earliest post-war years, as we shall see. *Pride* has been the positive spin to collective memory, applied to the whole experience from 1946 onwards.

The Channel Islands were one of the few places in Europe that were liberated peacefully. For this reason, the celebration of liberation is a wholly happy event in the islands today, unencumbered by memories of destruction, bombing, fighting and death that characterised the defeat of German forces in many other parts of Europe. These untroubled memories, coupled with the public memory of pride, are perhaps two reasons why Liberation Day is still immensely popular in the Channel Islands and show no sign of waning. It is a day for patriotism, parties and popular entertainment. As well as joyous celebration, it is also a time for commemoration, ceremony and solemnity. But has this always been the case?

Since the end of the war, the focus of attention has changed topographically and commemoratively and the way it has been celebrated has gone through changes which have varied in scope, bringing it sometimes closer and sometimes further away from the events of 1945; there has been no clear linear progression. There is evidence that, through time, Guernsey and Jersey have used modes of celebration which have drawn upon each other's practices, yet they have also strived to be deliberately different. At times they have also borrowed elements from other countries and traditions and from their own distant pre-Occupation past. At the same time, they have maintained now-traditional elements from the earliest days of celebration, calling upon these most especially at key moments of change, most likely in a subconscious effort to mask that change.

Important anniversaries of liberation now take place every five or ten years, and special efforts are made at these times. These anniversaries, especially the 40th, 50th and 60th, have also marked important watersheds and changes in modes of remembrance. Thus, the narratives and memories produced and consumed for and by the public have also changed at this time. Changes from year to year are often incremental and are, for most people, imperceptible. Thus, when looking back, it is hard for islanders to distinguish changes between one year and the next, or to identify precisely what was different about the Liberation Days of their child-hoods, especially in Guernsey where the changes have been less dramatic. That people were unable to pinpoint when exact changes took place or what they were is in itself revealing and speaks to the invisibility of incremental change.

In both Jersey and Guernsey, liberation celebrations and commemorations have gone through four distinct phases where different commemorative narratives have dominated and shaped public memory, although these have been articulated in different ways on each island. Through examining the key events of liberation in 1945 and the years that followed, I hope to explore these phases and the memory narratives that dominate them. My aim is to tease out the causes of the changes, linking these with wider memory politics. I also seek to explore the differences in the way Guernsey and Jersey celebrate, why this has widened over the last 25 years, and what and who have been the causal agents.

It is important to emphasise that this chapter focuses on Liberation Day alone. The narratives that take place on 9 May in Guernsey and Jersey have been preceded, ignored, emphasised or contradicted at other Occupation-related heritage sites across the islands and at other commemorative events. This emphasises the importance of studying all aspects of the legacy of occupation together, as I attempt in this volume, in order to gain a true appreciation and understanding of the wider picture before passing judgement. The failure of previous studies to do this has contributed to superficial or inaccurate interpretations (e.g. Bunting 1995: 336; Lennon and Foley 2007: 66–76).

Analysing Liberation Day, 1946 to the Present

In this chapter, I am interested in way that the two largest Channel Islands celebrate Liberation Day and what events, memories and narratives are recalled at this time. To understand what stories are told and passed on to the next generation is also to gain an insight into generational memory and the sources of pride and identity in the Channel Islands today. This in turn helps us to understand how this aspect of island heritage is used in identity creation and maintenance and helps shape self-perception.

In order to analyse the events which have taken place on Liberation Day between 1946 and the present day, information has been taken from two key sources: local newspapers (the *Guernsey Evening Press and Star* or GEP[1] and the *Jersey Evening Post* or JEP) and souvenir programmes. Newspapers provide reports both of what was organised and how it was received, thus offering an insight into both official, public and popular narratives and memories. Events which took place in the islands' capital towns were the focus of research and particular attention was paid to events on large anniversaries, as these were of particular interest when it came to changes in the way that Liberation Day has been celebrated.

While the local newspapers also report on international and British news, they are predominantly locally focused and inwards looking. The *Guernsey Press and Star* in particular has a reputation (perhaps undeserved) for being non-controversial, wary of criticising or upsetting those in positions of power, and thus tends to maintain the status quo. The local papers are also inevitably constrained by what is deemed acceptable in small islands, where everyone seems to know each other and where news travels quickly by word of mouth. Thus, there is little chance of privacy or anonymity. The newspapers are often fuelled by the kinds of stories and events that result from such conditions.

[1] The Guernsey Evening Press and The Star newspapers merged on 1 November 1965. The paper was renamed as the Guernsey Press and Star in September 1999.

Using participant observation, I also attended Liberation Day celebrations in the Channel Islands on six consecutive years between 2007 and 2012. While I alternated between islands, starting in Jersey in 2007 and finishing in Guernsey in 2012, I was in Guernsey for the 65th anniversary of liberation in 2010. This was an opportunity to witness a cavalcade, a special form of procession or parade which now happens in Guernsey on Liberation Day every five years.

Today, Liberation Day celebrations take place in Guernsey and Jersey on 9 May every year, and the day is a local bank holiday not observed in the UK. The island of Sark celebrates on 10 May, although the commemorations among this small population, numbering only a few hundred, were not part of Liberation Day research. Alderney does not recognise this day as nearly all of the population had evacuated to the UK for the duration of the war. They were not to return to their island until late 1945; Alderney had been devastated during the Occupation and the island became uninhabitable. Thus, it was not until major repair work was carried out (largely by German POWs and British soldiers) that they were able to return en masse. These Channel Islanders have 'Homecoming Day' on 15 December as their day of celebration, and their attitudes towards the Occupation are very different to those in other islands. Homecoming Day has only been a bank holiday in Alderney since 2005, has not been commemorated with special events annually since 1945 and is a low-key affair (Marriner 2009).

The first few Liberation Days after the war were clearly highly influential and set the tone for how all future celebrations should be conducted; it was inevitable that each succeeding celebration would be compared with the one that came before. It was also important that the day would be celebrated and commemorated in the 'right' way and that the 'right' message about the meaning of Allied victory and German defeat was transmitted to the local people. Judt (2002: 160) has remarked that 1945–1948 was 'the period during which Europe's post-war memory was moulded'; the Channel Islands were no exception. As with other European nations, there was an urgent need to frame the memory of war through the lens of patriotism in order to help the post-war reconstruction of their own self-esteem as much as of the islands themselves.

Although by no means clear-cut, various successive and overlapping layered themes have dominated Liberation Day over the years, with new modes of celebration creeping in slowly and growing in dominance over time. At the same time, large anniversaries have been the occasion during which major changes in celebration have been ushered in, although these often look both backwards and forwards in their elements and nowadays are accompanied by the unveiling of memorials, monuments and new museum exhibitions. There are also many elements—commemorative narratives—which characterised both the earliest years and the celebrations today, such as military parades, patriotism expressed through bunting and flag waving, the design of the souvenir programme covers and the displays in shop windows.

All of these elements of Occupation heritage—books, memorials, souvenir programmes and the commemoration of Liberation Day itself—have been characterised by Assmann (1995: 130–132) as stores of 'cultural memory' which 'preserve(s) the store of knowledge from which a group derives an awareness of its unity'. Like collective memory, cultural memory is not fixed and is reconstructed by a society in each era, within its frame of reference. It is something that needs to be 'cultivated' or performed regularly in order to shape and convey that society's self-image. As this form of memory is durable and can be transmitted from generation to generation, it makes it of special interest to me. In this chapter, I hope to show how cultural memory in the Channel Islands, expressed and performed through Liberation Day, is annually 'cultivated' as part of islanders' self-identity and passed down through the generations from 1945 to the present.

Assmann contrasted cultural memory with 'communicative memory', a form of memory based exclusively on the everyday communications which constitute the field of oral history. This sort of memory has a lifespan of 80–100 years at the most, corresponding to a maximum human lifespan of three or four generations. While these two categorisations are useful in helping us to understand the different forms of memory at play on Liberation Day, it must also be emphasised that they are not especially distinct from each other at this time. The period around Liberation Day is a prime time for journalists to collect oral histories from the Occupation generation and publish them in the local papers. These then become part of the cultural memory of the society and are stored as part of their corpus of knowledge about the Occupation and are thus involved in the construction and evolution of cultural memory. Similarly, speeches, radio interviews and broadcasts captured at the time of liberation have, in Jersey especially, been woven into the annual commemorative rituals of Liberation Day. Where communicative and cultural memory still remains distinct in the islands today is in the home or the local pub, where stories are passed down through the generations. Together, both cultural and communicative memory can be considered as the collective memory of the Occupation of the Channel Islands.

Every kind of memory has a narrative. In addition to discussing memory politics, in this chapter I follow Zerubavel (1995: 6, 8, 11–12) in using the concepts of 'commemorative narratives', 'master commemorative narratives' and 'commemorative density' to talk about Liberation Day themes. A commemorative narrative describes a story about a particular past that accounts for an act of remembrance and is used to describe an individual act of commemoration either within Liberation Day, or to describe the narrative of the day as a whole. A master commemorative narrative is used to describe the overarching theme produced by a series of similar commemorative narratives over a number of years which have thus acquired a commemorative density by dint of the consecutive similarity of their theme. As we shall see, the master commemorative narrative of public memory bears a different or partial relationship to the history of the Occupation and gives us an insight into the way in which different generations choose to confront or narrate their history.

While for Zerubavel, the master commemorative narrative represented the political elite's construction of the past, I use it here to describe the narrative of public memory (which may be dominated by either by official/elite or popular memory). While in the Channel Islands the public and official memory narrated on

Liberation Day may sometimes amount to one and the same thing, it is important to acknowledge the contribution that ordinary people can play in contributing to the overall memory narrative.

While it may give the wrong impression of the Channel Islands to overplay the contrast between the wishes of the political elites and that of the people on Liberation Day, sometimes they are at odds in Occupation-related heritage, as this book explores. Liberation Day remains an immensely popular day in the islands and some of the celebrations are organised by the people, for the people, although it is still possible to tease out narratives imposed from above as most official aspects of Liberation Day are organised by local government and special committees. It is also important to note that narratives from above and below overlap; after all, many of those in local government are often from families who experienced occupation and so themselves espouse and vocalise popular memory. Their position in the community does not automatically change the memories and narratives they vocalise.

Events where official narratives and speeches take place are also opportunities for counter-narratives to be expressed among attendees and for people to correct the speech-givers or to verbally express non-recognition of memories evoked. In this way, at a single occasion, memories and narratives from above and below can be and are expressed at the same time and in parallel, even if one is delivered into a microphone and another is murmured *sotto voce* among those listening. Memories are contested continuously and informally as well as formally.

Where commemorative narratives of the Occupation are seriously at odds, running counter to the hegemony of the master commemorative narrative, I use the term 'counter-memory' to describe them. Counter-memories in the Channel Islands have sought to draw attention or to commemorate those who have been otherwise excluded, suppressed or marginalised. They are almost exclusively those of the non-elites; yet thanks to the (sometimes strategic) inclusion of elites during the commemorations of these groups, some have, over time, increased in popularity and even become incorporated into the master commemorative narrative.

The First Liberation Day, 1945

Liberation in the Channel Islands was anticipated. Radio sets had been confiscated by the Germans in June 1942 and retention and discovery carried severe penalties; in fact, some islanders died in penal prisons for radio-related offences (e.g. Sanders 2004: 21–27). Despite this, large numbers of islanders held on to spare sets; in fact, this was probably the most widespread example of defiance in the Channel Islands throughout the Occupation. It has been estimated that as many as one household in four retained their sets.[2] Thus, islanders were able to keep abreast of the war news,

[2] Letter from Bob Le Sueur to author, 23 May 2011.

either directly or through friends. It is clear from Occupation diaries that, just as islanders were aware of the events of D-Day in June 1944—although they could see and hear the evidence of this from the islands and many reported being kept awake at night by planes overhead and the sound of bombs and heavy guns—they knew that the end of the war was coming.

Monthly, from December 1944 onwards, the International Red Cross ship, the *SS Vega*, arrived in both St Helier and St Peter Port to bring food and aid to the starving islands after they were cut off by the Allied invasion of Normandy. Before the war, the Channel Islands had looked to the UK for the import and export of food; during the Occupation such relationships were no longer possible and so the islands had to build up new trading relationships with France, through the port of Granville. After June 1944, this avenue of food procurement was also closed and so the islanders had to rely solely on the food grown in the islands. The occupiers starved along with the islanders, although once parcels arrived from the Red Cross, civilian rations were cut further by the Germans (Cruickshank 2004: 296–299).

As the war progressed, there was an increasing breakdown in law and order (clearly visible in court and prison records) and the local prisons quickly filled up. As an indication of local circumstances towards the end of the war, by April and May 1945 hungry occupying soldiers were begging and stealing from islanders which even the German authorities had to admit was a problem (von Aufsess 1985: 186).

When the outcome of the war was clear, probably after Hitler's death on 30 April but also before this date, islanders grew more daring and risked wearing patriotic symbols openly, as local diarists recorded (Carr 2014). Leslie Sinel reported that, by 1 May 1945, 'some shops were openly selling Union Jacks and other patriotic emblems, and people were carrying these through the streets with the Germans looking on' and by 4 May, people were queuing 'to buy flags and red-white-and-blue favours'. On 5 May, Sinel tells us that these shops were besieged with purchasers. In Guernsey, Violet Carey tells us that, on 5 May, 'all the babies in the prams were waving Union Jacks and the prams were decorated'. Rumours of an imminent surrender preceded the actual event by several days (e.g. Leslie Sinel, 4 May 1945; Violet Carey, 6 May Unpublished).

Meanwhile, the military operation to liberate the Channel Islands was waiting for the signal from SHAEF.[3] Operation Nestegg, as it was called, was to be carried out by the British troops of Force 135. Channel Islanders were deliberately chosen to be among these men, both because of the appropriateness of the decision and so that the men could act as guides for the liberation force. On 7 May, the General Officer Commanding-in-Chief of Southern Command in England sent a message to Vice-Admiral Friedrich Hüffmeier, the officer commanding the German armed forces in the Channel Islands. This message informed him of the signing of the unconditional surrender of all German forces that day and requested him to sign the surrender of the Channel Islands on 8 May. He was also requested to guarantee

[3] Supreme Headquarters Allied Expeditionary Force.

a safe passage for the two British destroyers, HMS *Bulldog* and *Beagle*, which were setting off for the islands. This was acknowledged and agreed. On board both ships were some of the advance party of Force 135, codenamed 'Omelette', which was to act as a token force until the arrival of the main body of the force on 12 May (Lamerton 2000: 101).

On 8 May, Hüffmeier sent his senior naval Staff Officer, Zimmerman, via a minesweeper to meet the *Bulldog*. Zimmerman told those on board that he was not empowered to sign the surrender, but to negotiate the conditions of armistice. He was told that the British would only deal with Hüffmeier or his representative empowered to sign unconditional surrender. Zimmerman then replied that the continued presence of the ships would be taken as a hostile act and they would be fired upon. He was sent away with a letter for Hüffmeier (ibid.: 101–102). The ships withdrew until the *Bulldog* received word that Hüffmeier would send his second in command, General major Heine (commander of the German garrison in Guernsey), to meet them and would guarantee safe passage.

Meanwhile, on land, on the morning of 8 May, Baron von Aufsess (head of civil affairs in the Channel Islands) told Bailiff Victor Carey in Guernsey that the war was over and that an announcement could be made to the States[4] members and the population. A States meeting was then convened at midday, during which the Bailiff announced that flags could be flown from 3 p.m., after the Prime Minister's speech, and that thanksgiving services could take place in churches, but that no further celebration should take place until the Allies arrived. The islanders were also told the good news via the *Guernsey Star*.

Around midnight on 8 May, Heine and Zimmerman arrived on board the *Bulldog*, which had arrived just off Guernsey, with the *Beagle*. The surrender documents were signed by Heine and Brigadier Snow (who was in overall charge of the military aspects of the liberation) at 7.15 a.m. on 9 May off St Peter Port. Snow deliberately wanted to keep the German waiting, both to exercise his authority and so that it could be captured clearly on film in natural daylight (Lamerton personal communication 2011). Heine was told that all swastikas in the Channel Islands should now be lowered and removed (ibid.: 106).

In Guernsey, crowds had been waiting since dawn at the harbour area, from where the two British destroyers were visible. People poured into St Peter Port from all parts of the island, decked in patriotic colours and bunting and waited for the troops. An advance party soon arrived at St Julian's Pier and the two senior officers were taken to the house of Jurat John Leale, head of the Controlling Committee (which carried out the administrative and executive wishes of the States), but as it was early in the morning and he was still in his pyjamas, arrangements were made for them to meet the Bailiff at the Court House later that morning (ibid.: 107). Meanwhile, the rest of the advance party made their way through the cheering crowds to the Royal Hotel on the Glategny Esplanade in

[4] The States of Guernsey and the States of Jersey are the local governments and parliaments of the islands.

St Peter Port, which was to be their temporary headquarters. At 10.15 a.m., the two senior officers met the Bailiff at the Court House and the Union Jack was ceremonially raised just outside as the crowds looked on, some gaining a good vantage point from the top of the war memorial (Harvey 1995: 283). Church bells were rung and the crowds celebrated, besieging the Royal Hotel all day as the soldiers gave out autographs, cigarettes and chocolate (Lamerton 2000: 108).

From sources such as private diaries and the memoirs of Bailiff Alexander Coutanche, we learn that in St Helier, the crowds started to gather in Royal Square as early as 5 May in anticipation of a speech by the Bailiff. On 7 May, Bailiff Coutanche issued a statement urging the population to 'keep calm and dignified and refrain from any sort of demonstration'. On 8 May, VE Day in Europe, the Bailiff announced that it would be appropriate to hoist flags on the conclusion of Winston Churchill's speech (Cruickshank 2004: 319). Loud speakers were erected in Royal Square in St Helier (Pocock 1975: 46) and thousands gathered there to listen. A cheer went up when he announced that 'our dear Channel Islands will be free today', perceived by Channel Islanders today to be the most famous of Churchill's speeches. The Union Jack, American flag and Jersey flag were raised from the Courthouse in Royal Square, the Bailiff announced that Royal Naval units were approaching the Channel Islands, and the national anthem was sung. The Bailiff then went to the prison to release political prisoners (photographic evidence of the freed prisoners exists in Lamerton 2000: 97); to the POW camp, to free the American and British sailors, soldiers and airmen who had made forced landings in the island or who had been captured in the Granville raid of March 1945; and to Pier Road, to free the Algerian POWs (Pocock 1975: 47; although Leo Harris (2004: 137) claims that this latter act was done by his father, John Harris). Although we do not know whether Bailiff Victor Carey freed the political prisoners in Guernsey personally, his relative, Violet Carey, recorded in her diary that the Germans would not allow prisoners in Guernsey to be freed until midnight on 8 May (Evans 2009: 211).

After the surrender had been signed in Guernsey in the early morning of 9 May, Brigadier Snow transferred to the *Beagle* and, leaving the *Bulldog* in Guernsey, set off for Jersey, where the German Commander had been ordered to come by boat to meet him. Knowing the traditional rivalry between the two islands, a second set of surrender documents had been drawn up for Jersey (Lamerton 2000: 110).

After being briefed on events, the Bailiff of Jersey was requested to come on board the *Beagle*. Along with his Attorney General (Charles Aubin) and Solicitor General (Cecil Harrison) he, and Major General Wulf and two of his staff, set off in a German pinnace. The surrender documents were signed on board, where the Bailiff took the opportunity to send a signal to the King and Prime Minister while on board (Pocock 1975: 48). It is likely that Coutanche was invited on board, whereas Carey was not because senior officers came to meet him instead at the Royal Court.[5]

[5] Mark Lamerton, personal communication, June 2011.

At the same time as the Bailiff and Wulf set out for the *Beagle*, they were passed by a launch from the destroyer. Two naval officers and four naval ratings landed at the Albert Pier in St Helier. After being swamped and carried by the cheering crowds, they arrived at the harbour office and hung a Union Jack out of the window. The crowds cheered again when a forced worker from the Organisation Todt (OT) also appeared at the window (Lamerton 2000: 116; Société Jersiaise photographic archive ref. 1000015). The national anthem was sung by the crowds below. Later, RAF formations flew over the island and the advance party of troops arrived, led by Lieutenant Colonel Robinson, the military commander responsible for the surrender of German troops. They headed to the Pomme D'Or hotel, which they took over as a temporary headquarters; it had previously been used as the German naval headquarters. The swastika was lowered and the Union Jack was raised from the hotel's balcony by the harbour master in a spontaneous ceremony as the crowd sang the national anthem again.

Captain Hugh Le Brocq, the first Jersey officer to land, climbed up to Fort Regent, which overlooks St Helier. He lowered the swastika and raised the Union Jack with his batman, which virtually coincided with the landing of the remainder of the troops from the advance party. The celebrations of the population in both islands continued for many days, and over the following weeks and months, people worked hard to get the islands back to normal and ready for the return of evacuees and deportees later that summer, and for the arrival of the first tourists in 1946.

Phase 1: 1946–1949: Master Commemorative Narrative: Military Victory, Patriotism and the War Dead

In the early post-war years, there was much similarity between the celebrations in both Guernsey and Jersey, although Jersey celebrated on 9 May from the beginning, whereas Guernsey chose the second Wednesday in May (because this was when 9 May fell in 1945) until around 1970. In both islands, Liberation Day comprised both solemn acts of commemoration and light-hearted, celebratory elements in different parts of the islands, but most especially in the islands' capitals. From the beginning, the commemorative memory was intensely religious, patriotic and closely tied to both the military (and through this, to the British war memory) and to the island's war dead and veterans.

The day started in Jersey with a service of thanksgiving in each of the island's churches, characterised by patriotic songs and songs of thanksgiving. In St Helier, this was held in St Luke's church next to Howard Davis Park, chosen for its proximity to the Allied War Cemetery and also because many of those in the cemetery had lain overnight in the church before their interment.[6] Among those in the congregation were an assembly of ex-servicemen of two wars, school children,

[6] *Jersey Evening Post,* 2 April 1946.

men from Force 135 and various other dignitaries, including the Lieutenant-Governor, the Bailiff and, as Churchill had declined to visit the island, Home Secretary James Chuter Ede. Battleships docked in the harbour for a few days, and a fly-past of RAF Meteors, Mosquitoes and Spitfires were part of the commemorations. In other parts of the island, liberation carnivals, fetes and a fairground provided entertainment for all. The overriding emotion, the JEP reported, was of a heartfelt thankfulness that the island was indeed free of the enemy and that it was on its way to complete recovery.

In 1946 in Guernsey, the Lieutenant-Governor's office invited representatives of the armed forces to visit to help commemorate the first anniversary of liberation. It was deemed that the pleasure of the people of Guernsey would be 'very greatly enhanced' by their presence.[7] The invitation was readily accepted, and the island was visited by HMS *George V* and the Commander-in-Chief of the Home Fleet, Admiral Sir Edward Syfret. Six squadrons from the RAF also flew over St Peter Port. Church services of thanksgiving took place all over the island, including the town church in St Peter Port, which was decorated with the British Legion flag and attended by detachments from the army and navy. As part of a narrative that included acts of homage to the war dead, wreaths were laid on the island's war memorial; this was a practice that was joined, from 1950, by the laying of a wreath at the White Rock, where 34 islanders died in the bombing raid at the harbour on 28 June 1940. As the wreath-laying on Liberation Day was no longer reported in the paper after 1953, it is assumed here that the practice moved to Armistice Day alone at around this time.

While music, dancing and fireworks characterised the evening celebrations, once the solemnity of the church service and wreath laying had passed, the cavalcade took place. From the beginning, this has involved a parade of themed floats of a celebratory nature, with various classes of entry often related to age groups, mode of transport or parish of entry (such as decorated bicycles for children under 10 years of age, or decorated floats from a certain parish). As Heaume (2006) has discussed, decorated floats and parades have a long pre-war tradition in the island for a range of events and so was, perhaps, a natural choice for the celebration of liberation. The theme of cavalcade floats also provides us with a very useful lens through which to observe the articulation of war memory, as we shall see.

Guernsey's cavalcade of 1946 was reported to have been half a mile in length[8] and led by the traditional patriotic figure of John Bull, who was to lead all future cavalcades in the early days (Fig. 5.1). Behind him came marching military bands and parades, including a local training corps, a band from HMS *George V* and a squadron of the RAF, followed by the cavalcade of 22 classes of bikes, fancy dress and floats and ex-servicemen. Disabled ex-servicemen were not given a part in the cavalcade but watched from the pavement. At the back of the cavalcade, followed only by a solitary motorbike, the penultimate class was titled 'Hitler's Guests—open

[7] Guernsey Archives reference BF/19–28/11, Liberation and Victory celebrations, 1945–1948.

[8] *Jersey Evening Post*, 10 May 1946.

Fig. 5.1 Liberation Day cavalcade by Eric Sirett (© and courtesy Peter Sirett)

to anyone imprisoned by the Germans'.[9] This had just one entry: Roy Machon, who was deported to a German prison, where he was ill-treated for making V-for-victory badges in support of an Allied victory. Styling himself as the 'V King' at the cavalcade, Roy expressed his resistance record with pride. That such a class of entry was incorporated into the Liberation Day commemorative narrative would prove to be an anomaly rarely repeated. As it was, Machon could only frame his narrative in terms that were acceptable at that time.

The competitors and the spectators alike made it an intensely patriotic occasion and the Guernsey Evening Press commented that the 'Liberation Day Anniversary will go down as Guernsey's day of red, white and blue'.[10] The *prix d'honneur*, awarded to the best float, was titled 'At Last', depicting a sailor hoisting the Union Jack above a bedraggled swastika. The rear of the lorry showed a German soldier seeking shelter in a foxhole with a bulldog biting his retreating hindquarters. A child dressed as Winston Churchill won first prize in his class.

If the commemorative part of the proceedings in Jersey focused on the war dead, veterans, military might, victory and the armed forces, then the celebrations that followed could potentially allow other narratives to come forth. Jersey celebrated with a carnival procession which took place only twice, in 1946 and 1949. As in Guernsey's cavalcade, narratives of patriotism and of victory over the enemy predominated and entries in 1946 included 'Britannia—Long Live our King',

9 *Guernsey Evening Press*, 7 May 1946: 2.

10 *Guernsey Evening Press*, 10 May 1946: 1.

'St George and the Dragon', 'Jersey at Peace, Swastika in Pieces'. Other entries made references to the last desperate months of the war. These included 'The Vega', 'A Canadian Red Cross Parcel' and 'Desperation, Liberation, Deliverance'.

In 1947, Field Marshall Montgomery visited the islands and, in 1948, the front page of the GEP was taken up with the story of how Guernseyman Major Wallace Le Patourel, who was awarded the Victoria Cross in 1942, was officially welcomed home to his native island and honoured by the Lieutenant-Governor, Sir Philip Neame, another holder of the same award. In ways such as this, the narrative of the veteran was accorded high status on Liberation Day in this period.

The annual cavalcade in Guernsey was still immensely popular in 1948. The *Guernsey Evening Press* records that there were 22 classes of entries marching, cycling or driving behind the figure of John Bull, including decorated cycles with cyclists in costume; pedestrians in costume; school tableaux; decorated agricultural vehicles; decorated lorries and motor cars; old military uniforms and Occupation transport. The float which garnered the most attention in the GEP and the *prix d'honneur* was one featuring a bulldog with his master (dressed in naval uniform), reclaiming his kennel from a man dressed as Hitler, with the caption 'Total Surrender'. The junior section was won by a boy in a dual costume that was Winston Churchill on one side of his body and Field Marshall Montgomery on the other.

It is interesting to observe that the themes of floats and costumes in the first few years of Guernsey's cavalcades were fairly fluid. There was a predominance of patriotic and victory-related floats and these were rewarded with prizes, which give us an insight into the subtle ways in which official memory was encouraged during this period. Other tableaux, characters and float themes, however, were also part of the cavalcade. These were perhaps most apparent in 1946, where clowns, nursery rhyme characters and children in general fancy dress made an appearance. By 1948, the cavalcade gained a good number of floats submitted by local businesses, who managed to advertise their products in a relevant way, such as the Guernsey Brewery Company who had a float titled 'Pony Ale Liberates Energy'. This was also a sign that the island was coming back to life and businesses were re-establishing themselves.

Although general fancy dress and floats unrelated to the master commemorative narrative were in evidence for the first few years, there is a clear indication that certain cavalcade themes were beginning to be cemented in tradition, and certain characters and floats frequently reappeared. The personification of John Bull and Winston Churchill were always taken on by islanders, and the float winner in 1949, for example, featured a re-enactment of a German walking down the pier steps to a waiting naval vessel, obviously to be taken away as a POW. Warships, soldiers and the national anthem were also dominating features of Liberation Day in the early years.

In Jersey over the next few years, the same formula was repeated in the morning as in 1946, with a service of thanksgiving in the Howard Davis Park and the 'Act of Homage', as it was called, at the Allied War Cemetery. While this was to become a fixed aspect of Liberation Day for decades to come, by 1950

Liberation Day was described (despite the now-annual funfair) as a 'quiet one, with few special arrangements and attractions'. Islanders 'took the matter in their own hands and celebrated in their own way—chiefly on the beaches and bays of the island',[11] suggesting that quiet introspection and family-focused modes of remembrance were chosen by the population in the absence of fixed events. The quiet nature of the fifth anniversary of liberation was also noted in Guernsey, where the day was described as a 'complete flop' because of the lack of organised events.[12] For the first time since the war there was no cavalcade, but it returned in 1951 (and then disappeared until 1960), which was described as 'the most outstanding Liberation Day to date'.[13]

For the first four years in Guernsey, liberation celebrations were organised by a two committees: the Cavalcade Committee and the States Liberation Committee, who ensured coordination of events (Heaume 2006: 41). But to what extent did these committees dictate how the event was celebrated, and did the local population appreciate and agree with the mode of celebration? A Guernsey newsletter published in the JEP on 11 May 1950 shows us that people were criticising the event because it did not take place on 'the great day' itself (as in Jersey), but a day or two later to suit 'business convenience' and decided upon by 'mere Statesmen' who treated it as a 'moveable feast'. It is clear that people in the two islands were being kept abreast of how the other island was celebrating, were suspicious that events were better in the rival island and also perhaps found it easier to complain to a non-local audience. This is borne out in the Guernsey correspondent's newsletter, which is worth quoting at length here:

> Watching the correspondence columns of the 'Evening Post' recently I see that there was considerable perturbation in the minds of several Jersey people because Jersey was not miming Guernsey and marking the occasion of Liberation with public rejoicing and festivity … I must dispel from the minds of Jersey people any fallacious belief they may be holding that Guernsey is making any big public manifestation of the day. That is entirely wrong—it is officialdom and island officials who staged big 'to-do's' on Guernsey's May 10. The general public, the man and woman in the street, are not being specially catered for at all.

The correspondent went on to state that, despite the military presence, the visiting battleship and the visiting dignitaries, there was nothing for the enjoyment of the young and old in the way of 'general festivity and rejoicing'. He went on to describe the military and 'warlike' events as 'abhorrent', 'antiquated' and 'out of place' as they glorified war and bloodshed (Liberation Day events of this era included the arrival of HMS Victorious in 1948 and HMS Illustrious in 1950; a parachute jumping display in 1950 and a football match with the British army in 1953). The correspondent requested, instead, that 9 May be made a bank holiday to 'revere memory' and so that people could have a day of 'real peace, remembrance

---

[11] *Jersey Evening Post*, 10 May 1950.

[12] *Guernsey Star*, 11 May 1950: 1.

[13] *Guernsey Evening Press*, 11 May 1951.

and thanksgiving' to do what they pleased with the 'same freedom that was once again ours on that Great Day, 9 May 1945'.[14]

If this correspondent was representative of the average person on the street in Guernsey, and there is little evidence to either support or contradict this, then it seems clear that this mode of celebration and commemoration was imposed from above. Despite this, the popularity of Liberation Day was clear, and people were freely taking part in the cavalcade and decorating and submitting their own floats. It is unclear how free the choice of design was and what informal or formal pressures may have been brought to bear upon choices which today are vetted by a special committee. It is possible that they may have had to be first cleared by the Cavalcade Committee or parish representatives. In any case, themes which conformed to narratives of victory, patriotism and military superiority were certainly favoured and may have needed little encouragement. Jersey's commemorations, too, were led by elites and dominated by military narratives in this period. Just how were the events on Liberation Day during those first few years being moulded?

Sanders (2005: 235) has explored how, immediately after the war, the Occupation was presented by Home Secretary Herbert Morrison to the House of Commons after his trip to the Channel Islands. His speech was 'devoid of the humiliation, desperation or compromise of principle occurring across the rest of Europe' and failed to include the forced and slave labourers, resisters and other eventual victims of Nazism. 'It was', he wrote, 'a view of history that left no place for the complexities and contradictions of enemy occupation'. The islanders were encouraged to 'lock into the British wartime history rather than dwell on the "dark years"'.

Sanders suggested that the UK government felt a sense of embarrassment over the abandonment of the islands in 1940 and so wanted to improve relations by 'adopting a conciliatory position'. Thus, after the war, with no other place to fit their war memory than the 'straightjacket of UK war memory—the Churchillian paradigm—islanders locked into the celebration of sublime heroism and unwavering steadfastness' (Sanders 2005: 256). And, as the Churchillian paradigm dictated that the British were a nation of victors not victims, this is why and how the first few years of Liberation Day celebrations focused on patriotic narratives of thankfulness and loyalty towards the British, military victory, and the remembrance of islanders who had died while fighting in the British armed forces. The UK actively contributed to this narrative by sending not just warships and soldiers to the islands for Liberation Day celebrations, but also government officials and royalty. In 1946, the Home Secretary was sent to the islands to give the first Liberation Day address in Guernsey. In his speech, he emphasised the high proportion of Channel Islanders who had served in the armed forces (more than one in ten of the population, as the GEP noted),[15] thus strongly reinforcing the link between the islands and the UK.

[14] *Jersey Evening Post*, 11 May 1950: 1.

[15] *Guernsey Evening Press*, 10 May 1946: 1.

It seems clear that this commemorative narrative was imposed from above for the first four or five years of the celebration of Liberation Day. We know that special committees oversaw the events: they did not occur spontaneously, even if the desire of the population to celebrate in some way was real and spontaneous. It is also clear that the British government was prepared to send across warships, war leaders, royalty and military personnel to take part in the celebrations. Complaints in the local papers about the military nature of the celebrations hint that this is not how the average islander necessarily wished to celebrate; in fact, after the first five years when the big displays were removed (or the narrative was deemed to need no reinforcement), Liberation Day became a noticeably quieter affair. The form of memory being articulated most strongly during this period can thus be characterised as an elite or official memory, encouraged by political leaders and supported by the British government and armed forces.

Official memory was also shaped by and expressed through the front cover designs of souvenir programmes. Guernsey's programmes from this period are interesting to observe. While the illustration for 1946 was of a red, white and blue sunrise over the island with the word 'LIBERTY' emerging from the sun's rays, by 1948 the patriotic figure of John Bull with his Union Jack waistcoat graced the front cover. He was flanked by two shields showing Guernsey's crest and the flag of England and St George depicted with a sword in the centre, presumably the sword with which St George slew the dragon. The following year, a knight on horseback, sword in hand, and the same two shields made up the patriotically coloured programme. By 1951, the programme featured the island's war memorial, complete with St George standing on top, the dragon's head under his foot and the Union Jack flying behind him. Again, the colour scheme is patriotic. We can see that the themes of patriotism, the war dead, and military might and victory over a dangerous enemy echo the same themes as the Liberation Day celebrations during this period. This was the positive war narrative that the Channel Islands wished to project.

In examining the overwhelmingly positive war narratives of formerly occupied countries, Confino (2005: 46) has explored how, in the wake of the Second World War, Europeans' 'inaccurate' memories helped them interpret their post-1945 world. He discusses how, in many countries, certain heroic and proud memories were fundamental to national recovery and creating and sustaining identity after the war. Unlike the Channel Islands, most countries focused on narratives of victimhood, which Confino argues was a 'defence mechanism to avoid moral responsibility for their roles as Holocaust perpetrators, bystanders and collaborators' (ibid.: 50). To invoke a similar argument to explain the blinkered focus on unwavering patriotism and pride in military victory would undoubtedly prove dissonant to Channel Islanders, but these are the kinds of issues which represent the complexities of occupation, and which the British government helped the islands to sweep under the carpet while at the same time helping them into the 'straightjacket of UK war memory'.

Just as the master commemorative narrative during those early years focused on military victory and patriotism, it also focused on the cult of the fallen soldier just as much as on veterans, even though Gillis (1994: 13) consigned such a cult to the pre-war years because of the impossibility of ignoring the civilian casualties of war of the Second World War. However, because the acknowledgement of civilian casualties in the Channel Islands would have involved a focus on resisters, political prisoners, Jews and forced workers, it seems to have been deemed safer to focus on the war dead in the commemorative narratives of Liberation Day and to keep the cemetery pilgrimages alongside the military parades.

Despite their famed peaceful and tranquil nature today, the Channel Islands were rather tense places to be immediately after the war. In his study of Israeli national traditions, Zerubavel (1995: xix) found that the commemoration of historical events was 'not only a powerful means of reinforcing social solidarity but also an arena of struggle over power and control'. Given the borderline civil unrest in Jersey and the complaints and disquiet in Guernsey immediately after the Occupation (e.g. Sanders 2005: 237f), social solidarity was certainly in need of reinforcement at this time, and getting the islands back under control would have been of paramount importance. Liberation Day was also an opportunity for civic and religious leaders to give speeches which could attempt to heal divisions in society, such as those which existed between returned evacuees and those who had stayed in the islands. These leaders were interested in loyalty to the status quo and the continuity of their own institutions, which were threatened with reform at this time (Cruickshank 2004: 346–349).

By reinforcing official memory from above through successive and repetitive ceremonies and modes of celebration, the authorities were encouraging the general population to accept and adopt official memory as their own. Public memory and official memory were thus one and the same during this period. That local people were willing to accept this is indicated in their similar willingness to take part; as Connerton (1989: 44) argues, to take part in a ceremony or ritual is to assent to its meaning. Pushing aside their darker memories associated with the 'complexities and contradictions' of occupation, they were willing to embrace narratives which celebrated British victory. As the official memory overlapped with real experience (in that islanders did fight and die on the side of the Allies, and that during the Occupation the vast majority were patriotic and loyal), many islanders were, it seems, also prepared to accept this partial version of events in favour of a narrative which involved the full story, warts and all. In any case, the 'full story' of the years of occupation has only in recent years begun to be been incorporated into Liberation Day events, even if it has been incorporated at an earlier date into other sites of memory elsewhere in the islands.

This master commemorative narrative or partial version of events was clearly acceptable to the people because it was and has been immensely long-lasting; elements from the very earliest days of commemoration still continue today. It can thus be described as a highly successful narrative. Gildea (2002) has explored the success or failure of the 'myths' or narratives of the past that the politicians, media and intellectuals told in post-war France in order to rally the public to their policies. Those which were only weakly connected to collective memory were likely to be overridden by those which had a powerful connection with collective memory. Thus, the long-term success of the British war narrative in the Channel

Islands suggests that it chimed strongly with collective memory—or, at least, with a *desired* collective memory. People in the Channel Islands were happy, it seems, to keep at arm's length the darker aspects of Occupation memory, which were not to resurface for many decades.

Phase 2: The 1950s and 1960s: Master Commemorative Narrative: Collective Amnesia

I characterise the period of the 1950s and 1960s as the years of 'collective amnesia'. This is not to suggest that the population of the Channel Islands had actually forgotten the events of the years of Occupation; indeed, silence can often be associated with remembering just as much as forgetting (Passerini 2003: 248). However, islanders found that it was easier not to talk about it if they were to successfully put the past behind them and move forward. As Jerseyman Bob Le Sueur, who was a young man during the Occupation, put it, 'there was almost a subconscious wish to repress memories which had been unpleasant, to close a disagreeable interlude, to get on with a future. Also most of us were incredibly busy at work ... there simply was no time'.[16]

To a certain extent, this era of amnesia grew out of the immediate post-war years' commemorations, which did not allow a narrative of the full realities of Occupation. However, once this version of events was impressed on the population as the way that 'traditional' commemoration would take place, and once the days of cavalcades and large military presences had diminished (although not vanished), celebrations of the 1950s and 1960s became relatively quiet affairs, although the patriotic nature of celebrations did not vanish. The day was still an occasion for bunting, flags and, in Guernsey, the military church parade which comprised many veterans. It was also marked by an increasing number of sporting events, such as football matches and cycling races, and became a day for healthy, family fun, unrelated to war memory. In Jersey, this included a gymnastics display and fireworks (1951), a football match (1953), a horse show and gymkhana (1956), a car rally, cycling race, golf competition and carnival ball (1957), a Liberation Day Walk (1962); and, in Guernsey, a funfair (1954), a youth rally (1958), a bed-pushing race (1961) and an inter-school race (1962).

The growing quietness of the day was duly noted by local reporters, who commented that it was 'typical of the people of Guernsey that, by and large, they will celebrate Liberation Day quietly, without fuss, but with a sincerity which can never be doubted and a gratitude that is immeasurable'.[17] Three years later, it was observed that 'the spectacular demonstrations with which we used to celebrate Liberation Day are things of the past. Many deplore the fact, but their absence is

[16] Letter from Bob Le Sueur to author, 23 May 2011.

[17] *Guernsey Evening Press*, 13 May 1954.

no proof that we are already beginning to forget. Thanksgiving can assume other forms'.[18]

In Jersey, the old mode of commemoration was also on the wane. By 1956, the JEP reported that the service in the Howard Davis Park had been discontinued and the British Legion pilgrimage to the Allied War Cemetery had had an 'extremely poor response' from the public.[19] Yet, 2 years later, a letter to the editor of the JEP complained that there was 'no opportunity to gather and share these thoughts and prayers and to recapture for one day the comradeship of an imprisoned people', and that the day should be made into a real day of remembrance and thanksgiving 'both for those who died and for those who lived, not just another day off work to do anything'.[20] Not everyone appreciated the demise of the old modes of remembrance of war.

Even before the war began to fade in people's memories, Liberation Day began to be a time when the Occupation itself was not explicitly invoked. While the exception to this could have been in the pageantry and cavalcades at large anniversaries, which might have provided an outlet for traumatic memories, in the event they were hijacked by other concerns. It is perhaps no coincidence that cavalcades were mostly discontinued in Guernsey during this period, taking place only in 1951, 1960 and not again until 1975. The 1960 cavalcade was described as 'small but good'.[21] All thirteen floats were described in the local press and not one had an occupation or liberation theme, which made this cavalcade almost unique in Liberation Day history. It was, however, accompanied by veteran and youth marching bands.

In Jersey, the only event of this type during this period was the tenth anniversary celebrations, when the 'Pageant of Jersey: from Viking to V-day' was held in 1955. The pageant was held in an arena and told the story of Jersey in ten vignettes or 'chapters' of key events of each century of the island's history, read out by a commentator. Chapter ten was, inevitably, 'The Liberation, 1945', and events of the Occupation were depicted, centring on the backdrop of Royal Square. The tableau started with a re-enactment of the surrender of the island, which took place through the painting of a large white cross painted in the Square. This was then transformed into a swastika as actors, dressed as German soldiers and riding motorbikes and marching, circled the arena as one read out the proclamation of occupation. A Gestapo arrest, the dire food shortage and starvation were depicted or invoked, as were the fortifications, the forced workers and the confiscation of radios. The chapter ended with the arrival of liberating soldiers in Royal Square and the Union Jack and flag of Jersey flown over the Royal Court. Although this tableau formed the grand finale of the pageant, it was but one of ten, and thus echoed the marginalisation of the occupation years that characterised this period.

[18] *Guernsey Evening Press*, 8 May 1957: 2.

[19] *Jersey Evening Post*, 10 May 1956.

[20] *Jersey Evening Post*, 10 May 1958: 4.

[21] *Guernsey Evening Press*, 10 May 1960: 1.

It is also interesting to observe that two categories of victims of Nazism (political prisoners and forced workers) featured in this pageant. Like the appearance of Roy Machon, the 'V King', in the 1946 cavalcade in Guernsey, we can see these as the exertions of popular memory upon the stage of public memory.

Such periods of amnesia were paralleled elsewhere in formerly occupied Europe. Rousso (2007: 29) has identified strong similarities between the evolution of public memories since the end of the war in European countries that had been occupied by the Germans, the second phase of which was also characterised by official silence and forgetting and which lasted until the late 1960s. In the Channel Islands, this era of forgetting was no different to that which had been imposed since 1946. The UK war narrative still held without the sturdy and visible props of visiting battleships and regiments from the armed forces, but local veterans and youth corps combined with local elites to keep the Churchillian paradigm alive.

Phase 3: 1970–1984: Master Commemorative Narrative: Remembering and Reliving the Occupation

Judt (2010: 448) has remarked how, at the beginning of the 1960s, Europe was run by and for old men (such as Churchill, Adenauer and De Gaulle) and their authority passed unquestioned; yet, by the end of the decade, these men were dead and their authority had been withdrawn from most spheres of social life.

The 1960s was a decade in which Europeans began to turn away from ideological politics; it was a time of protest, especially by students, against the status quo, against those in authority and against their parents' generation in general. Among a number of other things, they protested against the post-war ideologies that prevailed in their countries, often connected with the war narratives upon which their governments legitimised their right to rule. In France, for example, students protested against the De Gaulle government about the 'myth' of the resistance and the silence over collaboration (Rousso 1991: 99). In Italy, students protested against the portrayal of the memory of the anti-Fascist partisan resistance (Fogu 2006). In West Germany, too, the post-war generation spoke out about the silence of their parents' generation surrounding the subject of the Third Reich, and the failure of the country to come to terms with and to accept moral responsibility for Nazism (Kansteiner 2006: 119; Judt 2010: 416–417). The period between the late 1960s and the mid-1980s was one of profound change all over Europe as the post-war generation challenged the memories that 'were collectivised, officialised and institutionalised by the survivors of the war' (Fogu and Kansteiner 2006: 296).

In the Channel Islands, this period was also marked by the departure from the stage of the 'old men' who had been in positions of power during the Occupation. For example, Jersey wartime Bailiff, Alexander Coutanche, died in 1973; Cecil Harrison, his Solicitor General during the Occupation who later went on to become Bailiff, died in 1962. In Guernsey, Victor Carey, already an old man during the

Occupation, died in 1957. His successor as Bailiff, and first wartime president of the Controlling Committee, Ambrose Sherwill, died in 1968. His successor on the Controlling Committee, John Leale, died in 1969.

Yet, during this period, the first post-war generation and those who had been children during the Occupation did not seek to cast off the shackles of the British war memory that had dominated the Channel Islands. They did, however, begin to look back towards the dark years of 1940–1945 and open up a new field of discourse and research. As Sanders (2005: 257) has observed, this focused upon German fortifications, which he describes as a 'superficially apolitical domain where it was valid to ask questions and be curious'. Of course, these 'apolitical' fortifications were nothing of the sort as we saw in Chap. 3; yet this is how they were treated.

While this generation had no experience of the Occupation, their knowledge of this period was shaped not only by stories told in the home, but also by witnessing annual Liberation Day commemorations. While many from this generation speak of the reluctance of their parents to speak about the Occupation, others have inherited only light-hearted anecdotes which invariably tell of times when the occupiers were outwitted by the cunning of the islanders. However, as they grew up during a period when Liberation Day commemorations were small scale, localised or low key, their curiosity was piqued about a period that was discussed obliquely at home and was not alluded to in the popular celebrations on 9 May each year.

As they reached maturity in the mid-1960s and 1970s, their way of working through the legacy of Occupation manifested itself through a desire look back and reanimate or vicariously experience the event that they had missed, rather than to look forward resolutely as their parents had done. This was expressed in several ways, such as through a craze for collecting Occupation militaria, which led to the opening of a small number of second-generation private Occupation Museums in the mid-1960s and explored in Chap. 2. They also started the Channel Islands Occupation Society (CIOS) in Guernsey in 1961, the Jersey branch of which was set up 10 years later, as a forum where they could get together and discuss their interests. The society was not restricted to those born after the Occupation; leading lights included men such as Michael Ginns, who had, as a teenager, been deported from Jersey to Wurzach civilian internment camp in Germany in 1942. Such men were and still are very highly respected for their experiences, knowledge and stories of the Occupation years.

The membership of these organisations grew in number and influence, garnered increasing respect, and was at least partly responsible for ushering in a new era in Liberation Day celebrations in the 1970s. It is perhaps not surprising that the return of Liberation Day celebrations in Guernsey to 9 May (rather than the second Wednesday in May) took place at this time.

The first post-war generation exhaustively excavated, restored, refurbished and wrote books and articles about bunkers during this period, work they continue today. On the continent, such research might have resulted in questions being asked about forced and slave labour and the associated abuse of their human rights, about the role of Jews as labour, or about the role of local people in working for the OT—or conversely, in sheltering or feeding escaped OT workers. However, in Guernsey and Jersey, the research focused on the German soldiers who manned the fortifications; the type and capacity of the guns attached to the emplacements which dotted the islands; and the correct type of fittings and fixtures which should be used to restore the bunkers authentically. The interpretation of these structures was sanitised so that it would not offend or challenge visitors. It was not emotionally engaged; rather, it was decidedly detached, objective and cold (c.f. Uzzell and Ballantyne 2008). Thus, the work of the CIOS did not emerge as any kind of counter-memory to the British war narrative which still held sway in the islands at this time.

We can argue that, during these decades, the British war narrative was still strong enough to shelter the Channel Islanders' collective memory from the changes that were happening elsewhere on the continent. That they are inward-looking and perceive themselves as almost immune to events elsewhere in Europe is an accusation that is often levelled at the islands, despite historical evidence to the contrary; however, to have an insular mentality is probably an inescapable part of islands everywhere. Such perceived disconnection from the rest of the world contributes to the longevity of narratives, and when that narrative is especially dominant, it is unsurprising that the Channel Islands did not probe as deep into the years of Occupation as did others on the continent.

If the celebrations of Liberation Day during the 1970s and early 1980s included an investigation into the past, but one that did not dig too deep, this manifested itself primarily by reliving the past (especially on Liberation Day), using the material culture of the past, but the vision of the past that was invoked was a selective one.

The 1970s and the first post-war generation were to usher in a departure from the mode of celebration of the previous decades but, before their influence began to dominate by the mid-1970s, old themes still held sway at the 25th anniversary of liberation in 1970, especially in Jersey. This was the first opportunity for the post-Occupation generation to witness a grand spectacle of the immediate post-war celebrations which were invoked on this anniversary. It was this as much as anything else which fuelled the interest and participation of a new generation. Ironically, it seems that a re-invocation of the oldest modes of celebration was responsible for inspiring something new in the years that followed.

The programme for the 25th anniversary in Jersey, described in the JEP of 8 May 1970, included a visit by a Royal Naval landing craft and frigate; military displays by the Royal Corps of Signals and the Royal Hussars; a fly-past of a Spitfire and Lancaster and a parade of military bands. One of the largest gatherings at Howard Davis Park for many years took place. There was also a parade of floats with themes such as 'Distribution of Red Cross parcels' (St John's Ambulance), 'We carried on' (Girl Guides) and 'Vega arriving in Jersey' (Girls Brigade), 'Progress since the Liberation' (Scouts), 'Farming implements of the Occupation years' (Young Farmers club), representing a mixture of Liberation Day phases. Marching bands were represented by cadet corps and youth associations, and regiments from the visiting ships.

While official memory still dominated, popular memory found a voice in the parade line-up, as Jersey internees deported to Wurzach camp in Germany marched, as did the *Anciens Combattants* and *Prisonniers de Guerre* in Breton costume (who had presumably come across from France). The Jersey Trades Council, led by Jersey Communist Party member Norman Le Brocq, had a float depicting the illegal printing and distribution of leaflets and news during the Occupation. That this number of counter-narratives were articulated at a single time and allowed to become part of displayed public memory attests to a weakening in official memory at this time, caused by the demise of the older generation. However, as the parade was the place where popular memory was allowed a greater voice, it is unsurprising that it emerged most strongly here. Elsewhere, official memory still held strong in other memory arenas associated with the military.

The following year, more new narratives were literally cemented into the Liberation Day commemorations in Jersey by the erection of a public memorial at the former Strangers' Cemetery at Westmount in St Helier, now a crematorium. This commemorated the 101 forced and slave workers who died in the island and were buried in this location during the Occupation. Although the memorial instigators had been meeting on Liberation Day at Westmount for a number of years, the previous focus of their commemoration had been the two moveable slabs which remembered the Spanish Republican and Russian dead.

The ceremony at Westmount was attended only by Jersey Communist Party members, people from the Spanish Republican communities, and by people in the island who had helped to shelter workers during the Occupation. It was a low-key affair and no island dignitaries attended because it was also an occasion for political speeches by members of the Jersey Communist Party. During the Cold War, no politician wished to be associated with such meetings. Thus, the ceremony formed an alternative, a counter-narrative, to the celebrations in town for these communities, and the feeling of 'them and us' was to continue for many years to come.[22]

As the authority of the wartime generation faded with their passing or their retirement, the voices and desires of the post-war generation were increasingly given space. This became particularly noticeable from about 1975 onwards, when they used Liberation Day as a special day to recreate the event they had missed. The event in question, however, was not the original day of liberation in 1945, but the events of the Occupation. Thus, from this time, 9 May became a day for Occupation-related museum exhibitions, parades of wartime vehicles (1977 and 1979) and newspaper articles about the war years (1975). In 1983, Richard Heaume, Director of the German Occupation Museum in Guernsey and founder of the CIOS, held a Liberation Field Day, featuring military and 1940s vehicles and uniforms. The local paper noticed that some attendees even arrived in German uniform. In 1984, this event was repeated as a Liberation Day Rally of military and vintage vehicles, organised by the Guernsey military vehicle group, again with some people appearing in German uniforms. Those who took part in such rallies and parades

[22] Interview with Gary Font, 10 May 2011.

were probably CIOS members, whose collections of militaria included vehicles and uniforms just as much as guns and swastikas. Such events provided a good excuse to show off their collections and indulge in role-playing, which was how their vicarious desire to re-experience the Occupation years expressed itself.

In 1975 in Guernsey, the cavalcade was reinstated after an absence of several years. Richard Heaume led the committee (Heaume 2006: 42). Old favourites dominated the show, including the Vega (which won first prize), a Guernsey donkey[23] kicking a Nazi invader, and a scene aboard HMS *Bulldog* of the Germans signing the surrender. Other floats had titles such as 'We kicked them out!', 'Liberation from Starvation', 'We Were Prepared' and 'Guernsey Donkey—Free at Last'. New elements which reflected the passage of time since the war were reflected in two of the entries: 'Grandad—survivor of the occupation' and 'Grandad goes to war'. By 1980, the cavalcade comprised nearly 100 wartime cars, lorries, jeeps, bicycles and motorcycles, and one of these vehicles was used as the design for the souvenir programme. The bulk of the vehicles belonged to the military conservation group, showing that even though the tradition and the themed floats continued, the transport used to model the floats was no longer chosen at random. The old theme was given a new twist. While elements of the cavalcade paid homage to those who suffered during the Occupation, this was restricted to just two entries: a decorated bicycle entitled 'Return from Biberach' (the civilian internment camp to where many hundreds of islanders were deported) and a pedestrian in costume parading under the theme of 'Prisoners' Peace'. It should be noted that both of these groups chose to represent themselves through a post-war, post-Liberation lens rather than focusing on wartime suffering.

By the end of the 1970s, the growing curiosity in the war years of the post-war generation peaked in the restoration and refurbishment of German bunkers at Noirmont Point in Jersey by enthusiasts in the CIOS. Jersey led the way in this activity, with Guernsey following soon after. Members of the society started conducting special tours around the bunkers at Noirmont on Liberation Day in 1979, and this became an annual event, with other open or renovated bunkers and fortifications substituted or added to the itinerary. In Guernsey, the German naval tower at Pleinmont in the southwest coast of the island was restored and reopened on Liberation Day in 1982 by Willi Hagedorn, a former German naval signals officer. The restoration of several other fortifications in the island followed.

In the 1970s and 1980s, the memorial service at the Westmount crematorium in Jersey slowly grew in size as representatives from other associations started to attend, such as the French consul and the RAF association (1981), a Russian air force officer, a former Soviet slave worker and a representative from the UN association (1982) and a representative from the Polish consulate (1984). In 1981,

[23] Traditional inter-island rivalry dictates that those from Jersey call those from Guernsey, 'donkeys', while Jersey people are called 'crapauds' (toads) in return. In addition to recognising it as a term of abuse, Guernsey people also proudly refer to themselves as 'donkeys'. A 'Guernsey donkey' connotes either someone with long Guernsey ancestry or else someone who is incredibly stubborn (and often both). Stubbornness is held to be a typically 'donkey-ish' (i.e. Guernsey) trait.

70–80 people attended.[24] By 1985, people from five different countries are reported to have attended[25] including, for the first time, a member of the island's establishment, deputy Bailiff Peter Crill, although Philip Bailhache (later to be Bailiff) attended in 1980, the year after the death of Francisco Font, spokesperson of the Spanish Republican community, to pay his respects. This support of OT workers and other victims of Nazism by Bailhache were to become more visible after he became Bailiff in 1995.

Visiting Soviet attachés were also a regular feature. Because this was still the era of the Cold War, few islanders not directly involved with the memory of forced and slave workers wished to attend a service frequented by Communist Party members. The organisers were met with opposition by individuals who branded them left-wing agitators. Some islanders warned the organisers not to attend and sent them hate-mail.[26]

The increasing coverage in the local press of the ceremony at Westmount had a negative effect. In 1986, the ceremony attended by a crowd of around 100 people was interrupted by what was described as an 'anti-Soviet protest group', who tried to leave their own controversial floral tribute. Unfortunately, the event nearly ended in violence. The counter-memory status of the ceremony at this time reached its furthest point away from the collective memory celebrated in the centre of St Helier.

At a time when people on the continent were beginning to question the Occupation generation, overturn official memory and discuss aspects of collaboration and the hitherto neglected and marginalised victims of Nazi persecution, in the Channel Islands there was still violent opposition, in some quarters at least, to such counter-memories. The status quo still held sway and the unthreatening unearthing of bunkers and display of wartime vehicles were welcomed into the public memory. Although it was in the power of the post-war generation to destabilise collective memory, this did not happen. Rather, by working within a pre-existing interpretative framework which privileged the military capabilities and power of the bunkers, the guns and the military vehicles, the revivification of the Occupation years by this generation slotted into official memory without a hiccup.

Phase 4: 1985 to Present: Master Commemorative Narrative: Liberation

As the 1980s progressed, the older themes did not vanish entirely but no longer dominated the narrative. The military theme, for example, continued with events such as the church parade in Guernsey, which comprised marching bands and cadet corps. Other Liberation Day celebrations in the islands included acrobatic

---

[24] *Jersey Evening Post*, 11 May 1981:9.

[25] *Jersey Evening Post*, 10 May 1985.

[26] Speech by Gary Font at the annual ceremony at Westmount memorial, 9 May 2009.

flying displays and displays of prowess by visiting regiments. Patriotism was also still very much in evidence in the flags and bunting which decorated the islands. The entertainment still involved funfairs and sporting activities alongside military vehicle rallies, bunker visits and special open days at the Occupation museums (sometimes with all three of these events combined together with rallies outside bunker-museums). All of these kinds of events are still part of Liberation Day today. The successive phases of Liberation Day celebrations were (and are) successive superimposed layers, a veritable palimpsest of commemorations.

Although I have taken 1985 to mark the beginning of a new phase or layer in celebrations, this corresponds only to the first year in which the dominating theme of 'liberation' first made an appearance. It did not become the norm for every year that followed; in fact, it was only in 2000 that it became cemented in tradition in Jersey.

The year 1985 was the 40th anniversary of liberation and it was the first time that a large anniversary was marked by the erection of commemorative stones in both islands. This, I argue in the next chapter, was significant, as both the new elements in the celebrations and the stones remembered the important events of May 1945. They did not proclaim military might, victory and patriotism, nor did they discuss the events of the war years. Rather, they marked the beginning of a new focus in celebrations, quite literally, by subtly altering the commemorative landscapes of St Peter Port and St Helier. This became increasingly the case after the addition of new monuments in 1995, the 50th anniversary of liberation.

In 1985, the previous collective memories were still very much in evidence. The turn towards the Occupation years, ushered in during the previous decades, still grew in strength. Old wartime and occupation films were shown; interviews with the Occupation generation were published in number in the local paper (something which still happens annually today), and another Occupation exhibition was held at Jersey Museum. By the later 1980s, however, the 'Liberation' suffix was increasingly in evidence to describe events; thus, annual Liberation parties, Liberation balls and Liberation tea dances were held, especially for the Occupation generation. As the remainder of those who had been in positions of authority during the Occupation came to the ends of their lives, this generation was increasingly valued by the population, especially at this time of year, for their memories and experiences.

Looking back from the present, from a time when the liberation motif saturates all aspects of 9 May, we can see how and why the 40th anniversary marked something of a turning point in Liberation Day memory. For the first time, narratives from all four phases of celebration and commemoration were articulated on the same day, with the oldest modes coming back into play. A parade of servicemen on the streets of St Helier was described as 'the biggest seen in decades—perhaps since the Liberation itself'.[27] This was coupled with the now-annual contribution from the post-war generation and their military vehicles. The newly

[27] *Jersey Evening Post*, 10 May 1985.

Fig. 5.2 Bust of Jersey's Occupation-period Bailiff, Alexander Coutanche (© Gilly Carr)

emerging theme of liberation was set to affect and, later, dominate memory until the present day: the narrative of the original liberation itself, marked by an emphasis on re-enactment.

The liberation narrative was underscored in 1985 by the unveiling of two new liberation-themed commemorative plaques in Royal Square in Jersey. In this square, Bailiff Alexander Coutanche gave an impassioned speech on 8 May from a window in the States Building, following that of Winston Churchill, who had announced that the Channel Islands were to be liberated that day. That speech was repeated from the same balcony in 1985, where the then-Bailiff, Frank Ereaut, was joined by John Coutanche, the son of the wartime Bailiff.

A plaque, placed underneath the balcony where the original speech was given, was unveiled by the Duchess of Kent; it would be joined 5 years later by a bronze bust of Coutanche himself (Fig. 5.2). The Duchess also unveiled a frame that had been placed around what had once been, in May 1945, a symbol of protest. Close to the time of liberation, Mr Joseph Le Guyader had been repairing the paving in the Square after tree roots buckled some of the slabs. While his workman's shelter was erected over the repairs, he placed the paving slabs in the shape of a V for victory, also adding the letters 'EGA' so that, if he was caught and challenged by the Germans, he could claim that he was commemorating the arrival of the Red Cross ship, the Vega. The shelter was removed only at the time of liberation. Le Guyader's son and grandson made the frame around the V-sign and it was this that the Duchess of Kent was able to unveil at the 40th anniversary.

The focus on liberation and re-enactment was also underscored by a reunion of the original liberation veterans. The Union Jack was also ceremonially raised at the

Pomme D'Or hotel, just as it had been on 9 May 1945 after it was commandeered as the headquarters of the liberating forces. It is clearly no coincidence that the events of 9 May 1945 were turning into a re-enacted pageant just when those remaining witnesses of the original event were departing the stage.

In 1985 in Guernsey, the multiple phases of celebration were also in evidence and the day was declared the best Liberation Day for 40 years. The traditional military elements were represented by displays which included the Red Arrows and the parachute regiment; tank rides; a Liberation air-show; a 21-gun salute from Castle Cornet and marching displays by military bands. There was the usual cavalcade, dances and fireworks. The increased focus upon the act of liberation was marked by the unveiling of a commemorative stone in the marina where the liberating forces came ashore,[28] and a time-capsule was placed under a granite block on the slipway up which the forces climbed. There was also a re-enactment of the reading of the proclamations of King George VI and Brigadier Snow.

The celebrations of 1985 had, indeed, marked a turning point in the way memory of Liberation Day was to be articulated. After this date, the morning service of thanksgiving in Jersey moved from Howard Davis Park to the Royal Square, attended (as usual) by the Bailiff, the Lieutenant-Governor and the Dean.

Until the restructuring of Liberation Day in Jersey became fixed in 1995, the second half of the 1980s and the early 1990s followed the theme of the preceding years. In 1988, the Liberation Day committee proposed that, after the 50th anniversary in 1995, Liberation Day should be renamed Jersey Day.[29] The organisers were clearly out of step with popular opinion; the idea was met with such disfavour that it was withdrawn just a few days later. The new theme of 'liberation' had caught on and had public backing.

In 1990, Liberation Square was completed and unveiled by Bailiff Sir Peter Crill and Churchill's historic speech was re-enacted in Royal Square. The site for Liberation Square was chosen because this was where thousands had gathered to celebrate on the first Liberation Day in 1945, and because it was overlooked by the Pomme D'Or hotel, from where the Union Jack was raised (Young 1993: 10–11).

The war narrative articulated by Liberation Day was still in a state of flux, however, and even in the early 1990s the new theme had yet to achieve real commemorative density or be cemented in place as the commemorative master narrative. The early 1990s in Jersey were celebrated was with a funfair, show jumping, a charity walk, a display of military vehicles at the Channel Islands Military Museum, a special opening by the CIOS of the bunkers at Les Landes and Noirmont Point, and HMS *Jersey* was moored in the harbour and the Royal Hampshire Regiment marched through St Helier.

---

[28] This memorial is actually in the wrong place. While the advance party of liberating forces actually arrived at St Julian's Pier on 9 May, other units of the force arrived at the Connaught Landing on 12 May.

[29] *Jersey Evening Post*, 11 October 1988.

In Guernsey, the theme of the re-enactment of liberation again found favour in 1990 in the two-mile-long cavalcade which featured the Battle Re-enactment Association dressed as the members of Force 135. Yet at the same time, the crowds were treated to a Field Marshall Montgomery impersonator and a fly-past by two Nimrods. Other themes were represented with the participation of children dressed as evacuees, military and vintage cars, floats, a military parade, and a parade of decorated boats. Multiple commemorative narratives were in evidence at the same time in both islands.

The newly introduced theme of liberation was to prove so popular that people began to complain about the previous phase of celebration (espoused by the first post-war generation), contrasting it with celebratory forms of an even earlier post-war era. It was as if, once the origin of the earliest narratives had been lost in memory and become 'heritage', they were beyond criticism. An anonymous comment in the GEP recorded that

> 'People are divided about whether military vehicles should have a place in a celebration of peace. Some feel that they have, some that they have not … On one level we fear the glorification of war; we fear that young people who have never experienced it might be captivated by the display of fighting power. On another level we have to accept that our freedom could not have been regained without those instruments of war … Perhaps our unease about displays of military vehicles is an even greater anomaly than we realise, for we do not have similar concerns about military bands … but we do not see them in that light. We see them as part of our heritage, an essential part of our tradition and ceremony'.[30]

If 1985 and 1990 were still transitional markers in the change in narrative, the huge celebrations of the 50th anniversary of 1995 firmly entrenched the new mode of celebration and commemoration in a form that was to be continued up until the present day. This form, we were told by the *Jersey Evening Post*, had the capacity to stir 'the deepest of emotions and the most powerful of feelings'.[31] The celebrations of 1995 were described as striking 'a delicate and entirely appropriate bitter-sweet balance'. They were also seen as a 'watershed', marking a transformation of the Occupation years from 'the stuff of memory to the stuff of history' as the occupation generation grew older and fewer.[32]

The dedication of Liberation Square, the focus of which was the new Liberation Monument unveiled in 1995 by Prince Charles, sealed the location of the new site of memory in Jersey. The remit of the monument was that 'it must be a symbol of liberation and not occupation'; a 'permanent celebration of the freeing of this Island which was, along with its sister Isles, the only part of Britain to be occupied by the Third Reich' (Young 1993: 10–11). Although Royal Square was still to be

[30] *Guernsey Evening Press*, 10 May 1990: 1.

[31] *Jersey Evening Post*, 8 May 1996:8.

[32] Ibid.

used during subsequent Liberation Days, the main focus of public ceremony and the open air service moved to Liberation Square.

Re-enactment was now key to major Liberation Day celebrations in Jersey. The 50th anniversary celebrations included a broadcast of Churchill's speech, a re-enactment of Bailiff Coutanche's response in Royal Square by his son Jurat John Coutanche and a re-enactment of the landing of the Liberation forces. Two Royal Naval officers arrived at the Albert Pier and made their way to Liberation Square. They hung a Union Jack out of the window of the old harbour office and then raised the flag at the Pomme D'Or hotel. The souvenir programmes of Jersey and Guernsey in 1995 also featured photographs from May 1945, reflecting the importance of allowing new generations to synthetically 'witness' the past.

At the same time, other events included Occupation-related exhibitions at local museums, special openings of bunker sites and the parades of military and vintage vehicles. There was also a memorial fly-past of a Lancaster, Spitfire and Hurricane, and church bells continued to be rung in the morning, a practice going back to 1468 when they celebrated the liberation from French occupation.

Prince Charles also visited Guernsey for the 50th anniversary celebrations and unveiled the new Liberation Monument in St Peter Port. This was placed by the Weighbridge, which had been bombed during the harbour raid which took place just before the arrival of the Germans. It was also the area where the advance party had come ashore on 9 May, and where the crowds had gathered that day; thus, it was in a place directly equivalent to that unveiled in Jersey.

A commemorative stone was unveiled by former Bailiff Charles Frossard, along with a 'Liberation Avenue' of trees newly planted at Delancy Park in St Sampson, the parish north of St Peter Port. At another tree-planting ceremony in the parish of St Saviour, two of the trees were planted by former forced and slave workers, an unusual incursion into public memory for Guernsey, and the first time for decades that other narratives had been represented in Liberation Day public memory. This was echoed in the parish of St Andrew, where a special service of reconciliation and remembrance was held at the German Underground Hospital, a set of labyrinthine tunnels made by forced and slave labour.

The old themes continued but were given a liberation-themed twist; thus, when the Fort Hommet casemate on Guernsey's west coast was opened after restoration that year, it was performed by a senior surviving officer from Force 135. And the cavalcade, which in 1995 had a cast of thousands, also had a huge parade of military vehicles and foot soldiers representing Force 135. Also that year, Guernsey struck a medal for all surviving members of that Force. It seems that as the theme of liberation emerged as the master commemorative narrative during this period, official and popular memory began to converge as the general population embraced it as strongly as the islands' elites. With regard to the influence of the adopted British war narrative which emphasised 'pride in endurance until liberation by the victorious British' as one of its major tenets, this new collective memory was, in fact, not new at all.

Liberation Day Today and Tomorrow

While re-enactments on Liberation Day are currently in vogue in Jersey, Guernsey has not followed down this path. There is, perhaps, no need, as the decorated floats of the cavalcade held every five years play a similar role in narrating the important parts of the story of 1945 and inculcating the next generation. There are also practical reasons for the lack of re-enactment: the Royal Hotel, the headquarters of Force 135 in St Peter Port, burnt down in the early 1990s and has since been demolished. The area outside the Royal Court from where the Union Jack was hoisted is (unlike Royal Square or Liberation Square in Jersey) not especially suitable or large enough for vast crowds (although it somehow coped in 1945!). It is also at the top of a steep street and close to the island's war memorial, which belongs to another narrative; the crowds today are used to the celebrations being held along the flat esplanade by the harbour. However, the harbour front also has its historic precedents: on 12 May 1945, the main body of Force 135 arrived on a series of ships and the population waited in this area. When the troops disembarked, they marched along the esplanade, surrounded by the crowds, and a military band also came ashore to entertain them. In the very first celebrations of Liberation Day in the late 1940s, the cavalcades paraded along the same route. This area today is now topped and tailed by the liberation monuments erected in 1985 and 1995.

While the theme of liberation now dominates in Jersey on 9 May, in Guernsey this is perhaps less strongly articulated. In Guernsey, while the liberation label is attached to everything, the four phases of celebration are performed together. New elements from other cultures are periodically brought in, such as giant carnival heads (1988, 1990 and 2005, although one also appeared in the 1950 cavalcade), which are more characteristic of France or Belgium. The Normandy Markets, hosted by traders who come over from France laden with local produce, are also a popular feature of Liberation Day today. Older cultural traditions unrelated to Liberation Day are also included, such as the old Guernsey market and the Chevauchée de Ste Michel.

After the 50th anniversary in 1995, the Liberation Committee took the decision that they would need to change the emphasis of the day and to bring 'a carnival atmosphere' to St Peter Port in the afternoon after the serious commemorations of the morning (Ogier 1997: 3). Thus, the afternoon was taken over by a fairground and the International Festival of Street Entertainers for the next few years. The Committee believed that the day should be 'moved on' to become 'Guernsey's national day and a celebration of freedom' (Mellors quoted in Davies 1999: 1). While a similar statement in Jersey (albeit with a proposed name change for 9 May) was reversed in a matter of days after public protest, the Committee has been partially successful in Guernsey. The result is that the celebrations in non-anniversary years are now mostly indistinguishable from any which have taken place since the 1970s. Yet, despite three calls made by the Committee since 1996 for changes to Liberation Day, to make it a national day rather than exclusively about liberation (e.g. Oliphant 2004: 1), this has not quite happened yet. This, surely, is a

Fig. 5.3 Liberation Day cavalcade float, Guernsey 2010, Vega (© Gilly Carr)

Fig. 5.4 Liberation Day cavalcade float, Guernsey 2010, Red Cross parcel (© Gilly Carr)

reflection of the contestation between official and popular memory, the desire of the population to keep celebrating in the ways that have now become established over the decades, and especially of the post-war generation, who are not ready to let go even if the Occupation generation are rapidly passing from the scene.

At the last big anniversary, in 2010, the traditional military church parade took place in the morning, inspected by the then-Bailiff, Sir Geoffrey Rowland, and the Lieutenant-Governor, Sir Fabian Malbon. The afternoon cavalcade was a mixture of old and new themes. Floats patriotically decked with bunting and flags included old favourites such as a trailer pulling a replica of the Vega (Fig. 5.3); a lorry float decked with the giant-size contents of a Red Cross parcel (Fig. 5.4); a scarecrow in a field dressed in German uniform (apparently a common view after the Occupation); a gun battery; and non-liberation themes such as a float titled 'Guernsey's sporting heroes'. In addition to the usual flag-covered military and vintage vehicle and bicycle displays, a few Lanz bulldog tractors had come over from Germany to

Fig. 5.5 Re-enactment of the unfurling of the flag from the harbour master's office, Liberation Day, Jersey (© Gilly Carr)

join the parade, and this raised a few eyebrows. They pulled behind them some wheeled Occupation-era military equipment such as searchlights and guns, and these had white flags of surrender attached to them. 'Proper thing too', I heard the person next to me in the crowd mumble. The involvement of Germans in Liberation Day celebrations in Guernsey continues to be controversial. Unlike St Helier, which is twinned with Bad Wurzach, to where hundreds of islanders were deported in 1942, St Peter Port is not yet twinned with its opposite number in Biberach (although this has been on the agenda for a while). It is likely that, with more exposure and more acts of reconciliation, this may change.

In Jersey, despite the inauguration of a commemorative narrative of liberation in 1985, 1990 and 1995, it was not to become a fixed, *annual* motif until 2000. Bailiff Philip Bailhache, who had been in office since 1995, argued that Liberation Day should be brought to life annually rather than just every five years. From that date onwards, the public service moved from Royal Square to Liberation Square, where a detailed re-enactment of liberation has taken place annually, including the flag unfurling at the harbour master's office by two naval officers (Fig. 5.5), the arrival of Force 135 (played by members of the Jersey field squadron or, more recently, members of the island cadet forces) throwing sweets to the cheering crowd, and the raising of the Union Jack at the Pomme D'Or hotel and at Fort Regent (Fig. 5.6). A commentary accompanies this pageant, interspersed with snatches from original radio broadcasts of 9 May 1945, or quotes from the locally well-known Occupation diary of Leslie Sinel. This re-enactment includes the national anthem and patriotic songs and sometimes a fly-past of Second World War planes.

Fig. 5.6 Raising of the Union Jack at the Pomme D'Or hotel, Liberation Day, Jersey (© Gilly Carr)

Major changes to the sea front, harbour and esplanade have taken place in St Helier since the Occupation. The bus station has moved and is now round the corner from Liberation Square and renamed Liberation Station; the main road in front of the esplanade and out of the town is named La Route de la Liberation; and the old wharf next Liberation Square is now renamed Liberty Wharf. The narrative of liberation is now well and truly fixed in the landscape of the town.

During Bailhache's period of office (1995–2009), Liberation Day has become more inclusive of narratives of victims of Nazism, with special reference made to the fate of deportees, Jews, forced and slave workers and political prisoners. In 2002, 'reconciliation' was the dominant theme and the mayor of Bad Wurzach, Helmut Morczinietz, was welcomed by Bailhache to St Helier to mark the twinning of the two towns. In Bailhache's words, 'Liberation Day has become an occasion for bridge building and for the assertion of a national identity which embraces everyone whose heart is in the Island'.[33]

'Liberation 60', in 2005, continued in the same vein and was also inclusive of victims of Nazism. If the Liberation Tapestry unveiled in 1995 by Prince Charles included scenes from the darker side of the Occupation, such as the deportations and the fate of political prisoners, in 2005 these people were made more visible. In the Charing Cross area of St Helier, twelve banners were hung depicting people who performed brave acts or who were deported to concentration camps. Included among these were Albert Bedane (who hid a Jewish woman), Harold Le Druillenec (sent to Belsen), Dennis Vibert (who successfully escaped to Britain), Maurice

[33] Email of 8 November 2010, to author from Sir Philip Bailhache.

Fig. 5.7 Westmount memorial ceremony, Liberation Day, Jersey (© Gilly Carr)

Gould (caught while escaping, deported, and died in Wittlich prison) and Claude Cahun (artist and imprisoned resister).

At the slave worker memorial at Westmount things have also moved on, especially since the end of the Cold War, which has had a big effect on how the plight of Soviet slave workers were perceived. In 2001, Gary Font, son of Spanish Republican forced worker Francisco Font, took over as Master of Ceremonies. He has worked hard to increase numbers and encourage more people to attend; he has also invited foreign ambassadors and island dignitaries and so, since 2005, the Bailiff and (since 2007) the Lieutenant-Governor have laid wreaths for the 101 known forced and slave workers who died in the island during the Occupation. Over the years, more plaques commemorating different forced and slave worker groups have been added to the memorial. In 2009, for example, the Belarusians were remembered and in 2011, the French North Africans. Around 40 wreaths are laid today and about a quarter are from families of former Spanish Republican forced workers who stayed in the island (Fig. 5.7). The ceremony has changed from being a counter-narrative to Liberation Day to becoming one of the most important wreath-laying events in the island's calendar. It is now, for some, an integral part of the experience of Liberation Day, not an alternative to it. In Jersey at least, the victims of Nazism are now an accepted part of public memory and even regularly figure in the Bailiff's public address on 9 May. While the sceptical might interpret this as an attempt by elites to 'neutralise competing interpretations of the past that might threaten social unity … and fidelity to the established social order' (Burgoyne 2003: 2010), this would be to ignore the genuinely felt desire of individuals in positions of authority to change and adapt the status quo. Change has not just been pushed through from below. Victims of Nazism certainly do not dominate collective memory, but are a noticeable part of the commemorative landscape of Liberation Day. As Jersey has learned, 'even a shameful past may earn self-admiration for facing up to it' (Lowenthal 1994: 46).

This is not to say that the island could not do more to cement a commitment to these causes. It would be an accurate part of history to re-enact the release of political prisoners. While the prison has now been demolished, a plaque has been placed on the wall outside and a small act of commemoration could take place here, as it does at Westmount. As mentioned earlier, there is evidence that at least one OT worker[34] showed himself from the window of the harbour master's office after the flag was hung at the window; the JEP records that the crowds below cheered when they saw him (Lamerton 2000: 116).[35] This is not included in the re-enactment on Liberation Day.

In Guernsey, no entry onto the commemorative stage of Liberation Day has yet been mounted by former victims of Nazism. While these groups are now being remembered in memorials (a process that is not yet complete), Liberation Day today is seen as appropriate mainly for remembering the events of 9 May 1945, rather than any other event. An exception includes 2003, when the mayor of Biberach, Thomas Fettback, attended Liberation Day celebrations to apologise for his country's actions during the war. He laid a wreath on the island's war memorial and gave a plaque to the Bailiff to commemorate the deportation of islanders to the civilian internment camp in his town.

Another group whose absence on Liberation Day is even more obvious, although not entirely unexpected, is the occupiers. While they are alluded to in speeches which refer to the 'dark years of occupation', they do not appear in re-enactment in Jersey. We do not see swastika flags being lowered before the raising of the Union Jack at the Pomme D'Or hotel or at Fort Regent. No German soldiers skulk in the background as the liberators come ashore, and none are led away as POWs. Such re-enactment would be seen as very bad taste and a retrograde step as far as reconciliation is concerned.

Yet the occupiers are not *entirely* excluded at this time. A drive-past by Allied and German military vehicles are included in the annual celebrations in St Helier, although those driving them always dress in American or British uniforms or in camouflage gear. In Guernsey, the Germans have often been depicted on cavalcade floats, caricatured as POWs or shown in the act of being humiliated by the liberators or locals in some way. In the 2010 cavalcade, there were three representations of the occupiers. One was shown sitting in an outside privy with his trousers round his ankles; the uniform of a second was used on a post-war scarecrow; and a third was painted as part of the design on the back of float, being kicked out of the island by a Guernsey donkey. The appearance in the cavalcade of vehicles from Germany pulling wheeled, surrendered items of military equipment confirmed the only permitted memory of the occupiers on this day: as a humiliated

[34] While the JEP records that a group of Moroccans showed themselves at the window, later interviews conducted with those present at the time, coupled with photographic evidence and a signature recorded in the Naval Officer's pay book, suggests that the a solitary Russian POW named Alexander Galub was the person at the window (Lamerton personal communication, 20 June 2011; my thanks to Nikolai Ssorin-Chaikov for translating the signature).

[35] *Jersey Evening Post*, 9 May 1945.

Fig. 5.8 German vehicles on display in the Liberation Day cavalcade, Guernsey (© Gilly Carr)

and defeated people (Fig. 5.8). Once again, this fits neatly with the collective memory of Liberation Day which has promoted a pride in Allied military victory since the earliest days of commemoration.

It is not yet clear whether Jersey and Guernsey are taking truly divergent paths, with Jersey entering a fifth commemorative phase and moving towards a narrative which embraces victims of Nazism, and Guernsey continuing to focus on liberation. It is perhaps more likely that Guernsey is simply taking longer than its sister island to face its wartime demons and talk about them on Liberation Day. It is generally acknowledged that former Jersey Bailiff Philip Bailhache was particularly instrumental in addressing the 'complexities and contradictions of enemy occupation', and in memorialising victims of Nazism. In small islands, individuals are listened to (especially if they are influential) and can make a difference. Until somebody in a similar position of influence in Guernsey makes it their mission to publically address, discuss and digest the mistakes of the past, and to diverge, at least partially, from the UK war narrative as Jersey has begun to do, then Guernsey will find it difficult to fully progress to the next phase of commemoration. It will also find itself increasingly at odds with the rest of formerly occupied Europe. Such progress is dictated by the agendas of individuals, whether those individuals are Bailiffs, former victims of Nazism, or historians. The timing of when these groups push for recognition, or receive it without asking, cannot always be predicted.

Conclusion: The Politics of Memory on Liberation Day

The beginning of a fifth commemorative narrative on Liberation Day suggests that new agendas are emerging in the Channel Islands. New generations are being educated differently to their predecessors. Unlike the first post-war generation in the Channel Islands who were educated before the days of the National Curriculum, the subsequent generations have been and are taught about the Second World War and the Occupation at school. While some in the Channel Islands are inevitably being taught by members of the first and second post-war generation, nearly all teachers in the islands today were trained at universities and colleges in the UK. It remains to be seen whether the prevalent modes of display of history and heritage in the islands will unduly influence local research among the younger generation.[36] These generations have no parents or grandparents who lived through the Occupation, although half-remembered family stories are still passed down to them. Assmann (2008: 65) has suggested that, for these generations, memory of the traumatic past will become 'more and more homogeneous as it is reconstructed by historians and accessed through the shared representations of public narratives', of which Liberation Day is just one example.

In Jersey today, through their own observations on Liberation Day, the young are still growing up with a sanitised, second-hand and nostalgic idea of what it was like to experience a little of the Occupation, even if it was just its closing chapter. Things, however, are changing. In Guernsey, the cavalcade floats serve a very similar didactic purpose. While Guernsey and Jersey rarely seek to emulate each other, especially publically, they have mechanisms to tell the same story, keeping it alive for the future generations who will find it hard to change cherished collective memories. As Sanders has observed with reference to the construction of the Occupation narrative, 'attacking or questioning any of these building blocks has been next to impossible as, over the years traditionalists have feared that even minute changes would lead to a collapse of the entire structure' (2005: 235). It remains to be seen whether the straps which bind the straightjacket of the Churchillian paradigm will be loosened with the passing of the Occupation generation or their children.

Whether or not a change in the war narrative in the UK would have a knock-on effect in the Channel Islands is an interesting question. The longevity of the narrative in the UK has often been seen as due to the prevalent view that the Second World War was 'fought on the continent by continentals', which is why memories of 'heroic and positive memories of the war and remembrance of solidarity in suffering' continue (Berger 2010: 128–129). Given that the Channel Islands (especially Jersey) are now embracing its victims of Nazism, it is possible that pressure may be being applied in the opposite direction, i.e. from the islands to the UK. For example in 2010, 27 British 'Hero of the Holocaust' honours were awarded for the first time after campaigning by the Holocaust Educational Trust. These awards were given to Britons who had saved the lives of Jews and other persecuted groups during the Holocaust. Four people from Jersey were among those honoured,[37] thanks to advice from historian Paul Sanders to Downing Street.

[36] At the Liberation Day 2010 celebrations, the author saw a small exhibition mounted by local school children in the Tourist Information offices. It focused entirely on the arrival of the Red Cross ship, the Vega, bringing parcels to starving Islanders, helping them to endure the last few months of Occupation. This was a good example of the younger generation being taught about the Occupation along traditional lines.

[37] Albert Bedane, Ivy Forster, Louisa Gould and Harold Le Druillenec.

Because these honours were given to only a small number of people, they have little chance of making a major and lasting impact on the national consciousness. There are, however, other voices which exist in much greater number. At the time of writing, the testimonies of British (including Channel Islander) victims of Nazi persecution still exist as closed records in the Foreign and Commonwealth Office.[38] These records detail the sufferings in Nazi prisons and concentration camps for which Britons claimed compensation in the mid-1960s.[39] It is likely that, when and if these files are finally released, this will trigger a feeding frenzy among popular historians and academics alike, such is the well-known appetite for Second World War history in the UK. It will be interesting to observe what effect a new focus on the victims will have on the still-prevalent Churchillian paradigm.

At present, however, such is the continued power of the UK war narrative in the Channel Islands, new commemorative narratives that have entered the arena on Liberation Day are expressed within its framework and do not seek to challenge it. Such is the recognised strength and unity of focus of Liberation Day that the majority of victim groups have sought other occasions (such as Holocaust Memorial Day) and other foci (such as memorials) to express their own narratives. In this way, the status quo continues unchallenged on the most important day in the islands' commemorative calendar while at the same time the other occasions and memorials are sufficient both to satisfy most victim groups and to deflect any charges levelled at local government by outside journalists of continued collective amnesia or lack of interest in the plight of victims of Nazism.

Liberation Day today, especially in Guernsey, is simply not seen as an appropriate occasion for such groups to express their memories. While in Jersey the Bailiff makes a public address on Liberation Day and is able to mention or pay homage to those who suffered during the Occupation, no such address is made by the Bailiff in Guernsey on Liberation Day.[40] Elite narratives and official memory are thus tightly controlled by who is allowed to be present in the church parade (something decided by armed forces organisations in the island), who is allowed to have a float in the cavalcade, and what theme it should express. Cavalcade float themes are, today, vetted by the Cavalcade Working Party and have to be approved by the Liberation Day Core Working Group, a subgroup of the States of Guernsey Department of Culture and Leisure. The minister for Culture and Leisure is currently the chairman of the group, although can be any member of the Culture and Leisure board.[41] The official cavalcade application form for 2010 stipulated, in its conditions of entry, that 'the Cavalcade working party reserves the right to dis-

---

[38] The author is currently fighting for these to be released.

[39] Among this group we might include British Jews caught on the continent at the outbreak of war, SOE agents sent to occupied Europe from London, and Channel Islanders deported to prisons and concentration camps for acts of resistance.

[40] Sir Geoffrey Rowland personal communication, 17 June 2011.

[41] Email of 24 June 2011, to author from PF from the Department of Culture and Leisure.

allow any entry that is in their opinion un-safe, vulgar or of an objectionable nature'. While there is no guidance as to what theme would be considered appropriate for a float, photographs which illustrate the application form show an abundance of Guernsey flags and Union Jacks, marching veterans, people in wartime uniforms or costumes, a child dressed as a British Tommy and a float showing the theme of children being evacuated.[42] These are all clear examples of common themes enacted in cavalcades and on Liberation Day over the last 65 years. The kind of theme likely to be disallowed includes 'something which would convey anti-German feelings and featured swastikas, etc'.[43]

If there is no explicit pressure from above regarding the decoration of a cavalcade float on Liberation Day, how are decisions made? It is likely that such themes are dictated by 'tradition', which can be self-censoring and can dictate what is 'appropriate'. The repertoire of acceptable float themes has been built up over more than 65 years and informal discussions with islanders suggests that the selection of anything radically outside this corpus would be met with puzzlement or disapproval by the crowd.[44] It thus seems unlikely that any attempt would be made to break radically with tradition.

In this chapter, I have illustrated the longevity and stability of the British war narrative in the collective memory of the Channel Islands through successive and palimpsestic commemorative master narratives. I have also shown how official memory, imposed from above and with the direct help of the British government, has dominated public memory and the master commemorative narratives since 1945. Even where popular memory has been given a voice, especially since the 1970s onwards with the passing away of the older generation, it has rarely sought to challenge, nor has it acquired the commemorative density to challenge the dominance of narratives which continue to focus on themes of patriotism and pride in military might and victory. This is in direct contrast to elsewhere in Europe, where paradigm shifts in memory were observed between the late 1960s and mid-1980s (Fogu and Kansteiner 2006: 298). Instead, new or marginalised narratives have been expressed either within the confines of the pre-existing framework of Liberation Day or else, as in the case of the ceremony at the Westmount crematorium in St Helier, has mounted a separate, alternative commemorative space, providing an effective counter-memory which attracted those outside the establishment until the twenty-first century. Yet other groups have simply remembered their friends and family on different days and in different places, as we shall see in Chap. 6.

---

[42] My thanks to PF from the Department of Culture and Leisure for making this document available to me.

[43] Email of 28 June 2011, to author from PF from the Department of Culture and Leisure.

[44] In the 2010 cavalcade, the theme of one float was 'Guernsey's sporting heroes'. I heard those around me in the crowd mutter, 'What's that got to do with liberation or Occupation?'

References

Assmann, A. (1995). Collective memory and cultural identity. *New German Critique, 65*, 125–133.

Assmann, A. (2008). Transformations between history and memory. *Social Research, 75*(1), 49–72.

Von Aufsess, H. M. (1985). *The von Aufsess Occupation diary*. Chichester: Phillimore and Co. Ltd.

Berger, S. (2010). Remembering the Second World War in Western Europe, 1945–2005. In M. Pakier & B. Stråth (Eds.), *A European memory? Contested histories and politics of remembrance* (pp. 119–136). New York and Oxford: Berghahn Books.

Bodnar, J. (1992). *Remaking America: Public memory, commemoration, and patriotism in the twentieth century*. Princeton: Princeton University Press.

Bunting, M. (1995). *The Model Occupation*. BCA, London.

Burgoyne, R. (2003). From contested to consensual memory: The rock and roll hall of fame and museum. In K. Hodgkin & S. Radstone (Eds.), *Contested pasts: The politics of memory* (pp. 208–220). London and New York: Routledge.

Carey, V. Unpublished diary, island archives, Guernsey, ref. AQ 368.

Carr, G. (2010). The slowly healing scars of Occupation. *Journal of War and Culture Studies, 3*(2), 249–265.

Carr, G. (2012). Occupation heritage, commemoration and memory in Guernsey and Jersey. *History and Theory, 24*(1), 87–117.

Carr, G. (2014). Symbolic resistance. In G. Carr, P. Sanders, & L. Willmot (Eds.), *Protest, defiance and resistance in the Channel Islands* (pp. 1940–1945). London: Bloomsbury Academic.

Confino, A. (2005). Remembering the Second World War, 1945–1965: Narratives of victimhood and genocide. *Cultural Analysis, 4*, 46–75.

Connerton, P. (1989). *How Societies Remember*. Cambridge: Cambridge University Press.

Coser, L. A. (1992). Introduction. In M. Halbwachs (Ed.), *On collective memory* (pp. 1–34). Chicago and London: The University of Chicago Press.

Cruickshank, C. (2004) [1975]. *The German Occupation of the Channel Islands*. London: Oxford University Press/ Channel Islands: Guernsey Press.

Davies, P. (1999). *Liberation Day should be our national day* (p. 1). Guernsey: Guernsey Evening Press.

Evans, A. (2009). *Guernsey under Occupation: The Second World War diaries of Violet Carey*. Chichester: Phillimore and Co. Ltd.

Fogu, C. (2006). The legacy of fascist historical culture on Italian politics of memory. In R. N. Lebow, W. Kansteiner, & C. Fogu (Eds.), *The politics of memory in postwar Europe* (pp. 147–176). Durham and London: Duke University Press.

Fogu, C., & Kansteiner, W. (2006). The politics of memory and the poetics of history. In R. N. Lebow, W. Kansteiner, & C. Fogu (Eds.), *The politics of memory in postwar Europe* (pp. 284–310). Durham and London: Duke University Press.

Gildea, R. (2002). Myth, memory and policy in France since 1945. In J. Müller (Ed.), *Memory and power in post-war Europe* (pp. 59–75). Cambridge: Cambridge University Press.

Gillis, J. R. (1994). Memory and identity: the history of a relationship. In J. R. Gillis (Ed.), *Commemorations: The politics of national identity* (pp. 3–24). Princeton: Princeton University Press.

Halbwachs, M. (1992). *On collective memory*. Chicago and London: The University of Chicago Press (edited by L.A. Coser).

Harris, L. (2004). *A boy remembers*. Jersey: Channel Island Publishing.

Harvey, W. (1995). *The battle of Newlands*. Guernsey: The Guernsey Press Ltd.

Heaume, R. L. (2006). Liberation cavalcades and Le Chevauchée origins. *Channel Islands Occupation Review, 34*, 39–44.

Hobsbawm, E., & Ranger, T. (Eds.). (1983). *The invention of tradition*. Cambridge: Cambridge University Press.

Judt, T. (2002). The past is another country: myth and memory in post-war Europe. In J.-W. Müller (Ed.), *Memory and power in post-war Europe* (pp. 157–183). Cambridge: Cambridge University Press.

Judt, T. (2010). *Postwar: A history of Europe since 1945*. London: Vintage Books.

Kansteiner, W. (2002). Finding meaning in memory: a methodological critique of collective memory studies. *History and Theory, 41*, 179–197.

Kansteiner, W. (2006). Losing the war, winning the memory battle: the legacy of Nazism, World War II and the holocaust in the Federal Republic of Germany. In R. N. Lebow, W. Kansteiner, & C. Fogu (Eds.), *The politics of memory in postwar Europe* (pp. 102–146). Durham and London: Duke University Press.

Koonz, C. (1994). Between memory and oblivion: concentration camps in German memory. In J. R. Gillis (Ed.), *Commemorations: The politics of national identity* (pp. 258–280). Princeton: Princeton University Press.

Lamerton, M. (2000). *Liberated by force 135: The liberation of the Channel Islands*. Bradford-on-Avon: ELSP.

Lennon, J., & Foley, M. (2007) [2000]. *Dark tourism: The attraction of death and disaster*. London: Thomson Publishing [London and New York: Continuum].

Lowenthal, D. (1994). Identity, heritage and history. In J. R. Gillis (Ed.), *Commemorations: The politics of national identity* (pp. 41–57). Princeton: Princeton University Press.

Marriner, G. P. (2009) *Changing attitudes to Heritage and Identity in post-war Alderney, 1945–2009*. Unpublished undergraduate dissertation, Department of Archaeology, University of Cambridge.

Ogier, M. (1997). *Change of emphasis liberates carnival atmosphere* (p. 3). Guernsey: Guernsey Evening Press.

Olick, J. K. (1999). Collective memory: The two cultures. *Sociological Theory, 17*(3), 248–333.

Oliphant, M. (2004). *Liberation Day changes on way* (p. 1). Guernsey: Guernsey Evening Press.

Pakier, M., & Stråth, B. (2010). Introduction: A European memory?'. In M. Pakier & B. Stråth (Eds.), *A European memory? Contested histories and politics of remembrance* (pp. 1–20). New York and Oxford: Berghahn Books.

Passerini, L. (2003). Memories between silence and oblivion. In K. Hodgkin & S. Radstone (Eds.), *Contested pasts: the politics of memory* (pp. 238–254). London and New York: Routledge.

Pocock, H. R. S. (1975). *The memoirs of Lord Coutanche: A Jerseyman looks back*. London and Chichester Ltd: Phillimore and Co. Ltd.

Rousso, H. (2007). History of memory, policies of the past: what for? In K. H. Jarausch & T. Lindenberger (Eds.), *Conflicted memories: Europeanizing contemporary histories* (pp. 23–36). New York and Oxford: Berghahn Books.

Rousso, H. (1991). (trans A. Goldhammer), *The Vichy Syndrome: History and memory in France since 1944*. Cambridge: Harvard University Press.

Sanders, P. (2004). *The ultimate sacrifice*. Jersey: Jersey Heritage Trust.

Sanders, P. (2005). *The British Channel Islands under German Occupation 1940–1945*. Jersey: Société Jersiaise and Jersey Heritage Trust.

Sinel, L. (1945). *The German Occupation of Jersey: A complete diary of events from June 1940 to June 1945*. Jersey: The Evening Post.

Sontag, S. (2003). *Regarding the pain of others*. London: Penguin Books.

Uzzell, D., & Ballantyne, R. (2008). Heritage that hurts: interpretation in a postmodern world. In G. Fairclough, R. Harrison, J. H. Jameson, & J. Schofield (Eds.), *The heritage reader* (pp. 502–513). London and New York: Routledge.

Vitaliev, V. (1998). *Showing off the sites of shame* (p. 4). London: The Guardian.

Young, G. (1993). A monument to freedom. *Jersey Evening Post, 8*, 10–11.

Zerubavel, Y. (1995). *Recovered roots: Collective memory and the making of Israeli national tradition*. Chicago and London: University of Chicago Press.

Chapter 6
Interpreting Memorial Landscapes of Occupation and Liberation

In January 2009, I attended the Holocaust Memorial Day commemoration in St Helier. The museum gallery in which the service was held was packed with islanders and dignitaries. After the opening address was given by Bailiff Sir Philip Bailhache, members of the Jersey youth theatre read poems and extracts from memoirs of Holocaust survivors. The Dean of Jersey gave a final address after which we all went outside to the Lighthouse Memorial, which was erected in 1996 in memory of the 'Jersey 22': those who did not return after the war from Nazi camps and prisons. The island's dignitaries, including the Bailiff and Lieutenant Governor, and representatives of victims, lined up to lay wreaths on the memorial while the crowd watched.

Two years later, I was in St Peter Port for Holocaust Memorial Day. This open-air service was held in front of the Jewish memorial. Erected in 2001, it was the smallest plaque along the harbour wall and close to the town's 1995 Liberation Monument. The Jewish memorial had recently been restored after being damaged. Around twenty-five people attended the ceremony (a number which dwindled to twelve the following year), but no dignitaries were there. Representatives of the Channel Islands Occupation Society and the Guernsey Deportees Association attended, and two bouquets of flowers were placed by the plaque during the ceremony. The deputy Dean of the island took the service, and although the three Jewish women deported to Auschwitz were named and remembered, there was no discussion or mention of those who shared similar fates for acts of resistance, despite the publicity surrounding the discovery of a new resistance archive in Guernsey a few months before which had made international news.

During the service, I found myself wondering: why are some narratives highlighted and others ignored at certain times of the year? Why are some 'authorised' by the presence of dignitaries, and others fail to gain the same attention? Why do some commemorative events attract large crowds in one place and small numbers in another? Why are some events remembered with impressive monuments and others, with small plaques? Why are some memorials to some groups erected at an earlier date than others? Why should there be a difference between Guernsey and Jersey? Why should the same event be remembered so differently in neighbouring islands?

G. Carr, *Legacies of Occupation*, Contributions To Global Historical Archaeology 40,
DOI: 10.1007/978-3-319-03407-2_6,

Occupation Memorials in the Channel Islands

Occupation heritage in the Channel Islands represents an active and ongoing conversation with the past. Even into the twenty-first century, bunkers continue to be excavated and restored; collectors of German militaria continue to acquire more objects; Occupation museum owners add to and change their displays; commemorations of Liberation Day evolve, and new memorials are erected most years.

As this chapter will explore, memorialisation of the Occupation years has been a phenomenon which began in earnest in the mid-1980s and has since resulted in a plethora of memorials scattered over the streets of the capital towns of Jersey and Guernsey. A veritable landscape of memorials or 'memorialscape' has emerged over the last 30 years, but each time a memorial has been erected, it has represented either a termination or a transformation of the kind of conversation that the local population has (or refuses to have) with and about the past. For the most part, the erection of a memorial has represented the transition of a living memory of an event, held in the minds of the Occupation generation, onto an inscription on the surface of stone. As members of the Occupation generation pass on, their memories have been entrusted to a medium that is perceived to be durable: granite, the bedrock of the Channel Islands and the locally favoured material for memorials.

In Pierre Nora's terminology, we can describe this transition as an unavoidable move from a *milieu de mémoire*, a real environment of memory, to a *lieu de mémoire*, a site of memory (Nora 1989: 7). But even though granite is indeed durable, memorials themselves are not. They can be dismantled, moved, removed, ignored, boycotted, physically blocked and vandalised; their meanings can change; and they can also become overgrown and neglected. Sometimes town centres can shift because of new construction and once prominent memorials can find themselves marginalised. Only some memorials become incorporated within annual ceremonies during which dominant readings can become reinforced, but even this does not prevent them from fading from public consciousness for the rest of the year.

The problem with transferring living memory onto the surface of stone is that, as Young (1993: 5) has explored in depth, 'once we assign monumental form to memory, we have to some degree divested ourselves of the obligation to remember. In shouldering the memory-work, monuments may relieve viewers of their memory burden'. This has not always been the case in the Channel Islands, where the sheer number of memorials and the size of the most monuments daily provoke a particular and dominant understanding of the war years. Yet there exists other, dominated, narratives, as this chapter explores. Here, the attention that has been drawn away from the memories that certain memorials carry has led to them becoming forgotten and overgrown, with no guardian of memory left to champion their cause. Here, the conversation about and with the past has effectively been terminated or marginalised, although perhaps not always permanently.

Generally speaking, memorials in the Channel Islands have mostly been sited at the original and authentic locations of important historical events of the Occupation;

this has been of utmost importance to islanders as it helps to perpetuate and enshrine meaning and memory of a defining period within the landscape for future generations.

At the 40th anniversary of liberation in 1985, and every five years thereafter, markers were placed to help recall the happy events of the liberation. More recently, others have been erected to help remember dark events. The latter memorials acknowledge—and perhaps by their acknowledgement, seek forgiveness for—events that happened during the Occupation and which the local government failed—or was powerless—to prevent. While the blame for these events is nearly always placed squarely on German shoulders in the memorial inscriptions, these memorials can also perhaps be seen as acupuncture needles, puncturing and pinning down the difficult memories of trauma with the hope of somehow healing them and removing any potential stigma that may have resulted from the pointing fingers of outsiders.

Some events of the Occupation—those which have produced some of the most shameful and painful memories—have not yet been had a memorial erected to remember those who suffered. Now that almost all the original cast of actors has passed away, and their children, too, are growing old, it is possible that these darkest of legacies will never be turned into heritage.

Memory Boom and Memorialscapes

Memorial landscapes are found all over the world. The multiple aspects of memorials in any one landscape can inter-relate in a variety of different ways that allows them to be read as a narrative. Although such cumulative readings have been recognised before, in this chapter I formalise and explore the complex interplay of memorials within the concept of the 'memorialscape', presented here as a coherent methodology for reading those narratives. Such narratives are also influenced by memorial texts, functions and agency within the landscape, and thus can change through time. As Young (1993: 154) has observed, 'no memorial is everlasting: each is shaped and understood in the context of its time and place, its meanings contingent on evolving political realities'.

The idea that multiple memorials within a single landscape can combine to produce (a) dominant (and dominated) impression(s) or reading(s) has been identified in many case studies around the world (e.g. Ashton and Hamilton 2008; Bulbeck 1988; Hamilton 2003; Norkunas 1993; Nugent 2005; and Siblon 2009). A vast amount has also been written about the interpretation and history of individual monuments and memorials and memorial practices within landscapes and cityscapes (e.g. Foote 1997; Jordan 2006; Young 1993, 2000; and Doss 2010, to give but a small selection). These studies have been immensely valuable in giving us an insight into the overall impression that a quantity of memorials can produce, into the 'biography' of individual memorials, and into the emotional attitudes and practices of their audience that both are determined and transmitted by the memorials.

While they have offered us important insights yielded by *depth* of analysis, I believe that a rigorous analysis of the inter-relationship of memorials within a landscape, combined with the *breadth* of their many concomitant features, can produce new observations relating, in this particular instance, to the way in which a society or community has come to terms with its wartime past. To be specific, by exploring whether, how, when and why a legacy (in this case, the memory of the Occupation and the specific locations upon which events took place) is turned into heritage, and by whom, and by the placing of a memorial or monument upon that site or nearby, we can observe both which events have been incorporated into wartime narratives, and the resulting commitment to the memory of those events.

The need for a formalised concept of the memorialscape, as I outline it here, has gradually come into focus because of the growing density of memorials and monuments in many towns and cities. In the Channel Islands, the number of commemorative stones, statues and plaques erected to the memory of the German Occupation has risen rapidly since 1985, the 40th anniversary of liberation. Although this can be theorised in a number of ways, one very obvious reason for this increase in commemoration is likely to be a desire of the Occupation generation, who are dwindling in number, to have their memories cast in stone before it is too late, although sometimes this job has been completed by their children. The erection of many memorials has thus occurred only in recent years, on the cusp of passing of the last of this generation.

Such 'memory booms' are visible all over Europe, as has been highlighted by others (Winter 2000; Rousso 2007; Huyssen 2003: 18), although on the continent, this occurred at an earlier date than in the Channel Islands and came with an accompanying increase in recognition of the victims of the Second World War. Prime among the causes of this, Winter (2006: 60) has argued, is that the post-war narrative work of the Resistance (who had previously dominated the memorial scene) had, by then, done its job and the transition to post-war political stability was complete. There was thus room for other victims to come forward with their witness and push for recognition of their suffering. In the Channel Islands, we might suggest that once the post-war emphasis on the act of military victory and patriotism had done its job, then there was room, from around 1995 onwards, for victims of Nazism to come forward. It is their memorial plaques which now typify the memory boom of the last 25 years, as is discussed in more depth below.

Others have put forward different reasons for the rapid increase in memorialisation. Nora (1998) has argued that this 'era of commemoration' (in France at least) was prompted by a nostalgic desire to cling to what was passing away in the face of rapid change, and which has manifested itself through an increasing commemorative frequency at sites of memory. In America, Doss (2010: 2 and 19) has identified a 'memorial mania', which she describes as an 'obsession with issues of memory and history and an urgent desire to express and claim those issues in visibly public contexts' which represent 'heightened expectations of rights and representation among the nation's increasingly diverse publics'. She interprets this as stemming from a sense of 'entitlement' or 'ownership' that 'pervades today's memorial sphere' (ibid: 34). Such interpretations would not be wholly inapplicable to the Channel Islands, where representatives of groups of victims of Nazism and their families are also conscious of perceived past absences in the memorial record and have sought to rectify this.

Nora's concern with nostalgia is relevant to the Channel Islands. The Occupation is a time that is beginning to pass out of living memory. Like the London Blitz, terrible though it was, the Occupation is treated as a positive memory locally. It dominates war memory and historical re-enactment and, for those born after the event, it is commonly perceived as the most 'exciting' thing ever to happen in the islands. As we have already seen, the dominant war narrative in the Channel Islands is inextricably bound up with that of Britain rather than its continental cousins, despite the similarity of its wartime experiences with the latter. For most of the last 70 years, the dominant sites of memory in the islands have proclaimed a pride in endurance and survival until liberation and victory, and this has often predominated over the narratives of victims of Nazism. Despite this, these marginalised voices have been coming to the fore since the 50th anniversary of liberation.

That the German Occupation has popularly been presented through the selective commemorative lens of liberation over the last few decades can be attested by the successive monuments to this event being unveiled on Liberation Day every five years between 1985 and 2005. The dominant narrative of memorial erection during these two decades followed one in which younger islanders were beginning to look back at the Occupation years and ask questions about them for the first time. We should, perhaps, not be surprised that the narrative of liberation was so firmly and continuously emphasised during this time. This was promoted and supported by the islands' authorities who, one might imagine, were interested in keeping the focus away from certain dark events during the Occupation; dark events which might have provoked difficult questions and criticism of the behaviour of local government during the war years. Official narratives of liberation formed the new status quo until the 50th anniversary of liberation in 1995 and beyond. This aspect of commemorative heritage became the new 'tradition' until marginalised narratives, represented by the victims of Nazism, began to gain a voice and memorials of their own in the mid-1990s, with Jersey leading the way.

It is important to understand memorialisation in the Channel Islands as a practice that goes hand in hand with Liberation Day ceremonies, as the vast majority of all Occupation-related memorials in the islands have been inaugurated on, or in time for, Liberation Day, and the narratives espoused by memorials and by commemorative ceremonies have often been sung in unison. Where they have not, the discordant voices are worthy of further study.

Charting the Memorialscape

Throughout this chapter, I discuss how sites and events of suffering, death and celebration dating from the Occupation are written into the memorials and monuments of the Channel Islands. The vast majority of those that I consider here are of the traditional type; counter-monuments (as explored in Young 2000) have yet to be employed in the Channel Islands, although monumental and non-monumental artistic responses in sculpture to the Occupation exist.

While monuments and memorials are terms often used interchangeably in the popular sphere, memorials tend to be associated with loss and sadness while monuments are often associated with triumph, glory and positive memory. Such nomenclature is generally followed in the Channel Islands. Commemorative stones or sculpture associated with the memory of the act of liberation are invariably called 'monuments', while those erected to victims of Nazism are often 'memorials' and carry positive and negative memory associations, respectively.

For Rowlands (1999: 131), however, memorials can become monuments as a 'result of the successful completion of the mourning process', and where the 'temporal gap between mourning and memorial is the outcome of successful closure'. The transition of monuments back to memorials is also possible (ibid: 144). For Young (1993: 3), the same object can perform both functions: a statue, for example, can be both 'a monument to heroism and a memorial to tragic loss'. He suggests that there may be 'nothing intrinsic to historical markers that make them either a monument or a memorial'.

I have developed the concept of the 'memorialscape' in response to the complex and, indeed, complexity, of memorials in St Peter Port and St Helier and, to a lesser extent, in St Anne in Alderney. These have been installed, inaugurated or erected within a relatively small area, with all the associated implications of competitive memorial space, and it is this that lends them most readily to a memorialscape analysis. The majority of these memorials have been put up within a single generation, from 1985 onwards.

These memorials respect older monuments unconnected with the Occupation and commemorate events or acts that sometimes deliberately chose certain locations for their enactment because of their vicinity to an older memorial and earlier events. These Occupation monuments, memorials and plaques also have an influence upon how the space within the towns in which they are situated is encountered, experienced and negotiated by the inhabitants. They are mnemonic devices, which act to remind constantly the casual passer-by or visitor about the continued importance of the Occupation. As such, they are powerful and mostly high-profile objects which play an active role in society; their combined weight has frequently and recently acted to spur groups or individuals into erecting yet more memorials, each dedicated to their own particular groups who suffered during the Occupation.

These memorials can also be seen as examples of what Billig (1995: 6) terms 'banal nationalism', i.e. reminders or 'ideological habits' of nationhood which enable the nation to be reproduced. Such habits are not 'removed from everyday life' but are part of the endemic condition of established nations. In seeing these memorials daily, islanders are reminded of their place in history; however, these reminders are so familiar that they hardly register as reminders at all. People become blind to the memorials in their towns until certain times of the year when they become visible and important parts of ceremonies.

While most towns and cities contain a number of memorials and monuments, it is less usual to find a large number that record aspects of the same ‘event’ (if a military occupation of five years can be described in this way) and are thus inter-related. Given the potential unusualness of this phenomenon, but usefulness for other locations of conflict, occupation and liberation, it is appropriate to find a new term to describe it. This phenomenon may be found not only in other European countries that were occupied by the Germans in the Second World War, but also in places that have experienced an event or traumatic period that has had, or has the potential to have, a major impact on the memory and psyche of a population for several generations. A memorialscape analysis would be fruitful in towns and cities which recall the Spanish civil war (e.g. Viejo-Rose 2011a), the Troubles in Northern Ireland (e.g. Switzer 2005) and the conflict of the 1990s in the former Yugoslavia (e.g. Baillie-Warren 2011, 2013). The plethora of competitive, highly contested and provocative memorials that have resulted from these conflicts, and earlier ones that have been destroyed during later periods of unrest, would be highly suitable for such an analysis.

The concept of the memorialscape refers to a collection of memorials within a landscape that are inter-related in some way, whether in terms of space, time or event. The study of the memorialscape considers and incorporates 12 key features:

(1) the relative centrality or marginality of the memorial within the townscape/landscape; (2) the geographical/spatial/historical relationship to other memorials (or significant places and spaces) of the same ‘event’ or group; (3) the geographical/spatial/historical relationship to older monuments (or significant places and spaces) which commemorate other events; (4) the intervisibility of memorials to each other; (5) the shape, size, form and material chosen for the memorial; (6) the date at which the memorial was erected; (7) the condition of the memorial (as a sign of care or abandonment); (8) the use or visitation of the memorial; (9) the instigator and the person chosen to unveil the memorial (which both have implications of power and agency); (10) the memorial text; (11) the function of the memorial and (12) the biography of the memorial. These twelve features can together be read to provide overarching narratives (and counter-narratives) of the memorialscape.

Each of the memorials discussed in this chapter is an important Channel Island-specific site of memory within the townscapes of St Helier, St Peter Port and St Anne. They represent a desire to remember, at various levels, the events of, and the groups who suffered during, the Occupation. The sheer density of the memorialscape conspires to ensure that the memories of the event(s) that they commemorate exclude the possibility of forgetting.

In order to understand fully the memorialscape of these capital towns, I have built up a detailed historical study of every Occupation-related memorial or monument using the 12 features of the memorialscape as a guide. I restrict this chapter to the capital towns of Guernsey and Jersey only (Figs. 6.1 and 6.2), drawing upon St Anne in Alderney later as a contrast. As Sark has only one memorial, the island’s war memorial, it is not included in this analysis. Between 2007 and 2012, I recorded memorials, attending many unveilings and annual

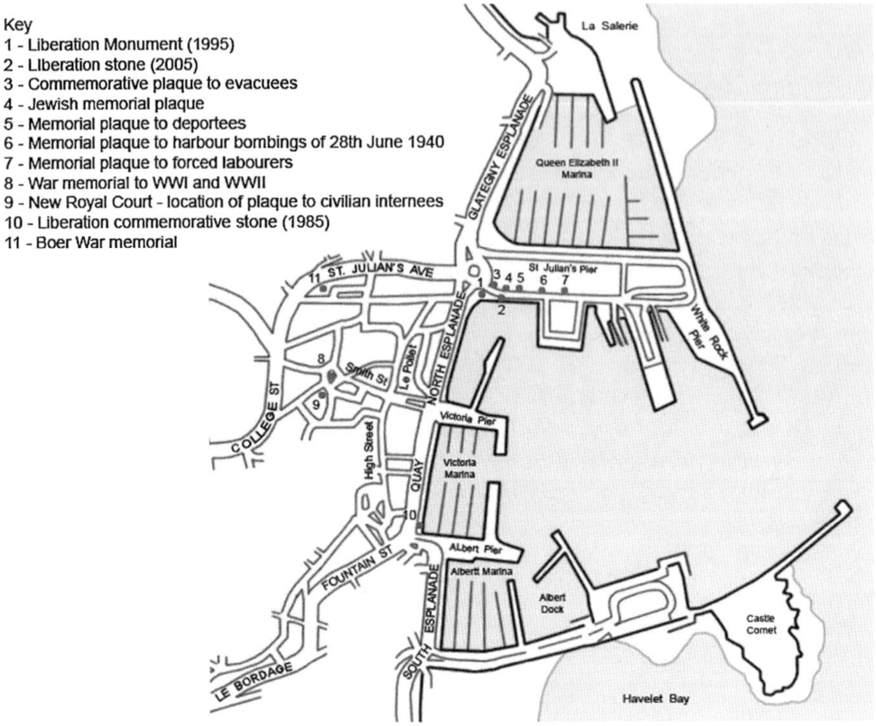

Fig. 6.1 Map of memorials in St Peter port, Guernsey (© Gilly Carr, courtesy Ian Taylor)

ceremonies. Informal interviews and discussions with people at various levels of authority within the island governments and with interest groups during the same period have also helped to inform the interpretations presented here.

Historical Background to the Victim Groups of the Occupation

In order to understand the people and events that have been given memorials or, conversely, have had to fight hard for them, it is important to remind ourselves who and what these are. While we might collectively refer to many of these groups (such as the Jews, political prisoners and those deported to civilian internment camps) as 'victims of Nazism', it is important to note that this is simply a term I have used for convenience and is not one commonly used in the Channel Islands; these groups are rarely referred to collectively at all and, as I discuss elsewhere in this volume, Channel Islanders do not see themselves as victims, but as victors in war. The term 'victim' is not entirely unproblematic in this context. It can be used

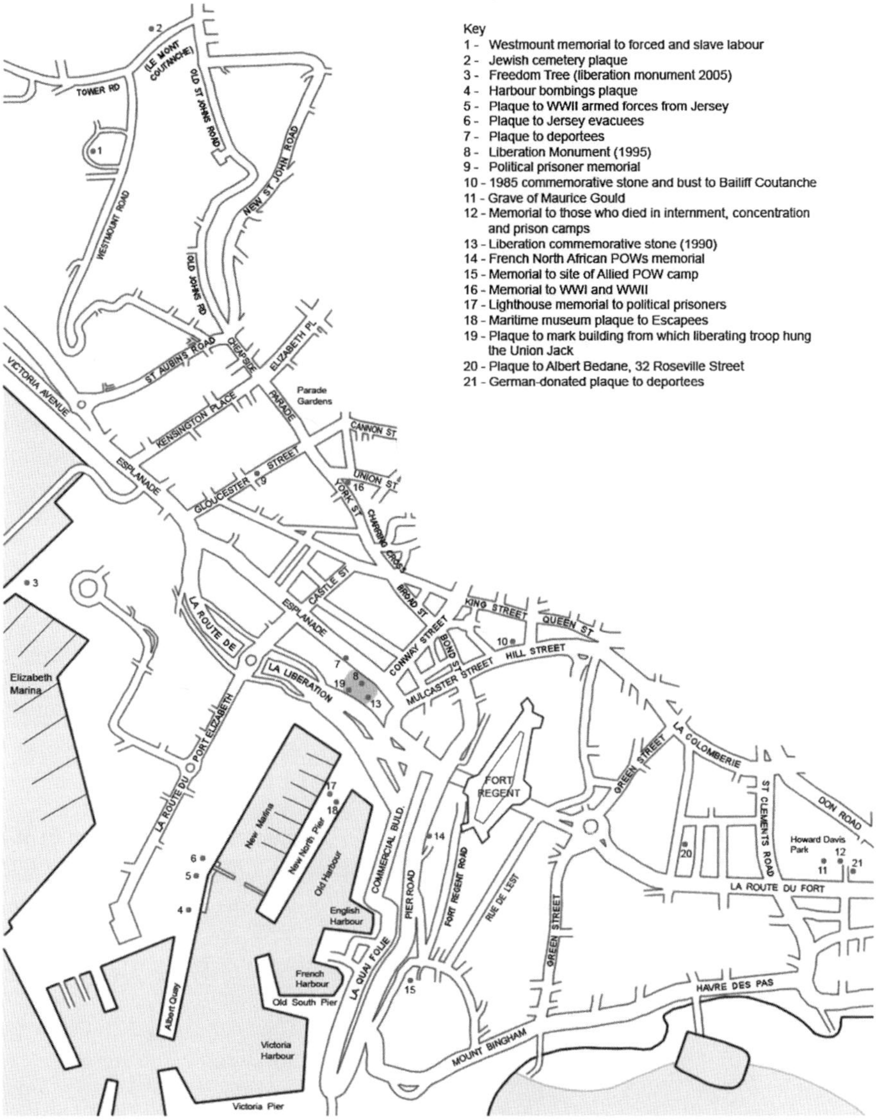

Fig. 6.2 Map of memorials in St Helier, Jersey (© Gilly Carr, courtesy Ian Taylor)

to manipulate people; to encourage them to contrast themselves with the 'perpetrator' and to perpetuate divisions, hatred and conflict. In an era of reconciliation, the perpetuation of perceived divisions and hatreds is hardly progressive, and yet people do not forget the identity of their former enemies.

In order to introduce these groups, most of whom have been touched upon already in this volume, I give here a brief historical overview of the German

Occupation of the Channel Islands, taking as my starting point the late spring and early summer of 1940, when German forces moved swiftly through Western Europe.

Occupying troops entered France, Belgium, Holland and Luxemburg on 10 May and the Channel Islands at the end of June and beginning of July. Nearly 25,000 islanders evacuated just before the Germans arrived, although nearly 70,000 stayed behind (Cruickshank 2004: 56). The evacuees, who, for the most part, arrived in Weymouth as homeless refugees, were the first victims of the German Occupation. Some Jewish Channel Islanders were among this group.

On 28 June 1940, the harbours of St Peter Port and St Helier were bombed and machine gunned from the air by German forces as a precursor to the Occupation. The 44 people who died as a result of those raids formed the next victim group.

Within the next few months, the Jews of the Channel Islands became the next group to be targeted by the German authorities. From October 1940 until January 1943, 12 consecutive anti-Jewish orders were enacted in the islands (Cohen 2000: 19–44). While around twenty Jews and their families suffered under these orders (Fraser 2000), in April 1942, three non-British Jewish women were deported from Guernsey to Auschwitz.

In September 1942 and February 1943, around 2,200 islanders were rounded up and sent to civilian internment camps in Germany, where 45 people died from diseases or natural causes. While the first wave of deportations targeted the English-born (i.e. non-indigenous) male islanders aged between 16 and 70 and their dependents, the second wave included British Jews, former military officers and ‘undesirables’ (i.e. political prisoners—those who had been imprisoned for acts of resistance). Both the deportees (or internees, as they are called in Jersey) and political prisoners are other important victim groups.

In 1942, many thousands of forced, slave and volunteer workers arrived in the islands as part of the OT, whose numbers in the Channel Islands eventually numbered 16,000 at their peak (Cruickshank 2004: 217, n. 59). These foreign labourers are another group long recognised in the islands as victims of Nazism. Of those who stayed behind in the islands after marrying local women, only one or two are still alive today.

In June 1944, after the Allied invasion of France, the Channel Islands were entirely cut-off. While food, fuel and raw materials had been scarce before, now the occupiers and the occupied had to exist only on what was still available in the islands and began to starve. Although some islanders had attempted to escape by boat before the D-Day landings, the number increased in the second half of 1944, and the names of all escapees are recorded in the islands today. The D-Day landings also netted a number of Allied POWs for the Germans, some of whom were brought to and interned in Jersey after a raid on the French coast.

When food, fuel and medical supplies in the islands had almost ceased, the Red Cross ship, the *SS Vega*, arrived from Lisbon in December 1944 and monthly thereafter, and saved the population from starvation. This ship has become the most famous in the islands’ history and has acquired almost mythical status, despite being scrapped long ago. It, along with the people of the islands who survived until liberation on 9 May 1945, is remembered annually.

There are clearly many groups of people in the Channel Islands today who are commemoratively recognised as victims of Nazism, although this has not always been the case. In the past, the islands, their museums and the one-time lack of memorials received criticism for having remembered and commemorated the perpetrators at the expense of the victims (e.g. Bunting 1995: 335–336; Vitaliev 1998; Lennon and Foley 2007: 76). However, as I argue elsewhere in this volume, the combined domination of the swastika and the German experience of occupation in the islands' museums has more to do with factors such as the proud display of battle scars; honouring of parents' and grandparents' experiences of occupation; vicarious re-experiencing of occupation and working through psychological traumas of occupation.

It is important to record here that some of the victims of Nazism might be considered problematic in so far as the wartime island governments could have done more to protect or help them, as discussed later. The potential embarrassment that this has subsequently caused and still has the potential to cause is likely to be a factor in explaining the absence or late erection of a memorial or monument to various groups.

Remembering the Occupation and Building the Memorialscape

While the criticism of the mid- to late- 1990s from Bunting, Vitaliev and Lennon and Foley drew attention to the lack of memorials to the victims of Nazism in the Channel Islands, this was not strictly accurate, as can be seen from Tables 6.1 and 6.2. The 1990s represented a decade of growth of the memorialscape of St Helier and St Peter Port, sparked by the 50th anniversary of liberation in 1995 and, before that, the 40th, in 1985, although a few had been erected earlier.

Broadly speaking, Occupation-related memorial and monument erection in the capitals of the Channel Islands can be divided into four phases:

- Phase 1: 1945–1950: Remembrance of the dead heroes (military war dead; bombing raid dead).
- Phase 2: 1950–1985: A time to forget. Virtually no new memorials erected by islanders; wreaths laid on existing memorials annually.
- Phase 3: 1985–2005: A nostalgic focus on living heroes, i.e. the occupation generation who experienced liberation (the unproblematic majority of the population).
- Phase 4: 1995–present: *Additional* focus on victims of Nazism (the problematic minority).

Table 6.1 Occupation-related monuments and memorials in St Peter Port and St Helier, 1945 to present, listed by theme

Group or event	St Helier	St Peter Port
Bombing raid dead	1990	1949
Foreign forced and slave workers	1960[e]	1999[b]
	1971	2001[c]
Jews	1999	2001
	2000	
Political prisoners	1986[a]	–
	1995	
	1996	
Individual resisters	2005	–
Deportees	1970[d]	2003[d]
	1985[b]	2010
	1986[a]	
	2003[c]	
Escapees	1995	–
Evacuees	2006	2010
Liberation	1985	1985
	1990	1995
	1995	2005
	2000	
	2005	
Vega/red cross	1985	–
	1994	
POWs	2005 × 2	–
Total extant today	22	9

[a] Memorials that did not name the victim group involved, but implied their inclusion
[b] Memorials that were taken down and amended after public pressure
[c] New memorials that replaced those taken down
[d] Memorials presented by visiting Germans dignitaries
[e] Memorial presented by visiting Russians

This table does not include the towns' war memorials, as these are not Occupation-related. It also excludes monuments and memorials outside St Peter Port and St Helier, and those which are not directly related to those people present in the islands during the occupation. Thus, military personnel washed up or shot down in the islands are excluded. Memorials which were taken down and later replaced by another to the same victim group have been counted as one in the total, and the date of their first erection is considered here to be the most important

Table 6.2 Occupation monuments and memorials erected in St Helier and St Peter Port from 1945 to present, listed by decade

Number of memorials	St Helier	St Peter Port
1945–1954	0	1
1955–1964	1	0
1965–1974	2	0
1975–1984	0	0
1985–1994	7	1
1995–2004	7	4
2005–2014	5	3
Total	22	9

Before the 40th anniversary of liberation, the celebration of Liberation Day, a public holiday in the Channel Islands, had petered out into just another bank holiday, with seemingly little relevance to memory surrounding the war years. This important anniversary became the spur for its reinvigoration in both Guernsey and Jersey, but as the even larger anniversary loomed in 1995, it acted to remind most victims of Nazism that they still had not yet been recognised.

Tables 6.1 and 6.2 summarise data about the large number of memorials and monuments that have been erected in St Peter Port and St Helier. As a combined group, together they constitute the memorialscape of these two towns. As I have outlined already, there are various analytical categories to help us make sense of the memorialscape in both analysing the importance of individual victim groups and in understanding the narrative of the memorialscape as a whole. With reference to the maps in Figs. 6.1 and 6.2, and Tables 6.1 and 6.2, I compare and contrast the two competing narratives of memorial-erection phases 3 and 4, exploring how they distanced themselves from phase 1. The theme of endurance and survival, expressed through a celebration of liberation and influenced by the British war narrative, is thus compared with the memorialscape of the victims of Nazism. The first occupies the centre stage but has, in recent years, conceded marginal ground to the counter-memories which compete with official occupation narratives.

The position of the military dead of the First and Second World Wars occupied prime commemorative space in St Peter Port and St Helier until 1995, although the first challenge to their physical dominance came in 1985. Before the 40th anniversary of liberation, only four Occupation-related memorials existed in St Helier and St Peter Port combined, and only two of these were provided by those who were resident in the islands. The first to be erected was to those who died in the bombing raid of 1940 on St Peter Port; it was inaugurated a week before Armistice Day in 1949, on the same day that Second World War additions to the town's war memorial were unveiled. St Helier's equivalent memorial, placed in two locations to mark where people died, was not erected until 1990, possibly because the raid on Jersey had had less impact, caused less damage, and killed fewer people than in Guernsey.[1]

A Soviet timber ship, the mv *Jarensk*, visited Jersey in 1960. Its crew members were taken by local members of the Communist Party (notably Norman Le Brocq) to the Strangers' Cemetery at Westmount, St Helier, to see where their dead comrades had been buried during the war. As Norman Le Brocq and his friends had been involved in helping escaped OT workers, a friendship still existed between the Jersey Communist Party and the OT workers (who mostly comprised the Spanish Republicans) who stayed in the island after the war.

Seeing that no proper memorial marked the spot, the visiting Russians were spurred to make a collection for a commemorative plaque. Although it was installed in the cemetery, it was moved when the German war graves commission,

---

[1] Interview with Michael Ginns, January 2009.

the *Volksbund Deutsche Kriegsgräberfürsorge*, visited the island the following year to remove their own war dead along with the OT workers (Ginns 2006: 154–155).

On the 25th anniversary of liberation, in 1970, the plaque (now with a concrete base) was placed in the island's crematorium. It, along with a portable plaque commemorating Spanish Republicans, was used once a year on Liberation Day. Francisco Font, a prominent Spanish Republican and former forced worker who had stayed in the island, kept the plaque in his home. On 9 May each year, he and his friends would put the two plaques in a wheel barrow to carry them to a patch of ground in the middle of the crematorium, put them on the ground, and place flowers on them[2] (Fig. 6.3). On Liberation Day, members of the Jersey Communist Party and the Spanish Republicans would gather to remember those who died. Although the Communist Party members used the occasion to give political speeches (something which deterred most islanders from attending), for the Spaniards it was a time to recall their struggle during the Spanish Civil War.[3]

After some difficulty, and a tussle over the wording, Font, along with some members of the Jersey Communist Party (Norman Le Brocq, Stella Perkins and Henny Prax), was given permission in 1971 to erect a granite horseshoe-shaped memorial in the crematorium grounds. The desire for a permanent memorial was most likely triggered by the original plaque paid for by the crew of the *Jarensk*.[4] The new memorial was installed with the *Jarensk* plaque, that of the Spanish Republican community, and one from the French Consulate. A new Russian plaque was later provided in 1978 by the Russian Naval attaché from the London Embassy.[5] In subsequent years, plaques to the Polish, Jewish, Belgian, French North Africans and Belarus labourers have been added (Fig. 6.4).

As with OT workers, the first memorialisation of those deported from Jersey was made by non-locals. In 1970, the people of the town of Bad Wurzach in Germany, to where deported Jersey people had been sent in 1942, gave a memorial plaque dedicated to those from the island who died in the camp. It was placed in St Luke's church in St Helier as one of the deceased islanders, the Reverend Atyeo, had been a vicar at that church.

While these four memorials were the only ones erected to mark the Occupation in the first 40 years after the war, the celebrations of the 40th anniversary of liberation in 1985 heralded a new memorial narrative in the Channel Islands (phase 3), and was instigated by the local government. It also signalled new sites of memory in the topography of the capitals of Jersey and Guernsey. Rather than being tied to memories of military valour and fighting overseas as promoted by the large war memorials in St Helier and St Peter Port, the first tendrils of the

[2] Interview with Gary Font, son of Francisco Font, 10 May 2011.

[3] Interview with Gary Font, son of Francisco Font, 22 September 2012.

[4] Interview with Gary Font, 22 September 2012.

[5] Jersey Evening Post 27 February 1978.

Fig. 6.3 Spanish republicans standing next to Spanish and Russian forced and slave worker memorials on Liberation Day (© and courtesy Gary font)

Fig. 6.4 Francisco Font standing by the new memorial in the 1970s (*Courtesy* Ron Robinson and Gary Font)

memorialscape moved the commemorative attention to places in the islands where significant events of the liberation took place, as described in Chap. 5.

In Guernsey, this was the harbour area of St Peter Port, where the liberating army came ashore, the site of which was marked by a stone unveiled by the Duchess of Kent. In Jersey, this was the Royal Square in St Helier, where Coutanche announced the liberation of the island. The location of the 40th anniversary memorial stone was also the location of what, before the Occupation, had been the most important event in Jersey history, namely the Battle of Jersey of 1781. However, Coutanche's speech from the balcony of the States Chambers in the square to the crowds below inscribed a new meaning into the space. The stone marking this speech was sited beneath the balcony, and the Duchess unveiled this and a curb around the V-sign in the square.

The 50th anniversary of the arrival of the *SS Vega* fell in December 1994. Jersey alone decided to mark this anniversary with a memorial, which was unveiled by Bailiff Sir Peter Crill on the Albert Pier in St Helier, the place where the ship had originally berthed. The design chosen for the memorial was a red cross overlapping a white-ringed golden V, thus playing upon double meaning of the V for Vega and for Victory, echoing that in Royal Square. A smaller polished granite plaque was also unveiled at the Maritime Museum on the New North Quay in St Helier to thank the people of Britain, Canada and New Zealand who gave food and medicine through the Red Cross.

Less than 6 months later, in 1995, the central focus of liberation both in the capital towns' geography and in the psyche of the islanders was well and truly established. Liberation Square in St Helier, very close the harbour and the area where liberating soldiers came ashore, was inaugurated with a commemorative stone in 1990 unveiled by Sir Peter Crill, and completed in 1995, providing the focus for all subsequent Liberation Day celebrations. In both St Peter Port and St Helier, monumental sculptures celebrating the 50th anniversary of liberation, again instigated by local government, were unveiled by Prince Charles, and both dominate the space of their erection. St Helier's is in Liberation Square, and St Peter Port's is by the harbour, next to the Weighbridge clock tower that was badly damaged in the bombing raid of June 1940, but also where rejoicing islanders met liberating troops.

The plans for both of these sculptures were controversial from the start for the form that they took. The States of Guernsey Liberation Committee, who oversaw the competition for the design in the island, specified that the sculpture must contain a water feature (to represent tears of joy), doves (to represent peace) and granite (to symbolise the steadfastness and endurance of islanders).[6] Predictably, the maquettes for the three best designs were all very similar (Crocker 1994: 7). They were also so unpopular with the public that, mere months before the monument was due to be unveiled, a non-figurative sundial monument was hurriedly designed instead by local artist Eric Snell.

The focal obelisk was made of 50 layers of grey Guernsey granite, one for each year of liberation. It was sited so that its shadow traced a specific path along a curved white granite bench on Liberation Day each year, highlighting inscriptions recording the major events of 9 May 1945 (Falla 1994: 1–2). In this way, 1945, 1995 and every Liberation Day in the future would be linked. The top five layers of the obelisk were sheared away at an angle to represent the five years of occupation and the trauma it caused. This design was eventually deemed to be broadly acceptable by the public, after some wrangling over the wording which failed to name the nationality of the occupiers (Leslie 1995: 1; Ogier 1995: 1–2).

---

[6] Guernsey Evening Press, 6 April 1994: 3.

Jersey's (eventual) sculpture by Philip Jackson to mark the 50th anniversary of liberation depicts a group of people waving a large Union Jack as a celebration of victory. It was also controversial,[7] and initial plans were changed in response to fierce public criticism after the Occupation and Liberation Committee originally chose a design which celebrated 50 years of peace and depicted people releasing doves—not what the public had anticipated. One of the bronze figures was altered to depict a man in British army battledress, and the women in the group were given a more active role. The group of figures were also separated slightly to allow members of the public to stand among them. They were also positioned to face the Pomme D'Or Hotel. This hotel had been the focal point for celebrations on 9 May 1945 after British soldiers had climbed onto the balcony, taken down the swastika, and raised the Union Jack, a scene that is re-enacted on Liberation Day today. In this way, the figures in the sculpture join the crowd in watching the re-enactment of liberation every 9 May (Fig. 6.5).

Monument committees on both islands had bowed to public pressure after clichéd and seemingly uncontroversial remits had deeply disappointed islanders. As an insight into the kind of design that islanders wanted, the Guernsey Evening Press ran an unofficial competition in 1994 for the public to design the monument after the original maquettes had been turned down by the public. Although there was no guarantee that the winner's idea would be used, in the end design elements were taken from many entries. The newspaper published all 45 submitted designs over several months.[8] While some stayed within the original, official remit of doves, water features and granite, most were explicit in their inclusion of patriotic symbols, military figures, trampled swastikas, excerpts from Churchill's speeches and statements of victory. Most entries were submitted by members of the Occupation generation. Although Jersey's final monument also included many of these popular elements, Guernsey's did not, much to the chagrin of the population. However, as the final decision was announced only 9 months before the unveiling, people appreciated that work needed to begin if the monument was to be ready by the 50th anniversary and the island was not to be embarrassed publically.

Both Guernsey and Jersey situated their monuments on hallowed ground that had played a momentous role on the first Liberation Day, and both islands ended up with sculptures that commemorated the liberation of ordinary people from occupation. While Guernsey's monument hinted at trauma (Fig. 6.6), no attempt was made to make the memorials explicitly inclusive of victims of Nazism or any other group whose memory might prove problematic to the authorities or the population more generally. While the public of both islands were able to change the design of their monuments within certain parameters, the final choice was still at least partly dictated by the appointed monument committees.

---

[7] http://members.societe-jersiaise.org/geraint/statues/lib.html [Accessed 28 March 2009].

[8] Guernsey Evening Press 18 May 1994: 5; 25 May 1994: 5; 1 June 1994: 5; 4 June 1994: 5; 8 June 1994: 4; 11 June 1994: 4; 24 June 1994: 21; 6 July 1994: 5; 20 July 1994: 4; 4 August 1994: 1.

Fig. 6.5 The centrality of the 1995 liberation monument, St Helier, on Liberation Day (© and courtesy Jersey Evening Post)

Fig. 6.6 Liberation monument, St Peter Port, Guernsey (© and courtesy Jonathan Bartlett)

Ten years later, in 2005, the Queen unveiled another commemorative stone in St Peter Port and another sculpture in St Helier. The link between the islands' loyalty to the Crown, especially in wartime, and the pervading influence of the

British war narrative of endurance and survival until victory (or liberation) has thus been repeatedly emphasised by the local authorities to form a master commemorative narrative.

Since 1995, and before that date in Jersey, victims of Nazism have begun to find a voice in the Channel Islands. The 50 year delay can be explained in many ways. The 50th anniversary was a catalyst for soul-searching about the events of the occupation[9] as those who experienced it first-hand teetered on the edge of living memory. This in itself was problematic, because at the very time when victims of Nazism were being given a voice, many had already died leaving only a few to agitate for memorials. We must also remember that an Occupation-related memorial culture only properly began in the Channel Islands in 1985, so it may not have occurred to some to ask for recognition in the form of a memorial before this date. An additional factor at the 50 year anniversary was the role of Jersey Bailiff, Sir Philip Bailhache, who proved to be a strong supporter of victims of Nazism, as discussed in the last chapter; many memorials were erected during his period of office, something that is now referred to locally as the 'Bailhache effect'. Bailhache also espoused a policy of openness with regard to the island's wartime record—something that no Guernsey Bailiff has yet done.

Months before Bailhache came to office, retiring Bailiff Sir Peter Crill was asked to unveil memorials to those who escaped from the islands. These were situated at the places of their departure. The impetus for their instigation was to mark Crill's retirement, as he had been one of the successful escapees himself. As unsuccessful and captured escapees were imprisoned and some deported to penal prisons and concentration camps, the unveiling of these memorials was important in kick-starting the acknowledgement of narratives other than those of liberation.

By 1995, dominant narratives were in any case secure enough to allow minority voices to be heard. This prominent anniversary, with the accompanying large expenditure of public money on monumental sculpture, made islanders from victim groups wonder why their money was not being spent on projects which represented their memories and experiences. As these groups reached the end of their lives, it became increasingly important to them to have their experiences publically recognised. Controversial publications of this time (e.g. Bunting 1995) challenged the secure position of established occupation memory and the absence of victims' voices, and these demanded a response.

In any event, a fourth phase in memorialisation began, but the ground set apart from its surroundings and made sacred—or 'sanctified', as denoted by Foote (2003: 8)—in 1985, and again in 1995 with a large monument which overshadowed and dominated the space around it, effectively blocked the ability of other memorials and alternative discourses to compete on an equal footing.

While nearly all memorials in the Channel Islands are placed at very specific locations for historical reasons, such sites of memory can often be moveable feasts and are often politically as well as geographically influenced. This resulting

[9] Email to author from Sir Philip Bailhache, former Bailiff of Jersey, 8 November 2010.

flexibility of location has been exploited. In St Peter Port, for example the harbour, now dominated by the 1995 Liberation Monument has become the key site of memory for the narrative of liberation. However, the harbours were also the place where Jews, political prisoners and deportees were sent away from both Guernsey and Jersey; they were also the place where forced and slave labourers arrived. They are thus legitimate potential sites of memory for these groups. However, while in Guernsey, space has now been given over to memorials to these groups in the harbour area, these are marginalised and unfortunately made to look insignificant by the Liberation Monument. This may not have been intentional, but it is nonetheless the end result. The Jewish memorial plaque (instigated by the Jewish community in Jersey) is small, scuffed (but restored in 2010) and is not part of the dominant view-shed of any visitor approaching the memorial area in the harbour. Instead, the 1995 and 2005 memorials to liberation and the 2010 memorial to the evacuees catch the eye first, an unproblematic triumvirate which accord with the dominant war narrative. The memorial plaque to forced workers, first erected in 1999 and instigated by a former forced worker, is not only a long way down the harbour wall and away from the main thoroughfare and other memorials, but is 'hidden' in a recess in the wall (Fig. 6.7). It and the large Liberation Monument are scarcely intervisible, with all the associated implications for the master commemorative narrative. The memorial to deportees is, however, closer to the Liberation Monument. Unlike the Jews and the forced workers, the deportees were islanders who had already endured 2 years of occupation. They thus occupy a middle ground between the victims of Nazism and the 'ordinary islanders who endured occupation'.

In Jersey, Liberation Square is the focus of commemoration. As this is by the harbour, memorials to the various victim groups could have been placed within this general area, as they have in Guernsey. However, in this island, commemorative plaques to Jews were erected in the island's synagogue and Jewish graveyard in 1998, and on the slave worker memorial the following year, which itself was established on the site of the burial place of this group. All of these memorials are on the edge of town, and the synagogue is in another parish.

The commemorative stone to internees, instigated by Michael Ginns of the Jersey ex-internee association who had been deported to Wurzach in 1942, was first put up in 1985. It is attached to the building in St Helier from which islanders were deported, is small, easily missed and around the corner from the later Liberation Monument rather than intervisible with it. A second, dedicated in 1986 to all those deported from the island between 1940 and 1945 (by implication, Jews, deportees and political prisoners, although none of these groups are named), was erected in Howard Davis Park, also on the edge of St Helier, and just outside the Allied War Cemetery, thus emphasising the exclusion and marginalisation of these groups from the dominant narratives of the first two phases of memorial erection. The failure of this memorial to name the separate victim groups and the different reasons why they were deported from the island was the reason why separate memorials to Jews and political prisoners were erected later.

Fig. 6.7 Memorials by the harbour in Guernsey (© Guernsey Museums and Galleries)

In Guernsey, there is no memorial to political prisoners or resistance, although the memorial erected to civilian deportees in 2010 remembers, as a postscript, those who 'for other reasons' were deported and died in labour camps and prisons in Europe. Instead or because of the lack of dedicated memorial, the prime site of memory for some former political prisoners has been the graveyard, where their status has been engraved on their headstones. Others have erected 'grass-roots' memorials to their family members. Sánchez-Carretero and Ortiz (2011: 107) argue that these have a 'firmly political nature, as silent witnesses to violence and pain'. Jean Harris, the daughter of Joseph Gillingham who died in a prison camp after being deported for his role in helping to run an underground newspaper, now places a wooden cross with her father's name on it alongside the others on St Peter Port's war memorial on Armistice Day (Fig. 6.8).

The key spokesperson for political prisoners in Guernsey was Frank Falla, who was responsible for getting compensation from the British government in the 1960s for Channel Islanders who had been sent to concentration camps or comparable institutions. Sadly, he died in the early 1980s, just before the era of memorialisation of the occupation began. Jersey's equivalent was Joe Mière, also a former political prisoner. He was the instigator of the first memorial to political prisoners in the island, erected in 1995 after much struggle with the authorities. It was important to Mière to place it in Gloucester Street, on the site of Jersey's Occupation prison, now demolished. In his private correspondence, he reveals that when the local government at last acceded to his request to erect a memorial, they

Fig. 6.8 Grass-roots memorial to Joseph Gillingham in front of Guernsey's war memorial in St. Peter Port (*front row, centre*) (© and courtesy Jonathan Bartlett)

initially wanted to place it in a less visible location.[10] Despite Mière's complaints, the local authorities also decided to give the official unveiling of the memorial little advance publicity, because of the 'perceived sensitivities' surrounding the belief that 'many of the offences (committed) would have been punishable under normal civilian law and indeed could have been described as criminal'[11]. The wording on the plaque, like all others erected in a public place, had to go through official channels of approval, and although it is highly likely that Mière would have submitted a text, this would have been sanitized. The available documents suggest that this occurred at the highest levels.[12] Although Mière got his wish, with the memorial unveiled by the new Bailiff, Sir Philip Bailhache, the memorial is on the edge of the commercial district of St Helier and is now neglected. It plays no part in annual commemorative ceremonies and the lettering is peeling and partially obscured by ivy, making it difficult to read (Fig. 6.9). Even when the hand of local government is forced in the erection of a memorial, they cannot be forced to hold ceremonies there and the population cannot be forced to attend. However, this was not the end of the story for Jersey's political prisoners—or at least, for those who died in captivity.

---

[10] My thanks to Joe's son, Mick Mière, for allowing me access to his late father's paperwork.

[11] Jersey Archives reference C/C/L/C9/1.

[12] Jersey Archives reference C/C/L/C9/1.

Fig. 6.9 Memorial to political prisoners, St Helier, Jersey (© Gilly Carr)

In 1996, a memorial sculpture was erected in St Helier in the form of a small, reused lighthouse and dedicated to the 'Jersey 22' who did not return from continental concentration camps and penal prisons. This is positioned in the harbour, close to the Maritime Museum which holds the Liberation Tapestry, which features some of the narratives of the Jersey 22 alongside the story of the Occupation. The location of this influenced the positioning of the Lighthouse Memorial (as it became known).[13] It is intervisible with the Liberation Monument although, ironically, the busy main road, La Route de la Liberation, separates and demarcates the two areas. The Lighthouse Memorial, while a little smaller, is broadly of a comparable size to the Liberation Monument and is the focus for the annual Holocaust Memorial Day ceremony, which is extremely well attended by wreath-bearing islanders and dignitaries alike (Fig. 6.10). In Guernsey, a small handful of islanders and no dignitaries attend the small open-air service on this day. The tiny Jewish memorial is the focus of the five-minute ceremony, and a single posy was placed by the plaque in 2009 and 2010. Political prisoners were mentioned for the first time only in 2012, on the direct intervention of the author, but this was not repeated the following year.

In Guernsey, the sites of memory of victims of Nazism are not visible or large enough to challenge the supremacy of the dominant Liberation Monument and were erected after it. In Jersey, the erection of the Liberation Monument made a clear statement about what and where the focus of attention should be. The sites of

[13] Email to author from Jon Carter, Director of Jersey Museum, 6 June 2011.

Fig. 6.10 The lighthouse memorial, Holocaust Memorial Day 2009, Jersey (© Gilly Carr)

memory of victims of Nazism have, like the Westmount memorial, become sites of counter-memory, despite other competing, dominant narratives and commemorative events. This memorial has also been a way for some minority groups in the historically monocultural Channel Islands to express themselves commemoratively on Liberation Day now that it has seen the addition of plaques and wreaths commemorating other nationalities over the last few years.

While in Guernsey, the 60th anniversary of liberation was an excuse to unveil two more stones commemorating the event, in Jersey, 2005 was a time for commemorating its heroes of the Occupation—a new status for people who had shown great courage during this period. This included, notably, Albert Bedane, who had sheltered a Jewish woman. A plaque was erected outside his house to mark his bravery. Also at this time, in the Charing Cross area of St Helier, pavement slabs were installed and engraved with Occupation quotations, as described in Chap. 4. Many were from victims of Nazism. This area of St Helier already contained two earlier monuments: one to commemorate the Queen's Silver Jubilee, and the other to mark the site of the town's first prison, and from both of which the town's cenotaph can be seen. These new pavement memorials have ensured that the space of this part of St Helier, previously untouched by public Occupation memory or memorial, has now been inscribed with the narrative of Occupation. Despite their effectiveness and degree of poignancy, it is sadly true to say that both their positions in the town and on the ground have meant that these pavement slabs are often ignored, walked on and thus marginalised in the memorialscape.

Although Guernsey has been slower than Jersey to move its memorial focus away from the act of liberation in any convincing way, Jersey has by no means successfully drawn a line underneath this popular narrative. As well as honouring brave individuals, in 2005 Jersey also chose to celebrate the 60th anniversary with another large piece of public sculpture, although this time steering clear of granite, doves and water features. This sculpture invited people to put an end to the glut of Occupation memorialisation by encouraging them to focus on the future, although many islanders still turn resolutely to the past.

On the new St Helier waterfront area, the bronze Freedom Tree designed by Richard Perry was erected to represent freedom, peace and hope for the future. It was placed in a new granite-paved public space named *La Pièche de L'Av'nîn* or the 'Place of the Future'. A tree was chosen because the Germans cut down 100,000 of them during the first four years of Occupation. The erection of the bronze tree was mirrored by the planting of a new wood in the island comprising 60 saplings to represent the anniversary.[14] The tree itself appears to be a charred trunk with short, cropped branches, no doubt symbolising the effects of occupation, but with newly sprouting leaves and acorns, symbolising new life. This tree clearly looked to the post-occupation future, both in its symbolism and in its location on the new Elizabeth Marina, which was built in 1998. According to tourist information, the tree is 'emblematic of fresh growth and continuity, pointing Jersey away from the past while still acknowledging its power and presence'.[15] However, its situation in such a marginal space in St Helier, hidden behind the architecturally much-maligned Radisson hotel (although visible from the next bay), seems to imply that Jersey is aware of the potential unpopularity of its intended move into its post-occupation future. Neither has the memorial found much favour with the public. Criticism has been scathing, mostly because of its cost. One man commented to me that it was 'just somewhere for the seagulls to sit'. The debacle over the liberation monuments show that many Channel Islanders, especially those of the Occupation generation, prefer their Occupation-related sculptures to be representational, looking back to the past and speaking of emotions and experiences at the time of liberation, rather than to be reinterpreted into more modern symbols and sentiments of peace and looking to the future.

Whatever the intentions of local government, the 60th anniversary of liberation did not draw a line under remembrance of the Occupation. Both Guernsey and Jersey accept that the Occupation remains a touchstone that inscribes and memorially dominates their landscape and may continue to do so into the future.

More memorials have been erected since 2005, all of which have been instigated by members of the Occupation generation. In 2006 in Jersey, two associated memorials were erected on the Albert Quay: one to evacuees and the other to islanders who died in the armed forces during WWII. Both of these were instigated

[14] Jersey Evening Post, 5 May 2005: 7.

[15] http://jersey.com/english/discoverjersey/occupationtoliberation/pages/occupationtrail.aspx [Accessed 7 August 2012].

Fig. 6.11 Deportee memorial, Guernsey, unveiled 2010 (© Gilly Carr)

by former evacuee Jean McLaughlin in memory of her mother and her father's experience of war. In Guernsey, two new memorials were unveiled in the spring of 2010. The first of these was erected to those deported to civilian internment camps in Germany in 1942 and 1943 and organised by the Guernsey Deportee Association (Fig. 6.11). The second was erected to remember the evacuation, instigated by former evacuees to mark the 70th anniversary of their traumatic flight from the island.

These are unlikely to be the last new Occupation-related memorials. There are still more groups to be honoured and remembered, most obviously those who committed acts of resistance in Guernsey and who were imprisoned, deported or killed for their actions. I return to the reasons for their memorial absence later.

Location, Marginality and Intentionality

We have seen in earlier chapters the manifestation in heritage of Paul Sanders' argument that, after the Occupation, the war memory of the Channel Islands were locked, by the British, into the 'straightjacket of UK war memory—the Churchillian paradigm … [of] sublime heroism and unwavering steadfastness' (2005: 256). As this paradigm stated that the British were a nation of victors not victims, there was no room to discuss the darker aspects of occupation. Thus, after memorials were first erected to the military war dead, commemorative and memorial attention was given to the ordinary civilian survivors of the Occupation.

Had attention been given to the civilian dead, traumatised or injured, this would have involved acknowledging victims of Nazism, and such acknowledgement would have run counter to the Churchillian paradigm.

That the plight of victims of Nazism has only begun to be properly addressed in the islands since the mid-1990s is reflected in the appearance of memorials to these groups from this date and the difficulties and controversies they have faced in their positioning and their wording. The British war memory has had great longevity and still dominates in the Channel Islands, even if this is now due to the influence of tradition more than anything else. It is very clear that there has been a direct link between identity and war memory, with its focus on endurance and survival until liberation/victory, and the kinds of memorials (and their size, shape, material chosen and location) which have been erected at certain times. Islanders are still learning how to embrace an uncomfortable past.

While I have suggested that memorials to victims of Nazism have been placed in marginal settings—perhaps unthinkingly—is this a fair assessment? The directors of both Guernsey and Jersey museums, who are both major players in the heritage of the islands, confirm that there is 'no set system'[16] or policy guidelines which determine the precise situation of memorials in St Peter Port and St Helier. Rather, the lack of process means that decisions are made 'ad hoc', 'at short notice', 'in un-minuted meetings' and in 'informal emails'. They are also the result of 'horse-trading' by all interest groups and stakeholders, including representatives from heritage, environment and marketing departments, the harbour office, the parish concerned, the media, petitioners, politicians and sometimes even the Bailiff.[17]

When deciding the exact positioning, this is variously dictated by 'political decision'[18] and 'aesthetics and practicalities', such as the avoidance of benches and 'not crowding the other plaques'.[19] Other factors include association with other relevant heritage sites[20] and the need to 'maintain a respectful distance' from other memorials[21] so as to avoid an 'unintended political or religious link'[22] or, conversely, the expression of a desire to place memorials within the same area because of 'appropriateness', due to a perceived link between them.[23]

Although local stakeholders have suggested to me that the concept of the memorialscape 'reads too much' into the positioning of memorials,[24] at the same

---

16 Email to author from Jon Carter, 6 June 2011.

17 Email to author from Jason Monaghan, Director of Guernsey Museum, 3 June 2011 and email to author from Jon Carter, 7 June 2011.

18 Email to author from St Peter Port Harbour Master, Peter Gill, 21 June 2011.

19 Email to author from Jason Monaghan, 3 June 2011.

20 Email to author from Jon Carter, 8 June 2011.

21 Email to author from Peter Gill, 21 June 2011.

22 Email to author from Peter Gill, 22 June 2011.

23 Email to author from Robert Barton, former Harbourmaster, St Peter Port, 23 June 2011.

24 Email to author from Jason Monaghan, 6 June 2011; email to author from Robert Barton, 23 June 2011.

time they also acknowledge locally significant concepts of 'appropriateness' and 'suitability' of situation and the perceived association between memorials caused by proximity. I propose that it is concepts such as these which allow practitioners to observe the nuances in memorialscape interpretation.

While the decision-making process is presented as the outcome of horse-trading and ad-hoc meetings, there is other evidence to suggest that things are less casual among those who agitate for memorials. Stakeholders who make it their business to champion the erection of a memorial, perhaps because of personal or family association, are much more particular when it comes to location. Three examples from Guernsey will suffice to illustrate this point.

In the mid-1990s, the Fortress Guernsey Steering Group[25] and former Spanish Republican forced worker, Juan Alarcon, helped to plan a memorial to foreign workers.[26] While the Steering Group suggested that the memorial should go next to the harbour-bombing plaque which had been erected in 1949, the Board of Administration (BoA)[27] was not in favour of such a positioning as it was not an 'appropriate' site.[28] The BoA also suggested that the proposed memorial was going to be too large to be appropriate to the site. As the size was in the end not an issue, it is more likely that the real concern was that the proposed memorial would be bigger than the harbour-bombing plaque, thus eclipsing it and its narrative.

Ultimately, the two memorials did share the harbour wall but the foreign worker memorial was placed in a recess, shielding it from the other. As an RAF-bombing raid, aimed at German ships delivering large guns, had inadvertently also killed 14 foreign workers at the harbour, the location was seen as appropriate. This location, within a recess and not intervisible with the Liberation Monument, might suggest marginalisation. However, it has also been read locally as being 'sheltered', making remembrance ceremonies 'more structured and visible', making it 'the most elegant and complete' of all memorial arrangements in the area, not to mention the first memorial that passengers from cruise liners encounter when they arrive in the island.[29]

When the Jewish memorial plaque was suggested in March 1999 to mark the deportation of three non-British Jews to Auschwitz, there was debate at the Heritage Committee about whether it should be placed in the German Occupation Museum or at the harbour with the other memorials.[30] The Jersey Jewish Congregation was later brought into the discussion, and they supported a memorial at

---

25 Heritage Committee minutes (Guernsey), 26 January 1996. (Fortress Guernsey are a subcommittee of the Channel Islands Occupation Society who concern themselves with German fortifications).

26 Guernsey Evening Press, 19 February 1997.

27 The BoA in Guernsey, now disbanded, had responsibility for the general administration relating to sites such as the harbour, the airport, the cliffs and common land.

28 Heritage Committee minutes (Guernsey), 8 October 1996 and letter from Committee to President of the Tourist Board, 10 October 1996.

29 Email from Peter Gill to author, 22 June 2011.

30 Heritage Committee (Guernsey) minutes 6 April 1999 and 4 May 1999.

the harbour. However, the Heritage Committee received a letter from Mr Van Grieken, a Dutch former OT worker who had been instrumental in getting the foreign worker memorial changed in 2001 because it had included the names of German overseers (Carrier 2000: 4; Locke 2001: 3). Van Grieken expressed the opinion that the Jewish memorial should not be placed near the memorial to foreign workers.[31] While his reasons are unknown, it seems likely that Van Grieken recognised the associated meanings and narratives that might be read from both memorials should their proximity be too close. The association of adjacent memorials and their narratives was also suggested to the author as a reason for the Jewish and forced worker memorials possibly to be placed closer together in future so that they would be separate from the recent memorials erected to both evacuees and deportees in Guernsey in 2010.[32] Similar acknowledgement is apparent in the views of the chairman of the Guernsey Deportees Association, who told the author that he was happy with the location of the deportees' memorial. 'It was', he said, 'quite suitable as it is near the memorial to the Jewish ladies ... down the far end [by the forced worker memorial] would have been very unsuitable'[33].

These three examples demonstrate that even when policies and guidelines are haphazard or missing, and even when stakeholders reject the influence of the principles of the memorialscape, local perceptions and interpretations of 'appropriateness', and an awareness of shared narratives for memorials in close proximity to each other, will still conspire to shape the resulting memorialscape. The flexible nature of sites of memory, already discussed, is also an important factor in allowing the movement of memorials in line with local perceptions of suitability.

Memorial Unveilers and Memorial Texts: Enforcing or Changing the Authorised Heritage Discourse

While aspects of the materiality of memorials and monuments such as their relative size, proximity and condition can affect their 'reading', one of the most powerful aspects of a memorial, in terms of manipulating emotion or people, is its text or message. Viejo-Rose (2011b: 5) has explored how, in the context of reconstruction in post-civil war Spain, commemorative practices and associated memorials were constructed in an attempt to 'mould memories in order to give legitimacy to the post-war administration'. This process was selective and choices were made about what to remember and what to deliberately silence.

---

[31] Undated letter from Van Grieken to Heritage Committee (Guernsey).

[32] Informal conversation between author and minister for Culture and Leisure, Guernsey, 1 April 2010.

[33] Phone call between Tom Remfrey, Chairman of the Guernsey Deportees Association and the author, 5 June 2011.

In the Channel Islands, the first post-war narratives were firmly fixed upon the war dead. In both Jersey and Guernsey, the First World War memorials were reused for the Second World War dead, as they are elsewhere in Britain. The First World War plaque on St Peter Port's memorial, erected in 1926, reminds passers-by that the soldiers gave up their own lives 'so that others might live in freedom. Let those who come after see to it that their names be not forgotten'. Above this is another plaque, erected in 1949. Its text reads '*Mon Dieu – Soyez Beni – Mon Dieu – Soyez Remercie* [My God - Bless You – My God – Thanks Be] for the liberation of Guernsey on the 9th May 1945 after 5 years of enemy Occupation'. At the same time as attention was to be focused upon the dead military war heroes, the attention of the people was also drawn to the act of liberation. The (perhaps unintentional) aim was to link the two narratives as cause and effect in islanders' subconscious.

While these narratives occupied public attention until 1985, when the first liberation monuments were erected in Jersey and Guernsey in a separate place to those of the war heroes, any focus of attention on other groups was not in evidence. However, not all islanders were liberated or in the island on 9 May. Neither those languishing in foreign prisons and labour camps to where they had been deported for acts of resistance, nor those deported to civilian internment camps, nor the island's Jews. In the post-liberation period, attention did not focus on these groups or other victims of Nazism such as the forced and slave workers. If it had, then the population (who were already expressing deep dissatisfaction with the wartime administration, especially in Jersey) may have been (even) less willing to accept the continued rule of the war-time government. This was a government who could perhaps have done more to prevent both the deportation of its citizens and the human rights abuses suffered by others brought forcibly to the islands.

There are many ways, in a democracy, that a government can show its support (or lack of it) for certain narratives of war. When it comes to memorials, support can be signalled in the British Isles in no higher way than by inviting members of the Royal Family to do the unveiling. Table 6.3 shows that six out of seven liberation monuments unveiled in St Peter Port and St Helier have been unveiled by royals: in 1985, by the Duchess of Kent; in 1995 by Prince Charles and in 2005 by the Queen. These memorials have also been instigated and often paid for by local government, sometimes with contributions by the public.

When we compare these to the memorials erected for victims of Nazism, not one has been unveiled by royalty. Most have been instigated by members of the victim group in question, unveiled by the Bailiff of the island and paid for through a combination of private sponsorship, members of the group instigating the memorial and local government. The implication here is that while liberation monuments are perceived to be for everyone, victims of Nazism are a minority group with only minority interest and therefore are not important enough to get the biggest memorials unveiled by the most important people.

We might also note that, while memorials to victims of Nazism have been unveiled by the Bailiffs, this fact has rarely been included within the memorial text. This contrasts with memorials that were unveiled by members of the Royal

Table 6.3 List of memorial, instigator and unveiler by island

Memorial	Island	Unveiler	Instigator	Perpetrator
Liberation 1985	Jersey and Guernsey	Duchess of Kent	Local government	German military (Jersey)
Liberation 1990	Jersey	Bailiff	Local government	Not mentioned
Liberation 1995	Jersey and Guernsey	Prince Charles	Local government	German forces
Liberation 2005	Jersey and Guernsey	The Queen	Local government	German forces (Guernsey)
Deportees 2010	Guernsey	Bailiff	Former deportees	German occupying forces
Deportees 1985	Jersey	Bailiff	Former deportees	Agent of deportation not named
Combined deported islanders 1986	Jersey	Bailiff	Former deportee	Agent of deportation not named
Jews 2001	Guernsey	Bailiff	Jewish community	German occupying forces
Jews 1998	Jersey	Lord Jakobovits (Emeritus Chief Rabbi)	Jewish community	Agent of deportation not named
Foreign workers 1999 (2001)	Guernsey	Bailiff	Former OT workers	German occupying forces
Foreign workers 1971	Jersey	No unveiling	Former OT workers	Germans/Nazism
Political prisoners 1995	Jersey	Bailiff	Former political prisoner	Agent of imprisonment and deportation not named
'Jersey 22' 1996	Jersey	Bailiff	Museum curator	Agent of deportation not named
Evacuees 2006	Jersey	Former evacuee	Former evacuee	Enemy not named
Evacuees 2010	Guernsey	Bailiff	Former evacuee	German forces

Family. The only exception to this is the memorial plaque to political prisoners in St Helier, unveiled by Sir Philip Bailhache in 1995. Those to Jews, deportees and foreign workers in both islands do not record who unveiled these memorials. Is it possible that any legitimacy conferred upon these memorials by the authority unveiling them is, at the same time, denied them through lack of acknowledgement in the memorial text? While in most cases, we might explain this discrepancy as due to the relative size of the memorials and the surface area available for inscription, this in itself is indicative of the importance attached locally to the memory of different groups. That elites have lent their names to dominant memorials, memories and narratives and not to marginalised others is likely to be an example of the way in which certain narratives have become dominant in the Channel Islands.

Let me give an example of this using Guernsey's most recent memorial plaque. In February 2013, a blue plaque[34] was unveiled on the former home of Marie Ozanne, a Guernseywoman in the Salvation Army who publically protested to the Germans about their actions towards the Jews, the forced and slave workers and the deportees.[35] She was put in prison and died in 1943 aged just 37. On the 70th anniversary of her death, a blue plaque was unveiled by the current Bailiff of Guernsey, Richard Collas. The group of islanders who gathered in the bitter cold for the ceremony was intimate, and in the narrow lane by Marie Ozanne's former home it seemed wholly appropriate and fitting that the island's Bailiff and not a member of the Royal Family, who had little to do with Guernsey, should be performing the unveiling. And yet why should this be? If, for example, the island had embraced the suffering of victims of Nazism as its master war narrative, not only would this memorial have been erected decades previously, but Marie Ozanne would have been a well-known local heroine and a large memorial bearing the names of those islanders who died in Nazi custody would perhaps have been unveiled soon after the war in a prominent location in St Peter Port. It would have been entirely appropriate in those circumstances for a member of the Royal Family to have unveiled that memorial as a token of thanks to islanders for their patriotism and loyalty to the Crown. However, this is not the trajectory taken by war memory in the Channel Islands. Once again, the sense of what is locally perceived to be 'appropriate' can be a useful tool in understanding the memorialscape.

One cannot help but feel that, in the eyes of many, the narratives of victims of Nazism might be perceived as less important in the Channel Islands because they were a minority. While this may be true numerically, in that while everyone present in the Channel Islands on 9 May 1945 was liberated, only some (albeit a couple of thousand of the population, many of whom were in camps at the time) were victims of Nazism. It is interesting (although perhaps not surprising), to see whose narratives are chosen by local government to speak for everyone and whose

[34] Blue plaques are historical markers put up on the front of houses or places of work of famous or important people or events to record a link between the place and person/event.

[35] http://www.bbc.co.uk/news/world-europe-guernsey-21557669

narratives are embraced as the dominant or most important narrative of occupation. Time and again, the heritage of occupation in the Channel Islands analysed in this volume has shown that, since 1985, liberation (with its associations of victory and endurance) has reigned supreme as the master narrative even if this is now beginning to be challenged. This contrasts sharply with memorials in Western Europe, where narratives of victimhood and martyrdom have historically predominated and are seen to speak for everyone, even though continental experiences of occupation were comparable with those in the Channel Islands.

The role of memorials in legitimising certain narratives in the Channel Islands can be seen in terms of an authorised heritage discourse (AHD). This concept was developed by Smith (2006: 4), who argued that 'at one level, heritage is about the promotion of a consensus version of history by state-sanctioned cultural institutions and elites to regulate cultural and social tensions in the present. On the other hand, heritage may also be a resource that is used to challenge and redefine received values and identities by a range of subaltern groups'. For Smith, the AHD is self-referential and 'draws on and naturalises certain narratives and cultural and social experiences—often linked to ideas of nation and nationhood' (ibid). We can see this in practice in the Channel Islands, where the AHD is that which is supported by and legitimates the role of elites and local government and their right to rule, and maintains the dominant narrative of liberation. Since the mid-1990s, these ideas have been effectively challenged by those who had alternative experiences of occupation or who were not liberated because they were in prison or internment or concentration camps. These people have campaigned to get memorials to represent their groups, and such memorials can be said to form a subaltern or dissenting heritage discourse, especially as those who champion them have not often been heritage professionals (with the exception of the Lighthouse Memorial in Jersey). As the AHD establishes who has the authority to speak for the past (i.e. local government), those who were outside this group of elites did not initially have a voice—or realise that it was possible for them to have one.

Earlier in this chapter, I examined how the size and location of liberation memorials have effectively marginalised those erected to victims of Nazism, and this, too, is part of the way that the AHD operates in the Channel Islands, as it works to 'exclude the historical, cultural and social experiences of a range of groups' while also working to 'constrain and limit their critique' (ibid: 30). Smith argues that the AHD excludes competing discourses by constructing heritage as something that is 'engaged with passively—while it may be the subject of the popular 'gaze', that gaze is a passive one in which the audience will uncritically consume the message…' (ibid: 31). In other words, because the narrative of occupation through the lens of liberation is portrayed in such a dominant way and all other readings obfuscated, the visitor or viewer will (it is assumed) passively and uncritically absorb this narrative and not question it or ask about the possibility of other readings.

The text on the memorials and monuments is not always reticent when it comes to pointing the finger of blame. The first thing to note from Table 6.3 is that in the Channel Islands, both on memorials and in daily parlance, the occupiers were and are always referred to as 'Germans' and not 'Nazis'. The only exceptions to this can be seen on several of the plaques on the Westmount slave worker memorial which were donated by different countries. The reason for this particular nomenclature is most likely to be attributable to the very high density of occupying soldiers in the islands. As German soldiers were billeted in the homes of many islanders, most people got to know individual soldiers as ordinary humans rather than as 'inhuman barbarian Nazis', 'the Boche' or other common epithets. This is not to say that Channel Islanders did not use these epithets; just to suggest that they often came to know the people behind the uniform.

The second observation of patterning from Table 6.3 is that the enemy, perpetrators, facilitators or forces responsible for the suffering of islanders and victim groups are either named as the German forces (in all seven Guernsey memorials listed) or else not named at all (in eight out of eleven memorials in Jersey). It is significant that at no point has any memorial attempted to lay any portion of blame on the actions or inactions of the local wartime government for not doing enough to protect its own people. This is not to accuse the local government of wartime collaboration, nor to give the impression that no one attempted to complain about deportations or the treatment of Jews and foreign workers—indeed, strong protests were made at various times. What I am suggesting, however, is that the text on memorials does not make any suggestion at all that local government could have done more to help or to protest—which indeed perhaps it could. As Paul Sanders (2005: 98) argues, while the authorities 'did the 'right thing', there was probably an even 'righter' thing—to resist, by whatever limited means available and, if necessary, behind the backs of those Germans with whom they had built relationships of trust but who were incapable of seeing through the criminal nature of the system they were serving'. The local authorities are not implicated on memorials and the AHD protects the status quo. By not naming the agents of deportation, however, a question mark is effectively drawn over the subject. As Jersey has been more open than Guernsey in discussing its wartime role because of the 'Bailhache effect', its seeming reticence to pin the blame squarely on the occupiers is interesting. Could this be due solely to political correctness which considers it bad manners to 'point the finger' at a country which is now a European allay?

As I have observed through discussing the subject with those involved in recent memorial erections in Guernsey, memorial texts are difficult political matters that must be authorised before they are committed to stone. The memorial instigator is not free to choose a wording of their own, but they must negotiate with local government and heritage authorities. Where memorial texts have, in the past, been deemed to offend, perhaps because of inaccuracies (the Jersey deportee memorial and the Guernsey foreign worker memorial) or because of a failure to name the perpetrators (the Guernsey 1995 liberation monument), they have been replaced. Where a memorial text has not gone far enough in acknowledging the groups who suffered (e.g. the 1986 Jersey memorial to those deported), then additional memorials have been erected at a later date. It is unthinkable, at present, that any Occupation-related memorial text in the Channel Islands should lay any blame at all at the door of the local authorities, and I am not suggesting that any memorial should do so, but perhaps in another generation, when and if narratives of victims of Nazism move centre stage, this may yet happen.

Different Islands, Different Responses

While I have explained the difference in attitudes towards victims of Nazism in Guernsey and Jersey in terms of the 'Bailhache effect', I have not yet adequately explained why Guernsey's Bailiffs have not followed suit, and why the island is less forthcoming in remembering these groups. Revealingly, the continued absence of a memorial to political prisoners is key to understanding the difference in the way that Occupation memory is constructed and supported in the islands.

It is well known that during the Occupation, Bailiffs of both Guernsey and Jersey strongly and publically denounced acts of resistance, preferring a cordial relationship with the occupiers as a method of self-preservation for their population (Bunting 1995: 78; Willmot 2000: 70–71). Thus, after the war, it was hard for the same government, still in power, to honour people who committed acts of resistance and who thus potentially risked the lives of the wider population.

In Guernsey, no Bailiff, member of local government or community leader has made it his or her cause to support these particular victims of Nazism. It is possible, however, that the long and prominent career in the island since the mid-1960s of respected former Bailiff, Sir de Vic Carey, who held office from 1999 to 2005, and who was the grandson of the wartime Bailiff, has indirectly, unintentionally, and through no fault of his own, suppressed activism in this area (the 'Carey effect', as it were). Sir de Vic is also known for his reticence to speak about his grandfather; as much as anything else, this is because he believes that the role of Bailiff should not be political.[36]

We might also add that some former Bailiffs and officials in local government who have held positions of authority since 1945 have also been descendants or relations of those who were part of the wartime administration during the Occupation, and one might speculate whether this has also acted to stifle criticism of the anti-resistance stance in the island.[37] It seems likely that a non-critical stance has been adopted both at the highest levels as well as among the general population. This would explain why Jersey has had proportionally more spokespeople (and resulting memorials) for victims of Nazism.

In the kind of small, close-knit community which is characteristic of the Channel Islands, to criticise the actions of the forebears of one's colleagues or predecessors would be unthinkable. Such criticisms are difficult to shake off or

[36] Informal conversation between Sir de Vic Carey and author, 12 May 2012.

[37] This observation was mentioned to the author by Sir Philip Bailhache, former Bailiff of Jersey, in an interview of 22 June 2009.

move past—and thus are less rarely made in the first place—when one has to live and/or work in close proximity with the subject of one's attack.

As a result of these factors and others, a Bailhache-like figure has yet to emerge in the island and a memorial to political prisoners has yet to be erected. While there is little to stop the children of Guernsey's political prisoners raising money for their own memorial and seeking permission to put it in a public place, this is not necessarily the answer. As Doss (2010: 363) argues, 'simply adding more memorials is not adequate, of course: commemorative accrual must be accompanied by a critical reconsideration of historical memory itself'.

We can see from this why Guernsey's memorials to victims of Nazism have been late to emerge, with forerunners emerging first in Jersey in the case of Jews, forced and slave labourers, deportees and political prisoners. We can also see why the text on Guernsey's memorials to these groups is explicit in naming the occupying forces as the agents of deportation, while Jersey's memorials have been more reserved in apportioning blame. As Viejo-Rose (2011b: 5) argues in her discussion of how memorials can be used to attempt social control, 'memorials can be used to construct a mythology for the emerging power structure, one that supports its claims of legitimacy and power'. In Guernsey and Jersey, this 'myth' is one that has traditionally focused on liberation and victory to the exclusion of all else. But what of Alderney, whose inhabitants' experience of war was the same as those from Guernsey and Jersey who evacuated, and which was covered in concrete fortifications and labour camps?

Narratives of War in Alderney

In Alderney, almost the entire population evacuated to the UK, where they lived as refugees, joined the armed forces or settled down for good in their new homes. Many, but not all, returned on 15 December 1945[38] to an utterly desecrated island that had been made just about habitable in time for their arrival. The next few years were spent getting their island back to some semblance of normality. During their absence, German forces had covered the island in concrete fortifications and had built concentration and labour camps. The traces of these were there when the population returned in 1945 and they are still there today.

While the Occupation is an integral part of Guernsey and Jersey identity and heritage today, and one that is remembered with great pride, it is still anathema in Alderney and has been thoroughly rejected by the population, as I have discussed elsewhere (Carr 2007) and earlier in this volume. While the details of the Occupation have been provided for Alderney's museum by a local military historian, it

[38] Homecoming Day in Alderney remembers not only the return to the island but the struggle of a generation in rebuilding the island and the community, which had been scattered across the UK during the evacuation. http://www.bbc.co.uk/news/world-europe-guernsey-11995020, accessed 3 August 2012.

is clear from the island's tourist brochure that the islanders are more interested in their natural history. Neither of the two reused bunkers in the island evokes the Occupation in the manner espoused by Guernsey and Jersey's bunkers, and one is currently used by the Alderney Wildlife Trust.

How, then, does Alderney's experience and narrative of war play out in the island's memorials and what impressions can be taken from the island's memorialscape? Memorials in Alderney which refer to the war years are to be found in two key locations: the memorial garden in Victoria Street in St Anne, and at the harbour. There is also a small sprinkling of other memorials at particular sites of memory around the island. Rather than any focus on liberation or victory, as is readily apparent in Jersey and Guernsey, the dominant narrative of memorials here is the importance of military service, especially relevant given that Alderney was a garrison island. This narrative applies both to islanders who served in the world wars, and to British military personnel who helped to demilitarise the island after the war, and whose collective experience is personified in the role of one man in particular: Sapper George Onions of the Royal Engineers who died on minefield clearance operations in June 1945.

The walled memorial garden in St Anne was originally founded as a place of reflection for the memory of the island's military war dead of the First World War (Fig. 6.12). Since then, in addition to the central obelisk war memorial, an additional four plaques have been added to the walls. The first remembers Alderney men and women who volunteered to serve in the armed forces during the Second World War. The second is dedicated to Sapper Onions. These two memorials are close to each other on the same wall, are the same size, and made out of the same material (polished blue granite) with lettering in the same font. It is likely that both were erected at the same time, and their proximity shows the equality in which the memories of both groups are held: the serving islanders and those who died in clearing the island ready for the return of those islanders.

On the wall furthest away from the entrance to the garden is a modest central plaque, of equivalent size to the first two, but made of bronze. This commemorates the 50th anniversary of the 'return from exile after the German Occupation' (i.e. the homecoming), and includes part of Winston Churchill's famous speech in which he announced the liberation of the Channel Islands. A couple of metres away from this plaque, and in a subordinate position lower down the wall, is a plaque commemorating 50 years of 'loyal voluntary service' to Alderney from 1951 to 2001 of the Women's Voluntary Service/Women's Royal Voluntary Service (WVS/WRVS). This organisation gives aid to civilians in need and plays an important role in helping people during the war, especially during the Blitz. For years, the WRVS in Alderney also tended Sapper Onions' grave, which is in St Anne's churchyard.

The importance of military service (of islanders and Sapper Onions) is twinned in Alderney's memorialscape with the narrative of evacuation and homecoming. That this is equally important is attested to its central position in the memorial garden but also at the island's harbour. Here, there are two memorials: one to remember the evacuation of the population to Weymouth in England and the

Fig. 6.12 Memorial garden, St Anne, Alderney (© Gilly Carr)

second, to remember the 60th anniversary of the 'return of the evacuees' in 2005. This was also the year that Homecoming Day became a holiday and returned to prominence as a day of memory in Alderney. Close to both of these is the 'Sapper Slipway', built in 1962.

Alderney also has a number of memorial sites related to the Occupation. Two of these are not in authentic locations: the Sapper Onions peace garden created by schoolchildren, and the plaque on the wall of Alderney museum marking the location of the labour camps. The other three memorials in the island remember the foreign slave and forced labourers at places where they suffered or were buried.

The first of these three memorials is on the wall of St Anne's church and explicitly records the nearby burial place (as opposed to the memory) of 45 'Soviet citizens'. It is perhaps more of a marker than a memorial; it appears to simply refer to the group rather than to commemorate them. There is no mention of how or why they came to be buried in the graveyard and only the dates on the memorial tell us that the dead date to the Second World War.

The second is the Hammond Memorial. This overlooks Longis Common where liberating troops found a large burial ground of forced and slave labourers. The memorial initially comprised a single small granite boulder given to the island by the French in 1951 to remember their citizens who died during the war. In 1966, a

Fig. 6.13 The Hammond Memorial, Alderney (© Gilly Carr)

member of the States of Alderney, Mr Bert Hammond, built a larger, two-tier memorial around the original boulder, with the addition of pots of flowers and nine plaques on the second tier to remember the people of different nationalities who died. On the first tier, a tenth memorial plaque, made of the same stone as those dedicated to the labourers, remembers three members of the Hammond family (including Mr Hammond himself), whose ashes were scattered at the site in the 1980s (Fig. 6.13).

The third and final memorial of this type was erected only in 2008, a massive 63 years after the war. A plaque was placed by former prisoners and their families (instigated by a Polish former inmate) on the concrete entrance post of *SS Lager* Sylt, the site of a former concentration camp near Alderney's airport. This is still the only labour camp in the Channel Islands to have any kind of memorial plaque.

In summary, then, we can see that where Alderney has commemorated the camps of forced and slave labourers, their hand was forced by other nationalities or former inmates. At the Hammond Memorial, the traumatic memory of their fate has been softened by the addition of a plaque remembering the islander who instigated the memorial. Where Alderney has put up memorial plaques without encouragement (at St Anne's church), the labourers have been identified only by their nationality; the reasons for their presence are unexplained. One cannot help but detect a slight historical reluctance to embrace narratives other than those which reflected the direct wartime experience and values of the islanders themselves.

Conclusion: A Changing Memorialscape

Memorialscapes are highly complex entanglements in space and time of competing and overlapping narrative layers. By exploring its 12 key features, I hope to have set out a methodology for successfully penetrating and interpreting these sites of memory and counter-memory in the landscape, allowing the resulting narratives to be read.

The two largest Channel Islands have seen four overlapping phases of memorialisation, each of which has built up the memorialscape and gradually changed the commemorative Occupation narrative. Despite dominating commemorative and non-commemorative space and inscribing its narrative on different parts of the islands' capitals, the master commemorative narrative of endurance until victory and liberation (as expressed through both 50th anniversary liberation monuments) has been increasingly challenged since 1995.

The success of this challenge, and the admission of the memory of victims of Nazism into the master narrative, has varied according to island. In St Peter Port, their memory has been allowed into the memorial space of the dominant narrative, but has not challenged it in any serious way. Instead, other memorials are small, marginalised or give the impression of having been hidden away, most especially those relating to non-islander groups such as forced and slave labourers or Jews. In St Helier, the main sites of memory of victims of Nazism and of liberation are spatially separate, both through historical accident or design. Despite this, the memorial to the 'Jersey 22', who were islanders and not foreigners and which, like the Liberation Monument, is now also a centre of large annual commemorations, has now effectively changed the reading of the town's memorialscape. Since 1995, Jersey has indeed been open about its wartime record and is more ready than its sister island to include victims of Nazism within its dominant narrative and to embrace them as fellow heroes of the occupation. In Alderney, the smaller number of memorials and the smaller size of the island have made it difficult to identify memorial phases, but we can clearly see how its narrative of war is strongly echoed in its memorials.

The concept of the memorialscape is likely to be useful in other conflict locations involving civilians, especially (but not limited to) those that have experienced occupation and liberation; continental Europe is full of such sites.

While I have focused on monuments and memorials here, any interpretation of a memorialscape should ideally also examine the wider memory landscape and other physical and non-physical sites of memory and counter-memory in order to gain a fuller understanding of how public and private memory works within any society. In the conclusion of this volume, I bring together these other threads of interpretation.

We have a tendency to prioritise memorials because of their public visibility and accessibility. It is all too easy to pass judgement upon a place, as others have done for the Channel Islands, for the presence or absence of certain memorials and monuments, but memorialscapes, memorial landscapes and intangible modes of commemoration which leave little or no trace can be complex in their interpretation. They are linked to other memorialscapes in other places with other narratives, through events such as evacuation and deportation. Untangling a memorialscape is not easy: many threads of history link plaques, memorial stones and monuments to the spaces that they inhabit; spaces that have seen other events at other times, and events that have dominated earlier narratives and have given rise to earlier memorials and earlier memorialscapes.

References

Ashton, P., & Hamilton, P. (2008). Places of the heart: Memorials, public history and the State in Australia since 1960. *Public History Review, 15*, 1–29.

Baillie, B. (2011). *The Wounded Church: War, destruction and reconstruction of Vukovar's religious heritage*. Unpublished PhD thesis, University of Cambridge.

Baillie, B. (2013). Memorialising the Martyred City: Negotiating conflict time in Vukovar. In W. Pullan & B. Baillie-Warren (Eds.), *Locating urban conflicts: Ethnicity, nationalism, religion*. London: Palgrave MacMillan.

Billig, M. (1995). *Banal nationalism*. London: Sage Publications.

Bulbeck, C. (1988). *The stone laurel: Race, gender and class in Australian memorials*. Queensland: Institute for Cultural Policy Studies, Division of Humanities, Griffith University.

Bunting, M. (1995). *The model Occupation*. London: BCA.

Carr, G. (2007). The politics of forgetting on the island of Alderney. *Archaeological Review from Cambridge, 22*(2), 89–112.

Carrier, D. (2000). *Take the German bosses off the workers' memorial* (p. 4). Guernsey: Guernsey Evening Press.

Cohen, F. (2000). *The Jews in the Channel Islands during the German Occupation 1940–1945*. Jersey: Jersey Heritage Trust.

Crocker, J. (1994). *Designs on our monument* (p. 7). Guernsey: Guernsey Evening Press.

Cruickshank, C. (2004) [1975]. *The German Occupation of the Channel Islands*. Stroud: Sutton Publishing (Oxford: Oxford University Press).

Doss, E. (2010). *Memorial Mania: Public feeling in America*. Chicago: University of Chicago Press.

Falla, J. (1994). *Obelisk to mark Liberation?* (pp. 1–2). Guernsey: Guernsey Evening Press.

Foote, K. E. (2003) [1997]. *Shadowed ground: America's landscapes of violence and tragedy*. Austin: University of Texas Press.

Fraser, D. (2000). *The Jews of the Channel Islands and the rule of law, 1940–1945*. Brighton: Sussex Academic Press.

Ginns, M. (2006) [1994]. *The Organisation Todt and the Fortress Engineers in the Channel Islands*. Jersey: Channel Islands Occupation Society Archive Book no. 8.

Hamilton, P. (2003). Memorial studies and cultural history. In H.-M. Teo & R. White (Eds.), *Cultural history in Australia* (pp. 81–97). Sydney: University of New South Wales Press.

Huyssen, A. (2003). *Present pasts: Urban palimpsests and the politics of memory*. Stanford: Stanford University Press.

Jordan, J. (2006). *Structures of memory: Understanding urban change in Berlin and beyond*. Stanford: Stanford University Press.

Lennon, J., & Foley, M. (2007). *Dark tourism: The attraction of death and disaster*. London: Thomson Publishing.

Leslie, K. (1995). *Fashions change, the facts don't* (p. 1). Guernsey: Guernsey Evening Press.

Locke, J. (2001). *'Nazi names' will be erased from memorial*. Guernsey: Guernsey Evening Press. 3.

Nora, P. (1989). Between memory and history: Les Lieux de Memoire. *Representations, 26*, 7–25.

Nora, P. (1998). The era of commemoration. In P. Nora (Ed.), *Realms of memory: The construction of the French past. Volume III: Symbols* (pp. 609–637). New York: Columbia University Press.

Norkunas, M. K. (1993). *The politics of public memory: Tourism, history and ethnicity in Monterey, California*. Albany: State University of New York Press.

Nugent, M. (2005). *Botany bay: Where histories meet*. Crows Nest: Allen and Unwin.

Ogier, M. (1995). *Monument wording will change: No U-turn, committee 'just did not want to overspend'* (pp. 1–2). Guernsey: Guernsey Evening Press and Star.

Rousso, H. (2007). History of memory, policies of the past: What for? In K. H. Jarausch & T. Lindberger (Eds.), *Conflicted memories: Europeanizing contemporary histories* (pp. 29–31). New York and Oxford: Berghahn Books.

Rowlands, M. (1999). Remembering to forget: Sublimation as sacrifice in war memorials. In A. Forty & S. Küchler (Eds.), *The art of forgetting* (pp. 129–145). Oxford: Berg.

Sánchez-Carretero, C., & Ortiz, C. (2011). Grassroots memorials as sites of heritage creation. In H. Anheier & Y. R. Isar (Eds.), *Heritage, memory and identity* (pp. 106–113). London: Sage.

Sanders, P. (2005). *The British Channel Islands under German Occupation 1940–1945*. Jersey: Jersey Heritage Trust and Société Jersiaise.

Siblon, J. (2009). 'Monument mania'? Public space and the Black and Asian presence in the London landscape. In P. Ashton & H. Keane (Eds.), *People and their pasts: Public history today* (pp. 146–162). Basingstoke: Palgrave Macmillan.

Smith, L. (2006). *The uses of heritage*. London: Routledge.

Switzer, C. (2005). Conflict commemoration among Protestants in Northern Ireland. In G. J. Ashworth & B. Graham (Eds.), *Senses of place: Senses of time* (pp. 119–132). Aldershot: Ashgate Publishing Ltd.

Viejo-Rose, D. (2011a). Destruction and reconstruction of heritage: Impacts on memory and identity. In H. Anheier & Y. R. Isar (Eds.), *Heritage, memory and identity* (pp. 53–69). London: Sage.

Viejo-Rose, D. (2011b). Memorial functions: Intent, impact and the right to remember. *Memory Studies, 4*(4), 1–16.

Vitaliev, V. (1998). *Showing off the sites of shame* (p. 4). London: The Guardian.

Willmot, L. (2000). The Channel Islands. In B. Moore (Ed.), *Resistance in Western Europe* (pp. 65–92). Oxford and New York: Berg.

Winter, J. (2000). The generation of memory: Reflections on the 'memory boom' in contemporary historical studies. *Bulletin of the German Historical Institute, 27*, 69–92.

Winter, J. (2006). Notes on the memory boom: Warm remembrance and the uses of the past. In D. Bell (Ed.), *Memory, trauma and world politics: Reflections on the relationship between past and present* (pp. 54–73). Basingstoke and New York: Palgrave Macmillan.

Young, J. E. (1993). *The texture of memory: Holocaust memorials and meaning*. New Haven and London: Yale University Press.

Young, J. E. (2000). *At memory's edge: After-images of the holocaust in contemporary art and architecture*. New Haven and London: Yale University Press.

Chapter 7
Conclusion

Heritage, Identity and Generations

During the Second World War, almost every nation was directly or indirectly associated with or affected by the impact of war. While the legacies of war of large nations and smaller regions alike are well researched, far less is understood about how small islands have reacted over the long term. Yet for many islands, such as the Channel Islands, war had an enduring impact on their memory, heritage and sense of identity. It seems that when war encroaches upon island shores, especially in the form of military occupation, the impact upon the local population is often disproportionate and continues to reverberate long after the conflict has passed. Yet is the legacy of war really more enduring in small islands compared with other places and, if so, is this perhaps because of closer ties of kinship and group identity? Do these enable collective memories to last longer and, in turn, more strongly shape identity and its resulting war-related heritage? Or is long-term impact ensured, instead, by the immense shock of the destruction of tranquil island life by the arrival of conflict and the forced necessity of hosting unwelcome guests for a number of years? I would suggest that the unavoidably insular nature of islands and an inward-looking character is, in the case of the Channel Islands, at least partly responsible for the long duration of war memory here. The densely packed and visibly ubiquitous nature of the occupationscape in the Channel Islands also plays a part.

What, if anything, can the study of island responses to war teach us about the longevity of war memories, legacies and the heritage of war? Is there any sense in which islands can act as bounded 'laboratories' which allow us to understand the macrocosm of the legacy of war in microcosm? The Channel Islands certainly provide a unique setting for the researcher, offering richly multifaceted Second World War landscapes within a tightly bound geographical context. They also seemingly continue to nurture the memory of the German Occupation more strongly than is apparent in Britain or in other Western European countries today.

G. Carr, *Legacies of Occupation*, Contributions To Global Historical Archaeology 40,
DOI: 10.1007/978-3-319-03407-2_7, © Springer International Publishing Switzerland 2014

The Role of Generations in Occupation Heritage

This volume has shown how the seeds of Occupation heritage were sewn both during the Occupation and in the years that followed. One of the earliest acts of creation of Occupation heritage began with the imaginative play of the first post-war generation of children—specifically little boys. Although their collections of German militaria were often encouraged and facilitated by adults, it was the children who sought to rescue objects that had been thrown away, dumped or destroyed by adults after the war. While the adults who lived through the war on the whole sought to remove its remnants, children were proactive in its rescue and retrieval. For them, collecting was a coping mechanism, a way of making sense of and controlling the material culture of war. It is rare for children to found, direct and shape future heritage strategy; yet this is effectively what has happened in the Channel Islands. Their experience of living in the post-Occupation era and the perception of occupation gained in childhood, influenced by the stories of those around them, directly influenced the shape of heritage that these children were later to create. The active encouragement of adults and their donation of militaria to childhood collections is perhaps difficult to understand in the safety-conscious twenty-first century. Yet one strand of traditional male identity in the Channel Islands has long focused on martial prowess, with all of its associated familiarity and competence with weaponry; generations of men were once required to serve in the Guernsey or Jersey Militias. The early induction of boys into a military role is thus not so surprising, especially as many of the men who encouraged it had probably themselves fought in the First or Second World War. The associations between masculinity and weaponry were, no doubt, consciously made.

These young boys grew up and founded museums of their own in which to display their prized collections—collections which portrayed a nostalgic image of a past that most of them had missed or were not old enough to understand fully and which they sought to recreate through museum displays. These museums were *primarily* venues for showing off their collections and not for giving a holistic and educational experience to tourists. While tourism was highly important in the post-war economic recovery of the Channel Islands, collectors believed that swastikas, helmets and guns would prove a bigger draw than wooden clogs worn by foreign labourers, which in any case rarely survived and were not part of their collections.

These museums have followed an almost formulaic pattern since their inception. As part of this, they have exhibited great cultural conservatism because of the systems of value espoused by collectors, where particular concepts of 'authenticity' and of 'closeness to the Occupation' are favoured. Occupation museums have had an important influence upon the popular collective memory of subsequent generations. The museum owners have also gone on to become some of the guardians of memory of the Occupation, and the German-dominated experience which is presented in museums has lead local people to become normalised or desensitised to images of soldiers and swastikas.

The later restoration of bunkers from the late 1970s onwards has been inspired and influenced by earlier presentations of the past in Occupation museums. Such occupier-heavy modes of restoration were simply a natural and unquestioned way to present the islands' heritage. Like the museum displays, the restored bunkers also present a nostalgic vision of the Occupation, in which mannequin soldiers carry out inoffensive and innocent tasks such as playing chess, listening to the radio and reading the paper. Embracing the same systems of value as the museum owners, the dioramas in bunkers also favour displays which give a selective view both of 'authenticity' and of temporal closeness to the Occupation which suggest to the visitor that the soldiers have left the room for only a few minutes.

For the first post-war generation, bunkers were restored as a way of discovering the Occupation for themselves and of honouring their parents and grandparents. For those who lived through the occupation, restoration was also a way not just of healing traumatic memories, but of making sure that the broader memories of military occupation would be kept alive. 'Scars on the landscape' slowly became 'stars in the landscape' as reclaimed bunkers made the transition to heritage. Bunkers have long been battlegrounds for control; first between the generations and later between enthusiasts and the heritage professionals. As the fight continues with regards to heritage listing and World Heritage Status, the ongoing conflict is still between the competing narratives of the past that these groups present.

Although bunkers have been places of pain and shame and of uncomfortable memories for islanders, this forms no part of the presentation of bunker enthusiasts. Instead, bunkers are proud battle trophies, part of the booty of the victors. All over Europe, bunkers have emerged as symbolic spaces where narratives of occupation are expressed and controlled by the groups who own them.

While bunkers have been deemed a heritage worth fighting for, labour camps have never been perceived as such. They are forgotten places; the outsider in the sites of memory of the occupationscape discussed in this volume. They do not reflect the experiences of the dominant group and so have been neglected. Unlike the other sites, the camps are now invisible, raising questions of whether *sites* of memory in the Channel Islands tend to dwell in *sights* of memory. At the same time, so used are islanders to the most visible sites, the bunkers, that they often seem to be invisible and taken for granted.

Even where the camps have been removed, they still have a presence, even if this is only archival or residing in memory, and even where excavation alone is the only kind of intervention that could turn them into heritage. The reasons for their exclusion from memory are various, but three dominant suggestions have been put forward in this volume. First, the workers tended to be and still are remembered by many islanders, especially by post-war generations, as undifferentiated 'Russians' at a time when sympathies for citizens of the USSR were at an all-time low, i.e. during the Cold War. Second, labour camps provoke dark memories of human rights abuses, starvation and ill-treatment. lurking in the background here are dangerous questions—or even accusations—of potential collaboration of local people who worked for the Germans. Third is the influence of the Churchillian paradigm, mostly in evidence on Liberation Day, which stresses narratives of victory over victimhood. This is perhaps why the spoils of the victor (the booty and the bunkers) have been valued more highly than the detritus of the victims and the places where they lived.

We might also suggest that over the last 20 years, since the emergence of victims of Nazism into the memorialscape, there has been a hierarchy of victims in the Channel Islands, where some have been remembered and ranked more highly in local collective memory. The relative position of groups has waxed and waned according to times of the year (such as Liberation Day or Holocaust Memorial Day) and at major anniversaries. At the time of writing, the 70th anniversary of the beginning of the 1942 deportations is upon us and museum exhibitions,[1] newspaper articles, special services and reunions will serve to promote these groups in local consciousness. Even so, the narrative told by former deportees is rarely one of victimhood, but of endurance and survival. Even these potential victims have learned to narrate their experiences in terms which minimise their own suffering.

With regards to the OT camps, it appears that the decision to destroy, remove and build over most of them was taken a long time ago. Wooden huts were sold to farmers for storage or recycled by people for firewood. The desire was to 'erase the mess', to 'clean it up' and to engage in 'deliberate amnesia'.[2] For the most part, this took place in the early days of the post-war period. By the 1960s and 1970s, when the first post-war generation was reaching adulthood and carrying out research on certain sites of the occupation as a way to satisfy their curiosity and re-engage with the Occupation, it seems that very little was still intact or recognisable as a camp site.[3] Because these structures were, for the most part, made of wood and not concrete and because the undergrowth had claimed that which had not been built over, there was not much left either to provoke excitement or to study. Additionally, the camps represented, for the most part, the experience and memory of outsiders and not of the islanders themselves. The dark anxieties and fears that camps had the potential to provoke were kept at arm's length. While the precise nature of the fears has faded with time, they have been contaminated with the Channel Islands' aversion to anything which could be remotely defined as collaboration. Because there were no post-war trials in the islands during which this concept might have been defined, unpicked and led to prosecutions, such fears have now grown out of all proportion and have eclipsed any positive narratives of local humanitarian aid to workers that might otherwise have emerged.

While camps are legacies that have been ignored and shunned, avoiding the imposition of any kind of narrative, the celebrations and commemorations of Liberation Day sit at the opposite end of this spectrum. Here, we can see the deployment of various external military props which were engaged by the local government as a natural and obvious way of framing official memory narratives of

---

[1] *Occupied behind Barbed Wire*, curated by the author, was on display in Jersey Museum in 2012 and Guernsey Museum in 2010.

[2] Telephone call between author and Bob Le Sueur, 21 August 2012.

[3] Telephone call between author and Michael Ginns, 16 August 2012.

occupation. As the act of liberation itself and the victory parades that followed were military affairs, the earliest annual celebrations that followed naturally sought to call upon the military once more almost as a form of re-enactment of the historic day itself. In this way, the military tradition was established.

While different aspects of Liberation Day narratives have moved in and out of focus over time, they have at the same time remained broadly stable and displayed great longevity. Commemorative narratives have moved from a focus on veterans, military might, victory and patriotism, through a period of what appears to have been deliberate amnesia, to the emergence once again of narratives of victory (through the lens of liberation), and a patriotism which never really went away. While victory was a concept which shone the light upon military personnel, liberation has the civilians at its heart. Memory has thus edged closer to the island experience rather than that of Britain, for whom the islands' sons fought in the armed forces.

Challenges from other quarters, from victims of Nazism, have instead sought different spaces or times for their counter-memories. Some have also cleverly integrated official memory with their own by inviting members of local government to play an important role in their ceremonies, a practice which has now become more common place in Jersey than in Guernsey. While Liberation Day was once about the imposition of official memory narratives upon the population, it too has also long become adopted as 'traditional' by ordinary people, so that official and popular memory has now become one and the same thing on this day.

Due to their popular acceptance, Occupation-related traditions are rarely questioned in the Channel Islands. This acceptance led, for the first 50 years after liberation, to a lack of questioning of dominant narratives. These narratives became encapsulated in the memorials and monuments which anchored them into the landscape at sites where key events took place. This became a way of cementing both official memory and the importance of certain narratives in the minds of the population, particularly those born after the war who did not experience the events for themselves. Even in the 1970s, when the post-war generation began to explore the Occupation for itself, the dominant narrative was not challenged. Research in this period did not seek to expose the difficulties and complexities of occupation.

From 1995 onwards, counter-narratives of victims of Nazism have found a voice that has been loud enough to become part of the memorialscape. While Guernsey has memorials to a number of different victim groups, they have not yet become part of the Liberation Day commemorations or celebrations, unlike in Jersey. Instead, these groups have found other occasions on which to meditate upon their past sufferings: 23 April for deportees (the date of the liberation of islanders from Biberach camp); Armistice Day for foreign workers; and Holocaust Memorial Day for the island's Jews. Jersey also marks these events.

One of the key differences between the two largest islands is likely to be the role of past and present Bailiffs and their willingness to critically address the darker aspects of the past. It is likely that this has also affected the way in which each island has instinctively or carefully chosen memorial texts. Spatial patterning indicates that dominant memorials have been steered or supported by elites or groups from local government, and sometimes this has been backed up by the deployment of members of Royal Family, who have unveiled memorials to help bring a sense of authority and official sanction to the memorials and the narratives which they espouse. This has not been the case for victims of Nazism. Further, the flexibility of positioning of the key authentic locations of their narratives has been used to its full advantage, allowing their memorials to be placed in marginal locations which do not interfere with the dominance of memorials to liberation.

The Evolution of Occupation Heritage

Three of the legacies of occupation discussed in this volume cannot easily be divided into clear generational phases for analysis. This is because of the lack of detailed archival data for labour camps and private museums, and the unsuitability of collections of militaria for this kind of comparative analysis. However, the study of bunkers, memorials and Liberation Day has revealed a clear but overlapping, four-phase evolutionary trajectory, summarised in Table 7.1.

The broad similarities between the phases of these legacies of occupation enable a single trajectory to emerge, as discussed below. This belies the apparent division between the narratives of popular and official memory in the Channel Islands; they are perhaps not as far apart as we might think and have come to converge due to their influence upon each other.

We can see that after the war and until the early 1950s, there was a tension between the islands' celebration of their freedom and victory while also mourning their dead. It was also a period of cleansing, when anything associated with military occupation was destroyed. After this was complete, the islands entered into a phase of deliberate and voluntary amnesia. This is not to suggest that people genuinely forgot the pain and suffering of occupation during this period. Simply, that it was politically and socially necessary for people to put the past (and its legacies) behind them and focus upon the future in order to rebuild the islands' economies and infrastructures and to find a way to heal a society that had become divided by accusations of collaboration.

From the mid-1970s onwards, the post-war generation grew interested in the war years and satisfied their curiosity through creating or rescuing Occupation heritage. This happened up to a decade earlier through the opening of private Occupation museums. I term this third phase 'Occupation nostalgia' as it characterises the way that the Occupation was presented by those who had (for the most part) missed it, invoking its positive aspects and repressing its more traumatic aspects, especially in bunker presentation. The focus upon liberation in memorials from 1985 onwards was also a part of this.

The final phase has been characterised by anamnesis, a deliberate calling to mind of the more traumatic aspects of war suffered by victims of Nazism. This was triggered, for the most part, by the 50th anniversary of liberation, which in turn

Table 7.1 Evolution of Occupation heritage

Heritage type	Phase 1	Phase 2	Phase 3	Phase 4
Bunkers	Erasure, 1945–1953	Amnesia and disguise, 1950s–1970s	Nostalgic rehabilitation and restoration, 1970s–present	Contestation and memorialisation, 1998 to present
Memorials	Dead heroes (military war dead, bombing raid dead): 1945–1950	Time to forget. Few new memorials. 1950–1985	1985–2005: focus on liberation (living heroes)	Additional focus on victims of Nazism, 1995+
Liberation Day	Military victory, patriotism and the war dead: 1946–1949	Collective amnesia: 1950s and 1960s	Occupation nostalgia: 1970–1984 (including liberation, 1985 to present)	Victims of Nazism, 1995+

encouraged introspection and self-analysis. The mammoth celebrations of 1995 also helped those find a voice who hitherto had been overlooked. These fresh narratives spurred new exhibitions at private museums a few years later, such as at the German Underground Hospital in Jersey (rebranded as Jersey War Tunnels at around this time) and at the German Occupation Museum in Guernsey.

During the consecutive periods of amnesia and nostalgia, how was it possible to repress traumatic memories of wrongdoing by the occupiers and some islanders? What stories or myths of occupation held currency in their stead? Sanders (2005: 234–235) suggests that the narrative of the 'official version of history', which lasted in some quarters well into the 1990s, was one in which the islanders behaved in an exemplary and dignified manner with no compromise of principle. Occupation government was done 'by the book' and the relationship with the Germans was 'correct'. Exceptions to the rule were Irish informers and the women who indulged in horizontal collaboration. The longevity of this myth undoubtedly contributed to the late arrival (compared with elsewhere in Europe) of the final phase of anamnesis.

These four phases of Occupation heritage can usefully be compared with those of France and of Western Europe more generally. While analysis on such a national or continental level may lack the nuance of more detailed regional or site-specific analyses, it none the less remains a useful comparison. In his study of the history of memory of the German occupation of France since 1944, Rousso (1991) observed that the French have also gone through four consecutive phases. His sources of memory were threefold and overlap in just one place with those I discuss in this volume, namely in the study of commemorations. His other two sources included film, and historical research and teaching (ibid: 219–221). These last two legacies of occupation are of a different ilk to mine, but can be equally subjected to similar types of chronological analysis.

Rousso termed his first phase 'unfinished mourning'. This was a period when the population had to deal with the aftermath of war, and the purge and subsequent amnesty of collaborators after they had served prison sentences. This period lasted from 1944 to 1954. From 1954 to 1971, the subject of the Vichy regime became less controversial. It was a period when the French repressed or minimised memories of the regime and its most negative aspects in favour of a focus upon the Resistance. Rousso termed this period as one of 'repressions'. This was followed by the third phase from 1971 to 1974, which Rousso termed 'the broken mirror'. This was when the myth of the Resistance was shattered and featured the 'return of the repressed'—those whose experience was not that of resistance—namely the prisoners of war, the workers of the Service Travail Obligatoire (STO) and the deportees (especially those who were Jewish). The fourth and final phase, which continued until the present (defined by the time of the publication of original French edition of Rousso's book in 1987), was characterised by 'obsession'. It was a period defined both by the obsessive importance that the Occupation had in French political debate, by the reawakening of Jewish memory (1991: 10 and 303–305), and by the 'duty to remember' (Rousso 1998: xi). The French are very much still haunted by the Occupation, just as are those in the Channel Islands.

In a later work, Rousso (2007: 29–31) further identified a three-phase model which charted the changing public memories of most countries which experienced German occupation (see Table 7.2). He argued that in general, they followed the same three-phase 'historical rhythm'. This started with a period of tension between the need to 'put the past behind them and push ahead with national reconstruction' on the one hand and the need to pay homage to heroes and victims on the other, which involved legal proceedings against collaborators. No such legal proceedings occurred in the Channel Islands, although there were calls for it to take place (Cruickshank 2004 [1975]: 339–340; Sanders 2005, Chap. 7).

The second phase on the continent was followed by a protracted period of official silence, repression and forgetting which lasted until the 1960s in Europe and the mid-1990s in the Channel Islands. Here, attention was diverted by Occupation nostalgia and the 'myth of a correct relationship' between the occupiers, islanders and local government.

The third phase, which Rousso argues began in the 1970s in Western Europe and after 1989 in the East, was a period of 'anamnesis and the return of ghosts from the past', which brought to the fore questions relating to the legacy of occupation, collaboration and anti-Semitism. In the Channel Islands, such ghosts returned, in the main and in force, only at and after the 50th anniversary of liberation.

The discrepancy between the first phases of the Channel Islands' and European war memory can be explained by the very different experiences of war and responses to occupation by mainland Britain and the continent. The time delay in the Channel Islands of something equivalent to the last two phases of Rousso's later model can be understood mostly by the insularity and inward-looking nature of the Channel Islands, which are neither part of the European Union nor the United Kingdom. They are fiercely independent, dislike outside interference and can be intolerant of ideas from outsiders. Despite this, the influence of the British war narrative is also likely to have played a part in causing a deviation from and

Table 7.2 A comparison of phases of evolution of European war memory

Channel Islands (4-phase model)	Mourning and cleansing (1940s–early 1950s)	Deliberate amnesia (1950s–1970s)	Occupation nostalgia (1970s–present)	Anamnesis of victims of Nazism (1995 to present)
France (4-phase model) (Rousso 1991)	Mourning (1944–1954)	Repression (1954–1971)	Return of the repressed/the broken mirror (1971–1974)	Obsession (mid-1970s—present)
Western Europe (3-phase model) (Rousso 2007)	Tension between purging and national reconstruction	Silence, repression and amnesia from mid-1950s to late 1960s	Anamnesis of ghosts of the past (1970s onwards)	

time delay to Rousso's model, although it is interesting to see that, despite its influence, the Channel Islands' trajectory of memory has not been entirely dissimilar to that of other countries.

British war memory is recognised as one of the most long lived and unbroken in Europe (Berger 2010: 130)—it is, after all, also an island and a traditionally Eurosceptic one at that. The influence of its war memory in the Channel Islands has been weakening since the 50th anniversary of the end of the war. While Jersey in particular has been embracing narratives of the perpetration of Nazi terror since then, it is also true to say that Britain was equally late, compared with mainland Europe, in developing a memorial culture around the Holocaust (ibid: 128–129). It is possible that the Channel Islands were influenced by Britain in this respect and by the beginning of the annual commemoration of Holocaust Memorial Day from 2001. It is perhaps also likely that emerging internal pressures from certain individuals within the islands were ultimately responsible for the shift in narratives in the Channel Islands.

The Organic Evolution of the Occupationscape

The overriding impression which emerges when examining the legacies of war as a whole in the Channel Islands is that the occupationscape has grown organically since 1946. No grand plan existed, which is not to say that the direction and contours of heritage and memory have not been manipulated, controlled or shaped by different groups at different times.

Using a broad brush, we can divide Occupation heritage narratives in the Channel Islands into two groups: those initially created at grass-root level by non-elites, representing popular memory; and those imposed from the start by local government, speaking for official memory. We might also observe that those involved in grass-root heritage have used the tangible legacies of Occupation (militaria and bunkers). Those in local government, on the other hand, have selectively used intangible (and thus more malleable) legacies, such as memory, and turned them into the ceremonies of Liberation Day. Over time, the narratives of these ceremonies have crystallised in the landscape as memorials, which themselves represent a palimpsestic view of liberation days from 1945 onwards. While, on the face of it, it is easier to be more selective with memories than with hard, objective 'facts' such as bunkers, we have seen how the stories told within bunkers can be just as selective or partisan as those narrated in ceremonies or memorials.

The power struggle between elites and non-elites for the control of public Occupation memory was more obvious between the post-war era (when the display of memory on Liberation Day was yet to become formalised) and the 1970s (when bunker restoration was controversial). By the time memorialisation became a popular way to cement Occupation memory from the mid-1980s onwards, with government elites showing ownership of memorial space, the struggle was over and the nostalgic theme of the Liberation memorials was uncontroversial. Ten years later, the contestation over public narratives was once more made visible as victims of Nazism began to seek greater recognition on the public stage.

Today, the division between elites and non-elites is perhaps more apparent than real. To set them in opposition as separate bounded entities is not necessarily appropriate in the small communities of the Channel Islands. Sometimes elites and non-elites are one and the same people. Sometimes they work together or advise each other on heritage issues and events, and the resulting memory narratives overlap and converge. Official memory has sometimes become popular memory, as the crowds on Liberation Day today attest. Increasingly, the contestation is not between official and popular memory, nor between elites and non-elites. Rather, it has been between professionally trained heritage specialists and the Occupation enthusiasts and has so far been apparent only in Jersey. Nonetheless, the long history of the dominance and ownership of Occupation heritage by the enthusiasts mean that they have had the upper hand in shaping popular memory.

Where does this leave the legacies of occupation which have not become heritage, such as labour camps? These are sites which have been seemingly shunned by both professionals and enthusiasts alike in the Channel Islands, even though the history and state of the camps were recorded in a CIOS publication in 1994 and later updated (Ginns 2006). Nobody has claimed ownership or fought for restoration of any camp at any time, even though the CIOS in Jersey complained against the recent partial destruction of the site of one camp by the construction of an electricity substation.

However, camps have not yet entirely been forsaken by all groups. Photographic evidence exists of members of the Jersey Communist Party and Spanish Republicans standing in front of the remains of various camps in around 1970[4]—possibly on the occasion of the 25th anniversary of the liberation. This suggests that these two groups, who had originally formed friendships during the Occupation, worked together later on to keep an eye on these sites through special

[4] Jersey Archive reference L/F/64/B/1/1

pilgrimages or tours. While they did not (or were not empowered to) do anything with them, they had not entirely forsaken or forgotten them. Further, former Spanish Republican forced worker Francisco Font unsuccessfully tried to garner support in 1970 for the erection of a plaque at Fort Regent in St Helier to mark the internment of slave workers of various nationalities in a camp at the fort. At the same time, he also explored the potential of a memorial at the site of the former burial place of OT workers, and this was in the end successful.

The Spanish Republicans and Communist Party members also kept faith with other similar sites of memory of their own private occupationscapes. These included the fortifications that the Spaniards helped to build[5] and, as mentioned, the burial ground where deceased forced and slave labourers were buried. This latter site is now the location of the memorial at Westmount which honours forced and slave labourers on Liberation Day each year. From this, we can observe how groups existing on the margins nurture memory in their own way. Even when memorials are not erected immediately after an event, it does not mean that sites have been forgotten or that they are not valued. By the time that marginalised groups get a voice or become empowered, the damage may already have been done to their legacies of occupation and it can be too late to rescue them from destruction.

With the passing of the wartime generation, the danger is that if their own personal occupationscapes do not become publically recognised—if the location of their sites of memory dies with them—then sites which were targeted for 'deliberate amnesia' risk becoming truly forgotten. Just as the Occupation now stands on the edge of living memory, so do sites such as the forced and slave labour camps.

We might pause to conjecture whether, if the Soviet ship had not arrived in the Channel Islands in 1960 and ordered a small memorial plaque at the site of the burial place of their dead kinsmen, then the trigger may not have been present for Spanish Republicans to fight, 10 years later, for a fixed memorial at the same location.[6] They might instead have considered restoring a camp, especially after bunker restoration began in the late 1970s. It is possible that that the current occupationscape in the Channel Islands might have looked very different today if it were not for certain serendipitous twists of fate. Similar analyses elsewhere in Europe should also take into account such contingencies.

While we cannot base analysis on what-ifs, my fieldwork research has strongly suggested that the organic growth of Occupation heritage has been shaped by certain key figures (whether members of the Occupation generation and their relatives, Bailiffs, individuals in local government, or other proactive people). It is a matter of chance that these characters happen to have been born in one

---

[5] Gary Font, son of Francisco Font, states that 'Spanish Republicans and others who wanted to remember forced and slave labourers would go to the Underground Hospital and lay flowers' in the entrance to the tunnel. This took place in the years prior to the arrival of the Russian ship in 1960, which generated a memorial plaque. Emails from Gary Font to author, 16 and 22 August 2012.

[6] It is also worth noting that Gary Font also independently offered this assessment.

island rather than another, but perhaps the social and political circumstances in that island nurtured or provided opportunities that simply did not exist elsewhere for them to find a voice at particular times.

These people have been united in their tenacity and desire to fight for an intervention in a particular legacy of occupation to turn it into heritage. While each of them has had their own agendas and has been influenced by (or fought against) dominant narratives, the current occupationscape is unique to the Channel Islands. It is the product both of circumstance, contestation and local power relations, and is still in flux. We should not perceive heritage as a fixed thing. New memorials get erected and others fall into disuse; Liberation Day narratives change; new museum exhibitions open; and the tussle for control of bunker presentation continues. We should not expect things to be the same in 10 years' time. What is neglected today can become remembered tomorrow and vice versa. Similarly, we should not expect the Channel Islands' occupationscapes to be identical to those of other Western European countries. They were each shaped by their own specific histories and by people motivated by their own experiences who, in turn, were operating within wider European trends. While examples of good practice and ethical heritage and tourism can be learned from other countries, we should not be surprised that Occupation heritage in the Channel Islands has not developed in the same direction as that of France, Belgium or Norway. There is no reason why it should. We should be alert to the formation of peculiarities and particularities of a place, because therein lies the key to understanding its legacies of occupation.

The Construction of Identity Through Heritage

Heritage, memory and identity are overlapping, interrelated and porous categories, and the diagram below, based on the analysis in this volume, offers just one way of understanding their relationship in the Channel Islands. It demonstrates how islanders draw upon their legacies of occupation, which themselves derive from certain selected wartime events and resulting memories (both popular and/or official) which are meaningful to them, into order to create and construct identities through heritage, as demonstrated in Chaps. 2–6 (Fig. 7.1).

I have stated throughout this volume that the German Occupation is an important part of Channel Islands identity; it was a defining part of local history and an experience that marked a generation and beyond, regardless of whether they evacuated or were occupied. However, there have been many post-war incomers to the islands whose families did not have these experiences. I have already noted that this has not necessarily been a bar to getting involved in Occupation heritage in one way or another, whether as a collector of militaria, a restorer of bunkers or as a member of the CIOS. In fact, the aspect that unites all of these activities and many similar ones is participation, active involvement and intervention in the legacies of war. These have created a sense of belonging for many (Fig. 7.2)

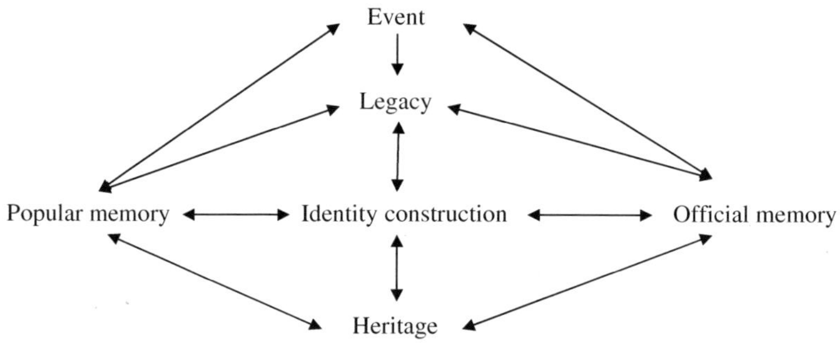

Fig. 7.1 The link between heritage, memory and identity in the Channel Islands

Those whose identity is most strongly influenced and defined by the Occupation today—those with whom I have been working most closely over the last 6 years—are those whose daily lives are entirely wrapped up in the Occupation. These include private museum owners, bunker restorers and collectors. Such groups will voraciously consume all aspects of the Occupation, and it forms their primary identity.

At the next level down are those who participate less actively. While this group may possess family stories and souvenirs dating from the Occupation years and may also attend Liberation Day celebrations, their consumption of heritage tends to be passive. I would estimate that they account for the majority of those who live in the Channel Islands. These are people who played in bunkers as children but have no interest in restoring them (even though are supportive of such endeavours); who watch but play little or no part in organising or participating in re-enactments or parades on Liberation Day; who own but do not trade in Occupation souvenirs; and who show visiting guests around Occupation museums and bunkers but are not necessarily regular visitors themselves. For these people, the Occupation still matters; they are by no means indifferent to it. At the third and lowest level are those who avoid all aspects of Occupation heritage, although this is actually quite difficult to do in the Channel Islands such is its pervasiveness. My own observations would suggest that recent migrants are among those who fall into this category; those who have not yet lived long enough in the Channel Islands to learn about or to be interested in or influenced by its culture.

Modern Channel Islands identity which is actively involved in its heritage draws upon memory (whether family, popular, public or official) and specific wartime events to dictate where and how that involvement is channelled. For example, for relatives of former forced workers, family memory of the treatment of those workers would mean that they are more likely to attend memorial ceremonies and lay wreaths for this group, and to visit fortifications with family and friends as a way of understanding wartime experiences and suffering. For the average islander whose family was occupied, it is important to attend Liberation Day celebrations, visit local museum exhibitions on Occupation themes, and often to buy books on the Occupation to display on their bookshelves (whether or not they actually read them). Time and again I have also seen family scrapbooks comprising wartime letters, photos and documents. The curation of family history is another important aspect of local identity and is often undertaken by the senior generation in each family, often themselves members of the Occupation generation. This group has also been active in agitating for memorials, attending commemorative ceremonies, celebrations and annual reunions or meetings of their particular interest group (such as, for example, the Guernsey Deportee Association).

For all of these different groups, identity claims are often made or cemented through legacies of occupation, whether through rescuing their particular legacies from destruction and oblivion, campaigning for recognition through heritage (most often these days through memorialisation) or through involvement in the organisation of commemorative events. People create and shape heritage and the resulting occupationscape to express their identity, just as that heritage or occupationscape will also influence and shape the identity of others.

Certain groups of islanders have sometimes been less accepting of heritage presented by trained heritage professionals rather than by themselves or other members of the community. Their resulting lack of involvement has sometimes acted to exclude them from newer heritage initiatives, such as those which represent victims of Nazism or whose modes of presentation are non-traditional or non-representational. This may lie behind disparaging remarks that I have heard aimed at ethical modern heritage presentation in Jersey, such as at the bunker memorial to forced workers at La Hougue Bie or at Jersey War Tunnels. Where the community has been more involved, such as in the Occupation tapestry on display in a gallery in Jersey's Maritime Museum, little or no local criticism has been forthcoming. While groups such as the CIOS have long been the guardian of Occupation knowledge, there is further capacity for them to share control of heritage with other organisations and to provide platforms for other voices to be heard.

Channel Islanders like to have a sense of ownership in and control over their heritage. They favour that which declares to a local audience 'this is who we are' rather than sanitised messages of 'this is how we want to be seen and judged by outsiders'; a narrative of 'this is what we experienced' versus a more holistic or educational experience for tourists. They prefer heritage statements that declare 'this is what and who we *want* to remember' rather than 'this is what and who we *should* remember'. The 'we' in these statements is usually the dominant majority who own or control the heritage sites. They are also the ones who have created the dominant public occupationscape.

In short, there are Channel Islanders who dislike having alternative, non-mainstream memory and heritage narratives imposed upon them—it is the *imposition* as much as anything else which is disliked. Independence and stubbornness are proudly acknowledged cultural character traits. It is likely that this has contributed to the cultural conservatism in heritage observed throughout this volume.

Despite the cultural conservatism and affection for traditional approaches among islanders, there are those among the heritage professionals in Jersey and

Guernsey who have expressed to me a desire to move into a post-Occupation future. They perceive the Occupation as increasingly 'old hat', in need of retirement, and perhaps just a little boring after 70 years of dominance. I wonder precisely how this is to be achieved given its dominance throughout island life, landscape and identity. Is it even theoretically possible or wise? There are legacies of occupation such as labour camps which have been shunned, hidden in the undergrowth and built over. Traumatic narratives of suffering, such as those of political prisoners, have yet to be fully and adequately acknowledged. Such restless ghosts as these are liable to continue to haunt islanders until they are dealt with, acknowledged publicly and incorporated into the occupationscape. Until this happens (and perhaps it never will) and until past injustices are confronted, we might question whether it is right to send the Occupation into retirement. The addition of these elements to Channel Island heritage might just help islanders fully to confront and come to terms with their traumatic past at last.

References

Berger, S. (2010). Remembering the Second World War in Western Europe, 1945–2005. In M. Pakier and B. Stråth (eds), *A European Memory? Contested histories and politics of remembrance*, pp. 119–136. New York and Oxford: Berghahn Books.

Cruickshank, C. (2004) [1975]. *The German Occupation of the Channel Islands*. London: Oxford University Press / Channel Islands: Guernsey Press.

Ginns, M. (2006) [1994]. *The Organisation Todt and the Fortress Engineers in the Channel Islands*. Jersey: Channel Islands Occupation Society Archive Book no. 8.

Rousso, H. (1991). *The Vichy Syndrome: History and memory in France since 1944*. Cambridge: Harvard University Press.

Rousso, H. (1998). *The haunting past: History, memory and justice in contemporary France*. Philadelphia: University of Pennsylvania Press.

Rousso, H. (2007). History of memory, policies of the past: What for? In K. H. Jarausch & T. Lindenberger (Eds.), *Conflicted memories: Europeanizing contemporary histories* (pp. 23–77). New York: Berghahn Books.

Sanders, P. (2005). *The British Channel Islands under German Occupation 1940–1945*. Jersey: Jersey Heritage Trust and Société Jersiaise.

Index

G. Carr, *Legacies of Occupation*, Contributions To Global Historical Archaeology 40, DOI: 10.1007/978-3-319-03407-2, © Springer International Publishing Switzerland 2014

The fruits of slave labour, Alderney, © Gilly Carr

Printed in Great Britain
by Amazon

32127383R00185